The Super Cute
AMIGURUMI
BIBLE

T0244301

1

Ebury Press, an imprint of Ebury Publishing
20 Vauxhall Bridge Road
London SW1V 2SA

Ebury Press is part of the Penguin Random House group of companies whose
addresses can be found at global.penguinrandomhouse.com

First published by Ebury Press in 2024

www.penguin.co.uk

A CIP catalogue record for this book is available from the British Library

ISBN 9781529938753

Commissioning Editor: Céline Nyssens
Design: maru studio G.K.
Production: Percie Bridgwater

Illustrations: © Adobe Stock (fromage; ricoco)

Printed and bound in China by C&C Offset Printing Co., Ltd

The authorised representative in the EEA is Penguin Random House Ireland,
Morrison Chambers, 32 Nassau Street, Dublin D02 YH68.

Penguin Random House is committed to a sustainable future for our business,
our readers and our planet. This book is made from Forest Stewardship
Council® certified paper.

The Super Cute

AMIGURUMI
BIBLE

A WHOLE WORLD OF CUDDLY CROCHET PATTERNS

EBURY
PRESS

Contents

~~~~~~

Easy Peasy

~~~~~~

A Bit Tricky

Go Pro!

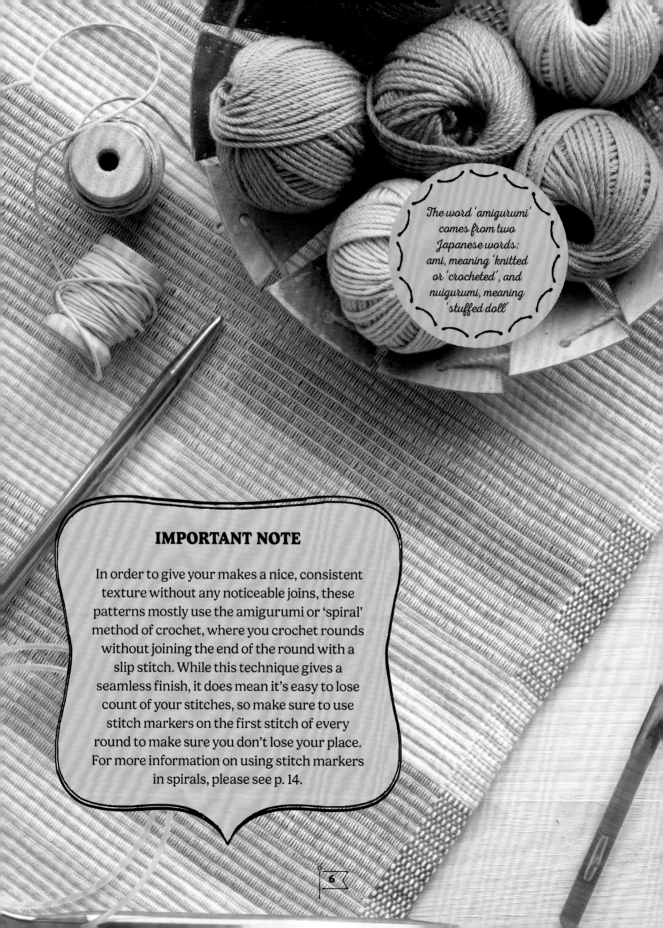

The word 'amigurumi' comes from two Japanese words: ami, meaning 'knitted or 'crocheted', and nuigurumi, meaning 'stuffed doll'

IMPORTANT NOTE

In order to give your makes a nice, consistent texture without any noticeable joins, these patterns mostly use the amigurumi or 'spiral' method of crochet, where you crochet rounds without joining the end of the round with a slip stitch. While this technique gives a seamless finish, it does mean it's easy to lose count of your stitches, so make sure to use stitch markers on the first stitch of every round to make sure you don't lose your place. For more information on using stitch markers in spirals, please see p. 14.

Introduction

Welcome to The Super Cute Amigurumi Bible, a bumper book of adorable, cuddly crochet projects for you to make, love and share with friends and family. From purr-fect pets like cats and dogs to delightful dinosaurs and loveable dragons, you can let your imagination – and your crochet hook – run wild!

The patterns in these pages are each unique in their own way, with many of them including fun accessories which you can choose to include or leave out. Switching up the colours or embroidering some fun details are also great ways to customise your projects and add a special finish to your makes – it's really up to you how your new crocheted critters look.

Tension – a term meaning how loose or tight your stitches are – is not critical for any of these projects, but may affect some of the yarn quantities stated in the patterns, as well as the size of your finished projects. Please just remember to make your stitches tight enough that the stuffing inside your new friends doesn't show through!

This book assumes some basic knowledge of how to crochet, but includes a section on key stitches, abbreviations, and a few top tips. The patterns that follow are divided into three sections – Easy Peasy, A Bit Tricky, and Go Pro! – so you can choose a level of difficulty that suits you. However experienced you are, there's sure to be a super cute project for you to get started on right away. So what are you waiting for? Grab your crochet hook, and let's get stitching!

LIST OF TOOLS

CROCHET HOOKS

Everything starts with your hooks, of course! You will need these in a variety of sizes to suit the yarn you're working with.

YARN

Each pattern tells you which weight (thickness) of yarn is most suitable for the project, as well as which fibre we recommend using. Most of the patterns use cotton yarn, but certain projects such as our Dapper Fox (p. 104) or Gorgeous Guinea Pig (p. 150) use a different kind of yarn to create a special effect.

STITCH MARKERS

These handy little things help you keep track of where you are. For instance, you can simply pop one into your work at the start of a round, and you'll know exactly where the round begins. If you don't have any stitch markers to hand, you can use paperclips or scraps of thread and yarn instead.

TOY STUFFING

This is what you'll use to stuff your new amigurumi critters and bring them to life! Most toy stuffing is made of polyester, but it's also possible to find stuffing that's made of cotton or wool. If you're looking for a greener alternative, you can also use fabric scraps, re-purpose old socks and tights or use the filling from a worn-out pillow.

SAFETY EYES

Throughout this book, we've recommended that you use safety eyes for your new amigurumi pals. This is particularly important if the recipient is a child, so please do keep this in mind when you're adding the eyes at the end of your project. If the recipient is a child aged 36 months or younger, do not use safety eyes, as these present a potential choking hazard – instead, embroider eyes onto your creation using black thread.

EMBROIDERY THREAD AND NEEDLE

You can use embroidery thread to embroider smiles, eyes, rosy cheeks, or anything else you like onto your new crochet creatures! You can also add someone's initials to one of your finished projects to add a special touch to a handmade gift.

EMBROIDERY SCISSORS

These handy little scissors are perfect for cutting your yarn.

ABBREVIATIONS

across	to end of the row
approx	approximate(ly)
beg	beginning
bl	insert hook under back loop only
BP	Back Post: work st indicated, inserting hook around post of st from back to front to back and not in top of st
ch(s)	chain/chain stitch(es)
ch-sp(s)	chain space(s)
ch-	refers to ch made previously, eg. ch-3
cl(s)	clusters
cont	continue
dc	double crochet
dc2tog	(insert hook in next st, yrh & draw a loop through) twice, yrh & draw through all 3 loops on hook
dec	decrease
dtr	double treble crochet
dtr2tog	work 2dtr together
fdc	foundation dc
ftr	foundation tr
fl	insert hook under front loop only
foll/folls	following/follows
FP	Front Post: As BP, inserting hook around post from front to back to front
htr	half treble
htr2tog	work 2htr together
in next	sts to be worked into the same stitch
inc	increase
LH	left hand
lp(s)	loop(s)
meas	measures
patt(s)	pattern(s)
pm	place marker
prev	previous
qtr	quadruple treble
rem	remain(s)/remaining
rep	repeat
RH	right hand
rnd(s)	round(s)
RS	right side
sk	skip
sp(s)	space(s)
ss	slip stitch
st(s)	stitch(es)
t-ch(s)	turning chain(s)
tog	together
tr	treble crochet
tr cl	(yrh, insert hook in sp/st, yrh & pull up loop, yrh & draw through 2 loops) number of times indicated, yrh & draw through all loops on hook
tr2tog	(yrh, insert hook in next st, yrh & pull up loop, yrh a& draw through 2 loops) twice, yrh & draw through all loops on hook
ttr	triple treble crochet
WS	wrong side
yrh	yarn round hook
*	work instructions immediately foll *, then rep as many more times as directed
()	work all instructions in the brackets as many times as directed

CROCHET HOOK CONVERSIONS

UK	metric	US
14	2mm	–
13	2.25mm	B/1
12	2.5mm	–
–	2.75mm	C/2
11	3mm	–
10	3.25mm	D/3
9	3.5mm	E/4
–	3.75mm	F/5
8	4mm	G/6
7	4.5mm	7
6	5mm	H/8
5	5.5mm	I/9
4	6mm	J/10
3	6.5mm	K/10½
2	7mm	–
0	8mm	L/11
00	9mm	M/13
000	10mm	N/15

UK/US CONVERSIONS

UK		US	
chain	ch	chain	ch
slip stitch	ss	slip stitch	ss
double crochet	dc	single crochet	sc
half treble	htr	half double	hdc
treble	tr	double	dc
double treble	dtr	treble	tr
triple treble	ttr	double treble	dtr

WHICH HOOK DO I USE?

Hook size	UK yarn weight
2.5-3.5mm hook	4ply yarn
3.5-4.5mm hook	double knitting yarn
5-6mm hook	aran yarn
7mm and bigger	chunky yarn

Crochet Essentials

Over the next few pages, you'll find simple step-by-step guides to many useful stitches and techniques that you'll use every time you pick up a hook

HOLDING THE HOOK
Try these methods and see which works best

PENCIL METHOD
Hold the hook like a pencil, in your right hand (if you're right-handed), about 3-5cm from the hooked end. If your hook has a flat area, you'll find it comfortable to hold it here.

KNIFE METHOD
Hold the hook between your thumb and forefinger, about 3-5cm from the hooked end, resting the end of the hook against your palm. This will give you lots of control.

HOLDING THE YARN
Even tension results in even stitches

METHOD ONE
Pass the ball end of the yarn between the little finger and third fingers of your left hand (if you are right-handed), then behind the third and middle fingers, over your index finger.

METHOD TWO
Loop the ball end of the yarn loosely around the little finger of your left hand, then take it over the third finger, behind the middle finger and over your index finger.

MAKING A SLIPKNOT THE FIRST LOOP ON THE HOOK

  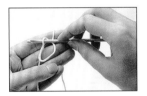 

1. Hold the tail of the ball of yarn in your left hand and drape the yarn clockwise over the top of it to form a loose, circular loop.

2. Hold the loop between left thumb and forefinger, then insert the crochet hook through the centre of the loop from front to back.

3. Catch the ball end of the yarn with the hook and pull it back through the centre of the loop, taking the yarn through with it.

4. Pull both ends of the yarn to tighten the knot, then pull just the ball end to tighten the loop so it's close to the hook, but not touching it.

CHAIN STITCH USE THIS STITCH TO MAKE YOUR FOUNDATION CHAIN

1. Hold the hook in your right hand, and both the yarn end and the working yarn in your left hand. Move the hook under and over the yarn to wrap it around anticlockwise.

2. Pull the hook towards the slipknot, catching the yarn in the hook, and pulling it through the slipknot loop. This forms your first chain (ch) stitch. Repeat steps 1 and 2 to form a chain length.

3. This is what your row of chains will look like. Hold the chain with your left hand near the hook, to keep the tension. Keep going until you have the number of chains that's stated in your pattern.

HOW TO COUNT CHAINS

Each chain or loop counts as one stitch. Never count your first slipknot or the loop on the hook (called the working loop). So that you can be accurate, make sure the chain is not twisted and that the front is facing you.

SLIP STITCH (SS)
This stitch has no height – often used to join rounds

1. You can make a slip stitch in any chain or stitch, to join it to the working loop on the hook. To make a slip stitch, simply insert the hook into the stitch indicated, from front to back.

2. Catch the ball end of the yarn with the hook, so the yarn wraps anticlockwise around it (yarn round hook, or yrh).

3. Gently pull the hook, and the yarn wrapped around it, back towards the 2 loops on the hook. Draw the yarn through both the loops on the hook.

4. This will finish the stitch and you'll see how the slip stitch has joined the working loop to the chain or stitch you inserted the hook into. You can also use slip stitch to form a neat edging.

DOUBLE CROCHET (DC) US TERM: SINGLE CROCHET
One of the key stitches in crochet, doubles are simple, compact stitches that form a dense fabric

1. To make a double crochet stitch, insert the hook under the top 2 loops of the next stitch on the previous row.

2. Wind the yarn around the hook (yrh).

3. Pull the yarn through the stitch, giving you 2 loops on your crochet hook.

4. Yarn round hook again, then pull the yarn through both loops. There's your double crochet made and you'll have one loop left on the hook, ready to do the next stitch.

HALF TREBLE CROCHET (HTR) US TERM: HALF DOUBLE CROCHET
A handy stitch that's between double and treble crochet in size, and looks slightly looser than double crochet

1. To make a half treble crochet stitch, work to where you want the htr and then wind the yarn round the hook (yrh).

2. Insert the hook under the top 2 loops of the next stitch in the previous row. Wrap yarn around the hook again (yrh).

3. Pull the yarn through the stitch only (3 loops on hook).

4. Yarn round hook again, pull the yarn through all 3 loops. You've made a half treble crochet. Continue working htr into next and following sts to the end of the row.

TREBLE CROCHET (TR) US TERM: DOUBLE CROCHET
One of the most popular stitches in crochet, this simple stitch is twice as high as a double crochet stitch

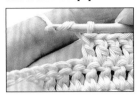   

1. To work a treble crochet, start by winding yrh and then insert the hook under the top 2 loops of the stitch on the previous row.

2. Wrap the yarn around the hook (yrh) and pull the yarn through the stitch only.

3. You will now have 3 loops on the hook. Yrh again, and draw the yarn through just the first 2 loops on the hook.

4. You will now have 2 loops on the hook. Yrh again and draw the yarn through the remaining loops on the hook. Your treble crochet is complete.

WORKING IN ROWS
Follow these simple rules to construct crochet fabric

1. The first row is made by working across the foundation chain from right to left. At the end of the chain or row, turn the work so that the yarn is behind the hook.

2. For the next row, first make the turning chain for the stitch you're about to work (see opposite). Now work the next stitch into the top of the stitches on your first row, missing the first stitch.

WORKING STITCHES INTO A RING
To make circles, tubes and other shapes

1. Make a foundation ring and work the t-ch (3ch for treble sts). Work a treble st as usual, but insert hook into centre of ring. For treble sts, yrh, insert hook into ring.

2. Finish the treble, as usual (yrh, pull yarn through ring, yrh, pull yarn through first 2 loops, yrh, pull yarn through 2 loops). Work more sts into the ring as needed.

DOUBLE TREBLE CROCHET (DTR) US TERM: TREBLE CROCHET

This is a stitch regularly used as an elongated version of the treble (described above). It's worked in a very similar way to the treble, as follows:

1. Make a foundation chain. Skip 4ch, *yrh twice, and insert the hook under the top loop of the next ch.
2. Yrh, pull the yarn through the ch loop only (4 loops on hook).
3. Yrh and pull the yarn through 2 loops only (3 loops on hook). Yrh and pull the yarn through 2 loops only (2 loops on hook).
4. Yrh and pull the yarn through the remaining 2 loops. Repeat from * to make more dtr sts.
5. To make the next row of dtr, turn work and ch4. This turning chain counts as the first dtr in a new row. Skip first st at the base of the t-ch, work 1dtr under the top 2 loops of the second stitch in previous row; continue to the end of the row.

TRIPLE TREBLE CROCHET (TTR) US TERM: DOUBLE TREBLE CROCHET

This is one of the longest standard crochet stitches and is mainly used in fancy stitch patterns. It's taller than a double treble crochet stitch (described left) and is worked in a very similar way, as follows:

1. Make a foundation ch. Skip 5 ch, *yrh 3 times, insert hook under top loop of next ch.
2. Yrh, pull yarn through ch loop only (5 loops on hook).
3. Yrh, draw loop through 2 loops only. Repeat from † 3 times more and your triple treble will be finished. Repeat from * to make more ttr sts.
4. To make the next row, turn work and ch5. This turning chain counts as the first triple treble in a new row. Skip first st at base of the t-ch. Work 1 triple treble, inserting hook under the top 2 loops of the second st in the previous row; continue to the end of the row.

HOW TO USE STITCH MARKERS IN SPIRALS

For most of the patterns in this book, you'll work the stitches in spiral rounds. If you've never done this before, don't worry, it's easy! At the end of a round, don't join the first and last stitches with a slip stitch. Instead, just work the first stitch of a new round into the top of the first stitch on the previous round. Using stitch markers will help you to keep track of spiral rounds. Our step-by-step guide (right) will show you how to do this.

1. Work the first stitch of a round and place a stitch marker in this first stitch.

2. Work a spiral round of double crochet stitches until you've worked the last stitch of the round. The next stitch you'll want to work into will have the stitch marker in it.

3. You'll need to remove the marker, work the first stitch of the new round and then replace the stitch marker in this first stitch, to mark the start of the round again.

HOW TO DECREASE IN DOUBLE CROCHET (DC2TOG)

1. Start by inserting the hook under the top two loops of the next stitch on the previous row. Begin to work a double crochet stitch in the usual way, working yrh and pull loop through (2 loops on hook).

2. Without finishing the first dc, begin the next dc by inserting the hook in the next stitch on the previous row. Again, work yrh and pull loop through (3 loops on hook).

3. Now complete both dc stitches together by working yrh and pull this loop through all 3 loops on the hook.

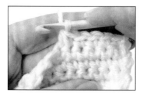

4. This is how your completed dc2tog should look. You will have neatly decreased one stitch. On subsequent rows, you can simply work a stitch into the top of the dc2tog stitch as usual.

HOW TO WORK CHAIN STITCH

1. Bring needle to the front of the fabric, after securing the thread at the back. Insert needle back into same hole (or very close to it) and pull gently to leave a small loop.

2. Bring needle to the front a little way to the right, making sure the needle passes through the loop. Insert the needle back into the same hole (or very close to it). Pull gently to leave a small loop.

3. Repeat Step 2 to make more loops.

4. After the final loop, make a small stitch over the last loop to secure it.

HOW TO WORK DOUBLE CROCHET IN A SPIRAL

 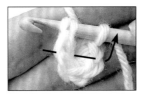  

1. Make a magic loop and work the t-ch (ch1 for dc). Now work 6 dc stitches into the loop, but do not join the last stitch and first stitch of this round with a slip stitch.

2. Instead, work the first dc stitch of the second round into the first stitch of the first round. To do this, insert the hook into the stitch, yrh, pull yarn through, yrh and pull the yarn through both loops.

3. You'll now be working in a spiral. Continue to work more rounds of dc stitches in a spiral, according to your pattern instructions.

4. On the last round, after you've worked the last dc stitch, you'll need to finish off the spiral with a slip stitch for a neat edge: insert the hook into the next stitch, yrh and pull through both loops.

HOW TO JOIN AMIGURUMI PARTS

1. Thread the yarn onto a tapestry needle. Secure the yarn to one piece with a small stitch. Insert the needle into the second piece where you wish to make the join.

2. Insert the needle through the first piece and back out. Next work through the second piece in the same way.

3. Repeat Step 2 until the pieces are securely joined. Insert the needle through and out at the back of one piece.

4. Weave the final tail inside one of the pieces.

HOW TO CHANGE COLOUR IN A SPIRAL

  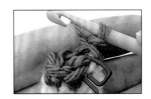 

1. If you need to work stripes in a spiral, your pattern will ask you to change colour. Always do this on the last yrh of the last stitch of the round in the previous colour.

2. Work the first stitch of the new round in the new colour and place a stitch marker in this first stitch.

3. Work a round of double crochet stitches until you've worked the last stitch of the round. The next stitch you'll want to work into will have the stitch marker in it.

4. You'll need to remove the marker, work the first stitch of the new round and then replace the stitch marker in this first stitch, to mark the start of the round again.

Easy Bunny

Even rookie crocheters will find this sweet little rabbit a breeze
to make. You can't get more easy – or fun – than this pattern, which involves
crocheting two squares of approx 15 x 15cms and then sewing up the two sides
using running stitch to pull the bunny into place. Although this is a super simple
pattern, the little bunny has lots of personality. Use the facial details
to make sure he has plenty of character!

TOP TIP

When you add the stuffing, if it shows through the stitches, you've overstuffed!

YOU WILL NEED

- Any DK or Aran weight yarn
- Small amount of toy stuffing
- Darning needle
- Scraps of black yarn for eyes and nose
- Pompom for tail

BUNNY
Using dc stitch make a square of crochet approx 15 x 15cms

TO MAKE UP
Step 1: Make a running stitch triangle in the top half of the square

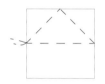

Step 2: Pull the triangle closed, pushing a small amount of toy stuffing into it. This forms the head and the ears. Tie off the ends securely.
Step 3: Sew up the remaining sides of the square to form the body and fill with stuffing.
Step 4: Make a running stitch around the bottom of the bunny and pull together to make the base.
Step 5: Embroider on eyes and nose and add a pompom for the tail. Darn in all ends.

Sugar Mice

Did you know that a group of mice is called a mischief?
These amigurumi sugar mice look like they're up to no good!

YOU WILL NEED

• DK weight cotton yarn, approximately one 50g ball of each colour you wish to use, and a small amount of bright pink yarn for the tail.

• A 3.5mm (US E/4) hook

• Toy stuffing

MEASUREMENTS

• 8cm (3in) long excluding tails

MOUSE

Using any colour except bright pink, make a magic loop.

Round 1 Ch1 (does not count as st throughout), 6dc into loop. [6 dc]

Round 2 2dc in each st around. [12 dc]

Round 3 *Dc in next st, 2dc in next st; repeat from * around. [18 dc]

Round 4 *Dc in next 2 sts, 2dc in next st; repeat from * around. [24 dc]

Round 5 *Dc in next 3 sts, 2dc in next st; repeat from * around. [30 dc]

Rounds 6-9 Dc in each st around. [30 dc]

Round 10 *Dc2tog, dc in next 3 sts; repeat from * around. [24 dc]

Rounds 11-12 Dc in each st around. [24 dc]

Round 13 *Dc2tog, dc in next 4 sts; repeat from * around. [20 dc]

Round 14 Dc in each st around. [20 dc]

Round 15 *Dc2tog, dc in next 3 sts; repeat from * around. [16 dc]

Round 16 *Dc2tog, dc in next 2 sts; repeat from * around. [12 dc]

Stuff mouse, and cont stuffing as you go.

Round 17 *Dc2tog, dc in next 2 sts; repeat from * around. [9 dc]

Round 18 *Dc2tog, dc in next st; repeat from * around. [6 dc]

Fasten off leaving a long tail. Weave yarn tail through all sts of Round 18 and pull to close. Weave in ends.

EARS
FIRST EAR

Row 1 Leave a tail of yarn (approx 10cm) and join yarn in Round 13 to work back towards mouse's tail. Using image as a guide for placement, ch1, dc in same Round, working diagonally away from nose, dc in Round 12, dc in Round 11, dc in Round 10, ss in Round 9, turn. [4 dc]

Row 2 Ch1, dc in each of next 4 dc.

Fasten off leaving a long tail. Sew tail to Round 14 using a tapestry needle to create a curve in Ear using the image as a guide.

SECOND EAR

Row 1 Leave a tail of yarn (approx 10cm) and join yarn in Round 10 to work back towards mouse's nose. Ch1, dc in same round, working diagonally away from nose, dc in Round 11, dc in Round 12, dc in Round 13, ss in Round 14, turn. [4 dc]

Row 2 Ch1, dc in each of next 4 dc.

Fasten off leaving a long tail.

Sew tail to Round 9 using a tapestry needle to create a curve in Ear using image as a guide. Weave in ends.

TAIL

Cut two lengths of bright pink yarn approx 36cm long. Thread needle from one side to the other between Rounds 1 and 2, so that there is an equal length each side.

Holding all ends tog, tie a knot close to body and trim yarn tails.

The ears are made in just two rounds and sewn to the head at a jaunty angle

An essential for any mouse, the pretty pink tail is knotted in position to finish the look

Puppy Pair

With their soft, sweet noses and ice cream colours, you can't help but fall for this adorable duo. Their dear little faces are so smiley and their black eyes seem to twinkle with glee. You'll have a fab time making them and kids will love them. This design is a great introduction to amigurumi – another perfect beginner project.

TOP TIP

Leave a tail of yarn at the end of each piece for sewing to the body

YOU WILL NEED

- Aran weight cotton yarn, approximately one 50g ball of each
  - Yarn A Turquoise
  - Yarn B Light Grey
  - Yarn C Beige
  - Yarn D Yellow
  - Yarn E Light Pink

- A 3.5mm (US E/4) hook

- Toy stuffing

- Scraps of felt in a mix of colours

- Grey, cream and black stranded cotton

- Black safety eyes, size 12mm

- Fabric glue

- Tapestry needle

MEASUREMENTS

20x10cm (8x4in)

EARS (MAKE 2)

Use Yarn A for the Boy Puppy and Yarn D for the Girl Puppy.
Make a magic loop and work 6dc into the loop. [6 sts]
Round 1 2dc in each st to the end. [12 sts]
Round 2 (Dc in the first st, 2dc in the next st), repeat to end. [18 sts]
Rounds 3-5 Dc in each st to the end. [18 sts]
Rounds 6-16 Dc2tog, dc in each st to end. [7 sts at end of row 16]
Fasten off.
Press flat to form the Ear shape.

ARMS AND LEGS (MAKE 4)

Use Yarn C for the Boy Puppy and Yarn E for the Girl Puppy.
Make a magic loop and work 6dc into the loop. [6 sts]

Round 1 (Dc in the first st, 2dc in the next st), repeat to end. [9 sts]
Rounds 2-8 Dc in each st to the end. [9 sts]
Fasten off.
Stuff well with toy stuffing.

BODY

Use the same colour as the Arms and Legs.
Make a magic loop and work 6dc into the loop. [6 sts]
Round 1 2dc into each st to the end. [12 sts]
Round 2 (Dc in the first st, 2dc in the next st), repeat to end. [18 sts]
Round 3 (Dc in the first 2 sts, 2dc in the next st), repeat to end. [24 sts]
Round 4 (Dc in the first 2 sts, 2dc in the next st), repeat to end. [30 sts]
Rounds 5-14 Dc in each st to the end. [30 sts]
Round 15 (Dc2tog, dc in next 2 sts), repeat to end. [24 sts]
Round 16 (Dc2tog, dc in next 2 sts), repeat to end. [18 sts]
Round 17 (Dc2tog, dc in next st), repeat to end. [12 sts]
Stuff firmly.
Round 18 Dc2tog, repeat to end. [6 sts]
Fasten off, leaving a long tail of yarn. Thread the cut yarn onto a wool needle and weave through the last 6 sts, pull the yarn tightly to close the hole. Weave in yarn and cut off any loose ends.

MUZZLE

Use Yarn D for the Boy Puppy and Yarn B for the Girl Puppy.
Ch5.
Round 1 Dc in second ch from hook, dc in next 2 sts, 3dc in last ch st, turn and work along the back of the ch, dc in 2 sts, 2dc in last st. [10 sts]
Round 2 (Dc in next st, 2dc in next st), repeat to end. [15 sts]
Round 3 (Dc in next two sts, 2dc in the next st), repeat to end. [20 sts]
Round 4 (Dc in next three sts, 2dc in the next st), repeat to end. [25 sts]
Rounds 6-9 Dc in each st to end. [25 sts]

For a quick and easy finish, cut a nose shape from felt and stitch on the mouth detail

Fasten off.
Stuff well with toy stuffing.

TAIL

Use the same colour as the Ears.
Make a magic loop and work 4dc into the loop. [4 sts]
Rounds 1-3 2dc in the first st, dc in each st to the end. [7 sts]
Change to Body colour after Round 3.
Rounds 2-13 Dc in each st to the end. [9 sts]
Fasten off.
Stuff well with toy stuffing.

BELLY PATCH

Use Yarn D for the Boy Puppy and Yarn B for the Girl Puppy.
Make a magic loop and work 6dc into the loop. [6 sts]
Round 1 2dc into each st to the end. [12 sts]
Round 2 (Dc in next st, 2dc in next st), repeat to end. [18 sts]
Round 3 (Dc in next 2 sts, 2dc in next st), repeat to end. [24 sts]
Round 4 (Dc in next 3 sts, 2dc in next st), repeat to end. [30 sts]
Fasten off and weave in ends.

HEAD

Use the same colour as Body, Arms and Legs.

Make a magic loop and work 6dc into the loop. [6 sts]

Round 1 2dc into each st to the end. [12 sts]

Round 2 (Dc in the next st, 2dc in the next st), repeat to end. [18 sts]

Round 3 (Dc in the next 2 sts, 2dc in the next st), repeat to end. [24 sts]

Round 4 (Dc in the next 3 sts, 2dc in the next st), repeat to end. [30 sts]

Round 5 (Dc in the next 9 sts, 2dc in the next st), repeat to end. [33 sts]

Round 6 (Dc in the next 10 sts, 2dc in the next st), repeat to end. [36 sts]

Round 7 (Dc in the next 11 sts, 2dc in the next st), repeat to end. [39 sts]

Round 8 (Dc in the next 12 sts, 2dc in the next st), repeat to end. [42 sts]

Round 9 (Dc in the next 13 sts, 2dc in the next st), repeat to end. [45 sts]

Round 10 (Dc in the next 14 sts, 2dc in the next st), repeat to end. [48 sts]

Round 11 (Dc in the next 15 sts, 2dc in the next st), repeat to end. [51 sts]

Round 12 (Dc in the next 16 sts, 2dc in the next st), repeat to end. [54 sts]

Mark the next round with a stitch marker.

Rounds 13-14 Dc in each st to the end. [54 sts]

Round 15 (Dc2tog, dc in next 7 sts), repeat to end. [48sts]

Round 16 (Dc2tog, dc in next 6 sts), repeat to end. [42 sts]

Insert the toy eyes 12 sts apart on the marked round.

Round 17 (Dc2tog, dc in next 5 sts), repeat to end. [36 sts]

Round 18 (Dc2tog, dc in next 4 sts), repeat to end. [30 sts]

Round 19 (Dc2tog, dc in next 3 sts), repeat to end. [24 sts]

Round 20 (Dc2tog, dc in next 2 sts), repeat to end. [18 sts]

Round 21 (Dc2tog, dc in next st), repeat to end. [12 sts]

Stuff firmly.

Round 22 Dc2tog, repeat to end. [6 sts]

Fasten off.

Thread the cut yarn onto a wool

needle and weave through the last 6 sts, pull the yarn tightly to close the hole. Weave in yarn and cut off any loose ends.

TO MAKE UP

With matching yarn, sew the Ears and Muzzle to the Head. Sew the Arms, Legs, Belly Patch and Tail to the Body. Sew the Head to theBody securely.
Fasten off and weave in ends.

FELT NOSE

Cut a triangle to fit neatly on the Muzzle (with outer points meeting the side of the Muzzle and the inner point meeting the foundation row). Glue or sew to Muzzle and, with stranded cotton, make a long stitch from inner point to the bottom of the Muzzle and work little stitches along the curve of the Muzzle for the mouth.

GIRL PUPPY EMBELLISHMENTS
COLLAR

With Yarn D, ch3.

Row 1 Dc in second ch from hook, dc in next 2 ch, turn. [2 sts]

Rows 2-20 Ch1, dc in each st to end. [2 sts]

Fasten off.

Sew in place round the Girl Puppy's neck.

FELT FLOWERS

Using a pencil, draw small flower shapes onto pieces of pastel felt. Cut out, place on top of each other in size order and sew together, then sew in place on the Girl Puppy's Head, where one of her Ears joins.

FELT BUCKLE

Cut a small 1-2cm square out of white felt. Fold in half and cut the centre out to form a buckle shape. Glue or stitch in place on the collar of the Girl Puppy.

BOY PUPPY EMBELLISHMENTS
FELT BOW TIE

Cut a rectangle 3x6cm out of aqua felt, then cut a long strip out of the same felt. Pinch the rectangle together in the middle, wrap the strip around this and glue or sew to hold in place. When dry, sew or glue in place on the Boy Puppy.

Owl Friends

This enchanting duo might be the best of friends, but opposites attract – one's a night owl while the other is wide-awake and ready to go. One thing's for sure, though – they're a hoot to make and definitely won't be ruffling any feathers if you're new to amigurumi.

YOU WILL NEED

LARGE OWL
• Aran weight cotton yarn, approximately one 50g ball of each:
- Yarn A Beige
- Yarn B Fuchsia
- Yarn C Light Pink
- Yarn D Orange
- Yarn E White

SMALL OWL
• Aran weight cotton yarn, approximately one 50g ball of each:
- Yarn F Cream
- Yarn G Turquoise
- Yarn H Teal
- Yarn D Orange
- Yarn E White

Note *If you are making both Owls you will only need one ball of Yarns D and E*

• A 4mm (US G/6) hook

• Toy stuffing

• 12mm black safety eyes

• Stitch markers

• Black stranded cotton

MEASUREMENTS
18x12x12cm (7x4¾x4¾in)

EYE PATCHES (MAKE 2)
Using Yarn E, make a magic loop.
Round 1 Ch1 (does not count as st throughout), 6dc into the loop. [6 sts]
Round 2 2dc into each st around. [12 sts]
Round 3 (Dc in next st, 2dc in next st) 6 times. [18 sts]
Fasten off.
Attach a safety eye to the centre of each Eye Patch.

LARGE OWL BODY
Using Yarn A, make a magic loop.
Round 1 Ch1, 6dc into the loop. [6 sts]
Round 2 2dc into each st around. [12 sts]
Round 3 (Dc in next st, 2dc in the next st) repeat to end. [18 sts]
Round 4 (Dc in next 2 sts, 2dc in the next st) repeat to end. [24 sts]
Round 5 (Dc in next 3 sts, 2dc in the next st) repeat to end. [30 sts]
Round 6 (Dc in next 9 sts, 2dc in the next st) repeat to end. [33 sts]
Round 7 (Dc in next 10 sts, 2dc in the next st) repeat to end. [36 sts]
Round 8 (Dc in next 11 sts, 2dc in the next st) repeat to end. [39 sts]
Round 9 (Dc in next 12 sts, 2dc in the next st) repeat to end. [42 sts]
Round 10 (Dc in next 13 sts, 2dc in the next st) repeat to end. [45 sts]
Round 11 (Dc in next 14 sts, 2dc in the next st) repeat to end. [48 sts]
Round 12 (Dc in next 15 sts, 2dc in the next st) repeat to end. [51sts]
Round 13 (Dc in next 16 sts, 2dc in the next st) repeat to end. [54 sts]

Mark Round 13 with a stitch marker.
Round 14-15 Dc in each st to the end. [54 sts]
From now on you will work some of the stitches in the back loop only. This will create the loops you need to work the feathers on the stomach.
Round 16 Dc in bl of next 12 sts, dc in each st to the end. [54 sts]
Round 17 Dc in bl of next 12 sts, dc to one st before the beginning of the bl dc. [54 sts]
Round 18 Dc in bl of next 14 sts, dc in each st to the end. [54 sts]
Round 19 Dc in bl of next 14 sts, dc to one st before the beginning of the blo dc. [54 sts]
Round 20 Dc in bl of next 16 sts, dc in each st to the end.

Place the Eye Patches so the safety eyes attach over the marked round, 10 sts apart. Remove st marker.
Round 21 Dc in bl of next 16 sts, dc to one st before the beginning of the bl dc. [54 sts]
Round 22 Dc in bl of next 18 sts, dc in each st to the end.
Round 23 Dc in bl of next 18 sts, dc to one st before the beginning of the bl dc. [54 sts]
Round 24 Dc in bl of next 20 sts, dc in each st to the end.
Round 25 Dc in bl of next 20 sts, dc to one st before the beginning of the bl dc. [54 sts]
Round 26 Dc in bl of next 22 sts, dc in each st to the end.
Round 27 Dc in bl of next 22sts, dc to one st before the beginning of the bl

dc. [54 sts]

Round 28 Dc in bl of next 24 sts, dc in each st to the end.

Round 29 (Dc2tog, dc in next 7 sts) repeat to end. [48 sts]

Round 30 (Dc2tog, dc in next 6 sts) repeat to end. [42 sts]

Round 31 (Dc2tog, dc in next 5 sts) repeat to end. [36 sts]

Round 32 (Dc2tog, dc in next 4 sts) repeat to end. [30 sts]

Round 33 (Dc2tog, dc in next 3 sts) repeat to end. [24 sts]

Round 34 (Dc2tog, dc in next 2 sts) repeat to end. [18 sts]

Round 35 (Dc2tog, dc in next st) repeat to end. [12 sts]

Stuff Owl with toy stuffing.

Round 36 (Dc2tog) 6 times. [6 sts]

Fasten off and use the tail to close the sts of Round 36.

OVERWORK FEATHER BELLY PATCH

Join Yarn C to the first unused fl from Round 15.

Row 1 Ch1, (dc in next st, dtr in next st) repeat to end, turn. [12 sts]

Change to Yarn B.

Row 2 Ch1, (dc in next st, dtr in next st) repeat to last unused fl, dc in last st, turn.

Change to Yarn C.

Repeat the last two rows until you have used up all the rows of back loop only stitches.

WINGS (MAKE 2)

WING TIPS (MAKE 6)

Using Yarn A, make a magic loop.

Round 1 Ch1, 6dc into the loop. [6 sts]

Round 2 (Dc in next st, 2dc in the next st) repeat to end. [9 sts]

Rounds 3-4 Dc in each st to end. [9 sts]

Fasten off.

JOIN WING TIPS

To make the Wings you will work around the sts of Round 4 of each of the Wing Tips to join them. Each Wing is made up of 3 Wing Tips.

Join Yarn A into any st on Round 4 of a Wing Tip.

Round 1 Ch1, dc in first 4 sts of the first Wing Tip, dc in the first 3 sts of the second Wing Tip, dc in the first 8 sts of the third Wing Tip, skip the next st on the middle Tip, dc in the next 3 sts on this Tip, skip the next st on the first Tip, dc in the last 4 sts on this Tip. [24 sts]

Round 2 Dc in each st to end. [24 sts]

Round 3 (Dc2tog, dc in next 10 sts) twice. [22 sts]

Round 4 (Dc2tog, dc in next 9 sts) repeat to end. [20 sts]

Round 5 (Dc2tog, dc in next 8 sts) repeat to end. [18 sts]

Fasten off and stuff lightly if required.

Sew each Wing in place on either side of the Body. You can use the images as a guide.

EARS (MAKE 2)
Using Yarn A, make a magic loop.
Round 1 Ch1, 4dc into loop. [4 sts]
Round 2 (Dc in next st, 2dc in the next st) twice. [6 sts]
Round 3 (Dc in next 2 sts, 2dc in the next st) twice. [8 sts]
Round 4 (Dc in next 3 sts, 2dc in the next st) twice. [10 sts]
Fasten off, sew in place either side of Head.

BEAK
Using Yarn D, make a magic loop.
Round 1 Ch1, 4dc into loop. [4 sts]
Round 2 (Dc in next st, 2dc in the next st) repeat to end. [6 sts]
Round 3 (Dc in next 2 sts, 2dc in the next st) repeat to end. [8 sts]
Round 4 (Dc in next 3 sts, 2dc in the next st) repeat to end. [10 sts]
Round 5 Dc in each st to end. [10 sts]
Fasten off and sew between the Eyes. You can use the image as a guide.

SMALL OWL BODY
Using Yarn F, make a magic loop.
Round 1 Ch1, 6dc into the loop. [6 sts]
Round 2 2dc into each st to the end. [12 sts]
Round 3 (Dc in next st, 2dc in the next st) repeat to end. [18 sts]
Round 4 (Dc in next 2 sts, 2dc in the next st) repeat to end. [24 sts]
Round 5 (Dc in next 3 sts, 2dc in the next st) repeat to end. [30 sts]
Round 6 (Dc in next 9 sts, 2dc in the next st) repeat to end. [33 sts]
Round 7 (Dc in next 10 sts, 2dc in the next st) repeat to end. [36 sts]
Round 8 (Dc in next 11 sts, 2dc in the next st) repeat to end. [39 sts]
Round 9 (Dc in next 12 sts, 2dc in the next st) repeat to end. [42 sts]
Rounds 10-12 Dc in each st to end. [42 sts]
Round 13 Dc in bl of next 10 sts, dc to one st before the beginning of the bl dc. [42 sts]
Round 14 Dc in bl of next 12 sts, dc in each st to the end. [42 sts]
Round 15 Dc in bl of next 12 sts, dc to one st before the beginning of the bl dc. [42 sts]

Round 16 Dc in bl of next 14 sts, dc in each st to the end. [42 sts]
Round 17 Dc in bl of next 14 sts, dc to one st before the beginning of the bl dc. [42 sts]
Round 18 Dc in bl of next 16 sts, dc in each st to the end. [42 sts]
Round 19 Dc in bl of next 16 sts, dc to one st before the beginning of the bl dc. [42 sts]
Round 20 Dc in bl of next 18 sts, dc in each st to the end. [42 sts]
Round 21 Dc in bl of next 18 sts, dc to one st before the beginning of the bl dc. [42 sts]
Round 22 Dc in bl of next 20 sts, dc in each st to the end. [42 sts]
Round 23 (Dc2tog, dc in next 5 sts) repeat to end. [36 sts]
Round 24 (Dc2tog, dc in next 4 sts) repeat to end. [30 sts]
Round 25 (Dc2tog, dc in next 3 sts) repeat to end. [24 sts]
Round 26 (Dc2tog, dc in next 2 sts) repeat to end. [18 sts]
Round 27 (Dc2tog, dc in next st) repeat to end. [12 sts]
Stuff with toy filling.
Round 28 (Dc2tog) repeat to end. [6 sts]
Fasten off as before.

FEATHER BELLY PATCH
Using Yarn G and Yarn H, work the feathering on the belly as for the Large Owl.

EARS, BEAK AND EYE PATCHES
Make Ears using Yarn F, a Beak and Eye Patches as for the Large Owl. Instead of using safety eyes, sew a U shape using small back stitches onto the Eye Patches. Use the photo as a guide and sew the Eyes onto the Owl above the belly feathers.
Attach the Ears and Beak as per the instructions for the Large Owl to finish.

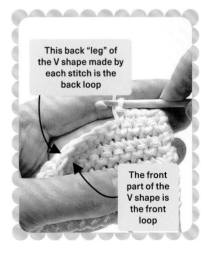

This back "leg" of the V shape made by each stitch is the back loop

The front part of the V shape is the front loop

Beach Bear

Say hello to this beach-ready teddy bear! He has headed to the beach for a spot of fishing but just can't resist jumping in for a splash about. With his arm bands on, of course.

YOU WILL NEED

- 4ply weight cotton yarn, approximately one 50g ball of each:
  - Yarn A Brown
  - Yarn B Yellow
  - Yarn C Orange
- Small amounts of Yarn D Black and Yarn E Blue

- A 3mm (US C/2 or D/3) hook

- Toy stuffing

- Stitch markers

MEASUREMENTS

20cm (7¾in) tall

ABBREVIATIONS

Invisible Decrease (inv dec)
Insert hook through the front loops of the next two sts, (yrh, pull through 2 loops on the hook) twice
Inv dec bl Work an invisible decrease as above, but using the back loops rather than the front loops of the stitches

HEAD

With Yarn A, ch2.
Round 1 (RS) 8dc in second ch from hook. [8 sts]
Round 2 2dc in each st around. [16 sts]
Round 3 (1dc, 2dc in next st) rep around. [24 sts]
Round 4 Dc in each st around.
Round 5 (2dc, 2dc in next st) rep around. [32 sts]
Round 6 (3dc, 2dc in next st) rep around. [40 sts]
Rounds 7-8 Dc in each st around.
Round 9 (4dc, 2dc in next st) rep around. [48 sts]
Rounds 10-11 Dc in each st around.
Round 12 (2dc in next st, 5dc) rep around. [56 sts]
Rounds 13-19 Dc in each st around.
Round 20 (5dc, inv dec) rep around. [48 sts]
Rounds 21-22 Dc in each st around.
Round 23 (4dc, inv dec) rep around. [40 sts]
Round 24 Dc in each st around.
Round 25 (3dc, inv dec) rep around. [32 sts]
Round 26 (2dc, inv dec) rep around. [24 sts]
Round 27 (1dc, inv dec) rep around. [16 sts] Stuff with toy stuffing.
Fasten off and leave long end for sewing Head to Body.

FOOT CONSTRUCTION

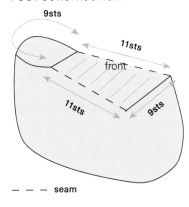

— — — seam

BODY

With Yarn A, ch2.
Round 1 (RS) 6dc in second ch from hook. [6 sts]
Round 2 2dc in each st around. [12 sts]
Round 3 (2dc in next st, 1dc) rep around. [18 sts]
Round 4 (2dc in next st, 2dc) rep around. [24 sts]
Round 5 (2dc in next st, 3dc) rep around. [30 sts]
Round 6 (4dc, 2dc in next st) rep around. [36 sts]
Round 7 (5dc, 2dc in next st) rep around. [42 sts]
Rounds 8-9 Dc in each st around.
Round 10 (2dc in next st, 6dc) rep around. [48 sts]
Rounds 11-15 Dc in each st around.
Round 16 (6dc, inv dec) rep around. [42 sts]
Rounds 17-18 Dc in each st around.
Round 19 (inv dec, 5dc) rep around. [36 sts]
Rounds 20-22 Dc in each st around.
Round 23 (Inv dec, 4dc) rep around. [30 sts]
Rounds 24-25 Dc in each st around.
Round 26 (Inv dec, 3dc) rep around. [24 sts]
Round 27 (Inv dec, 2dc) rep around. [18 sts]
Round 28 (Inv dec, 7dc) rep around. [16 sts]
Stuff body with toy stuffing.
Fasten off and weave in ends.

ARMS (MAKE 2)

With Yarn A, ch2.
Round 1 (RS) 6dc in second ch from hook. [6 sts]
Round 2 2dc in each st around. [12 sts]
Round 3 (2dc, 2dc in next st) rep around. [16 sts]
Round 4 Dc in each st around.
Round 5 (7dc, 2dc in next st) rep around. [18 sts]
Rounds 6-7 Dc in each st around.
Round 8 (4dc, inv dec) rep around. [15 sts]
Round 9 Dc in each st around.
Round 10 (3dc, inv dec) rep around.

[12 sts]
Round 11 Dc in each st around.
Round 12 (3dc, 2dc in next st) rep around. [15 sts]
Begin stuffing with toy stuffing as you go. Stuff lightly towards the end.
Rounds 13-18 Dc in each st around.
Round 19 1dc, 2dc in next st, 2dc, 2dc in next st, 4dc, (inv dec, 1dc) twice. [15 sts]
Round 20 Dc in each st around.
Round 21 (3dc, inv dec) rep around. [12 sts]
Round 22 Dc in each st around.
Round 23 (2dc, inv dec) rep around. [9 sts]
Finish stuffing, and shape arms so they arch a little. Sew open end tog and leave long end for sewing Arm to Body.

LEGS (MAKE 2)

With Yarn A, ch7.
Round 1 (RS) 5dc beg in second ch from hook, 3dc in last ch, rotate to work on other side of foundation ch, 4dc, 3dc in last ch. [15 sts]
Round 2 2dc in next st, 5dc, (2dc in next st)
3 times, 5dc, 2dc in next st. [20 sts]
Round 3 2dc in next st, 7dc, (2dc in next st)
4 times, 7dc, 2dc in next st. [26 sts]
Round 4 2dc in next st, 9dc, 2dc in next st, 3dc, 2dc in next st, 9dc, 2dc in next st, 1dc. [30 sts]
Rounds 5-8 Dc in each st around.
Remove hook from loop and place a st marker in loop to keep sts from unravelling. Do not cut this yarn as you will need it to cont later. Count back 12 sts from end of last Round and rejoin the other end of skein to 12th st, leaving a long tail.

FRONT OF THE FOOT

Now working in rows:
Row 1 Ch1 (does not count as st throughout), 9dc, turn leaving rem sts unworked. [9 sts]
Rows 2-3 Ch1, dc in each st to end, turn.
Row 4 Ch1, 1dc, inv dec bl, 3dc, inv dec bl, 1dc, turn. [7 sts]

Rows 5-6 Ch1, dc in each st to end, turn.

Row 7 Ch1, 1dc, inv dec, 1dc, inv dec, 1dc, turn. [5 sts]

Row 8 Ch1, dc in each st to end, turn.

Row 9 Ch1, 1dc, inv dec, 2dc.

Fasten off leaving a long tail.

SEWING UP THE FOOT

See diagram for Foot Construction on prev page. Turn foot WS out and sew one straight side of Front Foot to next 11 sts of Round 8, and the other straight side to prev 11 sts of Round 8. Turn RS out. This will leave 9 unworked sts of Round 8 and 4 sts across the top of the Front Foot to cont working for Leg. Pull foot into shape to smooth out any square angles. Pick up the prev working yarn at the beg of Round 8 to cont:

Round 9 Dc in each st around. [13 sts]

Round 10 1dc, (5dc, 2dc in next st) twice.[15 sts] Stuff with toy stuffing as you go.

Rounds 11-19 Dc in each st around.

Round 21 (1dc, inv dec) rep around. [10 sts] Finish stuffing.

Fasten off and leave long tail for sewing Leg to Body.

EARS (MAKE 2)

With Yarn A, ch2.

Round 1 (RS) 6dc in second ch from hook. [6 sts]

Round 2 2dc in each st around. [12 sts]

Round 3 (2dc in next st, 1dc) rep around. [18 sts]

Round 4 (2dc in next st, 2dc) rep around. [24 sts]

Round 5 (5dc, 2dc in next st) rep around. [28 sts]

Rounds 6-7 Dc in each st around.

Round 8 9dc, (inv dec) 5 times, 9dc. [23 sts]

Round 9 Dc in each st around.

Flatten Ear with last st in the centre and sew the open ends across the top. Leave a long tail for sewing the Ear to the Head. The front of the Ear will be the side with the Round 8 decreases.

TO MAKE UP

Pin Ears in place and mark the position of Eyes with pins. Make a small st at centre of each Eye (between Rnds 13 and 14, 9 sts apart). Pull the st tight to make an indentation and rep for 2nd eye. Take yarn inside head to base of the Head. **Fasten off** securely.

Using Yarn D, embroider eyes with small straight sts, then complete nose and mouth using image as a guide. Split a strand of yarn to make a finer line for the mouth. Check position of Ears. They should be pinched tog slightly and positioned in line with Round 6 at top of Head. Sew them in place. Position arms 4 Rounds from top of Body and sew in place. Position Legs with feet slightly turned out and sew in place. Pin Head and sew in place, adding stuffing as you sew to keep Head from tipping.

SHORTS

LEGS (MAKE 2)

With Yarn E, ch30.

Row 1 (RS) Dc in second ch from hook and in each ch to end. [29 sts] **Fasten off.**

Turn and join Yarn B in first st.

Rows 2-4 Ch1, dc in each st to end, turn. **Fasten off.**

Join the two Shorts Legs as follows:

Row 1 (RS) With Yarn B, ch2, with RS facing, dc in each st across the first Leg, ch2, dc in each st across the second Leg, do not fasten off. [62 sts] On next Round the Legs will be joined in to the Round, with the 'ch2' sections forming the centre front and centre back of Shorts. The side leg and crotch seam will be sewn up later.

Round 2 (RS) Join into the Round by working a dc st into first ch of Row 1, and cont working a dc st into each st and ch around. [62 sts]

Round 3 Dc in each st around.

Round 4 15dc, inv dec, 29dc, inv dec, 14dc. [60 sts]

Round 5 Dc in each st around.

Round 6 (Inv dec, 28dc) twice. [58 sts]

Round 7 Dc in each st around.

Round 8 (Inv dec, 27dc) twice. [56 sts]

Round 9 Dc in each st around.

Round 10 (Inv dec, 26dc) twice. [54 sts]

Round 11 Dc in each st around.

Round 12 (Inv dec, 25dc) twice. [52 sts]

Round 13 Dc in each st around. Change to Yarn E.

Round 14 Dc in each st around, ss in first st of next Round to finish.

Fasten off and weave in ends.

DRAWSTRING

With Yarn E, ch76.

Fasten off.

Thread drawstring onto a yarn needle and weave it in and out between sts of the last 2 rows of Shorts, starting at centre front. Tie a knot in each end of drawstring and cut off yarn ends. Sew up side legs and crotch seam in one.

ARM BANDS (MAKE 2)

With Yarn C, ch27 and ss into first ch to join into the Round, being careful not to twist.

Round 1 Ch1, dc into each ch around. [27 sts]

Rounds 2-16 Dc in each st around. Ss in first st of next Round to finish.

Fasten off leaving a long tail for sewing.

Fold Arm Band long edge to long edge and sew tog, adding stuffing as you go. Do not add any stuffing within 7 sts of the start of Round, so that one side of Band stays flatter. Back stitch across width of Band at this point to keep this section flat.

Itty-Bitty Bat

This tiny bat is a brilliant companion – he's always got a unique perspective on things and is more than content just hanging out.

YOU WILL NEED
• Any black DK yarn from your stash, approximately one 50g ball
• A 2.5mm (US B/1 or C/2) hook
• Safety eyes
• Toy stuffing
• Tapestry needle
• Stitch marker
• Small amount of black felt

MEASUREMENTS
13cm (5in) tall

HEAD
Using Black, make a magic loop.
Round 1 (RS) Ch1 (does not count as st), 8dc into loop. [8 sts]
Round 2 2dc in each dc around. [16 sts]
Round 3 (1dc in next dc, 2dc in next dc) 8 times. [24 sts]
Rounds 4-11 Dc in each dc around.
Round 12 (Dc in next st, dc2tog) 8 times. [16 sts]
Round 13 Dc in each dc around.
Round 14 (Dc in next 2 sts, dc2tog) 4 times. [12 sts]
Round 15 Dc in each dc around.

BODY
Round 16 (Dc in next 2 sts, 2dc in next st) 4 times. [16 sts]
Rounds 17-22 Dc in each dc around. Do not fasten off. Place eyes 6 sts apart between Rounds 10 and 11. Stuff Head and Body firmly. Press last Round of Body flat, making sure eyes are in centre of face. Work 8 ss across base of body to close, working each ss through both front and back of Body. Fasten off and weave in ends.

FEET
FIRST FOOT
Working into the ss seam, join Black in the first st.
Row 1 (RS) Ch1 (does not count as st), dc in same st and next 2 sts, turn, leaving rem sts unworked. [3 dc]
Rows 2-9 Ch1 (does not count as st), dc in each dc across, turn. [3 sts]
Fasten off leaving a long tail.

SECOND FOOT
Skip next 2 sts on ss seam. Join Black in next st and rep Rows 1-9.

Fasten off leaving a long tail.
Fold each foot in half and using the long tail and a tapestry needle sew the last row to the ss seam to create a loop for hanging the bat upside down.

EARS (MAKE 2)
Using Black, make a magic loop.
Round 1 (RS) Ch3 (counts as tr), 11tr into loop, ss to top of beg ch-3 to join. [12 sts]
Fasten off leaving a long tail.
Position ears onto head using the image as a guide and sew to secure.

WINGS
Using black felt, cut out wings using the image as a guide.
Glue or sew them in place onto head using the image as a guide and sew to secure.

Woolly Whale

With his distinctive stripy belly and freely flapping fins,
this delightful whale is an extremely lovable marine make.

YOU WILL NEED

• Aran weight cotton yarn,
approximately two 50g balls of:
- Yarn A Dark Blue
• A small amount of:
- Yarn B Light Green
- Yarn C Turquoise
- Yarn D Lilac

• A 4mm (US G/6) hook

• Safety eyes, approx 9mm
diameter

• Toy stuffing

• Stitch marker

MEASUREMENTS

22cm (8½in) long

NOTES

• The Whale Body is worked using
the amigurumi method. Work in a
continuous spiral without closing off
each round with a slip stitch.

• You may find it helpful to place a
marker in the first st of each round
and move it up as you work. The
Under Belly is worked as a separate
piece and sewn on afterwards

BODY

Using Yarn A, make a magic loop.
Round 1 (RS) 5dc into the loop, ss to
the first dc to join. [5 dc]
Round 2 2dc in each st around. [10
dc]
Round 3 (1dc in the next st, 2dc in the
next st) 5 times. [15 dc]
Round 4 (1dc in each of the next 2
sts, 2dc in the next st) 5 times. [20 dc]
Round 5 (1dc in each of the next 3

sts, 2dc in the next st) 5 times. [25 dc]
Round 6 (1dc in each of the next 4
sts, 2dc in the next st) 5 times. [30 dc]
Round 7 (1dc in each of the next 5
sts, 2dc in the next st) 5 times. [35 dc]
Round 8 (1dc in each of the next 6
sts, 2dc in the next st) 5 times. [40 dc]
Rounds 9-15 Dc in each st around.
Round 16 (1dc in each of the next 6
sts, dc2tog) 5 times. [35 dc]

Add the safety eyes between Rounds
15 and 16 approximately 15 sts apart.
These 15 sts will be located on the
belly side of the whale.

Rounds 17-19 Dc in each st around.
[35 dc]
Round 20 (1dc in each of the next 5
sts, dc2tog) 5 times. [30 dc]
Rounds 21-23 Dc in each st around.
Round 24 (1dc in each of the next 4
sts, dc2tog) 5 times. [25 dc]

TOP TIP

*You can use up any yarn
in your stash to make the
whale's striped belly*

Rounds 25-26 Dc in each st around.
Round 27 (1dc in each of the next 3 sts, dc2tog) 5 times. [20 dc]
Rounds 28-30 Dc in each st around.
Round 31 (1dc in each of the next 2 sts, dc2tog) 5 times. [15 dc]
Round 32 Dc in each st around.
Round 33 (1dc in the next st, dc2tog) 5 times. [10 dc]
Rounds 34-35 Dc in each st around. Stuff Body with toy stuffing.
Round 36 (Dc2tog) 5 times. [5 dc]
Fasten off.

UNDER BELLY
Using Yarn B, ch4.
Row 1 (RS) Dc in the second ch from the hook and each of the next 2 ch, turn. [3 dc]
From this point onwards, continue the colour sequence of: 2 rows Yarn C, 2 rows Yarn D, 2 rows Yarn B.
Row 2 Ch1 (does not count as st), 1dc in the first st, 2dc in the next st, 1dc in the last st, turn. [4 dc]
Row 3 Ch1, dc in each st across, turn.
Row 4 Ch1, 1dc in the first st, 2dc in the next st, 1dc in the last 2 sts, turn. [5 dc]
Row 5 Ch1, 1dc in the first 2 sts, 2dc in the next st, 1dc in the last 2 sts, turn. [6 dc]
Row 6 Ch1, 1dc in the first 2 sts, 2dc in the next st, 1dc in the last 3 sts, turn. [7 dc]
Row 7 Ch1, 1dc in each dc across, turn.
Row 8 Ch1, 1dc in the first 3 sts, 2dc in the next st, 1dc in the last 3 sts, turn. [8 dc]
Row 9 Ch1, 1dc in each dc across, turn.
Row 10 Ch1, 1dc in the first 3 sts, 2dc in the next st, 1dc in the last 4 sts, turn. [9 dc]
Row 11 Ch1, 1dc in each dc across, turn.
Row 12 Ch1, 1dc in the first 4 sts, 2dc in the next st, 1dc in the last 4 sts, turn. [10 dc]
Row 13 Ch1, 1dc in the first 4 sts, 2dc in the next st, 1dc in the last 5 sts, turn. [11 dc]
Rows 14-16 Ch1, 1dc in each dc across, turn.
Row 17 Ch1, 1dc in the first 5 sts, 2dc in the next st, 1dc in the last 5 sts, turn. [12 dc]
Row 18 Ch1, 1dc in the first 5 sts, 2dc in the next st, 1dc in the last 6 sts, turn. [13 dc]
Row 19 Ch1, 1dc in each dc across, turn.
Row 20 Ch1, 1dc in the first 6 sts, 2dc in the next st, 1dc in the last 6 sts, turn. [14 dc]
Rows 21-25 Ch1, 1dc in each dc across, turn.
Row 26 Ch1, 1dc in the first 6 sts, dc2tog, 1dc in the last 6 sts, turn. [13 dc]
Row 27 Ch1, 1dc in each dc across, turn.
Row 28 Ch1, 1dc in the first 5 sts, dc2tog, 1dc in the last 6 sts, turn. [12 dc]
Row 29 Ch1, 1dc in the first 5 sts, dc2tog, 1dc in the last 5 sts, turn. [11 dc]
Row 30 Ch1, 1dc in the first 2 sts, htr in the next 2 sts, tr in the next 3 sts, htr in the next 2 sts, 1dc in the last 2 sts. [11 sts]
Fasten off and weave in ends.

Pin this piece to the belly of the Body, making sure the eyes are evenly spaced on each side.
Sew in place.

TAIL (MAKE 4)
Using Yarn A, ch5.
Row 1 (RS) Dc in the second ch from the hook and each of the next 3 ch, turn. [4 dc]
Rows 2-6 Ch1 (does not count as st), dc in each st across, turn.
Row 7 Ch1 (does not count as st), skip the first st, dc in each st across, turn. [3 dc]
Row 8 Ch1 (does not count as st), skip the first st, dc in each st across, turn. [2 dc]
Fasten off.
Holding wrong sides together, sew around the edge of 2 pieces to create one side of the tail.
Repeat with the other 2 pieces and

The belly is crocheted separately then sewn onto the rest of his body

sew both to the tail end of the Body, using the image as a guide.

FLIPPERS (MAKE 4)
Using Yarn A, ch5.
Row 1 (RS) Dc in the second ch from the hook, htr in the next ch, tr in the next ch, dtr in the next ch, turn. [4 sts]
Rows 2-8 Ch1 (does not count as st), dc in each st across, turn. [4 dc]
Row 9 Ch1 (does not count as st), skip first st, dc in each st across, turn. [3 dc]
Row 10 Ch1 (does not count as st), skip the first st, dc in each st across, turn. [2 dc]
Fasten off.

Holding wrong sides together, sew around the edge of 2 pieces to create one flipper. Repeat with the other 2 pieces and sew both to the Body, using the photographs as a guide.

Chinese Cats

You won't need luck to get your new year off to a great start when you make these Chinese beckoning cats. The cats pictured here are decorated with a classic cherry blossom design made from felt and embroidery that adds a softness to these cheeky characters, but you can embellish them in any way you like. Made using just a few simple stitches, we can't think of a more enjoyable project for both newbie and experienced crocheters to try.

YOU WILL NEED

- 4ply weight cotton yarn, approximately one 50g ball of each:
- Yarn A Cream
- Yarn B Yellow
- Yarn C Red

- A 3mm (US C/2 or D/3) hook

- Wool needle

- Toy stuffing

- Black green and red embroidery thread

- Small buttons and gold bells

- Pink and red felt

- Air erasable pen

MEASUREMENTS

28x15cm (11x5¾in)

ABBREVIATIONS

Bobble stitch insert hook in stitch, draw loop through, draw through 2 loops on the hook, (insert hook in same space, draw loop through, draw through 2 loops on hook) repeat 3 times, draw through all 6 loops on hook

LARGE CAT

HEAD AND BODY

Using Yarn A, make a magic loop and work 6dc into the ring. [6sts]

Round 1 2dc into each st to the end. [12sts]

Round 2 (Dc in the first st, 2dc in the next st) repeat to end. [18sts]

Round 3 (Dc in the first 2sts, 2dc in the next st) repeat to end. [24sts]

Round 4 (Dc in the first 3sts, 2dc in the next st) repeat to end. [30sts]

Round 5 (Dc in the first 9sts, 2dc in the next st) repeat to end. [33sts]

Round 6 (Dc in the first 10sts, 2dc in the next st) repeat to end. [36sts]

Round 7 (Dc in the first 11sts, 2dc in the next st) repeat to end. [39sts]

Round 8 (Dc in the first 12sts, 2dc in the next st) repeat to end. [42sts]

Round 9 (Dc in the first 13sts, 2dc in the next st) repeat to end. [45sts]

Round 10 (Dc in the first 14sts, 2dc in the next st) repeat to end. [48sts]

Round 11 (Dc in the first 15sts, 2dc in the next st) repeat to end. [51sts]

Round 12 (Dc in the first 16sts, 2dc in the next st) repeat to end. [54sts]

Rounds 13-15 dc in each st to the end. [54sts]

Round 16 (Dc2tog, dc in next 7sts) repeat to end. [48sts]

Round 17 (Dc2tog, dc in next 6sts) repeat to end. [42sts]

Round 18 (Dc2tog, dc in next 5sts) repeat to end. [36sts]

Round 19 (Dc2tog, dc in next 4sts) repeat to end. [30sts]

Round 20 (Dc2tog, dc in the next 3sts) repeat to end. [24sts]

Stuff the head now.

Round 21 (Dc2tog, dc in the next 2sts) repeat to end. [18sts]

Round 22 (Dc2tog, dc in the next st) repeat to end. [12sts]

Round 23 (Dc in the first st, 2dc in the next st) repeat to end. [18sts]

Round 24 (Dc in the first 2sts, 2dc in the next st) repeat to end. [24sts]

Round 25 (Dc in the first 3sts, 2dc in the next st) repeat to end. [30sts]

Round 26 (Dc in the first 9sts, 2dc in the next st) repeat to end. [33sts]

Round 27 (Dc in the first 10sts, 2dc in the next st) repeat to end. [36sts]

Round 28 (Dc in the first 11sts, 2dc in the next st) repeat to end. [39sts]

Round 29 (Dc in the first 12sts, 2dc in the next st) repeat to end. [42sts]

Round 30 (Dc in the first 13sts, 2dc in the next st) repeat to end. [45sts]

Round 31 (Dc in the first 14sts, 2dc in the next st) repeat to end. [48sts]

Rounds 32-35 dc in each st to the end. [48sts]

Round 36 (Dc2tog, dc in next 6sts) repeat to end. [42sts]

Round 37 (Dc2tog, dc in next 5sts) repeat to end. [36sts]

Round 38 (Dc2tog, dc in next 4sts) repeat to end. [30sts]

Round 39 (Dc2tog, dc in the next 3sts) repeat to end. [24sts]

Stuff the head now.

Round 40 (Dc2tog, dc in the next 2sts) repeat to end. [18sts]

Round 41 (Dc2tog, dc in the next st) repeat to end. [12sts]

Round 42 (Dc2tog) repeat to end. [6sts]

Fasten off, then thread the cut yarn onto a wool needle and weave through the last 6sts, pull the yarn to close the hole. Weave in yarn and cut off any loose ends.

SMALL ARM

Using Yarn A, make a magic ring and work 6dc into the ring. 6sts.

Round 1 2dc into each st to the end. [12sts]

Rounds 2-3 Dc in each st to the end. [12sts]

Rounds 4-7 Dc2tog, dc in each st to the end. [8sts]

Rounds 8-14 Dc in each st to the end. [8sts]

Cut the yarn leaving a long tail and pull through loop to secure.

Stuff the arm firmly with toy stuffing and sew closed the gap at the top of the arm.

BECKONING ARM

Using Yarn A, make a magic ring and work 6dc into the ring. 6sts]

Round 1 2dc into each st to the end. [12sts]

Round 2 (Dc in the first st, 2dc in the next st) repeat to end. [18sts]

Rounds 3-4 Dc in each st to the end. [18sts]

Round 5 (Dc2tog, dc in the next st) repeat to end. [12sts]

Rounds 6-8 Dc2tog, dc in each st to the end. [9sts]

Rounds 9-17 Dc in each st to the end. [9sts]

Cut the yarn leaving a long tail and pull through loop to secure.

Stuff the arm firmly with toy stuffing and sew closed the gap at the top of

the arm.
Use Yarn A to make the detail on the paws. Anchor the thread to the base of the foot by sewing a few small stitches. Then use the photo as a guide to work long stitches 1cm (½in) apart, twice over the paw to create the pads (pull the thread really tight as you do this so that it shapes the paw). Secure thread as before to keep paw shape in place, then weave in and cut off any loose ends.

FEET
Make two in Yarn A.
Make a magic ring and work 6dc into the ring. 6sts.
Round 1 2dc into each st to the end. [12sts]
Round 2 (Dc in the first st, 2dc in the next st) repeat to end. [18sts]
Rounds 3-4 dc in each st to the end. [18sts]
Round 5 (Dc2tog) repeat to end. [9sts]
Fasten off as before and stuff firmly. Shape the feet as for the large arm.

EARS
Make two in Yarn A.
Make a magic ring and work 4dc into the ring. [4sts]
Round 1 (Dc in the first st, 2dc in the next st) repeat to end. [6sts]
Round 2 (Dc in the first 2sts, 2dc in the next st) repeat to end. [8sts]
Round 3 (Dc in the first 3sts, 2dc in the next st) repeat to end. [10sts]
Round 4 (Dc in the first 4sts, 2dc in the next st) repeat to end. [12sts]
Round 5 (Dc in the first 5sts, 2dc in the next st) repeat to end. [14sts]
Round 6 (Dc in the first 6sts, 2dc in the next st) repeat to end. [16sts]
Fasten off as before.
Cut a small triangle of red felt and glue inside the ear. Then use the photo as a guide to sew the ears to the cat's head. Pin the arms and feet in place and, when you are happy with the positioning, sew together. Weave in and cut off any loose ends.

COLLAR
Make one in Yarn C.
Ch 4.
Row 1 dc in second ch from hook, dc in next 2sts. [3sts]
Rows 1-30 ch 1 turn, dc in each st to end. [3sts]
Fasten off and sew around the cat's neck.

MEDALLION
Make one in Yarn B.
Make a magic ring and work 6dc into the ring. [6sts]
Round 1 2dc into each st to the end, sl st to join. [12sts]
Fasten off and weave in any loose ends then stitch the medallion to the collar.

WORK THE DETAILS
Using the photo as a guide, draw the face onto the head using water- or air-erasable pen. Use red embroidery thread to sew long stitches for the nose and mouth and black thread for the eyes, eyelashes and whiskers. Cut 4 small circles of pink felt, then cut 4 tiny slits out of them to turn them into flower shapes. Glue or sew onto the cat in a random pattern over the body and head, then join together with stitches of green embroidery thread for stems. Add tiny buttons as flower centres. Thread a gold bell onto red thread and tie around the cat's neck.

Cut 4 small circles of pink felt, then cut 4 tiny slits out of them to turn them into flower shapes. Glue or sew onto the cat in a random pattern over the body and head, then join together with stitches of green embroidery thread for stems. Add tiny buttons as flower centres. Thread a gold bell onto red thread and tie around the cat's neck.

SMALL CATS
HEAD AND BODY
Make two of each in Yarn A.
Make a magic ring and work 6dc into the ring. 6sts.

Round 1 2dc into each st to the end. [12sts]
Round 2 (Dc in the first st, 2dc in the next st) repeat to end. [18sts]
Round 3 (Dc in the first 2sts, 2dc in the next st) repeat to end. [24sts]
Round 4 (Dc in the first 3sts, 2dc in the next st) repeat to end. [30sts]
Rounds 5-7 dc in each st to the end. [30sts]
Round 8 (Dc2tog, dc in the next 3sts) repeat to end. [24sts]
Round 9 (Dc2tog, dc in the next 2sts) repeat to end. [18sts]
Round 10 (Dc2tog, dc in the next st) repeat to end. [12sts]
Stuff the head now.
Round 11 (Dc2tog) repeat to end. [6sts]
Round 12 2dc into each st to the end. [12sts]
Round 13 (Dc in the first st, 2dc in the next st) repeat to end. [18sts]
Round 14 (Dc in the first 2sts, 2dc in the next st) repeat to end. [24sts]
Rounds 15-16 dc in each st to the end. [24sts]
Round 17 (Dc2tog, dc in the next 2sts) repeat to end. [18sts]
Round 18 (Dc2tog, dc in the next st) repeat to end. [12sts]
Stuff the head now.
Round 19 (Dc2tog) repeat to end. [6sts]
Fasten off, then thread the cut yarn onto a wool needle and weave through the last 6sts, pull the yarn to close the hole. Weave in yarn and cut off any loose ends.

EARS
Make four in Yarn A.
Ch 4, dc in second ch from hook, htr in next st, tr in last st.
Fasten off as before. Cut small red felt triangles and glue into the ear then sew in place on the head of each cat.

BECKONING ARM
Make two in Yarn A (one for each cat).
Make a magic ring and work 6dc into the ring. [6sts]

Round 1 (Dc in the first st, 2dc in the next st) repeat to end. [9sts]
Rounds 2-3 dc in each st to the end. [9sts]
Round 4 (Dc2tog, dc in next st) repeat to end. [6sts]
Rounds 5-12 dc in each st to the end. [6sts]
Cut the yarn leaving a long tail and pull through loop to secure.
Stuff the arm firmly with toy stuffing and sew one to the right side of the body of each cat.

COLLAR
Make two in Yarn C.
Ch 16.
Ss in second ch from hook, sl st along ch to end.
Fasten off and sew one in place around each cat's neck. Weave in and cut off any loose ends.
Create the face as you did for the large cat.

THE POT OF GOLD
Make one in Yarn C.
Make a magic ring and work 6dc into the ring. [6sts]
Round 1 2dc into each st to the end. [12sts]
Round 2 (Dc in the first st, 2dc in the next st) repeat to end. [18sts]
Round 3 (Dc in the first 2sts, 2dc in the next st) repeat to end.[24sts]
Round 4 (Dc in the first 3sts, 2dc in the next st) repeat to end. [30sts]
Round 5 (Dc in the first 9sts, 2dc in the next st) repeat to end. [33sts]
Round 6 (Dc in the first 10sts, 2dc in the next st) repeat to end. [36sts]
Round 7 (Dc in the first 11sts, 2dc in the next st) repeat to end. [39sts]
Rounds 8-10 dc in each st to the end. [39sts]
Round 11 (Dc2tog, dc in the next 11sts) repeat to end. [36sts]
Round 12 (Dc2tog, dc in the next 10sts) repeat to end. [33sts]

Round 13 dc in each st to the end. [33sts]
Fasten off as before and weave in any loose ends. Stuff well.

GOLD
Make 1 in Yarn B.
Make a magic ring and work 6dc into the ring. [6sts]
Round 1 (bobble st, ch1) in each st to the end. 6 bobbles and 6chs.
Round 2 (bobble st, ch1, bobble st, ch1) in each chain space to the end, sl st to join. 12 bobbles and 12 ch.
Fasten off as before, then sew the gold onto the top of the pot. Weave in and cut off any loose ends, to finish.

Use an air- or water-erasable pen to draw the features onto the head before embroidering

Pretty Peacock

This perfect peacock with his proud plumage is bound to turn plenty of heads.
Hook one and keep him as your favourite, or create a whole flock
to give away as gifts ...

YOU WILL NEED

• 4ply weight cotton yarn,
approximately one 50g ball of
each:
- Yarn A Bright blue
- Yarn B Turquoise
- Yarn C Yellow

• A 2.5mm (US C/1 or B/2)
crochet hook

• 2 safety eyes or black beads
approx 5mm diameter

• Stitch markers

• Toy stuffing

MEASUREMENTS

11 cm (4¼in) tall

NOTES

• The Head and Body are worked as
one piece starting from the top of the
Head. All the other pieces are sewn
to the body.

HEAD AND BODY

Using Yarn A, make a magic loop.
Round 1 (RS) Ch1 (does not count as
st throughout), 6dc into the loop. [6
dc]
Round 2 2dc in each st around. [12 dc]
Round 3 (2dc in next st, dc in next st)
6 times. [18 dc]

Round 4 (2dc in next st, 2dc in next
st) 6 times. [24 dc]
Rounds 5-8 Dc in each st around.
[24 dc]
Round 9 7dc, (dc in next st, dc2tog)
3 times, 8dc. [21 dc]
Rounds 10-11 Dc in each st around.
[21 dc]
Round 12 8dc, (2dc in next st, dc in
next st) 3 times, 7dc. [24 dc]
Round 13 (Dc in next st, 2dc in next
st) 3 times, 12dc, (2dc in next st, dc in
next st) 3 times. [30 dc]
Round 14 (Dc in next 2 sts, 2dc in
next st) 3 times, 12dc, (2dc in next st,

*Simple but effective
chains are looped over
to make up the crest on
the peacock's head*

*The tail feathers are
sewn on in layers to
create that famous
peacock fan*

dc in next 2 sts) 3 times. [36 dc]
Insert the safety eyes between Rounds 6 and 7 approx 7 sts apart. If you're using black beads, sew the eyes when you have stuffed and finished the Body. Stuff the Head and continue stuffing as you go.
Round 15 Dc in each st around. [36 dc]
Round 16 (Dc in next st, 2dc in next st) 3 times, 24dc, (2dc in next st, dc in next st) 3 times. [42 dc]
Rounds 17-21 Dc in each st around. [42 dc]
Round 22 (5dc, dc2tog) 6 times. [36 dc]
Round 23 (4dc, dc2tog) 6 times. [30 dc]
Round 24 (3dc, dc2tog) 6 times. [24 dc]
Round 25 (2dc, dc2tog) 6 times. [18 dc]
Round 26 (1dc, dc2tog) 6 times. [12 dc]
Round 27 (Dc2tog) 6 times. [6 dc]
Fasten off and weave in ends.

BEAK
Using Yarn C, make a magic loop.
Round 1 (RS) Ch1, 5dc into the loop. [5 dc]
Round 2 2dc in next st, 4dc. [6 dc]
Round 3 2dc in next st, 5dc. [7 dc]
Fasten off, leaving a long tail for sewing.
Do not stuff. Pinch the Beak and sew it between Rounds 7 and 9 of the Head.

TAIL
LARGE FEATHER (MAKE 3)
Using Yarn A, make a magic loop.
Round 1 (RS) Ch1, 6dc into the loop. [6 dc]
Round 2 2dc in each st around. [12 dc]
Round 3 (2dc in next st, 5dc) twice. [14 dc]
Round 4 (2dc in next st, 6dc) twice. [16 dc]
Rounds 5-6 Dc in each st around. [16 dc]
Round 7 (Dc2tog, 6dc) twice. [14 dc]
Round 8 Dc in each st around. [14 dc]

Round 9 (Dc2tog, 5dc) twice. [12 dc]
Round 10 Dc in each st around. [12 dc]
Round 11 (Dc2tog, 4dc) twice. [10 dc]
Round 12 Dc in each st around. [10 dc]
Round 13 (Dc2tog, 3dc) twice. [8 dc]
Round 14 Dc in each st around. [8 dc]
Round 15 (Dc2tog, 2dc) twice. [8 dc]
Fasten off, leaving a long tail for sewing.
Do not stuff.

LARGE FEATHER DETAIL (MAKE 3)
Using Yarn C, make a magic loop.
Round 1 (RS) Ch1 (does not count as st), 6dc into the loop. [6 dc]
Change to Yarn B.
Round 2 2dc in each st around. [12 dc]
Round 3 Ch4, ss in second ch from hook, dc in next ch, htr in next ch, skip first 2 sts in Round 2, ss in next st.
Fasten off, leaving a tail for sewing this piece on to the Large Feather.

MEDIUM FEATHER (MAKE 3)
Using Yarn C, make a magic loop.
Round 1 (RS) Ch1, 6dc into the loop. [6 dc]
Change to Yarn B.
Round 2 2dc in each st around. [12 dc]
Round 3 Ch6, dc in second ch from hook and next ch, htr in next 2 ch, tr in next ch, skip first 3 sts in Round 2, ss in next st. Fasten off, leaving a tail for sewing.

SMALL FEATHER (MAKE 3)
Using Yarn A, ch7.
Row 1 (RS) Dc in second ch from hook, htr in next 3 ch, dc in next ch, ss in last ch. **Fasten off,** leaving a tail for sewing.

TO MAKE UP
Sew the Large Feather Detail onto the centre of the Large Feathers. Pin the Feathers to the base of the Body at the back, starting with the Large Feathers and layering the Medium

and Small ones on top, using the image as a guide. Sew securely into place.

CREST
Using Yarn A, ch5.
Ss in to the 5th ch from hook, ch8 and ss into the 8th ch from hook, ch5 and ss into the 5th ch from the hook.
Fasten off, leaving a tail. Sew to the centre back of the Head using the image as a guide.

FOOT (MAKE 2)
Using Yarn C, ch3.
Ss in second ch from hook and next ch. Ch4, ss in second ch from hook and next 2 ch, ch3, ss in second ch from hook and next ch, ch6, ss in second ch from hook and next 4 ch, ss in the first ch to join. **Fasten off** leaving a tail.
Sew the Feet to the Body.

Frog Prince

Quick and simple to make, this friendly frog is the perfect little gift to make for Valentine's Day, or if you just fancy a royal frog prince of your very own! A shiny gold crown perched on his head and a crimson heart brimming with love ensure we can't resist his froggy charms.

YOU WILL NEED

- Aran weight cotton yarn, approximately one 50g ball of each:
  - Yarn A Red
  - Yarn B Green
  - Yarn C Light Green
  - Yarn D Blue
  - Yarn E White

- A 4mm (US G/6) and 3mm (US C/2 or D/3) hook

- 9mm black safety eyes

- Toy stuffing

- Yarn needle

- Gold lamé embroidery thread

- Black embroidery thread

- Fabric glue

HEAD AND BODY

Starting in Yarn B, make a magic ring and work 6dc into the ring. 6sts

Round 1 2dc into each st to the end. 12sts

Round 2 (Dc in the first st, 2dc in the next st) repeat to end. [18sts]

Round 3 Dc in each st to end. [18sts

Round 4 (Dc in the first two sts, 2dc in the next st) repeat to end. [24sts]

Round 5 Dc in each st to end. [24sts]

Round 6 (Dc in the first three sts, 2dc in the next st) repeat to end. [30sts]

Round 7 Dc in each st to end. [30sts]

Round 8 (Dc in the first four sts, 2dc in the next st) repeat to end. [36sts]

Round 9-13 Dc in each st to end. [36sts]

Round 14 (Dc2tog, dc in the next ten sts) repeat to end. [33sts]

TOP TIP

Crochet a few extra little hearts to spread the love to everyone you care about!

Round 15 Dc in each st to end. [33sts]
Round 16 (Dc2tog, dc in the next nine sts) repeat to end. [30sts]
Round 17 Dc in each st to end. [30sts]
Round 18 (Dc2tog, dc in next three sts) repeat to end. [24sts]
Round 19 (Dc2tog, dc in next two sts) repeat to end. [18sts]
Round 20 (Dc2tog, dc in next st) repeat to end. [12sts]
Stuff firmly now.
Round 21 (Dc2tog) repeat to end. [6sts]
Fasten off and sew closed the gap at the bottom of the body. Weave in and cut off any loose ends.

LEGS
Make two of each size.
Starting in Yarn B, make a magic ring and work 6dc into the ring. [6sts]

SHORT LEGS
Round1-5 Dc in each st to end. [6sts]
Change to Yarn C.
Round 6-9 Dc in each st to end. [6sts]
Round 10 (Dc in the first two sts, 2dc in the next st) repeat to end. [8sts]
Round 11 (Dc in the first three sts, 2dc in the next st) repeat to end. [10sts]
Round 12 (Dc in the first four sts, 2dc in the next st) repeat to end. [12sts]
Round 13 (Dc in the first five sts, 2dc in the next st) repeat to end. [14sts]
Round 14 (Tr in first st, ch 2, dc in next two sts) repeat to last two sts, tr in next st, ch 2, dc in last st.
Fasten off, stuff with a pipe cleaner and sew closed the foot so that the treble stitches are lining up and forming the webbed foot.

LONG LEGS
Starting in Yarn B, make a magic ring and work 6dc into the ring. (6sts)
Round 1-15 Dc in each st to end. 6sts
Continue from round 6 of short legs pattern
Finish as before. Using the photo as a guide, bend the legs into shape and sew in place securely on the body. Weave in and cut off any loose ends.

EYES (MAKE TWO.)
Starting in Yarn E, make a magic ring and work 6dc into the ring. [6sts]
Round 1 (Dc in the first st, 2dc in the next st) repeat to end. [9sts]
Change to light green yarn
Round 2 Dc in each st to end. 9sts
Place a black safety eye through the centre of the eye. Stuff the eye and fasten off. Sew closed to form a ball, then sew in place on the head of the frog.

BOW (MAKE ONE IN YARN D.)
Ch 4
Row 1 Dc in 2nd ch from the hook, dc in the next two ch sts. [3sts]
Row 2-6 Ch 1, turn, dc in each st to the end. [3sts]
Fasten off leaving a long tail, thread the yarn to the centre of the long edge and wrap around, pulling tight to form a bow. Secure the yarn and then sew in place on the frog.
Using black embroidery thread on your wool needle, create a long stitch for the mouth with two short stitches either end. Fasten off and weave in loose ends where they can't be seen.

CROWN
Make one using gold lamé embroidery thread and a 3mm crochet hook.
Ch 14, Ss to form a ring
Round 1 1dc into each ch st. [14sts]
Round 2 (Tr in first st, ch 2, dc in next two sts) repeat to last two sts, tr in next st, ch 2, dc in last st
Fasten off and sew in place on the head.

HEART (MAKE ONE IN YARN A)
The heart is made by first making two circles then joining them together to form the heart in one piece.

1ST CIRCLE
Start with 6dc into magic ring. 6sts
Round 1 2dc into each st to the end. [12sts]
Round 2-3 Dc in each st to end. [12 sts]
Cut yarn and fasten off.

2ND CIRCLE
Make the same as circle 1 but do not cut off yarn at end.

JOINING CIRCLES
Round 1 Dc in the 12sts of circle 2, without breaking yarn dc in the 12sts of circle 1. [24sts]
Round 2 (Dc2tog, dc in next six sts) repeat to end. [21sts]
Round 3 (Dc2tog, dc in next five sts) repeat to end. [18sts]
Round 4 (Dc2tog, dc in next four sts) repeat to end. [15sts]
Round 5 (Dc2tog, dc in next three sts) repeat to end. [12sts]
Round 6 (Dc2tog, dc in next two sts) repeat to end. [9sts]
Stuff the heart now.
Round 7 (Dc2tog, dc in next st) repeat to end. [6sts]
Round 8 (Dc2tog) repeat to end. [3sts]

TO FINISH
Fasten off as before. Sew closed the hole at the base and top of the heart and sew in-between the frog's legs. Weave in and cut off any loose ends to finish.

Jolly Giraffe

Who wouldn't love the huge eyes and fluttering lashes on this charming animal character? This lovely giraffe is simple to crochet and uses fake eyelashes and felt to create eyes with a soft, droopy look. Grab your hook and get started now!

YOU WILL NEED

• 4ply weight cotton yarn, approximately 1 50g ball of each:
- Yarn A Beige
- Yarn B Brown
- Yarn C Yellow

• A 3mm (US C/2 or D/3) hook

• Black safety eyes, 15mm

• Wool needle

• Toy stuffing and pellets

• Beige felt

• Brown embroidery thread

• Clear fabric glue

• Fake eyelashes

MEASUREMENTS

• 30x20cm (11¾x8in)

EYES

Make the eyes first. Cut two circles of felt slightly larger than the safety toy eye and blanket stitch around the edge of each one with two strands of brown embroidery thread. Cut a hole in the centre of each felt circle to insert the post of the toy eye later. Cut two rectangles of felt slightly larger than the toy eye for eyelids. Coat the top third of the toy eyes with fabric glue. Mould a felt piece over the glued area, so it covers half the eye. Leave to dry, then cut off the excess. Attach fake eyelashes to the edge of the eyelid – stitch to the felt for extra security, then cut off any excess. Push the decorated eyes through the holes in the eye patches, then put to one side.

LEGS (MAKE 4)

Using Yarn B, make a magic loop.
Round 1 (RS) 6dc into the loop. [6 sts]
Round 2 2dc in each st around. [12 sts]
Round 3 (Dc in first st, 2dc in next st) 6 times. [18 sts]
Round 4 (2dc, 2dc in next st) 6 times. [24 sts]
Round 5 Dc bl in each st around.
Rounds 6-7 Dc in each st around.
Change to Yarn C.
Round 8 Dc2tog, dc in each st around. [23 sts]
Round 9 Dc in each st around.
Rounds 10-19 Repeat the last 2 rounds 5 more times. [18 sts after Round 19]
Rounds 20-27 Dc in each st around. Fasten off.
Stuff with toy stuffing pellets to make the finished giraffe stand up or with normal toy stuffing if you want a soft plush toy.

BODY

Using Yarn C, make a magic loop.
Round 1 (RS) 6dc into the loop. [6 sts]
Round 2 2dc in each st around. [12 sts]
Round 3 (Dc in first st, 2dc in next st) 6 times. [18 sts]
Round 4 (2dc, 2dc in next st) 6 times. [24 sts]
Round 5 (3dc, 2dc in next st) 6 times. [30 sts]
Round 6 (4dc, 2dc in next st) 6 times. [36 sts]
Round 7 (5dc, 2dc in next st) 6 times. [42 sts]
Rounds 8-21 Dc in each st around.
Round 22 (Dc2tog, 5dc) 6 times. [36 sts]
Round 23 (Dc2tog, 4dc) 6 times. [30 sts]
Round 24 (Dc2tog, 3dc) 6 times. [24 sts]
Round 25 (Dc2tog, 2dc) 6 times. [18 sts]
Round 26 (Dc2tog, 1dc) 6 times. [12 sts]
Stuff to this point.
Round 27 (Dc2tog) repeat 6 times. [6 sts]
Fasten off and sew closed the gap in the bottom of the Body.

HEAD

Using Yarn A, ch5.
Round 1 (RS) Dc in second ch from hook, dc in next 2 sts, 3dc in st, working along other side of foundation ch, dc in 2 sts, 2dc in last st. [10 sts]
Round 2 (Dc in first st, 2dc in next st) 5 times. [15 sts]
Round 3 (2dc, 2dc in next st) 5 times. [20 sts]
Round 4 (3dc, 2dc in next st) 5 times. [25 sts]
Round 5 (4dc, 2dc in next st) 5 times. [30 sts]

Round 6 (4dc, 2dc in next st) 6 times. [36 sts]
Round 7 (5dc, 2dc in next st) 6 times. [42 sts]
Round 8 (6dc, 2dc in next st) 6 times. [48 sts]
Rounds 9-13 Dc2tog, dc in each st around.
Change to Yarn C.
Rounds 14-26 Dc2tog, dc in each st around. [30 sts after Round 26]
Insert the Eyes now on Round 15 (one above the colour change) and 9 sts apart.
Round 27 (Dc2tog, 3dc) 6 times. [24 sts]
Round 28 (Dc2tog, 2dc) 6 times. [18 sts]
Round 29 (Dc2tog, 1dc) 6 times. [12 sts]
Stuff to this point.
Round 30 (Dc2tog) 6 times. [6 sts]
Fasten off and sew closed the hole at the back of the Head.

NECK
Using Yarn C, make a magic loop.
Round 1 (RS) 6dc into the loop. [6 sts]
Round 2 2dc in each st around. [12 sts]
Round 3 (Dc in first st, 2dc in next st) 6 times. [18 sts]
Round 4 (2dc, 2dc in next st) 6 times. [24 sts]
Round 5 Dc bl in each st around.
Round 6 (11dc, 2dc in next st) twice. [26 sts]
Rounds 7-9 Dc in each st around.
Round 10 (12dc, 2dc in next st) twice. [28 sts]
Rounds 11-12 Dc in each st around.
Fasten off and stuff well.
Use the image as a guide to sew the closed end to the underside of the Neck and the open end to the front of the Body. Sew the Legs on the underside of the Body.

EARS (MAKE 2)
Using Yarn C, make a magic loop.
Round 1 (RS) 4dc into the loop. [4 sts]
Round 2 (Dc in first st, 2dc in next st) twice. [6 sts]
Round 3 (2dc, 2dc in next st) twice. [8 sts]

Round 4 (3dc, 2dc in next st) twice. [10 sts]
Round 5 (4dc, 2dc in next st) twice. [12 sts]
Round 6 (5dc, 2dc in next st) twice. [14 sts]
Rounds 7-9 Dc in each st around.
Fasten off. Pinch the bottom edge together and sew in place on the sides of the Head.

HORNS (MAKE 2)
Using Yarn A, make a magic loop.
Round 1 (RS) 6dc into the loop. [6 sts]
Round 2 2dc into each st around. [12 sts]
Rounds 3-4 Dc in each st around.
Round 5 (Dc2tog) 6 times. [6 sts]
Rounds 6-7 Dc in each st around.
Fasten off, stuff and sew in place on the Head.

LARGE SPOTS (MAKE 8)
Using Yarn B, make a magic loop.
Round 1 (RS) 6dc into the loop. [6 sts]
Round 2 2dc into each st around, ss to first dc. [12 sts]

Fasten off and sew in place randomly over the Body and Neck.

SMALL SPOTS (MAKE 8)
Using Yarn B, make a magic loop.
Round 1 (RS) 6dc into the loop, ss to first dc. [6 sts]
Fasten off and sew in place randomly over the Body.

MANE
Using Yarn B, ch62.
Dc in second ch from hook and work along ch as follows:
(Ch1, dc in next st) 10 times, (ch2, dc in next st) 15 times, (ch3, dc in next st) 10 times, (ch2, dc in next st) 15 times, (ch1, dc in next st) 10 times.
Fasten off. Fold in half and sew in place along the Neck of the giraffe.

TAIL
Plait three lengths of Yarn C together. Knot the end and sew securely in place, to complete your giraffe. Weave in all ends.

Sleepy Sloth

This beady-eyed chap is never more than a few moments away from nodding off,
so he keeps his stripy nightcap on at all times. Will you give him a place to nap?

YOU WILL NEED

• 4ply weight cotton yarn,
approximately one 50g ball
of each:
- Yarn A Mid Brown
- Yarn B Dark Brown
- Yarn C Cream
- Yarn D Light Blue
- Yarn E Bright Blue
- Yarn F White

• A 2.5 mm (US B/1 or C/2) hook

• A pair of 6mm safety eyes

• An oval safety nose

• Black embroidery thread

• Stitch markers

• Tapestry needle

• Toy stuffing

• Pipe cleaners (optional)

MEASUREMENTS

26cm (10in) tall

ABBREVIATIONS

BL back loop only
FL front loop only

NOTES

• Arms and legs are made first and then joined to the body as you work.
• Insert pipe cleaners into the arms and legs to make them able to move in any position, otherwise stuff the limbs with toy stuffing.

LEGS (MAKE 2)

FEET

With Yarn B, ch4.
Row 1 (WS) Dc in second ch from hook and each ch across, turn. [3 dc]
Row 2 (Ch4, ss in second ch from hook and in each of next 2 ch, ss in bl of next st of Row 1) 3 times working last ss into beg ch-1 of Row 1. **Fasten off.**

LEGS

Round 1 Join Yarn A in fl of first st of Row 1, ch1, dc in fl loop only of each st in Row 1, continue along the other side of the foundation ch, dc in next 3 ch. [6 dc]
Round 2 (2dc in next st, 2dc) twice. [8 dc]
Rounds 3-5 Dc in each st around. [8 dc]
Round 6 2dc in next st, 7dc. [9 dc]
Rounds 7-8 Dc in each st around. [9 dc]
Round 9 2dc in next st, 8dc. [10 dc]
Rounds 10-11 Dc in each st around. [10 dc]
Round 12 2dc in next st, 9dc. [11 dc]
Rounds 13-14 Dc in each st around. [11 dc]
Round 15 2dc in next st, 10dc. [12 dc]
Rounds 16-20 Dc in each st around. [12 dc]
Fasten off.
Insert a pipe cleaner and stuff lightly.

ARMS (MAKE 2)

With Yarn B, ch4.
Rows 1-2 Work as Rows 1-2 of Feet.
Rounds 3-6 Work as Rounds 1-4 of Legs.
Round 7 (2dc in next st, 3dc) twice. [10 dc]
Round 8 Dc in each st around. [10 dc]
Round 9 (2dc in next st, 4dc) twice. [12 dc]

Rounds 10-11 Dc in each st around. [12 dc]
Round 12 Dc2tog, dc in next 10 dc. [11 sts]
Rounds 13-14 Dc in each st around. [11 dc]
Round 15 Dc2tog, dc in next 9 dc. [10 sts]
Round 16 Dc in each st around. [10 dc]
Round 17 Dc2tog, dc in next 8 dc. [9 sts]
Round 18 Join Yarn D in first st, dc in each st around. [9 dc]
Round 19 Dc in each st around. [9 dc]
Fasten off.
Insert a pipe cleaner and stuff lightly.

BODY

The Body is worked from the base upwards.
With Yarn A, make a magic loop.
Round 1 Ch1 (does not count as st), 6dc into the ring. [6 dc]
Round 2 2dc in each st around. [12 dc]
Round 3 (2dc in next st, 1dc) 6 times. [18 dc]
Round 4 (2dc in next st, 2dc) 6 times. [24 dc]
Round 5 (2dc in next st, 3dc) 6 times. [30 dc]
Round 6 (2dc in next st, 4dc) 6 times. [36 dc]
Round 7 2dc in next st, 4dc, 2dc in next st, to join the first leg work the next 6 dc in the sts of both the Body and Leg, 2dc in next st on body, 4dc, 2dc in next st, for the second leg work the next 6 dc in the sts of both the Body and Leg, (2dc in next st, 5dc) 2 times. [42 dc]
Round 8 (2dc in next st, 6dc, 2dc in next st, 6dc in the remaining sts of the leg) twice, (2dc in next st, 6dc) 2 times. [48 dc]
Rounds 9-18 Dc in each st around. [48 dc]
Round 19 (Dc2tog, 6dc) 6 times. [42 sts]
Fasten off.
Round 20 Join Yarn D in first st, dc in each st around. [42 dc]
Round 21 Dc in each st around. [42 dc]

Round 22 (Dc2tog, 5dc) 6 times. [36 sts]
Round 23 Dc in each st around. [36 dc]
Round 24 (Dc2tog, 4dc) 6 times. [30 sts]
Round 25 Dc in each st around. [30 dc]
Round 26 Dc in next 6 sts, to join the first arm work the next 3 dc in the sts of both the Body and Arm, 12dc, for the second arm work the next 3 dc in the sts of both the Body and Arm, 6dc. [30 dc]
Round 27 Dc in next 6 sts, dc in the remaining 6 sts of the first arm, 12dc, dc in the remaining 6 sts of the second Arm, 6dc. [36 dc]
Rounds 28-30 Dc in each st around. [36 dc]
Round 31 Rotate so that the Sloth is upside down, crochet the collar working in bl as follows: Ch1 (does not count as st), 13dc, 2htr, 2tr, (tr, ch3, ss) in next st, (ss ch3, tr) in next st, 2tr, 2htr, 13dc, ss in first dc to join. [36 sts]
Fasten off leaving a long tail for sewing. Fold the last Round to create the collar.

HEAD

With Yarn A, make a magic loop.
Round 1 Ch1 (does not count as st), 6dc into the loop. [6 dc]
Round 2 2dc in each st around. [12 dc]
Round 3 (2dc in next st, 1dc) 6 times. [18 dc]

Round 4 (2dc in next st, 2dc) 6 times. [24 dc]

Round 5 (2dc in next st, 3dc) 6 times. [30 dc]

Round 6 (2dc in next st, 4dc) 6 times. [36 dc]

Round 7 (2dc in next st, 5dc) 6 times. [42 dc]

Rounds 8-17 Dc in each st around. [42 dc]

Round 18 (Dc2tog, 5dc) 6 times. [36 sts]

Round 19 (Dc2tog, 4dc) 6 times. [30 sts]

Rounds 20-21 Dc in each st around. [30 dc]

Fasten off and weave in ends.

FACE PATCH

With Yarn C, ch6.

Round 1 Dc in second ch from the hook and each of next 3 ch, 5dc in last ch, working along opposite side of the starting ch, 3dc, 4dc in last st. [16 dc]

Round 2 (5dc, 2dc in each of next 3 sts) twice. [22 dc]

Round 3 5dc, (2dc in next st, 1dc) 3 times, 5dc, (2dc in next st, 1dc) 3 times. [28 dc]

Round 4 5dc, (2dc in next st, 2dc) 3 times, 5dc, (2dc in next st, 2dc) 3 times. [34 dc]

Fasten off leaving a long tail for sewing.

Pin the face patch between Rounds 9 and 17 of the Head and sew securely into place using the long tail.

EYE PATCHES (MAKE 2)

With Yarn B, ch8.

Round 1 Dc in second ch from hook and in next 5 ch, 5dc in last ch, working along opposite side of the starting ch, 5dc, 4dc in last st. [20 dc]

Round 2 (7dc, 2dc in each of next 3 sts) twice. [26 dc]

Fasten off leaving a long tail for sewing.

Insert the safety eyes into a corner of the eye patch, then insert between Rounds 2 and 3 of the face patch (Rounds 12 and 13 of the head)

approx 8 stitches apart. Rotate the eye patches downward before securing the safety eyes.

Insert the nose between the eyes into the very centre of the face patch. Using black thread, embroider a small mouth 2 rounds below nose.

Stuff the head with toy stuffing and sew it to the body using the remaining loops behind the collar to join them together.

HAT

Start with Yarn D, change colour after every two Rounds using Yarns D, E and F. Do not fasten off yarn, carry yarn up the hat on the WS.

Make a magic loop.

Round 1 Ch1 (does not count as st), 5dc into the loop. [5 dc]

Round 2 Dc in each st around. [5 dc]

Round 3 4dc, 2dc in next st. [6 dc]

Round 4 Dc in each st around. [6 dc]

Round 5 Dc in each st around to last st, 2dc in last st. [7 dc]

Round 6 Dc in each st around. [7 dc]

Rounds 7-12 Repeat (Rounds 5 and 6) 3 times. [10 dc]

Round 13 (4dc, 2dc in next st) twice. [12 dc]

Round 14 Dc in each st around. [12 dc]

Round 15 (5dc, 2dc in next st) twice. [14 dc]

Round 16 and all even rounds to Round 34 Repeat Round 14.

Round 17 (6dc, 2dc in next st) twice. [16 dc]

Round 19 (7dc, 2dc in next st) twice. [18 dc]

Round 21 (5dc, 2dc in next st) 3 times. [21 dc]

Round 23 (6dc, 2dc in next st) 3 times. [24 dc]

Round 25 (7dc, 2dc in next st) 3 times. [27 dc]

Round 27 (8dc, 2dc in next st) 3 times. [30 dc]

Round 29 (4dc, 2dc in next st) 6 times. [36 dc]

Round 31 (5dc, 2dc in next st) 6 times. [42 dc]

Round 33 (6dc, 2dc in next st)

6 times. [48 dc]

Rounds 34-40 Dc in each st around.

Fasten off and weave in ends.

POMPOM

With Yarn F, make a magic loop.

Round 1 Ch1 (does not count as st), 6dc into the loop. [6 dc]

Round 2 2dc in each st around. [12 dc]

Round 3 (Dc2tog) 6 times. [6 sts]

Fasten off leaving a long tail.

Stuff the small pompom. With a tapestry needle, weave the tail through the front loops of the last round, then pull to close the hole. Sew to the tip of the hat.

You'll make one face patch and two eye patches then add eyes, nose and a grin

Bear Brothers

There's double the sweetness with this project.
Take on a new toy challenge and hook these cookie-coloured
bear cub brothers.

YOU WILL NEED

- 4ply weight cotton yarn in dark brown
- A 2mm (US 4 steel) hook
- Tapestry needle
- 4 black round brads, 8mm in diameter
- 1 oval doll's nose, 5mm in diameter
- 1 oval doll's nose, 3mm in diameter
- Polyester toy stuffing
- Small pieces of felt in pink and white for cheeks and eyes
- Craft glue

MEASUREMENTS

Big bear: 10cm (4in) tall
Small bear: 8cm (3in) tall

ABBREVIATIONS

Inv dec Insert your hook into the front loop of the first st. Without putting the yarn round the hook, bring the hook to the front of the work and insert the hook into the front loop of the next st (3 loops on hook). Yrh and draw through all 3 loops.

BIG BEAR

HEAD

Make a magic loop, ch1, 6dc in loop. [6 sts]
Round 1 2dc in each st around. [12 sts]
Round 2 *2dc in next st, 1dc; rep from * another 5 times. [18 sts]
Round 3 *2dc in next st, dc in next 2 sts; rep from * another 5 times. [24 sts].
Round 4 *2dc in next st, dc in next 3 sts; rep from * another 5 times. [30 sts]

Round 5 *2dc in next st, dc in next 4 sts; rep from * another 5 times. [36 sts]
Round 6 *2dc in next st, dc in next 5 sts; rep from * another 5 times. [42 sts]
Round 7 *2dc in next st, dc in next 6 sts; rep from * another 5 times. [48 sts]
Rounds 8-14 Dc in each st around. [48 sts]
Round 15 *Inv dec, dc in next 6 sts; rep from * another 5 times. [42 sts)
Round 16 *Inv dec, dc in next 5 sts; rep from * another 5 times. [36 sts]
Round 17 *Inv dec, dc in next 4 sts; rep from * another 5 times. [30 sts]
Round 18 *Inv dec, dc in next 3 sts; rep from * another 5 times. [24 sts]
Round 19 *Inv dec, dc in next 2 sts; rep from * another 5 times. [18 sts]
Stuff head.
Round 20 *Inv dec, dc in next st; rep from * another 5 times. [12 sts]
Round 21 Inv dec all around. [6 sts]
Fasten off and thread tail of yarn through remaining stitches to close. Do not cut off the yarn.

EYE INDENTATIONS 01

With tapestry needle, bring rem yarn out to a stitch on left side of head, positioning it at the bottom of Round 11. Make one horizontal stitch and bring thread back down to bottom of head. Gently tug on yarn to create a slight indentation. Now repeat with the right side of the head – there should be 8 stitches in between the indentations. **Fasten off** ends at bottom of the head.

FACIAL FEATURES 02

Cut out two small half-moons of white felt – they should match the size of the black brads. Glue them near the indentations. Add glue onto the black brads and pop each of them into the st with the indentation. Centre the oval doll's nose between the eyes and glue on. Cut out two small circles of pink felt and glue them onto the cheeks.

BODY

Make a magic loop, ch 1, 6dc in loop. [6sts]
Round 1 Ch1, 2dc in each st around. [12 sts]
Round 2 *2dc in next st, 1dc; rep from * another 5 times. [18 sts]
Round 3 *2dc in next st, dc in next 2 sts; rep from * another 5 times. [24 sts]
Rounds 4-8 Dc in each st around. [24 sts]
Round 9 *Inv dec, dc in next 2 sts; rep from * another 5 times. [18 sts]
Fasten off and leave a long tail end for sewing up. Stuff body.

ARMS (MAKE 2)

Make a magic loop, ch1, 6dc in loop. [6 sts]
Rounds 1-5 Dc in each st around. [6 sts]
Fasten off and leave a long tail end for sewing up.

LEGS (MAKE 2)

Make a magic loop, ch1, 6dc in loop. [6 sts]
Round 1 2dc in each st around. [12 sts]
Rounds 2-3 Dc in each st around. [12 sts]
Round 4 Inv dec all around. [6 sts]
Rounds 5-6 Dc in each st around. [6 sts]
Fasten off and leave a long tail end for sewing up.

EARS (MAKE 2)

Make a magic loop, ch1, 6dc in loop. [6 sts]
Round 1 2dc in each st around. [12 sts]
Round 2 Dc in each st around. [12 sts]
Fasten off and make sure that you leave a long tail end for sewing up.

TAIL

Make a magic loop, ch1, 6dc in loop. [6 sts]
Round 1 2dc in each st around. [12 sts]
Round 2 Dc in each st around. [12 sts]
Round 3 *Inv dec all around. [6 sts]
Fasten off and leave a long tail end for sewing up.

TO FINISH
Pin pieces in place to gauge where each part should go. Sew body onto the head, sew on the ears and arms.

MAKE MOVEABLE LEGS AS FOLLOWS: ③
Thread long yarn end from one of the legs through a darning needle. Pierce body where this leg will be attached and bring it out on the other side where the other leg will go. Make a horizontal st and go back to the other leg. Remember not to tug too tightly. Do this one more time. Bring the needle out through the body and trim excess. Rep entire process with long yarn end from the other leg.

Position tail at a spot that will help the bear sit on his own. Sew in place.

SMALL BEAR
HEAD
Make a magic loop, ch1, 6dc in loop. [6 sts]
Round 1 2dc in each st around. [12 sts]
Round 2 *2dc in next st, 1dc; rep from * another 5 times. [18 sts]
Round 3 *2dc in next st, dc in next 2 sts; rep from * another 5 times. [24 sts]
Round 4 *2dc in next st, dc in next 3 sts; rep from * another 5 times. [30 sts]
Round 5 *2dc in next st, dc in next 4 sts; rep from * another 5 times. [36 sts]
Rounds 6-11 Dc in each st around. [36 sts]
Round 12 *Inv dec, dc in next 4 sts; rep from * another 5 times. [30 sts]

Round 13 *Inv dec, dc in next 3 sts; rep from * another 5 times. [24 sts]
Round 14 *Inv dec, dc in next 2 sts; rep from * another 5 times. [18 sts] Stuff head.
Round 15 *Inv dec, dc in next st; rep from * another 5 times. [12 sts]
Round 16 Inv dec all around. [6 sts]
Fasten off and thread tail of yarn through rem stitches to close.
Do not cut off yarn.

EYE INDENTATIONS
Follow instructions for Big Bear, but position them below Round 8, with 6 sts between each indentation.

FACIAL FEATURES
Follow instructions for Big Bear, glueing on brads, nose and felt pieces.

BODY
Make a magic loop, ch1, 5dc in loop. [5 sts]
Round 1 2dc in each st around. [10 sts]
Round 2 *2dc in next st, 1dc; rep from * another 4 times. [15 sts]
Round 3 *2dc in next st, dc in next 2 sts; rep from * another 4 times. [20 sts]
Rounds 4-7 Dc in each st around. [20 sts]
Round 8 *Inv dec, dc in next 2 sts; rep from * another 4 times. [15 sts]
Fasten off and leave a long tail end for sewing up.
Fill body with toy stuffing.

ARMS (MAKE 2)
Make a magic loop, ch1, 6dc in loop. [6 sts]

Rounds 1-4 Dc in each st around. [6 sts]
Fasten off and leave a long tail end for sewing up.

LEGS (MAKE 2)
Make a magic loop, ch1, 5dc in loop. [5 sts]
Round 1 2dc in each st around. [10 sts]
Rounds 2-3 Dc in each st around. [10 sts]
Round 4 (Inv dec) 4 times, dc in next 2 sts. [6 sts]
Round 5 Dc in each st around. [6 sts]
Fasten off and leave a long tail end for sewing up.

EARS (MAKE 2)
Make a magic loop, ch1, 5dc in loop. [5 sts]
Round 1 2dc in each st around. [10 sts]
Round 2 Dc in each st around. [10 sts]
Fasten off and leave a long tail end for sewing up.

TAIL
Make a magic loop, ch1, 5dc in loop. [5 sts]
Round 1 2dc in each st around. [10 sts]
Round 2 Dc in each st around. [10 sts]
Round 3 *Inv dec all around. [5 sts]
Fasten off and leave a long tail end for sewing up.

TO FINISH
Follow the assembly instructions given for Big Bear.

Baby Tapir

This little creature looks very detailed, but is simple to make. The horizontal marks are embroidered on after you've crocheted and stuffed the body, meaning it's easy to add the finishing touches.

YOU WILL NEED

• DK weight cotton yarn, approximately two 50g balls of each:
- Yarn A Black
• A small amount of each:
- Yarn B White
- Yarn C Grey

• A 2.75mm (US C/2) hook

• 2 safety eyes, 9mm

• Toy stuffing

MEASUREMENTS

14cm (5½in) tall

HEAD AND BODY

Using Yarn A, make a magic loop.
Round 1 (RS) Ch1 (does not count as st throughout), 8dc in loop. [8 sts]
Round 2 2dc in each st around. [16 sts]
Round 3 Dc in bl of each st around.
Round 4 Dc in each st around.
Round 5 7dc, 2dc in next 2 sts, 7dc. [18 sts]
Round 6 Dc in each st around.
Round 7 6dc, 2dc in next st, 1dc, 2dc in next 2 sts, 1dc, 2dc in next st, 6dc. [22 sts]
Rounds 8-9 Dc in each st around. Stuff as you go.
Round 10 2dc in fl of next 3 sts, 16dc, 2dc in fl of next 3 sts. [28 sts]

Round 11 Dc in each st around.
Round 12 (3dc, 2dc in next st) 7 times. [35 sts]
Round 13 (4dc, 2dc in next st) 7 times. [42 sts]
Round 14 Dc in each st around.
Round 15 (6dc, 2dc in next st) 6 times. [48 sts]
Rounds 16-24 Dc in each st around. Insert the safety eyes between Rounds 15-16, 20 sts apart.
Round 25 (Dc2tog, 1dc) twice, dc2tog, 14dc, (2dc in next st, 2dc) 3 times, 2dc in next st, 13dc, dc2tog, 1dc. [48 sts]
Round 26 Dc in each st around.
Round 27 *(2dc in fl of next st, dc in fl of next st) twice, 2dc in fl of next st**,

38dc; rep from * to ** once more. [54 sts]

Round 29 (1dc, 2dc in next st) 3 times, 42dc, (1dc, 2dc in next st) 3 times. [60 sts]

Rounds 30-32 Dc in each st around.

Round 33 1dc, 2dc in next st, 57dc, 2dc in next st. [62 sts]

Rounds 34-40 Dc in each st around.

Round 41 33dc, 2dc in next st, 1dc, 2dc in next st, 26dc. [64 sts]

Round 42 (7dc, 2dc in next st) 8 times. [72 sts]

Rounds 43-49 Dc in each st around.

Round 50 (7dc, dc2tog) 8 times. [64 sts]

Round 51 Dc in each st around.

Round 52 (6dc, dc2tog) 8 times. [56 sts]

Round 53 Dc in each st around.

Round 54 (5dc, dc2tog) 8 times. [48 sts]

Round 55 Dc in each st around.

Round 56 (4dc, dc2tog) 8 times. [40 sts]

Round 57 (3dc, dc2tog) 8 times. [32 sts]

Round 58 (2dc, dc2tog) 8 times. [24 sts]

Round 59 (1dc, dc2tog) 8 times. [16 sts]

Round 60 (Dc2tog) 8 times.

Fasten off.

Using Yarn B embroider a line on the side of each eye.

Using Yarn A, embroider the upper eye lid.

LEGS (MAKE 4)

Using Yarn A, make a magic loop.

Round 1 (RS) Ch1, 7dc in loop. [7 sts]

Round 2 2dc in each at around. [14 sts]

Round 3 Dc in bl of each st around.

Round 4-5 Dc in each st around.

Round 6 (6dc, 2dc in next st) twice. [16 sts]

Rounds 7-12 Dc in each st around.

Row 13 8dc, turn leaving rem sts unworked. [8 sts]

Row 14 (WS) Ch1, 8dc across.

Fasten off, leaving a long tail.

Stuff the Legs and sew to the Body.

EARS (MAKE 2)

Using Yarn B, make a magic loop.

Round 1 (RS) Ch1, 6dc in loop. [6 sts]

Round 2 (2dc, 2dc in next st) twice. [8 sts]

Change to Yarn A.

Round 3 (3dc, 2dc in next st) twice. [10 sts]

Round 4 Dc in each st around.

Round 5 (4dc, 2dc in next st) twice. [12 sts]

Round 6 (1dc, dc2tog) 4 times. [8 sts]

Fasten off.

Flatten the final round and sew to the Head over Rounds 23-25, approx 8 sts apart.

TAIL

Using Yarn A, make a magic loop.

Round 1 (RS) Ch1, 8dc in loop. [8 sts]

Round 2 Dc in each st around.

Round 3 (2dc, dc2tog) twice. [6 sts]

Flatten Round 3, work 3dc across both sides to close.

Row 4 Ch1, dc in first dc, dc2tog.

Fasten off.

Sew to the back of the Body.

TO FINISH

Using Yarn B, embroider the horizontal marks all over the Head, Body and Legs.

Using Yarn C, embroider 3 lines on the base of each Leg for nails.

Lovebirds

These friends are adorable and quick to stitch – ideal for amigurumi newbies.
These lovebirds are perched in a large glass jar, but you could keep your pocket-
sized pals free range, too. They'd make a lovely gift or a charming addition
to your craft area.

YOU WILL NEED

• A small amount of DK weight cotton yarn in:
- Yarn A Light Blue
- Yarn B Bright Blue
- Yarn C Pink

• A small amount of lace weight yarn:
- Yarn D Pale Yellow

• Black crochet thread

• A 2mm (US 4 steel) hook

• A 2.5mm (US B/1 or C/2) hook

• Tapestry needle

• Toy stuffing

MEASUREMENTS

5cm (2in) tall

ABBREVIATIONS

Invisible decrease (inv dec)
Insert hook into front loop of first st without putting yarn round hook, bring hook to front of work and insert hook into front loop of next st (3 loops on hook). Yrh and draw through all 3 loops

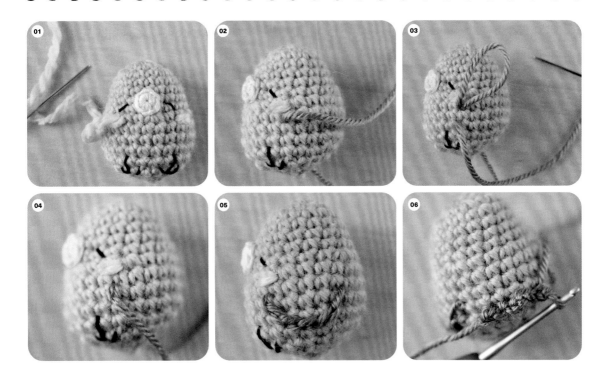

BODY

Using Yarn A and a 2.5mm hook, make a magic loop.

Round 1 (RS) Ch1 (does not count as st), 6dc in the loop. [6 sts]

Round 2 2dc in each dc around. [12 sts]

Round 3 (2dc in next dc, 1dc) 6 times. [18 sts]

Rounds 4-7 Dc in each st around.

Round 8 (2dc in next dc, 2dc) 6 times. [24 sts]

Rounds 9-12 Dc in each st around.

Round 13 (Inv dec, 2dc) 6 times. [18 sts]

Stuff Body.

Round 14 (Inv dec, dc in next dc) 6 times. [12 sts]

Round 15 (Inv dec) 6 times. [6 sts]

Fasten off, leaving a long tail, thread through the remaining sts to close.

BEAK

Using Yarn D and 2mm hook, make a magic loop.

Round 1 (RS) Ch1 (does not count as a st), 6dc in the loop. [6 sts]

Fasten off, leaving a long tail for sewing.

TO MAKE UP

Sew Beak onto the Body. The top of the Beak should fall below Round 5. Using black thread or embroidery floss, sew the eyes with a diagonal backstitch. They should fall below Round 6.

Add pink blushing cheeks with several backstitches of Yarn C below the eyes.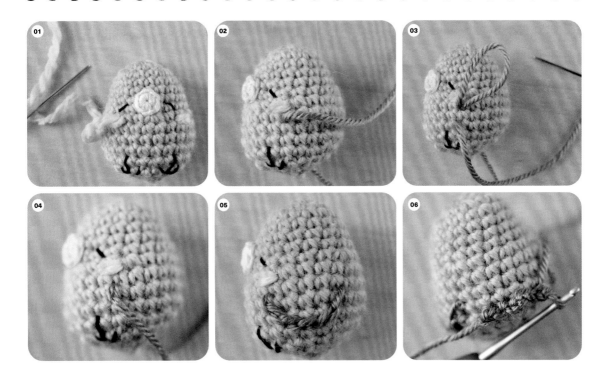

Use black thread to sew 3 straight stitches for each of the feet.

WINGS

The wings are worked using Yarn B and embroidered chain st.

Cut a 20cm length of yarn and thread it through a tapestry needle.

Bring the yarn up to a spot below the cheeks. **02**

Work 6 or 7 chain stitches to form a curved wing on each side of the Body. **03** **04** **05**

Bring the yarn ends out at the bottom of the body and trim the excess.

TAIL

The tail is surface crocheted onto the back of the body below Round 11, using Yarn B and a 2.5mm hook. The tail is worked across a total of 6 sts on the back of the Body, so identify these sts centrally on the back of your work and dc into first st. The following is worked in a continuous row over the next 5 sts: Ch2, ss to next st, 3htr in next st, ss to next st, dc in next st, ch2, dc in next st. **06**

Fasten off and weave in ends.

Perfect Panda

Ever wondered how a chap would carry his bamboo snacks when he's going about his important panda business? Well, this friendly little bear has the answer – this panda comes complete with a bag for his tasty bamboo treats. He's fun to make, with just a few techniques bringing this adorable creature to life.

YOU WILL NEED

• 4ply weight cotton yarn, approximately one 50g ball of each:
- Yarn A White
- Yarn B Black
• A small amount of each:
- Yarn C Yellow
- Yarn D Green
- Yarn E Dark Green

• Stranded cotton, pink

• A 2.5 mm (US B/1 or C/2) crochet hook

• 2 safety eyes or black beads approx 6mm diameter

• Stitch markers

• Toy stuffing

MEASUREMENTS

18cm (7in) tall

EYE PATCH

With Yarn B, ch4.

Round 1 Dc in second ch from hook and next ch, 5dc in last ch, rotate to work along opposite side of starting chain, dc in next st, 4dc in last st. [12 dc]

Round 2 (3dc, 2dc in next 3 sts) twice. [18 dc]

Round 3 3dc, (2dc in next st, dc) 3 times, 3dc, (2dc in next st, dc) 3 times. [24 dc]

Fasten off, leaving a tail for sewing.

HEAD

With Yarn A, make a magic loop.

Round 1 Ch1 (does not count as st), 6dc into the loop. [6 sts]

Round 2 2dc in each st around. [12 sts]

Round 3 (2dc in next st, 1dc) 6 times. [18 sts]

Round 4 (2dc in next st, 2dc) 6 times. [24 sts]

Round 5 (2dc in next st, 3dc) 6 times. [30 sts]

Round 6 (2dc in next st, 4dc) 6 times. [36 sts]

Round 7 (2dc in next st, 5dc) 6 times. [42 sts]

Round 8 (2dc in next st, 6dc) 6 times. [48 sts]

Round 9 (2dc in next st, 7dc) 6 times. [54 sts]

Round 10 (2dc in next st, 8dc) 6 times. [60 sts]

Round 11 (2dc in next st, 9dc) 6 times. [66 sts]

Rounds 12-19 Dc in each dc around.

Round 20 (Dc2tog, 9dc) 6 times. [60 sts]

Round 21 (Dc2tog, 8dc) 6 times. [54 sts]

Round 22 (Dc2tog, 7dc) 6 times. [48 sts]

Round 23 (Dc2tog, 6dc) 6 times. [42 sts]

Round 24 (Dc2tog, 5dc) 6 times. [36 sts]

Round 25 (Dc2tog, 4dc) 6 times. [30 sts]

Round 26 (Dc2tog, 3dc) 6 times. [24 sts]

Round 27 (Dc2tog, 2dc) 6 times. [18 sts]

Give your panda a characterful face with pink stranded cotton and black safety eyes

Insert one of the safety eyes into the Eye Patch (into the starting ch) then insert both safety eyes between Rounds 15 and 16 approx 14 sts apart using the image as a guide.

Fasten off and weave in ends.

MUZZLE

With Yarn B, make a magic loop.

Round 1 Ch1 (does not count as st), 6dc into the loop. [6 sts]

Round 2 2dc in each st around. [12 sts]

Round 3 (2dc in next st, 1dc) 6 times. [18 sts]

Round 4 (2dc in next st, 2dc) 6 times. [24 sts]

Round 5 4dc, 4htr, 8tr, 4htr, 4dc. [24 sts]

Round 6 Dc in each st around. [24 sts]

Fasten off, leaving a long tail.

Embroider the nose onto the Muzzle using the pink thread making long stitches to create a triangle between Rounds 3 and 5. Stitch the mouth using the image as a guide.

Sew the Muzzle to the Head between the eyes, stuff slightly as you stitch.

EARS (MAKE 2)

With Yarn B, make a magic loop.

Round 1 Ch1 (does not count as st), 6dc into the loop. [6 sts]

Round 2 2dc in each st around. [12 sts]

Rounds 3-5 Dc in each dc around. Do not stuff.

Fasten off leaving a long tail.

Sew the Ears on either side of the Head between Rounds 7 and 11.

BODY

The Body is worked from the base up.

Using Yarn B, make a magic loop.

Round 1 Ch1 (does not count as st), 6dc into the loop. [6 sts]

Round 2 2dc in each st around. [12 sts]

Round 3 (2dc in next st, 1dc) 6 times. [18 sts]

Round 4 (2dc in next st, 2dc) 6 times. [24 sts]

Round 5 (2dc in next st, 3dc) 6 times. [30 sts]

Round 6 (2dc in next st, 4dc) 6 times. [36 sts]

Round 7 (2dc in next st, 5dc) 6 times. [42 sts]

Round 8 (2dc in next st, 6dc) 6 times. [48 sts]

Round 9 (2dc in next st, 7dc) 6 times. [54 sts]

Rounds 10-18 Dc in each dc around.

Round 19 (Dc2tog, 7dc) 6 times. [48 sts]

Round 20 Dc in each dc around. Change to Yarn A.

Round 21 Dc in each dc around.
Round 22 (Dc2tog, 6dc) 6 times.
[42 sts]
Round 23 Dc in each dc around.
[42 sts]
Round 24 (Dc2tog, 5dc) 6 times.
[36 sts]
Round 25 Dc in each dc around.
[36 sts]
Round 26 (Dc2tog, 4dc) 6 times.
[30 sts]
Round 27 (Dc2tog, 3dc) 6 times.
[24 sts]
Round 28 (Dc2tog, 2dc) 6 times.
[18 sts]
Fasten off, leaving a long tail.

ARMS (MAKE 2)
With Yarn B, make a magic loop.
Round 1 Ch1 (does not count as st),
6dc into the loop. [6 sts]
Round 2 2dc in each st around. [12 sts]
Rounds 3-7 Dc in each dc around.
[12 sts]
Round 8 Dc2tog, 10dc. [11 sts]
Round 9 Dc in each dc around. [11 sts]
Round 10 Dc2tog, 9dc. [10 sts]
Round 11 Dc in each dc around.
[10 sts]
Round 12 Dc2tog, 8dc. [9 sts]
Round 13 Dc in each dc around.
[9 sts]
Round 14 Dc2tog, 7dc. [8 sts]
Round 15 Dc in each dc around.
[8 sts]
Fasten off, leaving a long tail.

LEGS (MAKE 2)
With Yarn B, make a magic loop.
Round 1 Ch1 (does not count as st),
6dc into the loop. [6 sts]
Round 2 2dc in each st around.
[12 sts]
Round 3 (partial) 1htr, 3tr in each of
next 2 sts, 1htr, 1dc, leave remaining
sts unworked. [9 sts]
Move stitch marker to next st for new
start of round.
Rounds 4-5 Dc in each st around.
[16 sts]
Round 6 7dc, dc2tog, 4dc, dc2tog,
1dc. [14 sts]
Round 7 7dc, dc2tog, 2dc, dc2tog,
1dc. [12 sts]

Rounds 8-13 Dc in each st around.
[12 sts]
Fasten off, leaving a long tail.

BAG
With Yarn C, ch7.
Round 1 Dc in second ch from hook
and next 4 ch, 3dc in last ch, rotate to
work along opposite side of starting
chain, dc in next 4 sts, 2dc in last st.
[14 dc]
Rounds 2-7 Dc in each dc around.
Do not fasten off.

STRAP
Row 1 Ch46, skip next 7 sts from
Round 7, ss in next st, turn.
Row 2 Dc in each ch of Strap.
Fasten off and weave in ends.

BAMBOO STICK (SHORT)
With Yarn D, make a magic loop.
Round 1 Ch1 (does not count as st),
5dc into the loop. [5 sts]
Rounds 2-4 Dc in each dc around.
[5 sts]
Change to Yarn E.
Round 5 1dc, ch3, dc in second ch
from hook and next ch, 4dc. [5 sts
and 1 leaf]
Change to Yarn D.
Rounds 6-7 Dc in each st around.
[5 sts]
Change to Yarn E.
Round 8 3dc, ch3, dc in second ch
from hook and next ch, 2dc. [5 sts
and 1 leaf]
Change to Yarn D.
Rounds 9-10 Dc in each dc around.
[5 sts]
Fasten off and weave in ends.

BAMBOO STICK (LONG)
Rounds 1-10 Work as Bamboo Stick
(Short).
Rounds 11-13 Repeat Rounds 5-7 of
Bamboo Stick (Short).
Fasten off and weave in ends.

TAIL
With Yarn B, make a magic loop.
Round 1 Ch1 (does not count as st)
5dc into the ring. [5 sts]
Round 2 2dc in each st around. [10 sts]

Round 3-4 1dc in each dc. [10 sts]
Round 5 (dc2tog, 3dc) repeat twice.
[8 sts]
Fasten off leaving a tail for sewing.
Stuff the tail.

TO MAKE UP
Stuff the Head and Body and use the
long tail to sew the Head onto the
Body.
Stuff the Arms and use the long tail
to sew them between Rounds 26 and
27 on either side of the Body.
Stuff the Legs and use the long tail to
sew them to the base of the Body
using the image as a guide.
Place Bag across Body and add
Bamboo.

Cuddly Schnauzer

Sit! Good boy. Stay! Excellent. This peppy schnauzer has already mastered two basic commands. The whiskers and and long toe stitches make this a nice easy project with some impressive finishing touches.

TOP TIP

Customise the button-on collar by stitching the name of your schnauzer on it

YOU WILL NEED

- DK weight acrylic yarn, approximately one 50 ball of each:
- Yarn A White
- Yarn C Light Grey
- A small amount of:
- Yarn B Dark Grey
- Yarn D Black
- Yarn E Light Brown

- A 3.25mm (US D/3) hook

- Toy filling

- 2 safety eyes, 9mm

- Button, 10mm

MEASUREMENTS

20cm (7¾in) tall

ABBREVIATIONS

inv dec (invisible dc2tog) Insert hook through fl of first st, yrh and pull up a loop, insert hook through fl of next st, yrh and pull through all loops on the hook

NOTES

• Change colour on the last yrh of st before colour change is indicated. See p. 15 for guidance on changing colour in a spiral.

BODY

Using Yarn C, make a magic loop.
Round 1 (RS) Ch1, 6dc into loop. [6 sts]
Round 2 2dc in each st around. [12 sts]
Round 3 (Dc in next st, 2dc in next st) 6 times. [18 sts]
Round 4 (Dc in next 2 sts, 2dc) 6 times. [24 sts]
Round 5 (Dc in next 3 sts, 2dc) 6 times. [30 sts]

Round 6 (Dc in next 4 sts, 2dc) 6 times. [36 sts]
Round 7 (Dc in next 5 sts, 2dc) 6 times. [42 sts]
Round 8 (Dc in next 6 sts, 2dc) 6 times. [48 sts]
Round 9 (Dc in next 7 sts, 2dc) 6 times. [54 sts]
Round 10 Dc in next 4 sts, 2dc in next st, (dc in next 8 sts, 2dc in next st) 5 times, dc in next 4 sts. [60 sts]
Rounds 11-15 Dc in each st around.
Round 16 (Dc in next 8 sts, inv dec) 6 times. [54 sts]
Round 17 Dc in next 24 sts, change to Yarn A, dc in next 6 sts, change to Yarn C, dc in rem 24 sts.
Round 18 Dc in next 23 sts, change to Yarn A, dc in next 8 sts, change to Yarn C, dc in remaining 23 sts.
Round 19 (Dc in next 7 sts, inv dec) twice, dc in next 4 sts, change to Yarn A, dc in next 3 sts, inv dec, dc in next 6 sts, change to Yarn C, dc in next st, inv dec, (dc in next 7, inv dec) twice. [48 sts]
Rounds 20-22 Dc in next 19 sts, change to Yarn A, dc in next 12 sts, change to Yarn C, dc in rem 17 sts.
Round 23 (Dc in next 6 sts, inv dec) twice, dc in next 3 sts, change to Yarn A, dc in next 3 sts, inv dec, dc in next 6 sts, inv dec, change to Yarn C, (dc in next 6 sts, inv dec) twice. [42 sts]
Rounds 24-25 Dc in next 18 sts, change to Yarn A, dc in next 10 sts, change to Yarn C, dc in rem 14 sts.
Round 26 (Dc in next 5 sts, inv dec) twice, dc in next 5 sts, change to Yarn A, inv dec, dc in next 5 sts, inv dec, change to Yarn C, (dc in next 5 sts, inv dec) twice. [36 sts]
Rounds 27-28 Dc in next 17 sts, change to Yarn A, dc in next 7 sts, change to Yarn C, dc in rem 12 sts.
Round 29 (Dc in next 4 sts, inv dec) 3 times, change to Yarn A, dc in next 4 sts, change to Yarn C, inv dec, (dc in next 4 sts, inv dec) twice. [30 sts]
Rounds 30-31 Dc in next 15 sts, change to Yarn A, dc in next 5 sts, change to Yarn C, dc in rem 10 sts.
Round 32 (Dc in next 3 sts, inv dec) 3 times, change to Yarn A, dc in next

3 sts, inv dec, change to Yarn C, (dc in next 3 sts, inv dec) twice. [24 sts]
Stuff body.
Fasten off with a ss in next st, leave a long tail to sew Head to Body.

HEAD

Using Yarn A, make a magic loop.
Rounds 1-6 (RS) As Rounds 1-6 of Body. [36 sts]
Round 7 Dc in each st around.
Fasten off with a ss in next st.
Join Yarn C into any st.
Rounds 8-13 As Round 7.
Round 14 Dc in next 15 sts, ss in fl of next 6 sts (marks top of muzzle), dc in rem 15 sts.
Round 15 (Dc in next 5 sts, 2dc) 6 times. [42 sts]
Rounds 16-23 As Round 7.
Round 24 (Dc in next 5 sts, inv dec) 6 times. [36 sts]
Round 25 (Dc in next 4 sts, inv dec) 6 times. [30 sts]
Add safety eyes between Rounds 16-17 approx 8 sts apart, make sure the top of the Muzzle sits centrally between the eyes.
Stuff Head, continuing to stuff as you go.
Round 26 (Dc in next 3 sts, inv dec) 6 times. [24 sts]
Round 27 (Dc in next 2 sts, inv dec) 6 times. [18 sts]
Round 28 (Dc in next st, inv dec) 6 times. [12 sts]
Round 29 (Inv dec) 6 times. [6 sts]
Fasten off with a ss in next st.
Thread yarn tail through last 6 sts to close.

NOSE

Using Yarn D, make a magic loop.
Round 1 (RS) Ch1, 8dc into loop. [8 sts]
Round 2 2dc in each st around. [16 sts]
Round 3 Dc in each st around.
Round 4 (Dc in next 2 sts, inv dec) 4 times. [12 sts]
Round 5 (Dc in next st, inv dec) 4 times. [8 sts]
Fasten off with a ss in next st, leaving a long tail.
Stuff the Nose and sew to the Head over Rounds 6-9.

Using Yarn D, make 1 long straight stitch from the bottom of the Nose to just below Round 1.

EARS (MAKE 2)
Using Yarn C, make a magic loop.
Round 1 (RS) Ch1, 6dc into loop. [6 sts]
Round 2 Dc in each st around.
Round 3 (Dc in next 2 sts, 2dc) twice. [8 sts]
Round 4 (Dc in next st, 2dc) 4 times. [12 sts]
Round 5 Dc in next 5 sts, 2dc in next 2 sts, dc in next 5 sts. [14 sts]
Round 6 Dc in next 6 sts, 2dc in next 2 sts, dc in next 6 sts. [16 sts]
Round 7 Dc in next 7 sts, 2dc in next 2 sts, dc in next 7 sts. [18 sts]
Rounds 8-9 Dc in each st around.
Round 10 Dc in next 8 sts, 2dc in next 2 sts, dc in next 8 sts. [20 sts]
Rounds 11-12 Dc in each st around.
Fasten off leaving a long tail.
Using the tail join the Ears to the Head over Rounds 17-22.

TAIL
Using Yarn C, make a magic loop.
Rounds 1-2 (RS) As Rounds 1-2 of Ears. [6 sts]
Round 3 Dc in each st around.
Round 4 2dc in next st, dc in each st around. [7 sts]
Rounds 5-6 Dc in each st around.
Rounds 7-15 Repeat Rounds 4-6 another 3 times. [10 sts]
Rounds 16-18 Dc in each st around.
Fasten off with ss in next st, leaving a long tail.
Stuff Tail and join to the back of the Body over Rounds 7-10.

FRONT LEGS (MAKE 2)
Using Yarn A, make a magic loop.
Rounds 1-5 (RS) As Rounds 1-5 of Body. [30 sts]
Rounds 6-8 Dc in each st around.
Round 9 (Dc in next 3 sts, inv dec) 6 times. [24 sts]
Round 10 (Dc in next 2 sts, inv dec) 6 times. [18 sts]
Rounds 11-16 Dc in each st around.
Fasten off with a ss in next st and weave in ends.

Join Yarn C into any st.
Rounds 17-23 Dc in each st around.
Round 24 (Dc in next 4 sts, inv dec) 3 times. [15 sts]
Fasten off with ss in next st, leaving a long tail.
Stuff the Leg up to Round 16, flatten the top of the Leg and use the tail to close the opening. Attach the Legs to the Body over Round 24.

HIND LEGS (MAKE 2)
Using Yarn A, make a magic loop.
Rounds 1-20 (RS) As Rounds 1-20 of Front Legs. [18 sts]
Round 21 (Dc in next 4 sts, inv dec) 3 times. [15 sts]
Fasten off with ss in next st, leaving a long tail.
Stuff the Leg up to Round 16, flatten the top of the Leg and use the tail to close the opening.
Attach to the side of the Body using the image as a guide.

COLLAR
Using Yarn E, ch37.
Row 1 (RS) Dc in 2nd ch from hook, dc in each ch across, turn. [36 sts]
Row 2 Ch1, dc in first 2 sts, ch1, skip 1 st (button hole made), dc in each st across, turn.
Row 3 Ch1, dc in next 33 sts, dc in ch-1 sp, dc in last 2 sts.
Fasten off.
Sew a button to the RS of the collar, at the opposite end to the button hole.

TO FINISH
To create the paws, use Yarn B to make three longs sts from Round 1 of the Leg to the top of the paw, pull the st tight to make indentation.
Join the Head to the top of the Body. To create the muzzle, cut 40 lengths of Yarn A, approx 20cm long. Fold in half and use your hook to thread folded end through fabric, take the 2 tails and thread through the loop pulling tight to secure. Work the muzzle either side of the Nose up to Round 14.
Secure the Collar around the neck.

Be sure to pull the stitches in the paws tightly to properly define the pupper's toes

Rainbow Unicorn

Hook this enchanting unicorn today, using yarn and supplies from your stash!
This on-trend design is packed with fun features, such as a glittery gold horn
and crinkly rainbow tresses. To make the magic happen, untwist the coloured
yarn strands to reveal their natural curl – it's unbelievably simple and effective!

YOU WILL NEED

- Approximately one 50g ball of any white DK yarn, plus oddments of any DK yarn in rainbow shades and gold
- 4mm (US G/6) hook
- Safety eyes
- Toy stuffing
- Extras: stitch markers

TOP TIP

Create the curls by splitting the yarn into strands

HEAD

With white, make a magic loop.
Round 1 Ch1 (does not count as st throughout), 6dc into the loop. (6 sts)
Round 2 2dc in each st around. [12 sts]
Rounds 3-4 Dc in each st around.
Round 5 (2dc in next st, 1dc) 6 times. [18 sts]
Round 6 3dc, (2dc in next st, 2dc) 3 times, 6dc. [21 sts]
Round 7 3dc, (2dc in next st, 3dc) 3 times, 6dc. [24 sts]
Round 8 3dc, (2dc in next st, 4dc) 3 times, 6dc. [27 sts]
Rounds 9-13 Dc in each st around. Secure eyes between Rounds 7 and 8, approx 8 sts apart. Stuff head with toy stuffing and continue stuffing as you go.
Round 14 (7dc, dc2tog) 3 times. [24 sts]
Round 15 (2dc, dc2tog) 6 times. [18 sts]
Round 16 (1dc, dc2tog) 6 times. [12 sts]
Round 17 (Dc2tog) 6 times. (6 sts) Fasten off and weave in ends.

EARS (MAKE 2)

With white, ch4.
Row 1 Dc in second ch from hook and in each ch to end, turn. (3 sts)
Row 2 Ch1, dc in each st to end, turn.
Row 3 Ch1, skip first st, 2dc, turn. [2 sts]
Row 4 Ch1, skip first st, 1dc. (1 st) Fasten off, leaving a tail for sewing ears to the head between Rounds 13 and 14.

HORN

With gold, ch7.
Row 1 Dc in second ch from hook and in each ch to end, turn. (6 sts)
Row 2 Ch1, skip first st, 5dc, turn. [5 sts]
Row 3 Ch1, skip first st, 4dc, turn. [4 sts]
Row 4 Ch1, skip first st, 3dc, turn. [3 sts]
Row 5 Ch1, dc in each st to end, turn.
Row 6 Ch1, skip first st, 2dc, turn. [2 sts]

Row 7 Ch1, dc in each st to end, turn. [2 sts]
Row 8 Ch1, skip first st, 1dc, turn. [1 st] Fasten off, leaving a tail for sewing. Fold piece in half and sew sides tog, then sew to head between Rounds 9 and 11.

BODY

With white, make a magic loop.
Round 1 Ch1, 6dc into the loop. [6 sts]
Round 2 2dc in each st around. [12 sts]
Round 3 (2dc in next st, 1dc) 6 times. [18 sts]
Rounds 4-8 Dc in each st around.
Round 9 (5dc, 2dc in next st) 3 times. [21 sts]
Round 10 (6dc, 2dc in next st) 3 times. [24 sts]
Rounds 11-13 Dc in each st around.
Round 14 (2dc, dc2tog) 6 times. [18 sts]
Stuff body with toy stuffing and continue stuffing as you go.
Round 15 (1dc, dc2tog) 6 times. [12 sts]
Round 16 (Dc2tog) 6 times. [6 sts] Fasten off and weave in ends.

NECK

With white, ch8, ss in first ch to join into a ring.
Round 1 Ch1, dc in each ch around. [8 sts]
Round 2 Dc in each st around. Fasten off, leaving a tail for sewing neck to head between Rounds 9 and 11.
Stuff with toy stuffing, then sew to body between Rounds 3 and 5.

FORELEG (MAKE 2)

With white, make a magic loop.
Round 1 Ch1, 6dc into the loop. [6 sts]
Rounds 2-8 Dc in each st around. Stuff lightly. Fasten off, leaving a tail for sewing legs to body between Rounds 4 and 5.

HIND LEG (MAKE 2)

With white, make a magic loop.
Round 1 Ch1, 6dc into the loop. [6 sts]
Rounds 2-7 Dc in each dc around.

Stuff lightly. Fasten off, leaving a tail for sewing legs to body between Rounds 12 and 13.

MANE AND TAIL

Cut rainbow yarns in half and in half again. You will have 4 pieces of each colour (approx 25cm each). Use 2 pieces of each colour for Mane and 2 for Tail. For Mane, fold each piece in half and knot it to Head like a fringe; use a crochet hook to pull loop of yarn through, and put ends of yarn through loop. Secure them behind Horn, using 2 pieces for each Round, starting from back of Horn for 6 Rounds. Create the curl effect by splitting the yarn into strands – they will be naturally curly. For tail, use a leftover piece of white, and knot all 12 coloured pieces tog in the middle as tightly as possible, leaving an end of white for sewing to Body.
Create curl effect as for the Mane.

Interesting Iguana

This rare banded iguana is sure to be a favourite among reptile fans of all ages! His variety of colours make him an interesting-looking make that isn't too challenging – perfect for a lizard-loving friend. Make sure you have a good variety of green yarns to hand before getting started.

YOU WILL NEED

• DK weight cotton yarn, approximately two 50g balls of:
- Yarn D Darker Green
• Approximately one 50g ball of each:
- Yarn C Mid Green
- Yarn D Dark Green
- Yarn E White
- Yarn F Beige
• A small amount of each:
- Yarn A Yellow
- Yarn B Light Green
- Yarn G Black

• A 2.75mm (US C/2) hook

• 2 safety eyes, 10mm

• Toy stuffing

• 15cm craft wire

MEASUREMENTS

20cm (7¾in) long

HEAD AND BODY

Using Yarn A, make a magic loop.
Round 1 (RS) Ch1 (does not count as st throughout), 8dc in loop. [8 sts]
Round 2 (RS) (1dc, 2dc in next st) 4 times. [12 sts]
Round 3 (2dc, 2dc in next st) 4 times. [16 sts]
Change to Yarn B.
Round 4 (3dc, 2dc in next st) 4 times. [20 sts]
Round 5 (4dc, 2dc in next st) 4 times. [24 sts]
Round 6 Dc in each st around.
Change to Yarn C.
Round 7 (3dc, 2dc in next st) 6 times. [30]

Round 8 12dc, 3htr in the next st, 4dc, 3htr in the next st, 12dc. [34 sts] Change to Yarn D.
Round 9 10dc, dc2tog, 2htr in next st, 1htr, 2htr in next st, 4dc, 2htr in next st, 1htr, 2htr in next st, dc2tog, 10dc. [36 sts]
Round 10 11dc, 5htr, 4dc, 5htr, 11dc. [36 sts]
Rounds 11-12 Dc in each st around.
Round 13 11dc, dc2tog, 1dc, dc2tog, 4dc, dc2tog, 1dc, dc2tog, 11dc. [32 sts]
Round 14 (Dc2tog) twice, 26dc, dc2tog. [29 sts]
Round 15 5dc, dc2tog, 16dc, dc2tog, 4dc. [27 sts]

Round 16 (Working in fl only) (7dc, dc2tog) 3 times. [24 sts]
Round 17 (1dc, 2dc in next st) 3 times, 12dc, (1dc, 2dc in next st) 3 times. [30 sts]
Round 18 2dc in next st, 28dc, 2dc in next st. [32 sts]
Place safety eyes between Rounds 10-11.
Stuff Head and Body as you work.
Change to Yarn E.
Round 19 Dc in each st around.
Round 20 (3dc, 2dc in next st) 8 times. [40 sts]
Change to Yarn D.
Rounds 21-23 Dc in each st around.
Round 24 (2dc in next st, 1dc) twice, 32dc, (1dc, 2dc in next st) twice. [44 sts]
Change to Yarn E.
Rounds 25-27 Dc in each st around.
Change to Yarn D.
Round 28 Dc in each st around.
Round 29 16dc, (dc2tog, 2dc) 4 times, 12dc. [40 sts]
Change to Yarn E.
Rounds 30-31 Dc in each st around.
Change to Yarn D.
Round 32 14dc, (dc2tog, 2dc) 4 times, 10dc. [36 sts]
Round 33 Dc in each st around.
Round 34 (4dc, dc2tog) 6 times. [30 sts]
Round 35 Dc in each st around.
Change to Yarn E.
Round 36 (3dc, dc2tog) 6 times. [24 sts]
Round 37 Dc in each st around.
Change to Yarn D.
Rounds 38-40 Dc in each st around.
Change to Yarn E.
Round 41 (6dc, dc2tog) 3 times. [21 sts]
Round 42 Dc in each st around.
Change to Yarn D.
Round 43 Dc in each st around.
Round 44 (5dc, dc2tog) 3 times. [18 sts]
Round 45 (4dc, dc2tog) 3 times. [15 sts]
Change to Yarn E.
Round 46 (3dc, dc2tog) 3 times. [12 sts]
Round 47 Dc in each st around.
Change to Yarn D.

Rounds 48-52 Dc in each st around, changing to Yarn E at beg of Round 50 and Yarn D at beg of Round 52.
Round 53 (4dc, dc2tog) twice. [10 sts]
Change to Yarn F.
Round 54 Dc in each st around.
Round 55 (3dc, dc2tog) twice. [8 sts]
Change to Yarn C.
Round 56 Dc in each st around.
Change to Yarn F.
Round 57 (2dc, dc2tog) twice. [6 sts]
Change to Yarn C.
Rounds 58-69 Dc in each st around, switching between Yarn F and Yarn C each round.
Insert metal wire into tail.
Cont with Yarn F.
Round 70 (2dc, dc2tog) twice.
Fasten off.
Thread tail through rem 4 sts, pull tight to close.

LEGS (MAKE 4)
Using Yarn D, make a magic loop.
Rounds 1-3 (RS) As Rounds 1-3 of Head and Body. [16 sts]
Round 4 4dc, skip 8 sts, 4dc. [8 sts]
The skipped sts will be worked on later in patt to form top of Leg.
Rounds 5-7 Dc in each st around.
Round 8 (2dc, dc2tog) twice. [6 sts]
Round 9 Dc in each st around.
Flatten final round and work 3dc evenly across to close.
Do not fasten off.

TOES
Row 1 Ch1, 2dc in first st, dc in next st, 2dc in next st, turn. [5 sts]
Row 2 Ch4, dc in second ch from hook, ss in next 2 ch, ss in first st from Row 1, ch5, dc in second ch from hook, ss in next 3 ch, ss in next st from Row 1, ch6, dc in second ch from hook, ss in next 4 ch, ss in next st from Row 1, ch5, dc in second ch from hook, ss in next 3 ch, ss in next st from Row 1, ch4, dc in second ch from hook, ss in next 2 ch, ss in next st from Row 1, ch5, dc in second ch from hook, ss in next 3 ch, ss in final st from Row 1.
Fasten off and weave in ends.

TOP OF LEGS
Join Yarn D in first skipped st from Round 3.
Round 1 Ch1, 2htr in first st, dc in next 6 sts, 2htr in final st, ss to beg htr. [10 sts]
Round 2 Ch1, htr in first 2 sts, dc in next 6 sts, htr in next 2 sts, ss to beg htr.
Fasten off.

TO MAKE UP
You can use the images as a guide when making up the Iguana.
Using Yarn D, sew the small holes either side of each Leg closed.
Lightly stuff the Legs and sew to the Body over Rounds 22-26 and Rounds 36-40.
Using Yarn C, embroider eyelids.
Using Yarn A and G, embroider the mouth and nostrils.

Merry Macaw

This beautiful blue-throated macaw is full of bright colours, and is a delight to create! With the fun crest detail on top of his head and his lovely wings, he's sure to swoop in and steal your heart.

YOU WILL NEED

- DK weight cotton yarn, approximately one 50g ball of each:
  - Yarn A Green
  - Yarn B Orange
  - Yarn C White
  - Yarn D Black
  - Yarn E Blue

- A 3mm (US C/2 or D/3) hook

- 2 safety eyes, 12mm

- Toy stuffing

MEASUREMENTS

18cm (7in) tall in sitting position

HEAD AND BODY

Using Yarn A, make a magic loop.
Round 1 (RS) Ch1 (does not count as st throughout), 6dc in loop.[6 sts]
Round 2 (RS) 2dc in each st around. [12 sts]
Round 3 (1dc, 2dc in next st) 6 times. [18 sts]
Round 4 (2dc, 2dc in next st) 6 times. [24 sts]
Round 5 (3dc, 2dc in next st) 6 times. [30 sts]
Round 6 (4dc, 2dc in next st) 6 times. [36 sts]
Round 7 (5dc, 2dc in next st) 6 times. [42 sts]
Round 8 (6dc, 2dc in next st) 6 times. [48 sts]
Round 9 (7dc, 2dc in next st) 6 times. [54 sts]
Rounds 10-11 Dc in each st around. Change to Yarn B.
Round 12 Dc in next 17 sts, change to Yarn C, dc in next 20 sts, change to Yarn B, dc in next 17 sts.
Rounds 13-17 16dc, change to Yarn C, 22dc, change to Yarn B, 16dc. Insert safety eyes between Rounds 14-15, approx 10 sts apart.
Round 18 17dc, change to Yarn C, 20dc, change to Yarn B, 17dc.
Round 19 18dc, change to Yarn C, 18dc, change to Yarn B, 18dc.
Round 20 18dc, change to Yarn D, 18dc, change to Yarn B, 18dc. Cont with Yarn B.
Round 21 Dc in each st around.
Round 22 (7dc, dc2tog) 6 times.[48 sts]
Round 23 (6dc, dc2tog) 6 times. [42 sts]
Round 24 (6dc, 2dc in next st) 6 times. [48 sts]
Round 25 (7dc, 2dc in next st) 6 times. [54 sts]
Round 26 2dc in next 4 sts, 50dc. [58 sts]
Round 27 2dc in next 8 sts, 50dc. [66 sts]
Rounds 28-38 Dc in each st around.
Round 39 (9dc, dc2tog) 6 times. [60 sts]
Round 40 Dc in each st around.
Round 41 (8dc, dc2tog) 6 times. [54 sts]

Round 42 (7dc, dc2tog) 6 times. [48 sts]
Stuff Head and Body as you work.
Round 43 (6dc, dc2tog) 6 times. [42 sts]
Round 44 (5dc, dc2tog) 6 times. [36 sts]
Round 45 (4dc, dc2tog) 6 times. [30 sts]
Round 46 (3dc, dc2tog) 6 times. [24 sts]
Round 47 (2dc, dc2tog) 6 times. [18 sts]
Round 48 (1dc, dc2tog) 6 times. [12 sts]
Round 49 (Dc2tog) 6 times. [6 sts]
Fasten off.
Thread tail through final 6 sts, pulling tight to close.

BEAK

Using Yarn D, ch5.
Round 1 (RS) 2dc in second ch from hook, dc in the next 2 ch, 4dc in the final ch, turn to work in opposite side of foundation ch, dc in the next 2 ch, 2dc in the next st. [12 sts]
Round 2 (RS) (2dc in next 2 sts, dc in the next 2 sts, 2dc in the next 2 sts) twice. [20 sts]
Round 3 (1dc, 2dc in the next st) twice, dc in next 2 sts, (1dc, 2dc in the next st) 4 times, dc in the next 2 sts, (1dc, 2dc in the next st) twice. [28 sts]
Rounds 5-7 Dc in each st around. Change to Yarn C.
Rounds 8-9 Dc in each st around.
Fasten off, leaving a long tail.

WINGS (MAKE 2)

Using Yarn D, make a magic loop.
Round 1 (RS) Ch1, 6dc in a loop.[6 sts]
Round 2 (RS) Dc in each st around.
Round 3 2dc in each st around. [12 sts]
Round 4 Dc in each st around.
Round 5 (1dc, 2dc in next st) 6 times. [18 sts]
Round 6 Dc in each st around.
Round 7 (2dc, 2dc in next st) 6 times. [24 sts]
Round 8 Dc in each st around. Change to Yarn E.
Round 9 (3dc, 2dc in next st) 6 times. [30 sts]
Round 10 Dc in each st around.

Round 11 (4dc, 2dc in next st) 6 times. [36 sts]
Rounds 12-15 Dc in each st around.
Round 16 (4dc, dc2tog) 6 times. [30 sts]
Round 17 (3dc dc2tog) 6 times. [24 sts]
Rounds 18-19 Dc in each st around.
Fasten off, leaving a long tail.

LEGS (MAKE 2)

Using Yarn D, make a magic loop.
Rounds 1-5 (RS) As Rounds 1-5 of Head and Body. [30 sts]
Rounds 6-10 Dc in each st around.
Round 11 9dc, (dc2tog) 6 times, 9dc. [24 sts]
Round 12 6dc, (dc2tog) 6 times, 6dc. [18 sts]
Round 13 3dc, (dc2tog) 6 times, 3dc. [12 sts]
Rounds 14-24 Dc in each st around.
Fasten off, leaving a long tail.

TAIL FEATHER

Using Yarn E, make a magic loop.
Rounds 1-8 (RS) As Rounds 1-8 of Wings. [24 sts]
Round 9 (3dc, 2dc in next st) 6 times. [30 sts]
Round 10 Dc in each st around.
Round 11 (4dc, 2dc in next st) 6 times. [36 sts]
Rounds 12-15 Dc in each st around.
Round 16 (4dc, dc2tog) 6 times. [30 sts]
Round 17 (3dc, dc2tog) 6 times. [24 sts]
Rounds 18-19 Dc in each st around.
Fasten off, leaving a long tail.

TO FINISH

Use the images as a guide when making up.
Stuff and pin the Beak and Tail Feather to the Body.
Once happy with the positions, sew into place.
Sew the Wings to the Body.
Stuff the Legs and pin in pace, ensuring the Macaw can sit before sewing into position.
Cut 5 strands of Yarn A approx 8cm long. Thread through the sts at the top of the Head and trim to desired length.
Using Yarn D, embroider straight stitches over the Head.

Royal Swan

If you're dreaming of a super-sized amigurumi project with deluxe details, look no further than this regal beauty, with her elegant neck and soft, fluffy wings. Hook up her crown and adorable flower necklace to give her a few pretty accessories.

YOU WILL NEED

• Super bulky weight wool blend yarn, approximately three 50g balls of:
- Yarn A White

• Aran weight cotton yarn, approximately one 50g ball of each:
- Yarn B Yellow
- Yarn C Pink

• Sport weight cotton yarn, approximately one 50g ball of each:
- Yarn D Green
- Yarn E Light Pink
- Yarn F Dark Pink

• Small amount of black embroidery thread

• 2.5mm (US B1 or C/2) crochet hook

• 3.5mm (US E/4) crochet hook

• 4.5mm (US 7) crochet hook

• 5mm (US H/8) crochet hook

• Soft toy stuffing

• Pet brush

• Stitch marker

• Yarn needle

ABBREVIATIONS (UK)

BLO work st through back loop only
FLO work st through front loop only
invdec invisible decrease – insert hook into the front loop of the next two sts in turn and pull a loop up through both, yrh and pull through both loops on hook
picot ch3, ss to 3rd ch from hook

MEASUREMENTS

26cm (10¼") high

NOTES

• If you substitute Yarn A, ensure the yarn includes natural fibre such as wool or alpaca so it can be brushed out. You could brush the whole body, not just the wings, to have the ultimate feathery swan.

BODY

Using Yarn A and 5mm crochet hook
Round 1 6dc in magic ring, pull ring tight. [6 sts]
Round 2 inc in each st around. [12 sts]
Round 3 (1dc, inc) 6 times.. [18 sts]
Round 4 (2dc, inc) 6 times.. [24 sts]
Round 5 (3dc, inc) 6 times.. [30 sts]
Round 6 (4dc, inc) 6 times.. [36 sts]
Round 7 (5dc, inc) 6 times.. [42 sts]
Round 8 (6dc, inc) 6 times.. [48 sts]

Round 9 (7dc, inc) 6 times. [54 sts]
Round 10 (8dc, inc) 6 times. [60 sts]
Rounds 11-15 1dc in each st around. [60 sts]
Round 16 28dc, 4htr, 28dc. [60 sts]
Round 17 26dc, invdec 4 times, 26dc. [56 sts]
Round 18 26dc, invdec 2 times, 24dc, invdec. [53 sts]
Round 19 invdec, 22dc, invdec 3 times, 21dc, invdec. [48 sts]
Round 20 invdec, 18dc, invdec 4 times, 18dc, invdec. [42 sts]
Form the neck:
Round 21 invdec, 7dc, ch2, miss 26 sts, 1dc into the next (27th) st
Replace the stitch marker and continue crocheting the neck

NECK

Round 1 1dc in each of next 14 sts, 1dc into BLO of each of the 2ch, 1dc into the last st. [17 sts]
Round 2 4dc, invdec 2 times, 9dc [15 sts]
Round 3 4dc, invdec, 7dc, inc, 1dc. [15 sts]
Round 4 1dc in each st around [15 sts]
Round 5 4dc, invdec, 6dc, inc, 2dc. [15 sts]
Round 6 4dc, invdec, 9dc. [14sts]
Round 7 4dc, invdec, 5dc, inc, 2dc. [14 sts]
Round 8 3dc, invdec, 9dc.. [13 sts]
Round 9 3dc, invdec, 5dc, inc, 2dc.. [13 sts]
Round 10 3dc, invdec, 3dc, 5htr. [12 sts]
1dc into next st, fasten off and leave a long tail for sewing

FINISHING THE BODY

Count back 6 sts on the body from the neck, join with a ss in this st and work 1dc into the same st, 5dc (you have now reached the neck with the front loops of ch2), invdec the 2 front loops, working continuously on the other side of the body, 10dc, invdec 2 times, 5dc. [25 sts]

Fasten off and leave a long tail. Stuff the body and sew the sides together by inserting the needle into the front loops only on both sides, weave yarn tail into the body

HEAD

Using Yarn A and 5mm crochet hook
Round 1 6dc in magic ring, pull ring tight. [6 sts]
Round 2 inc in each st around. [12 sts]
Round 3 (1dc, inc) 6 times. [18 sts]
Round 4 (2dc, inc) 6 times. [24 sts]
Round 5 (3dc, inc) 6 times. [30 sts]
Round 6 (4dc, inc) 6 times. [36 sts]
Rounds 7-11 1dc in each st around. [36 sts]
Round 12 (4dc, invdec) 6 times. [30 sts]
Round 13 (3dc, invdec) 6 times. [24 sts]
Round 14 (2dc, invdec) 6 times. [18 sts]
Round 15 (1dc, invdec) 6 times. [12 sts]
Round 16 invdec each st around [6 sts]
Stuff the head firmly, fasten off and leave a long tail for sewing. Close the hole by sewing back and forth across the opening, weaving the yarn tail into the head

BEAK

Using Yarn C and 3.5mm crochet hook
Round 1 6dc in magic ring, pull ring tight. [6 sts]
Round 2 (1dc, inc) 3 times. [9 sts]
Round 3 1dc in each st around. [9 sts]
Round 4 (2dc, inc) 3 times. [12 sts]
Fasten off and leave a long tail for sewing. Place the beak onto the head below Round 9 and above Round 12, and sew onto the head

EYES

Mark the eyes with two pins on Round 9, 2 sts apart. Embroider the eyes with black thread, using the

image as a guide. Pin the head onto the neck and sew into place

CROWN

Using Yarn B and 3.5mm hook
Work in but finish each round with a sl st
Round 1 ch20 and ss to form a ring
Round 2 ch1, 1dc in st at base of ch1, 1dc in each st around, join with ss to 1st dc. [20 sts]
Round 3 repeat Round 2
Round 4 ch1, 1dc in st at base of ch1, *miss 1 st, (2tr, picot, 2tr) in next st, miss 1 st, 1dc in next st; repeat from * another 4 times but on the last repeat omit the last dc. Join with a ss to the 1st dc, fasten off. Sew it to the head of the swan

WINGS (MAKE TWO)

Using Yarn A and 4.5mm hook
Round 1 6dc in magic ring, pull ring tight. [6 sts]
Round 2 (1dc, inc) 3 times. [9 sts]
Round 3 inc, 3dc, invdec, 3dc. [9 sts]
Round 4 (2dc, inc) 3 times. [12 sts]
Round 5 inc, 4dc, invdec, 5dc. [12 sts]
Round 6 (3dc, inc) 3 times. [15 sts]
Round 7 inc, 6dc, invdec, 6dc. [15 sts]
Round 8 (2dc, inc) 5 times. [20 sts]
Round 9 inc, 8dc, invdec, 9dc. [20 sts]
Round 10 (3dc, inc) 5 times. [25 sts]
Round 11 inc, 11dc, invdec, 11dc [25 sts]
Rounds 12-14 1dc in each st around. [25 sts]
Round 15 (3dc, invdec) 5 times. [20 sts]
Round 16 1dc in each st around. [20 sts]
Round 17 (2dc, invdec) 5 times. [15 sts]
Round 18 (1dc, invdec) 5 times. [10 sts]
Round 19 invdec in each st around [5 sts]
Fasten off leaving a long tail.
Use the yarn to close up the hole by sewing back and forth across the opening, weaving the yarn tail into the wing. Using the pet brush, brush both sides of the wings until fluffy – don't be afraid to brush vigorously, until you can't see the sts. Sew the wings onto the body.

FLOWER NECKLACE

NECKLACE
Cut a 15cm (6") length of Yarn D for the first tassel. Wrap Yarn D around a piece of paper approx. 3-4cm (1¼-15/8") wide, about 10 times. Using 2.5mm hook and the working yarn, make the top of a tassel by making a slip knot on the hook and working a ss through the top loops. Wrap the 15cm (6") length around the tassel to form the tassel head, ch100, then break yarn and fasten off with a long tail.

To form the second tassel, wrap yarn around the piece of paper again about 10 times, and use the long tail to tie the top securely. Cut another 15cm (6") length of yarn and wrap around the tassel to finish it. Trim the tassel ends to neaten.

FLOWERS
Using 2.5mm hook, make one flower with Yarn E and two with Yarn F as follows:
Row 1 ch11, turn
Row 2 2htr into the 2nd ch from hook, and in each st along. [20 sts]
Fasten off and leave a long tail. Roll each flower into a rose shape and secure with a few sts. Sew them onto the middle of the necklace and tie around the swan's neck.

Cheeky Monkey

This cheeky monkey is the perfect primate pal to hang out with the little ones in your life. With his own little banana to snack on, he won't need feeding either!

Use a chopstick or spoon handle when stuffing

TOP TIP

Master the magic ring technique to shape the monkey's head, body and limbs

YOU WILL NEED

- 4ply weight cotton yarn, approximately one 50g ball of each:
  - Yarn A Beige
  - Yarn B Orange
  - Yarn C Light Yellow
  - Yarn D Yellow

- 3.5mm (US E/4) hook

- 9mm safety toy eyes

- Wool and embroidery needle

- Toy stuffing

- Stitch markers

MEASUREMENTS

12x12x8cm (4¾x 4¾x3in)

MONKEY

Head part one
Make 1 in Yarn A
Start with 6dc into magic ring. [6sts]
Round 1 2dc into each st to the end. [12sts]
Round 2 (dc in the first st, 2dc in the next st) repeat to end. [18sts]
Round 3 (dc in the first two sts, 2dc in the next st) repeat to end. [24sts]
Round 4 (dc in the first three sts, 2dc in the next st) repeat to end. [30sts]
Round 5 (dc in the first nine sts, 2dc in the next st) repeat to end. [33sts]
Round 6 (dc in the first ten sts, 2dc in the next st) repeat to end. [36sts]
Round 7-10 dc in each st to the end. [36sts] *Mark rnd 8 with a stitch marker*
Round 11 (dc2tog, dc in next ten sts) repeat to end. [33sts]
Round 12 (dc2tog, dc in next nine sts) repeat to end. [30sts]
Round 13 (dc2tog, dc in next three sts) repeat to end. [24sts]
Round 14 (dc2tog, dc in next two sts) repeat to end. [18sts]
Pause to insert the toy eyes now. They go on the marked round 8 stitches apart
Round 15 (dc2tog) repeat to end. [9sts]
Fasten off. Stuff.
Sew closed the hole in base.

HEAD PART TWO

Make one in Yarn B
Start with 6dc into magic ring. 6sts
Round 1 2dc into each st to the end. [12sts]
Round 2 (dc in the first st, 2dc in the next st) repeat to end. [18sts]
Round 3 (dc in the first two sts, 2dc in the next st) repeat to end. [24sts]
Round 4 (dc in the first three sts, 2dc in the next st) repeat to end. [30sts]
Round 5 (dc in the first nine sts, 2dc in the next st) repeat to end. [33sts]
Round 6 (dc in the first ten sts, 2dc in the next st) repeat to end. [36sts]
Round 7-13 dc in each st to the end. [36sts]
Round 14 ss, dc, htr, tr, ch2, tr, htr, dc, ss. Rest of stitches are not worked.

Fasten off. Place over the head. Use photo as a guide for positioning and sew in place.
Use the photo as a guide for adding the monkey's features, and make sure he has a lovely wide smile!

BODY

Make 1 in Yarn B.
Start with 6dc into magic ring. 6sts
Round 1 2dc into each st to the end. [12sts]
Round 2 (dc in the first st, 2dc in the next st) repeat to end. [18sts]
Round 3 (dc in the first two sts, 2dc in the next st) repeat to end. [24sts]
Round 4-8 dc in each st to end. 24sts
Round 9 (dc2tog, dc in next two sts) repeat to end. [18sts]
Round 10 (dc2tog, dc in next st) repeat to end. [12sts] *stuff now*
Round 11 (dc2tog) repeat to end. [6sts]
Fasten off.
Sew closed the hole in base. Sew onto head.

ARMS AND LEGS

Make 4 starting in Yarn A.
Start with 6dc into magic ring. [6sts]
Round 1 2dc into each st to the end. [12sts]
Round 2 (dc in the first two sts, 2dc in the next st) repeat to end. [16sts]
Round 3 dc in each st to end. [16sts]
Round 4 (dc2tog) repeat to end. [8sts]
change to Yarn B at end of this round
Round 5-15 dc in each st to end. 8sts
Stuff firmly.
Sew in place on the body

BOTTOM

Make 1 in Yarn A.
Round 1 Ch 2, 8tr in 2nd ch from hook, ss in same st. Do not join.
Fasten off.
Sew in place.

TAIL

Make 1 in Yarn B.
Start with 7dc into magic ring. [7sts]
Round 1-18 dc in each st to the end. [7sts]

The bottom is added afterwards in Yarn A

Use a blunt-ended needle to insert the stuffing

Fasten off.
Sew in place.

BANANA

Make one starting in Yarn C.
Start with 4dc into magic ring. 4sts
Round 1 dc in each st to end.
Round 2-3 2dc in the first st, dc in each st to end. 6sts at end of round 3 *change to Yarn D at end of round 3
Round 4 Dc in bl in each st to end. 6sts
Round 5-6 dc2tog, dc in each st to end. 4sts at end of round 6
Round 7 dc in each st to end. 4sts
Stuff the banana here.
Fasten off.
Re-join yarn to loop created on round 4.
Round 1 (ch 6, ss in next st, skip next st) repeat to end.
Fasten off.

If you like, finish by sewing the banana to Marvin the Monkey's hand so that it won't get lost immediately.

Superhero Dog

Sure they're adorable, but who knew dachshunds had special powers?
This Superhero Dog is speeding through the sky to deliver an urgent
letter to a special someone. Will you hook this amigurumi cutie
and give him a place to land?

YOU WILL NEED

- 4ply weight cotton yarn, approximately one 50g ball of each:
  - Yarn A Brown
  - Yarn B Red
  - Yarn C Blue

- A 2.5mm (US B/1 or C/2) hook

- Safety eyes or black beads, approx 5mm diameter

- Plastic nose, approx 1cm diameter

- Black embroidery thread

- Tapestry needle

- Stitch markers

- Toy stuffing

MEASUREMENTS

- 19cm (7½in) tall

NOTES

· The Legs and Arms are made first, and joined into the Body as you work. All the other pieces are worked separately and then sewn in place.

ARMS AND LEGS (MAKE 4)

Using Yarn A, make a magic loop.
Round 1 (RS) Ch1 (does not count as st), 5dc into the loop. [5 sts]
Round 2 2dc in each dc around. [10 sts]
Rounds 3-10 Dc in each st around.
Fasten off.
Stuff lightly.

HEAD AND BODY

Worked from Head down.
Using Yarn A, make a magic loop.
Round 1 (RS) Ch1 (does not count as st), 6dc into the loop. [6 sts]
Round 2 2dc in each st around. [12 sts]
Round 3 (2dc in next st, 1dc) 6 times. [18 sts]

Round 4 (2dc in next st, 2dc) 6 times. [24 sts]
Round 5 (2dc in next st, 3dc) 6 times. [30 sts]
Round 6 (2dc in next st, 4dc) 6 times. [36 sts]
Round 7 (2dc in next st, 5dc) 6 times. [42 sts]
Rounds 8-15 Dc in each st around.
Round 16 (5dc, dc2tog) 6 times. [36 sts]
Round 17 (4dc, dc2tog) 6 times. [30 sts]
Round 18 (3dc, dc2tog) 6 times. [24 sts]
Round 19 (2dc, dc2tog) 6 times. [18 sts]

Secure the eyes between Rounds 11 and 12, approx 13 sts apart.
If you are using black beads for the eyes, you might like to wait until the Muzzle is attached before you sew them in place.
Round 20 Dc in each st around.
Stuff the Head with toy stuffing and continue stuffing as you go.
Round 21 (2dc in next st, 2dc) 6 times. [24 sts]
Round 22 (2dc in next st, 3dc) 6 times. [30 sts]
Round 23 5dc, join the first Arm, crocheting the next 5 dc of the Body and Arm together, 10dc, join second Arm, crocheting the next 5 dc of the Body and Arm together, 5dc. [30 sts]
Round 24 5dc, 5dc in the remaining 5 sts of the first Arm, 10dc, 5dc in the remaining 5 sts of the second Arm, 5dc. [30 sts]
Rounds 25-41 Dc in each st around.
Round 42 2dc in next st, 2dc, 2dc in next st, 22dc, 2dc in next st, 2dc, 2dc in next st. [34 sts]
Round 43 2dc, 2dc in next st, 28dc, 2dc in next st, 2dc. [36 sts]
Round 44 Dc in each st around.
Make sure to start the next Round from the centre back, so dc around to this position if you need to.
Round 45 7dc, join the first Leg, crocheting the next 5 dc of the Body and Leg together, 13dc, join the second Leg, crocheting the next 5 dc

of the Body and Leg together, 6dc. [36 sts]
Round 46 7dc, 5dc in the remaining 5 sts of the first Leg, 13dc, 5dc in the remaining 5 sts of the second Leg, 6dc. [36 sts]
Round 47 Dc in each st around.
Round 48 (4dc, dc2tog) 6 times. [30 sts]
Round 49 (3dc, dc2tog) 6 times. [24 sts]
Round 50 (2dc, dc2tog) 6 times. [18 sts]
Round 51 (1dc, dc2tog) 6 times. [12 sts]
Round 52 (Dc2tog) 6 times. [6 sts]
Fasten off and weave in ends.

EARS (MAKE 2)

Using Yarn A, make a magic loop.
Round 1 (RS) Ch1 (does not count as st), 5dc into the loop. [5 sts]
Round 2 2dc in each st around. [10 sts]
Round 3 (2dc in next st, 1dc) 5 times. [15 sts]
Rounds 4-8 Dc in each st around.
Round 9 Dc2tog, 13dc. [14 sts]
Round 10 Dc2tog, 12dc. [13 sts]
Round 11 Dc2tog, 11dc. [12 sts]
Round 12 Dc2tog, 10dc. [11 sts]
Round 13 Dc2tog, 9dc. [10 sts]
Round 14 Dc in each st around.
Fasten off, leaving a long tail.
Do not stuff.
Use the long tail to sew the Ears to each side of the Head, between Rounds 7 and 8.

MUZZLE

With Yarn A, make a magic loop.
Round 1 (RS) Ch1 (does not count as st), 6dc into the loop. [6 sts]
Round 2 2dc in each st around. [12 sts]
Round 3 (2dc in next st, 1dc) 6 times. [18 sts]
Round 4 (2dc in next st, 2dc) 6 times. [24 sts]
Round 5 (2dc in next st, 3dc) 6 times. [30 sts]
Round 6 (Dc2tog, 2dc) 3 times, 18dc. [27 sts]
Round 7 9dc.

Fasten off, leaving a long tail and the remaining sts unworked.
Secure the plastic nose between Rounds 4 and 5.
Stuff the Muzzle with toy stuffing.
Use the long tail to sew the Muzzle to the Head, between the Eyes.

TAIL
Using Yarn A, make a magic loop.
Round 1 (RS) Ch1 (does not count as st), 4dc into the loop. [4 sts]
Round 2 2dc in next st, 3dc. [5 sts]
Round 3 Dc in each st around.
Round 4 2dc in next st, 4dc. [6 sts]
Round 5 2dc in next st, 5dc. [7 sts]
Round 6 2dc in next st, 6dc. [8 sts]
Fasten off, leaving a long tail.
Stuff lightly.
Use the long tail to sew the Tail to the bottom of the Body, between Rounds 43 and 45.

CAPE
Using Yarn C, ch51.
Row 1 (RS) Dc in the second ch from the hook and in each ch across. [50 sts]
Fasten off and weave in ends.
Join Yarn B to the WS of the previous row in the 20th stitch.
Row 1 (WS) Ch1 (does not count as st), 12dc, turn leaving remaining sts unworked. [12 sts]
Row 2 Ch1 (does not count as st), 1dc, 2dc in next st, dc in each st to last 2 sts, 2dc in next st, dc in last st, turn. [14 sts]
Rows 3-4 Ch1 (does not count as st), dc in each st across.
Rows 5-22 Repeat (Rows 2-4) 6 more times. [26 sts]
Fasten off and weave in ends.

BORDER
With RS facing, rejoin Yarn B to top-left of cape, ch1 (does not count as st), dc in each row end and dc around to top-right of cape, working 3dc in each corner. Fasten off and weave in ends.

Super sausage 'S'
Using Yarn C, ch17.
Row 1 (RS) Skip the first ch, 3dc, dc2tog, 1dc, dc2tog, 2dc, 2dc in next st, 1dc, 2dc in next st, 3dc. [16 sts]
Fasten off and weave in ends.
Sew the 'S' on the centre back of the Cape.

The 'S' on Super Sausage's cape is a neat, but simple, addition

Sleepy Camel

With his doleful, sleepy expression, this camel would look great sitting on a child's bedroom shelf. Don't forget that you need to stuff the body and head as you go along – the last thing you want is a floppy camel!

Rounds 16-19 Dc in each st around
Round 20 (Dc in each of next 4 sts, dc2tog) 7 times. [35 sts]
Rounds 21-22 Dc in each st around
Round 23 (Dc in each of next 5 sts, dc2tog) 5 times. [30 sts]
Round 24 Dc in each st around
Round 25 (Dc in each of next 3 sts, dc2tog) 6 times. [24 sts]
Round 26 (Dc in next st, dc2tog) 8 times. [16 sts]
Round 27 (Dc2tog) 8 times. [8 sts]
Round 28 (Dc2tog) 4 times. [4 sts]
Fasten off.

HEAD
Using Beige, ch2.
Round 1 (RS) 8dc in second ch from hook. [8 sts]
Round 2 2dc in each st around. [16 sts]
Round 3 (Dc in each of next 3 sts, 2dc in next st) 4 times. [20 sts]
Rounds 4-15 Dc in each st around
Round 16 (Dc in each of next 4 sts, 2dc in next st) 4 times. [24 sts]
Round 17-20 Dc in each st around.
Round 21 (Dc in each of next 5 sts, 2dc in next st) 4 times. [28 sts]

BODY
Begin at the base of the Body.
Using Beige, ch2.
Round 1 (RS) 6dc in second ch from hook. [6 sts]
Round 2 2dc in each st around. [12 sts]
Round 3 (Dc in next st, 2dc in next st) 6 times. [18 sts]
Round 4 (Dc in each of next 2 sts, 2dc in next st) 6 times. [24 sts]
Round 5 (Dc in each of next 3 sts, 2dc in next st) 6 times. [30 sts]
Round 6 (Dc in each of next 4 sts, 2dc in next st) 6 times. [36 sts]
Round 7 (Dc in each of next 5 sts, 2dc in next st) 6 times. [42 sts]
Round 8 (Dc in each of next 6 sts, 2dc in next st) 6 times. [48 sts]
Rounds 9-14 Dc in each st around
Round 15 (Dc in each of next 6 sts, dc2tog) 6 times. [42 sts]

Pick any four colours from your stash to make the back cloth

Rounds 22-24 Dc in each st around.
Round 25 (Dc in each of next 2dc, dc2tog) 7 times. [21 sts]
Round 26 (Dc in next st, dc2tog) 7 times. [14 sts]
Round 27 (Dc2tog) 7 times. (7 sts)
Fasten off, leaving a 5cm tail. Using a wool needle, weave the yarn tail through the last round of stitches and pull tight to close. Weave in ends and trim.

EARS (MAKE 2)
Using Beige, ch2.
Row 1 (RS) 8dc in second ch from hook, turn. [8 sts]
Row 2 Dc in each st to end, turn. Repeat Row 2 once more.
Fasten off.

NECK
Using Beige, ch22, ss to first ch to join into a ring.
Round 1 (RS) Ch1 (not counted as st), dc in same st at base of beg ch-1, dc in each ch around. [22 sts]
Rounds 2-15 Dc in each st around.
Round 16 (Dc in each of next 2 sts, dc2tog) 5 times, dc in each of next 2 sts. [17 sts]
Round 17-18 Dc in each st around.
Round 19 (Dc in next dc, dc2tog) 5 times, dc in each of next 2 sts. [12 sts]
Round 20 (Dc2tog) 6 times. [6 sts]
Fasten off. Using a wool needle, weave the yarn tail through the last round of stitches and pull tight to close. Weave in ends and trim.

LEGS (MAKE 4)
Using Beige, ch16, ss in first ch to join into a ring.
Round 1 (RS) Ch1 (not counted as st), dc in same st at base of beg ch-1, dc in each ch around. [16 sts]
Rounds 2-19 Dc in each st around.
Round 20 (Dc in each of next 3 sts, 2dc in next st) 4 times. [20 sts]
Rounds 21-23 Dc in each st around. Now decrease for base.
Round 24 (Dc in each of next 2 sts, dc2tog) 5 times. [15 sts]
Round 25 (Dc in next st, dc2tog) 5 times. [10 sts]

Round 26 Dc in each st around.
Round 27 (Dc2tog) 5 times. [5 sts]
Fasten off. Using a wool needle, weave the yarn tail through the last round of stitches and pull tight to close. Weave in ends and trim.

HALTER AND LEAD REIN
Using Gold, make a chain long enough to fit around the Camel's nose and then around the back of the Head. Use the photo as a guide when sewing in place. Make a longer chain for the Lead Rein.

TAIL
Using Beige, ch15.
Row 1 (RS) Dc in second ch from hook, dc in each ch to end, turn. [14 sts]
Row 2 Ch1 (not counted as a st), dc in each st to end.
Fasten off. Cut a few lengths of Beige and add to one end of the Camel's Tail.

BACK CLOTH
Using Red, ch2.
Round 1 (RS) 6dc in second ch from hook. [6 sts]
Round 2 2dc in each st around. [12 sts]
Round 3 (Dc in next st, 2dc in next st) 6 times. [18 sts]
Round 4 (Dc in each of next 2 sts, 2dc in next st) 6 times. [24 sts]
Round 5 (Dc in each of next 3 sts, 2dc in next st) 6 times. [30 sts]
Round 6 (Dc in each of next 4 sts, 2dc in next st) 6 times. [36 sts]
Round 7 (Dc in each of next 5 sts, 2dc in next st) 6 times. [42 sts]
Rounds 8-9 Dc in each st around, changing to Green on last yrh of last dc.
Round 10 (Dc in next st, 1ch, miss next st) around, ss to first dc to join, changing to Gold on yrh of ss. [21 dc, 21 ch-1 sps]
Round 11 (Dc in next ch-1 sp, 2dc in next ch1-sp) around, ss to first dc, changing to Turquoise on yrh of ss. [30 sts]
Round 12 (Dc in next st, 2ch, miss next st) around, ss to first dc,

changing to Green on yrh of ss. [15 dc, 15 ch-2 sps]
Round 13 Ch1 (not counted as st), dc in same st at base of ch-1, (5tr in next 2-ch loop, dc in next 2-ch loop) to last 2-ch loop, 5tr in last 2-ch loop, ss to top of first dc. [8 5-tr groups, 8 dc]
Fasten off and weave in ends.

UNDER BODY STRAP
Using Turquoise, ch38.
Row 1 (RS) Dc in second ch from hook, dc in each ch to end, turn. [37 sts]
Row 2 Dc in each st to end.
Fasten off.

TO FINISH
Make the Head first. The widest part is the back of the Head. Take the Ears and curl them into semi circles, then sew one to each side of the Head. Using black yarn, embroider an eye onto each side, using the image as a guide. Embroider nostrils onto the Camel's nose. Take the gold chain Halter and sew in place on the Head. The tassels are made by winding a few lengths of yarn together and knotting them. Attach a tassel to each side of the Halter. Add the Lead Rein to the sides of the Head.

The Body and Head will already be stuffed. Stuff each Leg firmly, but do not close the tops. Stuff the Neck quite firmly but do not close the top. This is the part of the Neck that you will sew the Head onto. Take the Body and pin the Legs in place onto the base. Angle them outwards slightly to make the Camel stand well. Aim to get all the Legs level. Sew each one in place. Take the Neck and sew the Head to the open end; the Head should sit onto the Neck. Sew in place. Carefully pin the Neck onto the front of the Body, sew firmly in place. Attach the Tail to the back of the Camel. Place the Back Cloth onto the back of the Camel, sew neatly in place. Sew the Under Body Strap in place.

Cat Pair

These amigurumi kittens have been raiding the dressing-up box for their favourite outfits! Ballerina Bella is ready to twirl in her ruffled tutu, while Bow is snuggled up in a cosy hooded sleepsuit. Just purr-fect.

Bella's dress bodice is made as part of the body, and the skirt is crocheted separately

YOU WILL NEED

- DK weight cotton yarn, approximately one 50g ball of each:
- Yarn A White
- Yarn B Yellow
- Yarn C Pink
- Yarn D Green

- A 3.5mm (US E/4) hook
- Stitch markers
- Safety eyes or black beads, approx 15mm (½in) diameter
- Black embroidery thread
- Wool and embroidery needle
- Pink felt
- Fabric glue
- Small buttons in yellow and green

MEASUREMENTS

18x12x12cm (7x4¾x4¾in)

HEAD AND BODY (MAKE 1 PER CAT)

Using Yarn A, ch5.
Round 1 (RS) Dc in second ch from hook, dc in each of next 2 ch, 3dc in last ch, rotate and work along opposite side of ch, dc in each of next 2 ch, 2dc in next ch. [10 sts]
Round 2 (Dc in next st, 2dc in next st) 5 times. [15 sts]
Round 3 (Dc in each of next 2 sts, 2dc in next st) 5 times. [20 sts]
Round 4 (Dc in each of next 3 sts, 2dc in next st) 5 times. [25 sts]
Round 5 (Dc in each of next 4 sts, 2dc in next st) 5 times. [30 sts]
Round 6 (Dc in each of next 9 sts, 2dc in next st) 3 times. [33 sts]
Round 7 (Dc in each of next 10 sts, 2dc in next st) 3 times. [36 sts]
Round 8 (Dc in each of next 11 sts, 2dc in next st) 3 times. [39 sts]

Round 9 (Dc in each of next 12 sts, 2dc in next st) 3 times. [42 sts]
Round 10 (Dc in each of next 13 sts, 2dc in next st) 3 times. [45 sts]
Round 11 (Dc in each of next 14 sts, 2dc in next st) 3 times. [48 sts]
Round 12 (Dc in each of next 15 sts, 2dc in next st) 3 times. [51 sts]
Round 13 (Dc in each of next 16 sts, 2dc in next st) 3 times. [54 sts]
Place 2 stitch markers on the next round 12 sts apart to mark the position of the eyes.
Rounds 14-17 Dc in each st around.
Round 18 (Dc2tog, dc in each of next 7 sts) 6 times. [48 sts]
Round 19 (Dc2tog, dc in each of next 6 sts) 6 times. [42 sts]
Round 20 (Dc2tog, dc in each of next 5 sts) 6 times. [36 sts]
Round 21 (Dc2tog, dc in each of next 4 sts) 6 times. [30 sts]
Round 22 (Dc2tog) around. [15 sts]
Put working loop onto a stitch holder and fix the toy safety eyes to the marked stitches on Round 14. Stuff the head with toy filling.
Replace working loop back on hook and continue.
Round 23 (Dc in each of next 4 sts, 2dc in next st) 3 times. [18 sts]
Round 24 Dc in each st around, changing to Yarn D on last yrh of last dc for Bow's sleepsuit.
Round 25 (Dc in each of next 5 sts, 2dc in next st) 3 times. [21 sts]
Round 26 Dc in each st around, changing to Yarn B on last yrh of last dc for Bella's dress.
Round 27 (Dc in each of next 6 sts, 2dc in next st) 3 times. [24 sts]
Round 28 Dc in each st around.
Round 29 (Dc in each of next 7 sts, 2dc in next st) 3 times. [27 sts]
Round 30 Dc in each st around.
Round 31 (Dc in each of next 8 sts, 2dc in next st) 3 times. [30 sts]
Round 32 Dc in each st around.
Round 33 (Dc in each of next 9 sts, 2dc in next st) 3 times. [33 sts]
Round 34 Dc in each st around, changing to Yarn A on last yrh of last dc for Bella or continue in Yarn D for Bow's sleepsuit.

Round 35 (Dc in each of next 10 sts, 2dc in next st) 3 times. [36 sts]
Round 36 Dc in each st around.
Round 37 (Dc2tog, dc in each of next 10 sts) 3 times. [33 sts]
Round 38 (Dc2tog, dc in each of next 9 sts) 3 times. [30 sts]
Round 39 (Dc2tog, dc in each of next 3 sts) 6 times. [24 sts]
Round 40 (Dc2tog, dc in each of next 2 sts) 6 times. [18 sts]
Round 41 (Dc2tog, dc in next st) 6 times. [12 sts]
Round 42 (Dc2tog) 6 times. [6 sts]
Fasten off, leaving a long tail. Stuff the Body firmly with toy filling. Thread yarn onto wool needle and weave through the last 6 stitches, pull the yarn to close the hole at the bottom of the Body, weave in yarn ends and trim.

LEGS (MAKE 2)

Using Yarn A, make a magic loop.
Round 1 (RS) 6dc into the loop. [6 sts]
Round 2 2dc in each st around. [12 sts]
Round 3 Dc in each of next 2 sts, 2dc in next st, dc in each of next 2 sts, 3htr in next st, htr in each of next 2 sts, 3htr in next st, dc in each of next 2 sts, 2dc in next st. [18 sts]
Round 4 Dc in each of next 3 sts, 2dc in next st, dc in each of next 2 sts, htr in next st, 2htr in next st, htr in each of next 4 sts, 2htr in next st, htr in next st, dc in next st, 2dc in next st, dc in each of next 2 sts. [22 sts]
Round 5 2dc in next st, dc in each of next 8 sts, 3htr in next st, htr in each of next 5 sts, 3htr in next st, dc in each of next 6 sts. [27 sts]
Round 6 Dc in each st around.
Round 7 Dc in next st, dc2tog, dc in each of next 8 sts, dc2tog, dc in each of next 6 sts, dc2tog, dc in each of next 6 sts. [24 sts]
Round 8 Dc in each of next 11 sts, htr3tog, htr in each of next 3 sts, htr3tog, dc in each of next 4 sts. [20 sts]
Round 9 Dc in each of next 3 sts, dc2tog, dc in each of next 4 sts, dc2tog, dc in next st, dc2tog, dc in

next st, dc2tog, dc in each of next 3 sts. [16 sts]

Round 10 Dc in each of next 8 sts, dc2tog, dc in next st, dc2tog, dc in each of next 3 sts. [14 sts]

For Bow, change to Yarn D and work a round of slip stitches so Round 10 is worked into the dc stitches of Round 9, leaving a decorative edge.

Round 11 Dc in each st around.

Round 12 Dc2tog, dc in each remaining st around. [13 sts]

Rounds 13-22 Rep Rounds 11 and 12 another 5 times. [8 sts after Round 22]

Fasten off, leaving a long tail. Stuff firmly with toy filling.

Finish as before. Cut hearts out and dots out of pink felt and, using image as a guide, stick to the underside of the foot. Sew the Legs to the underside of the Body so that the cat is in a sitting down position.

ARMS (MAKE 2)

Using Yarn A, make a magic loop.

Round 1 (RS) 6dc in the loop. [6 sts]

Round 2 2dc in each st around. [12 sts]

Rounds 3-4 Dc in each st around.

Round 5 Dc2tog, dc in each remaining st around. [11 sts]

Round 6 As Round 5. [10 sts]

Round 7 Dc in each of next 5 sts, dc2tog, 1dc in each of next 3 sts. [9 sts]

For Bow, change to Yarn D now and work a round of slip stitches so Round 8 is worked into the dc stitches of Round 7 leaving a decorative edge.

Round 8 Dc2tog, dc in each remaining st around. [8 sts]

Rounds 9-17 Dc in each st around.

Fasten off, leaving a long tail. Stuff the Arm firmly with toy filling and finish as before. Sew in place on the Body.

EARS (MAKE 2)

Using Yarn A for Bella and Yarn D for Bow, make a magic loop.

Round 1 (RS) 4dc into the loop. [4 sts]

Round 2 (Dc in next st, 2dc in next st) twice. [6 sts]

Round 3 (Dc in each of next 2 sts, 2dc in next st) twice. [8 sts]

Round 4 (Dc in each of next 3 sts, 2dc in next st) twice. [10 sts]

Round 5 (Dc in each of next 4 sts, 2dc in next st) twice. [12 sts]

Round 6 (Dc in each of next 5 sts, 2dc in next st) twice. [14 sts]

Round 7 (Dc in each of next 6 sts, 2dc in next st) twice. [16 sts]

Fasten off, leaving a long tail. Cut triangles of pink felt and glue inside the Ears. Sew in place on the Head (do not sew Bow's Ears on until you've made her Hood).

TUTU (FOR BELLA ONLY)

Using Yarn B, ch37.

Row 1 (RS) 2dc in second ch from hook, dc in each ch to end, turn. [36 sts]

Row 2 Ch1 (not counted as st), 2dc in each st to end, turn. [72 sts]

Row 3 Ch1 (not counted as st), 2dc in each st to the end. [144 sts]

Fasten off, leaving a long tail. Sew in place around the waist of the Cat, making sure it doesn't twist.

DRESS STRAP (FOR BELLA ONLY)

Using Yarn B, ch20.

Fasten off, leaving a long tail. Sew one end to one side of the Top, wrap chain round the back of the Head and sew the other end to the opposite side of the Top. Weave in ends and trim.

Sew or glue a small yellow button to each end of the Strap to decorate.

HOOD (FOR BOW ONLY)

Using Yarn D, ch5.

Round 1 (RS) Dc in second ch from hook, dc in each of next 2 ch, 3dc in last ch, rotate and work along the opposite side of the ch, dc in each of next 2 ch, 2dc in next ch. [10 sts]

Round 2 (Dc in next st, 2dc in next st) 5 times. [15 sts]

Round 3 (Dc in each of next 2 sts, 2dc in next st) 5 times. [20 sts]

Round 4 (Dc in each of next 3 sts, 2dc in next st) 5 times. [25 sts]

Round 5 (Dc in each of next 4 sts, 2dc in next st) 5 times. [30 sts]

Round 6 (Dc in each of next 9 sts, 2dc in next st) 3 times. [33 sts]

Round 7 (Dc in each of next 10 sts, 2dc in next st) 3 times. [36 sts]

Round 8 (Dc in each of next 11 sts, 2dc in next st) 3 times. [39 sts]

Round 9 (Dc in each of next 12 sts, 2dc in next st) 3 times. [42 sts]

Round 10 (Dc in each of next 13 sts, 2dc in next st) 3 times. [45 sts]

Round 11 (Dc in each of next 14 sts, 2dc in next st) 3 times. [48 sts]

Round 12 (Dc in each of next 15 sts, 2dc in next st) 3 times. [51 sts]

Round 13 (Dc in each of next 16 sts, 2dc in next st) 3 times. [54 sts]

Rounds 14-19 Dc in each st around.

Fasten off, leaving a long tail, and pull through loop to secure. Sew in place on the Head.

PINK BOW (FOR BOW ONLY)

Using Yarn C, ch6.

Row 1 (RS) Dc in second ch from hook, dc in each ch to end, turn. [5 sts]

Rows 2-7 Ch1 (not counted as st), dc in each st to end.

Fasten off, leaving a long tail. Wrap yarn tightly around the middle of the rectangle and fasten off securely to create a bow shape. Sew in place on the Head. Sew or glue 3 small green buttons down the front of the sleepsuit to decorate.

TO FINISH

Use the photographs as a guide when creating the face. Glue a pink felt heart to the centre of the face to make a nose. Using two strands of black embroidery thread and long stitches, create the mouth and whiskers.

Deer Duo

This adorable mum and baby deer tick all the amigurumi boxes with their cute spots, sticky-up ears and stubby tails. They're quick to make up with a minimal amount of stitching.

YOU WILL NEED

- DK weight cotton yarn approximately one 50g ball of each:
  - Yarn A Burgundy
  - Yarn B White
  - Yarn C Black
- A 3mm (US D/3) hook
- Toy stuffing
- Two pairs of safety eyes or beads, approx 6mm (¼in) diameter
- Wool needle

NOTES

- Each part (except for the Belly) is worked using the amigurumi method as explained on p. 6.

BABY DEER

SPOTS (MAKE 6)

Using Yarn B, make a magic loop.
Round 1 (RS) 5dc into the loop, ss to first dc to join. [5 sts]
Fasten off.

EARS (MAKE 2)

Using Yarn A, make a magic loop.
Round 1 (RS) 4dc into the loop. [4 sts]
Round 2 (2dc in next st, dc in next st) twice. [6 sts]
Round 3 (Dc in next st, 2dc in next st) 3 times. [9 sts]
Round 4 (Dc in each of next 2 sts, 2dc in next st) 3 times. [12 sts]
Rounds 5-12 Dc in each st around.
Fasten off. Flatten the Ear, fold and stitch the bottom together to make Ear shape.

BODY

Add stuffing as you go.
Using Yarn A, make a magic loop.
Round 1 (RS) 5dc into the loop. [5 sts]
Round 2 2dc in each st around. [10 sts]
Round 3 (Dc in next st, 2dc in next st) 5 times. [15 sts]
Round 4 (Dc in each of next 2 sts, 2dc in next st) 5 times. [20 sts]
Round 5 (Dc in each of next 3 sts, 2dc in next st) 5 times. [25 sts]
Rounds 6-10 Dc in each st around.

Take your time to shape the ears before sewing them into position on your deer

Round 11 (Dc in each of next 4 sts 2dc in next st) 5 times. [30 sts]
Rounds 12-13 Dc in each st around.
Round 14 (Dc in each of next 5 sts, 2dc in next st) 5 times. [35 sts]
Rounds 15-17 Dc in each st around.
Round 18 (Dc in each of next 5 sts, dc2tog) 5 times. [30 sts]
Round 19 (Dc in each of next 4 sts, dc2tog) 5 times. [25 sts]
Round 20 (Dc in each of next 3 sts, dc2tog) 5 times. [20 sts]
Round 21 (Dc in each of next 2 sts, dc2tog) 5 times. [15 sts]
Round 22 (Dc in next st, dc2tog 5 times. [10 sts]
Round 23 (Dc2tog) 5 times. [5 sts]
Fasten off.

HEAD
Add stuffing as you go.
Using Yarn C, make a magic loop.
Round 1 (RS) 4dc into the loop.
Round 2 Dc in each st around, changing to Yarn B on last yrh of last dc.
Round 3 2dc in each st around. [8 sts]
Round 4 Dc in each of next 4 sts, 2dc in each of next 4 sts. [12 sts]
Round 5 Dc in each of next 6 sts, 2dc in each of next 4 sts, dc in each of next 2 sts. [16 sts]
Round 6 Dc in each st around.
Round 7 Dc in each of next 3 sts changing to Yarn A on last yrh of 3rd dc, dc in each of next 7 sts, 2dc in each of next 4 sts, dc in each of next 2 sts. [20 sts]
Round 8 Dc in each of next 10 sts, 2dc in each of next 8 sts, Dc in each of next 2 sts. [28 sts]
Round 9 Dc in each st around.
Fix toy safety eyes to front Head, using image as a guide for placement.
Round 10 (Dc in each of next 6 sts, 2dc in next st) 4 times. [32 sts]
Rounds 11-13 Dc in each st around.
Round 14 (Dc in each of next 6 sts, dc2tog) 4 times. [28 sts]
Rounds 15-17 Dc in each st around.
Round 18 (Dc in each of next 5 sts, dc2tog) 4 times. [24 sts]

Round 19 (Dc in each of next 4 sts, dc2tog) 4 times. [20 sts]
Round 20 (Dc in each of next 3 sts, dc2tog) 4 times. [16 sts]
Round 21 (Dc in each of next 2 sts, dc2tog) 4 times. [12 sts]
Round 22 (Dc in next st, dc2tog) 4 times. [8 sts]
Round 23 (Dc2tog) 4 times. [4 sts]
Fasten off.

NECK
Using Yarn A, ch22, ss to first ch to join into a ring.
Round 1 (RS) Ch1 (not counted as st), dc in same st at base of beg ch-1, dc in each ch around. [22 sts]
Rounds 2-3 Dc in each st around.
Fasten off.

BELLY
Using Yarn B, ch5.
Row 1 (RS) Dc in second ch from hook, dc in each ch to end, turn. [4 sts]
Row 2 Ch1 (not counted as st here and throughout), 2dc in first st, dc in each of next 2 sts, 2dc in last st, turn. [6 sts]
Row 3 Ch1, 2dc in first st, dc in each of next 4 sts, 2dc in last st, turn. [8 sts]
Row 4 Ch1, 2dc in first st, dc in each of next 6 sts, 2dc in last st, turn. [10 sts]
Row 5 Ch1, 2dc in first st, dc in each of next 8 sts, 2dc in last st, turn. [12 sts]
Row 6 Ch1, 2dc in first st, dc in each of next 10 sts, 2dc in last st, turn. [14 sts]
Rows 7–14 Ch1, dc in each st to end, turn.
Row 15 Ch1, dc in each of next 6 sts, dc2tog, dc in each of next 6 sts, turn. [13 sts]
Row 16 Ch1, skip first st, dc in each of next 10 sts, dc2tog, turn. [11 sts]
Row 17 Ch1, skip first st, dc in each of next 8 sts, dc2tog, turn. [9 sts]
Row 18 Ch1, dc in each st to end, turn.
Row 19 Ch1, skip first st, dc in each of next 6 sts, dc2tog, turn. [7 sts]
Row 20 Ch1, skip first st, dc in each of next 4 sts, dc2tog, turn. [5 sts]

Row 21 Ch1, dc in each st to end, turn.
Row 22 Ch1, ss across the stitches of the top row and then continue down the row ends, across the foundation chain and up the opposite row ends to make a neat border all the way round. **Fasten off.**

TAIL
Using Yarn A, make a magic loop.
Round 1 (RS) 4dc into the loop. [4 sts]
Round 2 (2dc in next st, dc in next st) twice. [6 sts]
Round 3 (Dc in next st, 2dc in next st) 3 times. [9 sts]
Rounds 4-5 Dc in each st around.
Fasten off.

LEGS
Stuff as you go, stuffing the top half of the Legs very lightly, as you need to bend them when you sew them on.
Using Yarn C, make a magic loop.
Round 1 (RS) 4dc into the loop. [4 sts]
Round 2 2dc in each st around. [8 sts]
Round 3 Dc in each st around, changing to Yarn A on last yrh of last dc.
Rounds 4-13 Dc in each st around.
Fasten off.

TO FINISH
Sew Ears onto Head, Neck onto Body and Head onto Neck (adding a little extra toy filling to create a firm neck). Sew Belly Patch onto Body then sew legs onto Body, pinning them first so you can check the Deer sits properly as the Head is a little heavy. Sew Tail onto Body, then attach the Spots.

MOTHER DEER
SPOTS
Make as for Baby Deer.

HEAD
Add stuffing as you go.
Using Yarn C, make a magic loop.
Round 1 (RS) 4dc into the loop.
Round 2 (2dc in next st, dc in next st) twice. [6 sts]
Round 3 Dc in each st around, changing to Yarn B on last yrh of last dc.

Round 4 2dc in each st around. [12 sts]

Round 5 Dc in each of next 6 sts, 2dc in each of next 6 sts. [18 sts]

Round 6 Dc in each of next 9 sts, 2dc in each of next 6 sts, dc in each of next 3 sts. [24 sts]

Rounds 7-8 Dc in each st around.

Round 9 Dc in each of next 4 sts, changing to Yarn A on last yrh of 4th dc, dc in each of next 10 sts, 2dc in each of next 6 sts, dc in each of next 4 sts. [30 sts]

Round 10 Dc in each of next 13 sts, 2dc in each of next 2 sts, dc in each of next 6 sts, 2dc in each of next 3 sts, dc in each of next 4 sts, 2dc in each of next 2 sts. [37 sts]

Round 11 Dc in each st around. Fix toy safety eyes to front Head, using image as a guide for placement.

Round 12 Dc in each of next 6 sts, 2dc in next st, dc in each of next 12 sts, 2dc in next st, dc in each of next 11 sts, 2dc in next st, dc in each of next 5 sts. [40 sts]

Rounds 13-16 Dc in each st around.

Round 17 (Dc in each of next 6 sts, dc2tog) 5 times. [35 sts]

Rounds 18-20 Dc in each st around.

Round 21 (Dc in each of next 5 sts, dc2tog) 5 times. [30 sts]

Round 22 (Dc in each of next 4 sts, dc2tog) 5 times. [25 sts]

Round 23 (Dc in each of next 3 sts, dc2tog) 5 times. [20 sts]

Round 24 (Dc in each of next 2 sts, dc2tog) 5 times. [15 sts]

Round 25 (Dc in next st, dc2tog) 5 times. [10 sts]

Round 26 (Dc2tog) 5 times. [5 sts]
Fasten off.

EARS

Using Yarn A, make a magic loop.

Round 1 (RS) 4dc into the loop. [4 sts]

Round 2 2dc in each st around. [8 sts]

Round 3 (Dc in next st, 2dc in next) 4 times. [12 sts]

Round 4 (Dc in each of next 2 sts, 2dc in next) 4 times. [16 sts]

Round 5 (Dc in each of next 3 sts, 2dc in next) 4 times. [20 sts]

Rounds 6-10 Dc in each st around.
Fasten off. Flatten out piece, fold and sew bottom edge together to make Ear shape.

BODY

Add stuffing as you go.
Using Yarn A, make a magic loop.

Round 1 (RS) 6dc into the loop. [6 sts]

Round 2 2dc in each st around. [12sts]

Round 3 (Dc in next st, 2dc in next st) 6 times. [18 sts]

Round 4 (Dc in each of next 2 sts, 2dc in next st) 6 times. [24 sts]

Round 5 (Dc in each of next 3 sts, 2dc in next st) 6 times. [30 sts]

Rounds 6-10 Dc in each st around.

Round 11 (Dc in each of next 4 sts, 2dc in next st) 6 times. [36 sts]

Rounds 12-15 Dc in each st around.

Round 16 (Dc in each of next 5 sts, 2dc in next st) 6 times. [42 sts]

Rounds 17-20 Dc in each st around.

Round 21 (Dc in each of next 5 sts, dc2tog) 6 times. [36 sts]

Round 22 (Dc in each of next 4 sts, dc2tog) 6 times. [30 sts]

Round 23 (Dc in each of next 3 sts, dc2tog) 6 times. [24 sts]

Round 24 (Dc in each of next 2 sts, dc2tog) 6 times. [18 sts]

Round 25 (Dc in next st, dc2tog) 6 times. [12 sts]

Round 26 (Dc2tog) 6 times. [6 sts]
Fasten off.

NECK

Using Yarn A, ch30, ss to first ch to join into a ring.

Round 1 (RS) Ch1 (not counted as st), dc in same st at base of beg ch-1, dc in each ch around. [29 sts]

Rounds 2-3 Dc in each st around.
Fasten off.

BELLY

Using Yarn C, ch4.

Row 1 (RS) Dc in second ch from hook, dc in each of next 2 ch, turn. [3 sts]

Row 2 Ch1 (not counted as st here and throughout), 2dc in first st, dc in next st, 2dc in last st, turn. [5 sts]

Row 3 Ch1, 2dc in first st, dc in each of next 3 sts, 2dc in last st, turn. [7 sts]

Row 4 Ch1, 2dc in first st, dc in each of next 5 sts, 2dc in last st, turn. [9 sts]

Row 5 Ch1, 2dc in first st, dc in each of next 7 sts, 2dc in last st, turn. [11 sts]

Row 6 Ch1, 2dc in first st, dc in each of next 9 sts, 2dc in last st, turn. [13 sts]

Row 7 Ch1, 2dc in first st, dc in each of next 11 sts, 2dc in last st, turn. [15 sts]

Row 8 Ch1, 2dc in first st, dc in each of next 13 sts, 2dc in last st, turn. [17 sts]

Rows 9-20 Ch1, dc in each st to end, turn.

Row 21 Ch1, skip first st, dc in each of next 14 sts, dc2tog, turn. [15 sts]

Row 22 Ch1, skip first st, dc in each of next 12 sts, dc2tog, turn. [13 sts]

Row 23 Ch1, skip first st, dc in each of next 10 sts, dc2tog, turn. [11 sts]

Row 24 Ch1, skip first st, dc in each of next 8 sts, dc2tog, turn. [9 sts]

Row 25 Ch1, skip first st, dc in each of next 6 sts, dc2tog, turn. [7 sts]

Row 26 Ch1, skip first st, dc in each of next 4 sts, dc2tog, turn. [5 sts]

Row 27 Ch1, ss across the top row and then down the rows, across the foundation chain and up the rows to make a neat border all the way round.
Fasten off.

LEGS

Stuff as you go, stuffing the top half of the Legs very lightly, as you need to bend them when you sew them on.
Using Yarn C, make a magic loop.

Round 1 (RS) 5dc into the loop. [5 sts]

Round 2 2dc in each st around. [10 sts]

Round 3 Dc in each st around, changing to Yarn A on last yrh of last dc.

Rounds 4-16 Dc in each st around.
Fasten off.

TO FINISH

Sew together following instructions as given for Baby Deer.

Little Lion

This lion is way too cute to be a fiercesome beast! Despite his thick mane,
he's more like a cub looking for a friend ... could it be you?
He's obviously a team player.

YOU WILL NEED

• 4ply weight cotton yarn, approximately one 50g ball of each:
- Yarn A Yellow
- Yarn B Dark Brown
- Yarn C White
- Yarn D Green
- Yarn E Orange

• A 2.5mm (US B/1 or C/2) hook

• A 3 mm (US C/2 or D/3) hook

• Black stranded cotton

• 2 safety eyes (9mm)

• A safety nose (10mm)

• Stitch markers

TOY STUFFING MEASUREMENTS

• Approx 14 cm (5½in) tall

Add a special touch to your make by embroidering a name onto the cap

HEAD

With Yarn A and a 2.5mm hook, make a magic loop.

Round 1 Ch1 (does not count as st), 6dc into the loop. [6 dc]

Round 2 2dc in each st around. [12 dc]

Round 3 (1dc, 2dc in next st) 6 times. [18 dc]

Round 4 (2dc, 2dc in next st) 6 times. [24 dc]

Round 5 (3dc, 2dc in next st) 6 times. [30 dc]

Round 6 (4dc, 2dc in next st) 6 times. [36 dc]

Round 7 (5dc, 2dc in next st) 6 times. [42 dc]

Round 8 (6dc, 2dc in next st) 6 times. [48 dc]

Round 9-14 Dc in each st around. [48 dc]

Round 15 (Dc2tog, 6dc) 6 times.
[42 sts]
Round 16 (Dc2tog, 5dc) 6 times.
[36 sts]
Round 17 (Dc2tog, 4dc) 6 times.
[30 sts]
Round 18 (Dc2tog, 3dc) 6 times.
[24 sts]
Round 19 (Dc2tog, 2dc) 6 times.
[18 sts]
Round 20 Dc in each st around.
[18 dc]
Fasten off.
Do not stuff Head yet.

MUZZLE

With Yarn A and a 2.5mm hook, make
a magic loop.
Round 1 Ch1 (does not count as st),
6dc into the loop. [6 dc]
Round 2 2dc in each st around. [12 dc]
Round 3 (1dc, 2dc in next st) 6 times.
[18 dc]
Round 4 (2dc, 2dc in next st) 6 times.
[24 dc]
Round 5-6 Dc in each st around. [24
dc]
Fasten off leaving a long tail for
sewing.

EAR (MAKE 2)

With Yarn A and a 2.5mm hook, make
a magic loop.
Round 1 Ch1 (does not count as st),
6dc into the loop. [6 dc]
Round 2 2dc in next st, 5dc. [7 dc]
Round 3 2dc in next st, 6dc. [8 dc]
Round 4 2dc in next st, 7dc. [9 dc]
Round 5 2dc in next st, 8dc. [10 dc]
Round 6 (2dc in next st, 4dc) twice.
[12 dc]
Round 7 Dc in each st around. [12 dc]
Fasten off leaving a long tail for
sewing.

BODY

With Yarn A and a 2.5mm hook, make
a magic loop.
Round 1 Ch1 (does not count as st),
6dc into the loop. [6 dc]
Round 2 2dc in each st around. [12
dc]
Round 3 (1dc, 2dc in next st) 6 times.
[18 dc]

Round 4 (2dc, 2dc in next st) 6 times.
[24 dc]
Round 5 (3dc, 2dc in next st) 6 times.
[30 dc]
Round 6 (4dc, 2dc in next st) 6 times.
[36 dc]
Round 7-12 Dc in each st around.
[36 dc]
Round 13 (Dc2tog, 1dc) 4 times.
[32 sts]
Round 14 Dc2tog 4 times, 24dc.
[28 sts]
Round 15 (5dc, dc2tog) 4 times.
[24 sts]
Round 16-17 Dc in each st around.
[24 sts]
Round 18 (2dc, dc2tog) 6 times. [18 sts]
Round 19 Dc in each st around, ss to
first st to join. [18 sts]
Fasten off leaving a long tail for
sewing. Stuff the Body.

TAIL

With Yarn A and a 2.5mm hook, ch11.
Row 1 Dc in 2nd ch from hook and
each ch across. [10 dc]
Fasten off leaving a long tail for
sewing.

Use three 2cm strands of Yarn E to
add a fringe at the end of the tail.

ARM (MAKE 2)

With Yarn A and a 2.5mm hook, make
a magic loop.
Round 1 Ch1 (does not count as st),
5dc into the loop. [5 dc]
Round 2 2dc in each st around.
[10 dc]
Round 3-4 Dc in each st around.
[10 dc]
Round 5 3dc, dc2tog twice, 3dc.
[8 sts]
Round 6-9 Dc in each st around.
[8 dc]
Stuff the arm.
Fasten off leaving a long tail for
sewing.

LEG (MAKE 2)

With Yarn A and a 2.5mm hook, ch5.
Round 1 Dc in second chain from the
hook, dc in next 2 ch, 3dc in last ch,
rotate to work along opposite side of
starting ch, 2dc, 2dc in last ch. [10 dc]
Round 2 (4dc, 2dc in next st) twice.
[12 dc]

Each limb is worked
separately and
stitched together
at the end

Round 3 (4dc, 2dc in each of next 2 sts) twice. [16 dc]
Round 4-5 Dc in each st around. [16 dc]
Round 6 5dc, dc2tog twice, 7dc. [14 sts]
Round 7 4dc, dc2tog twice, 6dc. [12 sts]
Round 8 (Dc2tog, 2dc) 3 times. [9 sts] Stuff the leg.
Round 9 Dc in each st around. [9 dc]
Fasten off leaving a long tail for sewing.

MANE
With Yarn E and a 3mm hook, make a magic loop.
Round 1 Ch1 (does not count as st), 6dc into the loop. [6 dc]
Round 2 2dc in each st around. [12 dc]
Round 3 (1dc, 2dc in next st) 6 times. [18 dc]
Round 4 (2dc, 2dc in next st) 6 times. [24 dc]
Round 5 (3dc, 2dc in next st) 6 times. [30 dc]
Round 6 (4dc, 2dc in next st) 6 times. [36 dc]
Round 7-10 Dc in each st around. [36 dc]
Do not fasten off.
Continue with the lower part of the Mane (it will look like a beard). Ch15, dc in second ch from hook and each ch across, ss into the next st of Round 10, turn to work back along Lower Mane, dc in next 15 sts.
Fasten off leaving a long tail for sewing.

CAP
With Yarn D and a 2.5mm hook, make a magic loop.
Round 1 Ch1 (does not count as st), 6dc into the loop. [6 dc]
Round 2 2dc in each st around. [12 dc]
Round 3 (1dc, 2dc in next st) 6 times. [18 dc]
Round 4 (2dc, 2dc in next st) 6 times. [24 dc]
Round 5-8 Dc in each st around. [24 dc]
Change to Yarn C.

Make a wild woolly mane for your little lion by looping orange yarn through your stitches

Round 9 8ss, 2dc in next st, 1htr, 2tr in each of next 3 sts, 1htr, 2dc in next st, 9ss.
Fasten off leaving a long tail of yarn and decorate the cap with some long stitches.

TO MAKE UP
Place the safety nose on the Muzzle between Rounds 3 and 4.
Stitch the mouth to the Muzzle, under the nose, using the black stranded cotton.
Sew the Muzzle between Rounds 9 and 18 of the head, stuffing lightly while sewing.
Insert the safety eyes between Rounds 12 and 13 of the Head, 2 stitches away from the muzzle.
Stuff the Head with toy stuffing.
Sew the Head to the Body.
Position Legs and Arms. Sew the Arms between Rounds 12 and 13 of the Body approximately 2 stitches apart. Sew the Legs between Rounds 4 and 6 of the Body.
Sew the tail to the bottom.
Sew the Mane on the Head with the wrong side up, positioning the narrow strap under the Muzzle and sewing the end to the other side of the Mane. This piece is used as a base for securing the hair of the Mane. Cut several strands of Yarn E (approx 6 cm long). Fold each strand in half and use the crochet hook to join it in a stitch into the visible loops. Cover the last round of the Mane completely and approx. half of the total stitches.
Sew the Ears on the Mane.

Lovely Lamb

Leaping for joy, this lovely little lamb is an adorable addition to your crochet menagerie. She has a wonderfully tactile coat that just begs to be stroked, made using a clever combo of bobble stitches. Truly baa-rilliant.

YOU WILL NEED

- DK weight cotton yarn, approximately two 50g balls of
- Yarn A Cream
- One 50g ball of
- Yarn B Taupe
- Small amounts of:
- Yarn C Pink
- Yarn D Yellow
- Yarn E Green

- A 2.5mm (US B/1 or C/2) hook

- A 3mm (US C/2 or D/3) hook

- A pair of safety eyes, 6mm diameter

- Toy stuffing

- Black embroidery thread

- An embroidery needle

MEASUREMENTS

20cm (8in) tall (excluding ears) and 14cm (5½in) long

ABBREVIATIONS

Bobble (Yrh, insert hook into next st, yrh and pull up loop, yrh and draw through 2 loops) 4 times, inserting hook in same st each time, yrh and draw through all 5 loops on hook.

Petal Ss into next st, ch3, yrh, insert hook into same st, yrh and pull up loop, yrh and draw through 2 loops, yrh, insert hook into same st, yrh and pull up loop, yrh and draw through 2 loops, yrh, draw through all 3 loops, ch3, ss into the same st

NOTES

- The Head, Tail and the first part of the Body and Legs are worked using the amigurumi method as explained on p. 6, while the front of the Body and Legs are worked in rows.
- The bobble pattern appears on the reverse side of the Lamb as you crochet.

BODY

Using a 3mm hook and Yarn A, make a magic loop.

Round 1 (RS) Ch1 (does not count as st throughout patt), 6dc into loop. [6 sts]

Round 2 (Dc and Bobble in next st) 6 times. [12 sts]

Round 3 (2dc in next st, dc in Bobble) 6 times. [18 sts]

Round 4 (2dc in next st, Bobble in next st, dc in next st) 6 times. [24 sts]

Round 5 (2dc in next st, dc in next 3 sts) 6 times. [30 sts]

Round 6 (2dc in next st, Bobble in next st, dc in next 2 sts, Bobble in next st) 6 times. [36 sts]

Round 7 (2dc in next st, dc in next 5 sts) 6 times. [42 sts]

Round 8 (2dc in next st, Bobble in next st, dc in next 3 sts, Bobble in next st, dc in next st) 6 times. [48 sts]

Round 9 Dc in each st around.

Round 10 Dc in next st, (Bobble in next st, dc in next 3 sts) 11 times, Bobble in next st, dc in next 2 sts. [48 sts]

Round 11 Dc in each st around.

Round 12 (Bobble in next st, dc in next 3 sts) 12 times.

Round 13 Dc in each st around.

Round 14 (Dc in next 3 sts, Bobble in next st) 12 times.

Round 15 Dc in each st around.

Round 16 Dc in next 2 sts, (Bobble in next st, dc in next 3 sts) 11 times, Bobble in next st, dc in next st.

Rounds 17-24 Repeat Rounds 9-16. Ss into next st, turn.

SHAPE FRONT

The following is worked in rows:

Row 1 (RS) Dc in same st as ss, dc in next 3 sts, dc2tog, dc in next st, dc2tog, dc in next 5 sts, ss into next st, turn. [13 sts]

Row 2 (WS) Ch1, dc in same st as ss, dc in next st, Bobble in next st, dc in next 2 sts, Bobble in next st, dc in next 3 sts, Bobble in next st, dc in next 2 sts, Bobble in next st, dc in next 2 sts of Round 24, ss into next st, turn. [16 sts]

Row 3 Ch1, dc in same st as ss, dc in next 5 sts, dc2tog, dc in next st, dc2tog, dc in next 5 sts, dc in next st of Round 24, ss into next st, turn. [16 sts]

Row 4 Ch1, dc in same st as ss, dc in next st, Bobble in next st, (dc in next 3 sts, Bobble in next st) 3 times, dc in next st, dc in next st of Round 24, ss to the next st, turn. [18 sts]

Row 5 Ch1, dc in same st as ss, dc in next 6 sts, dc2tog, dc in next st, dc2tog, dc in next 6 sts, dc in next st of Round 24, ss into next st, turn. [18 sts]

Row 6 Ch1, dc in same st as ss, dc in next st, Bobble in next st, dc in next 3 sts, (Bobble in next st, dc in next 2 sts) twice, Bobble in next st, dc in next 3 sts, Bobble in next st, dc in next st, dc in next st of Round 24, ss into next st, turn. [20 sts]

Row 7 Ch1, dc in same st as ss, dc in next 7 sts, dc2tog, dc in next st, dc2tog, dc in next 7 sts, dc in next st of Round 24, ss into next st, turn. [20 sts]

Row 8 Ch1, dc in same st as ss, dc in next st, Bobble in next st, (dc in next 3 sts, Bobble in next st) 4 times, dc in next st, dc in next st of Round 24, ss into next st, turn. [22 sts]

Row 9 Ch1, dc in same st as ss, dc in next 8 sts, dc2tog, dc in next st, dc2tog, dc in next 8 sts, dc in next st of Round 24, ss into next st, turn. [22 sts]

Row 10 Ch1, dc in same st as ss, dc in next st, Bobble in next st, (dc in next 3 sts, Bobble in next st, dc in next 2 sts, Bobble in next st) twice, dc in next 3 sts, Bobble in next st, dc in next 2 sts, ss into next st, turn. [24 sts]

Row 11 Ch1, dc in same st as ss, dc in next 9 sts, dc2tog, dc in next st, dc2tog, dc in next 9 sts, dc in next st of Round 24, ss into next st, turn. [24 sts]

Row 12 Ch1, dc in same st as ss, dc in next st, Bobble in next st, (dc in next 3 sts, Bobble in next st) 5 times, dc in next st, dc in next st of Round 24, ss into next st, turn. [26 sts]

Row 13 Ch1, dc in same st as ss, dc in next 10 sts, dc2tog, dc in next st, dc2tog, dc in next 10 sts, dc in next st of Round 24, ss into next st, turn. [26 sts]

Row 14 Ch1, dc in same st as ss, dc in next st, Bobble in next st, (dc in next 3 sts, Bobble in next st) twice, (dc in next 2 sts, Bobble in next st) twice, (dc in next 3 sts, Bobble in next st) twice, dc in next st, dc in next st of Round 24, ss into next st, turn. [28 sts]

Row 15 Ch1, dc in same st as ss, dc in next 11 sts, dc2tog, dc in next st, dc2tog, dc in next 11 sts, dc in next 6 sts of Round 24, do not turn. [32 sts]

SHAPE NECK

Next Round (RS) (Dc2tog, 2dc) 3 times, dc2tog, dc in next st, (dc2tog, 2dc) 4 times, dc in next st, ss to first st to join into the round. [24 sts, not including ss]
Fasten off, leaving a long tail.

HEAD

Starting at Lamb's nose, using a 2.5mm hook and Yarn B, make a magic loop.

Round 1 (RS) Ch1, 6dc into loop. [6 sts]
Round 2 (2dc in next st) 6 times. [12 sts]
Round 3 (2dc in next st, dc) 6 times. [18 sts]
Round 4 (2dc in next st, 2dc) 6 times. [24 sts]
Rounds 5-6 Dc in each st around.
Round 7 (2dc in next st, 3dc) 6 times. [30 sts]
Rounds 8-9 Dc in each st around.
Round 10 (2dc in next st, 4dc) 6 times. [36 sts]
Rounds 11-12 Dc in each st around.
Round 13 (2dc in next st, 5dc) 6 times. [42 sts]
Rounds 14-18 Dc in each st around.
Round 19 (Dc2tog, 5dc) 6 times. [36 sts]
Round 20 (Dc2tog, 4dc) 6 times. [30 sts]
Round 21 (Dc2tog, 3dc) 6 times. [24 sts]
Round 22 (Dc2tog, 2dc) 6 times. [18 sts]
Round 23 (Dc2tog, dc) 6 times. [12 sts]
Ss next st.
Fasten off, leaving a long tail of yarn.

EARS (MAKE 2)

INNER EAR
Using a 2.5mm hook and Yarn C, ch9.
Row 1 (WS) Dc in second ch from hook, dc in next 6 ch, 3dc in next ch, working along opposite side of starting ch, dc in next 7 ch, turn. [17 sts]
Row 2 (RS) Ch1, dc in first 8 dc, 3dc in next st, dc in next 8 dc, turn. [19 sts]
Row 3 Ch1, dc in first 9 dc, 3dc in next st, dc in next 9 dc, turn. [21 sts]
Fasten off.

OUTER EAR
Using a 2.5mm hook and Yarn B, ch9.
Rows 1-3 Work as Rows 1-3 of Inner Ear. Do not fasten off.

JOIN EAR PIECES

Place WS of Inner and Outer Ear together, with the Inner Ear facing up.
Row 4 With Yarn B, ch1, inserting the hook under both loops of each stitch of the Inner Ear first, then the Outer Ear to join, dc in each of first 10 dc, 3dc in next st, dc into each of the next 10 dc. [23 sts]
Ss to the first dc of Row 4 to join the lower corners and shape the Ear.
Fasten off, leaving a long tail.

FRONT LEGS (MAKE 2)

Starting at the foot, with a 2.5mm hook and Yarn B, make a magic loop.

The pretty pink flower is threaded carefully through stitches that form the lamb's mouth

Round 1 (RS) Ch1, 6dc into loop. [6 sts]

Round 2 (2dc in next st) 6 times. [12 sts]

Round 3 Dc in back loop only of each st around.

Rounds 4-16 Dc in each st around.

Round 17 (2dc in next st, 3dc) 3 times. **Fasten off.** [15 sts]

SHAPE TOP OF LEG

The following is worked in rows:

Row 1 (RS) Join Yarn A in first st, dc in first 2 dc, (2dc in next dc, 1dc) 6 times, dc in next dc, turn. [21 sts]

Row 2 (WS) Ch1 (does not count as st throughout), dc in first 2 dc, (Bobble in next st, 1dc in next 3 sts) 4 times, Bobble in next st, dc in next 2 sts, turn.

Row 3 Ch1, dc in each st, turn.

Row 4 Ch1, dc in first 4 sts, (Bobble in next st, dc in next 3 sts) 4 times, dc in next st, turn.

Row 5 Dc in each st, turn.

Rows 6-7 Repeat Rows 2-3.

Fasten off, leaving a long tail.

HIND LEGS (MAKE 2)

Starting at the foot, using a 2.5mm hook and Yarn B, make a magic loop.

Rounds 1-17 As Rounds 1-17 of Front Legs.[15 sts]

SHAPE TOP OF LEG

The following is worked in rows:

Row 1 (RS) Join Yarn A in first st, dc in next dc, (2dc in next dc, 1dc) 3 times, dc in next 2 dc, (2dc in next dc, dc) 3 times, turn. [21 sts]

Row 2 (WS) Ch1, dc in next 2 dc, (Bobble in next st, dc in next 3 sts) 4 times, Bobble in next st, dc in next 2 sts, turn.

Row 3 Ch1, (2dc in next st, 1dc) 3 times, dc in next 9 sts, (1dc, 2dc in next st) 3 times, turn. [27 sts]

Row 4 Ch1, (dc in next 3 sts, Bobble in next st) 6 times, dc in next 3 sts, turn.

Row 5 Ch1, (2dc in next st, 1dc) 3 times, dc in next 15 sts, (1dc, 2dc in next st) 3 times, turn. [33 sts]

Row 6 Ch1, dc in next 4 sts, Bobble in next st, (dc in next 3 sts, Bobble in next st) 6 times, dc in next 4 sts, turn.

Row 7 Ch1, dc in each st across.

Fasten off, leaving a long tail of yarn.

TAIL

Using a 2.5mm hook and Yarn A, make a magic loop.

Round 1 (RS) Ch1, 5dc into loop, ss into first dc to join. [5 sts]

Round 2 (2dc in next dc) 5 times. [10 sts]

Round 3 (2dc in next dc, 1dc) 5 times. [15 sts]

Rounds 4-8 Dc in each st around.

Round 9 (Dc2tog in next dc, 1dc) 5 times. [10 sts]

Rounds 10-12 Dc in each st around.

Fasten off, leaving a long tail of yarn.

FLOWER (MAKE 5 IN YARN A AND 6 IN YARN C)

Using a 2.5mm hook and Yarn D, make a magic loop.

Round 1 (RS) Ch1, 5dc into loop, ss into first dc to join. Fasten off. [5 sts]

Round 2 Join Yarn A or C in first st, Petal 5 times, ss into first st to join.

Fasten off, leaving a long tail.

STEM AND LEAF (MAKE 1 FOR EACH FLOWER)

Using 2.5mm hook and Yarn E, ch21.

Row 1 (RS) Ss into second ch from hook and next 13 ch, ch7, ss into second ch from hook, dc in next ch, htr in next ch, tr in next ch, htr in next ch, dc in next ch, ss in remaining 6 ch of the starting ch21.

Fasten off.

TO MAKE UP

BODY

Stuff the Body, filling it up to the opening at the neck.

HEAD

Attach the safety eyes to the Head in Round 8 approx 8 sts apart. Stuff the Head firmly. Thread the tail of the yarn onto a needle and run a gathering stitch around the last round of stitches, draw up tightly.

Fasten off.

Embroider the nose in fly stitch (see opposite), using 4 strands of embroidery thread.

Sew the Head to the Body, stitching all around the neck edge and neatly inserting more stuffing into the neck before closing, if necessary.

EARS

Using the long tail, sew each ear neatly to the top of the Head, stitching all around the edges to attach them securely in place.

LEGS

Use the long tail, sew together the seam of the top shaping. Stuff the Legs firmly, filling them to the top and keeping the base flat. Stitch the front Legs side by side, just before the front shaping of the Body, with the seam facing towards the back. Sew the hind Legs next to each other at the back of the Body, with the seam in the Leg facing towards the front. Stitch all around each Leg to hold them securely in place, inserting more stuffing if necessary.

TAIL

Use the end of the crochet hook to push a small amount of stuffing into the end of the Tail. Using the yarn tail, run a gathering stitch around the last round of stitches, draw up to close.

Fasten off.

Sew the Tail to the back of the Body.

Stitch the Flowers to the top of the Stems. To attach a pink Flower to the Lamb's mouth, thread a short length of yarn through the end of the Stem. Thread the ends of the yarn through a needle and draw the needle between the stitches on one side of the front of the face, below the nose, and through to the other side pulling the Stem through. Secure in place with a few hidden stitches.

Tie together the remaining Flowers into bunches of 5 Flowers with a crocheted cord of ch60.

Weave in all yarn ends.

Dinosaur Duo

With such amiable expressions, there's nothing scary about these amigurumi dinosaurs. You can go all out on the accessories for this dynamic duo, with a cute crochet collar for the girl dinosaur and a snazzy orange bow tie for the boy. Easy to make, this pair of prehistoric critters will be popular with everyone.

YOU WILL NEED
• Aran weight cotton yarn approximately one 50g ball of each:
- Yarn A Pink
- Yarn B Blue
- Yarn C Light Green
- Yarn D Light Yellow
- Yarn E White
- Yarn F Orange

• A 3.5mm (US E/4) hook

• Safety eyes or beads, approx 12mm (½in) diameter

• Toy stuffing

• Wool and embroidery needle

• Black embroidery thread

MEASUREMENTS
18x12x12cm (7x4¾x4¾in)

NOTES
• The Body starts at the base by joining together the Feet and working up.

〰〰〰〰〰〰〰〰〰〰〰〰

FEET (MAKE 2)
Using Yarn A or B, make a magic loop.
Round 1 (RS) 6dc into the loop. [6 sts]
Round 2 2dc in each st around. [12 sts]
Rounds 3-6 Dc in each st around.

Fasten off on the first Foot but leave the yarn attached to the second Foot, then continue from Round 1 of the Body.

BODY
Round 1 Dc in each st of the first Foot, dc in each st of the second Foot. [24 sts]
Round 2 2dc in each of next 3 sts, dc in each of next 18 sts, 2dc in each of next 3 sts. [30 sts]
Round 3 (2dc in next st, dc in next st) 3 times, dc in each of next 18 sts, (2dc in next st, dc in next st) 3 times. [36 sts]
Round 4 (2dc in next st, dc in each of next 11 sts) 3 times. [39 sts]
Round 5 (2dc in next st, dc in each of next 12 sts) 3 times. [42 sts]

Rounds 6-8 Dc in each st around.
Round 9 (Dc2tog, dc in each of next 12 sts) 3 times. [39 sts]
Round 10 Dc in each st around.
Round 11 (Dc2tog, dc in each of next 11 sts) 3 times. [36 sts]
Stuff the legs with toy filling.
Round 12 Dc in each st around.
Round 13 (Dc2tog, dc in each of next 10 sts) 3 times. [33 sts]
Round 14 Dc in each st around.
Round 15 (Dc2tog, dc in each of next 9 sts) 3 times. [30 sts]
Round 16 Dc in each st around.
Round 17 (Dc2tog, dc in each of next 8 sts) 3 times. [27 sts]
Round 18 Dc in each st around.
Round 19 (Dc2tog, dc in each of next 7 sts) 3 times. [24 sts]

The tail is key to keeping your dino upright, so pay particular attention when stuffing it

Round 20 Dc in each st around.
Round 21 (Dc2tog, dc in each of next 6 sts) 3 times. [21 sts]
Rounds 22-25 Dc in each st around.
Round 26 (Dc2tog, dc in each of next 5 sts) 3 times. [18 sts]
Rounds 27-28 Dc in each st around.
Round 29 (Dc2tog, dc in next st) 6 times. [12 sts]
Stuff rest of Body.
Round 30 (Dc2tog) 6 times. [6 sts]
Fasten off and weave in ends.

TAIL

For Pink Dino, using Yarn A, make a magic loop.
Round 1 (RS) 6dc into the loop. [6 sts]
Round 2 2dc in first st, dc in each remaining st around. [7 sts]
Round 3 Dc in each st around.
Rounds 4-13 Rep Rounds 2 & 3 another 5 times. [12 sts after Round 13]
Rounds 14-26 2dc in first st, dc in each st to end. [25 sts after Round 26]
Fasten off. Stuff and sew in place on Body.

For Blue Dino, using Yarn B, make a magic loop.
Round 1 (RS) 6dc into the loop. [6 sts]
Round 2 2dc in each st around. [12 sts]
Round 3 (Dc in next st, 2dc in next st) 6 times. [18 sts]
Round 4 Dc in each st around. [18 sts]
Round 5 (Dc2tog, dc in next st) 6 times. [12 sts]
Stuff the end of the Tail.
Round 6 (Dc2tog) 6 times. [6 sts]
Rounds 7-31 Continue as per instructions for Pink Dino's Tail from Round 2 to the end.
Fasten off. Stuff and sew onto Body. Use Yarn C to work French knots over the ball at the end of the Tail to create spikes.

HEAD

For Pink Dino, using Yarn A, ch5.
Round 1 Dc in second ch from hook, dc in each of next 2 ch, 3dc in last ch, rotate and work along the opposite side of the ch, dc in each of next 2 ch, 2dc in last ch. [10 sts]

Round 2 (Dc in next st, 2dc in next st) 5 times. [15 sts]
Round 3 (Dc in each of next 2 sts, 2dc in next st) 5 times. [20 sts]
Round 4 (Dc in each of next 3 sts, 2dc in next st) 5 times. [25 sts]
Round 5 (Dc in each of next 4 sts, 2dc in next st) 5 times. [30 sts]
Round 6 (Dc in each of next 4 sts, 2dc in next st) 6 times. [36 sts]
Rounds 7-9 Dc in each st around.
Rounds 10-21 Dc2tog, dc in each remaining st around, marking Round 19 with a stitch marker. [24 sts after Round 21]
Insert the toy safety eyes on the marked round at the top of the Head, 14 sts apart.
Round 22 (Dc2tog, dc in each of next 2 sts) 6 times. [18 sts]
Round 23 (Dc2tog, dc in next st) 6 times
Stuff Head.
Round 24 (Dc2tog) 6 times. [6 sts]
Fasten off and sew onto the Body. Using black embroidery thread, use the image as a guide to create a long mouth and two lines for the nostrils.

For Blue Dino, make basic Head using Yarn B, following instructions as given for Pink Dino.

BACK HORN (BLUE DINO ONLY)

Using Yarn B, make a magic loop
Round 1 (RS) 6dc into the loop. [6 sts]
Rounds 2-10 2dc in first st, dc in each remaining st around. [15 sts after Round 10]
Fasten off. Stuff and sew to the back of the Head.

GREEN HORN (BLUE DINO ONLY)

Using Yarn C, make a magic loop.
Round 1 (RS) 4dc into the loop. [4 sts]
Rounds 2-5 2dc in first st, dc in each remaining st to end. [8 sts after Round 5]
Fasten off. Stuff and sew to the front of the Head.

ARMS (MAKE 2)

Using Yarn A or B, make a magic loop.
Round 1 (RS) 6dc into the loop. [6 sts]

Rounds 2-6 Dc in each st around.
Fasten off and sew in place on the Body.

BELLY PATCH (BLUE DINO ONLY)

Using Yarn C, make a magic loop.
Round 1 (RS) 6dc into the loop. [6 sts]
Round 2 2dc in each st around. [12 sts]
Round 3 (Dc in next st, 2dc in next st) 6 times. [18 sts]
Round 4 (Dc in each of next 2 sts, 2dc in next st) 6 times. [24 sts]
Round 5 (Dc in each of next 3 sts, 2 in next st) 6 times. [30 sts]
Fasten off and sew in place on the belly of the Dino.

BOW TIE (BLUE DINO ONLY)

Using Yarn F, ch7.
Row 1 (RS) Dc in second ch from hook, dc in each of next 5 ch, turn. [6 sts]
Rows 2-8 Ch1 (not counted as st), dc in each st to end. [6 sts]
Fasten off and weave in ends.
Wrap yarn around the centre of the rectangle to form a bow. Sew in place on the neck of the Dino.

COLLAR (PINK DINO ONLY)

Using Yarn E, ch25.
Row 1 (RS) Ss in second ch from hook, dc in next ch, hrt in next ch, tr in next ch, hrt in next ch, dc in next ch, *ss in next ch, dc in next ch, hrt in next ch, tr in next ch, hrt in next ch, dc in next ch; rep from * to end, turn. [24 sts]
Row 2 (Ch3, dc in next st) to end.
Fasten off and sew in place around the neck of the Dino.

TO FINISH

For Pink Dino, using Yarn D, sew long stitches across the front Body and Tail to form the stripes, using image as a guide.

Sunshine Snail

It's all about the details for this happy little snail, with a shell embellished using slip stitches worked in a contrasting colour, plus curly crocheted streamers and tiny flowers decorating the hat. It's also a fantastic project to practise your shaping on – in fact, once complete, you'll feel as if you've totally snailed it …

YOU WILL NEED

• DK weight cotton yarn, approximately one 50g ball of each:
- Yarn A Yellow
- Yarn B Berry
- Yarn C Teal

• A 2.5mm (US B/1 or C/2) hook

• A pair of safety eyes, 6mm diameter

• Toy stuffing

• Black embroidery thread

MEASUREMENTS

18cm (7in) in length

NOTES

• The Body is made in two pieces that are joined and then edged. The shaping at the front is worked in rows, working into one extra stitch on each side of every row and decreasing the stitches.

• The Head and most of the Shell are worked using the amigurumi method as explained on p.6.

• The rest of the shell is crocheted in rows. Slip stitches are worked into the front loops of the stitches to produce three decorative bands on the surface of the Shell.

BODY
TOP
Using Yarn A, ch24.
Row 1 (WS) Dc into second ch from hook, dc into next 21 ch, 3dc in last ch, working along the opposite side of the starting ch, dc in next 22 ch, turn. [47 sts]
Row 2 (RS) Ch1 (does not count as st throughout patt), dc in first 23 dc, 3dc in next st, dc in next 23 dc, turn. [49 sts]
Row 3 Ch1, dc in first 24 dc, 3dc in next st, dc in next 24 dc, turn. [51 sts]
Row 4 Ch1, dc in first 25 dc, 3dc in next st, dc in next 25 dc, turn. [53 sts]
Row 5 Ch1, dc in first 26 dc, 3dc in next st, dc in next 26 dc, turn. [55 sts]
Row 6 Ch1, dc in first 27 dc, 3dc in next st, dc in next 27 dc, turn. [57 sts]
Row 7 Ch1, dc in first 28 dc, 3dc in next st, dc in next 28 dc, turn. [59 sts]
Row 8 Ch1, dc in first 29 dc, 3dc in next st, dc in next 29 dc, turn. [61 sts]
Row 9 Ch1, dc in first 30 dc, 3dc in next st, dc in next 30 dc, turn. [63 sts]
Row 10 Ch1, dc in first 31 dc, 3dc in next st, dc in next 31 dc. [65 sts]
Fasten off.

FOOT
Using Yarn A, ch29.
Row 1 (WS) Dc into second ch from hook, dc into next 26 ch, 3dc in next ch, working along the opposite side of starting ch, dc in next 27 ch, turn. [57 sts]
Rows 2-5 Work as Rows 7-10 of the Top of the Body.
Do not fasten off.

The snail has a double crochet edging around its foot to help it glide along

JOIN BODY PIECES
Place WS of Top and Foot together, with the top facing up.
Row 1 (RS) Ch1, inserting hook under both loops of each stitch of Top first, then Foot to join, dc in first 32 dc, 3dc in next st, dc into next 32 dc. Do not fasten off. [67 sts]

SHAPE FRONT
Round 1 (RS) Rotate Body to work into Row ends of Top, work 20 dc evenly into Row ends of Top, then work 10 dc evenly into Row ends of Foot, ss to first dc to join, turn. [30 sts]
Row 1 (WS) Ch1, dc in same st as ss, dc in next 11 dc, ss into next st, turn leaving rem sts unworked. [12 dc, 1 ss]
Row 2 (RS) Ch1, dc in same st as ss, dc in next 12 dc, dc in next st of Round 1, ss into next st, turn. [14 dc, 1 ss]
Row 3 Ch1, dc in same st as ss, dc in next 14 sts, dc in next st of Round 1, ss into next st, turn. [16 dc, 1 ss]
Row 4 Ch1, dc in same st as ss, (dc, dc2tog, dc) 4 times, dc in next st of Round 1, ss into next st, turn. [14 sts, 1 ss]
Rows 5-8 Repeat Rows 3-4 twice.
Row 9 Repeat Row 3.
Row 10 Ch1, dc in same st as ss, dc in next 16 dc, dc in next st of Round 1, turn. [18 dc]
Row 11 Ch1, dc in each dc of previous row, turn. [18 dc]
Row 12 Ch1, 2dc in first dc, dc in next 6 dc, (dc2tog) twice, dc in next 6 dc, 2dc in next dc, turn. [18 dc]
Rows 13-14 Repeat Rows 11-12.
Fasten off, leaving a long tail of yarn at the end.

FOOT EDGING
With the Foot facing up, join Yarn A with a ss to the first dc in Row 1 that joined Foot to Top of the Body.
Row 1 (WS) Dc into same st as ss, dc in next 32 dc, 3dc in next dc, dc in next 33 dc, ss into front shaping, turn. [69 dc]
Row 2 (RS) Ch1, dc in next 34 dc, 3dc in next dc, dc in next 34 dc, ss into front shaping. [71 dc]
Fasten off.

HEAD
Using Yarn A, make a magic loop.
Round 1 (RS) Ch1, 6dc into loop. [6 sts]
Round 2 2dc in each st around. [12 sts]
Round 3 (2dc in next st, 1dc) 6 times. [18 sts]
Round 4 (2dc in next st, 2dc) 6 times. [24 sts]
Round 5 (2dc in next st, 3dc) 6 times. [30 sts]
Round 6 (2dc in next st, 4dc) 6 times. [36 sts]
Rounds 7-16 Dc in each st around.
Round 17 (Dc2tog, 4dc) 6 times. [30 sts]
Round 18 (Dc2tog, 3dc) 6 times. [24 sts]
Round 19 (Dc2tog, 2dc) 6 times. [18 sts]
Round 20 (Dc2tog, 1dc) 6 times. [12 sts]
Fasten off, leaving a long tail.

ANTENNAE (MAKE 2)
Using Yarn A, make a magic loop.
Round 1 (RS) Ch1, 6dc into loop. [6 sts]
Round 2 2dc in each st around. [12 sts]
Round 3 Dc in each st around.
Round 4 (Dc2tog) 6 times. [6 sts]
Rounds 5-12 Dc in each st around.
Fasten off, leaving a long tail.

SHELL
Using Yarn B, make a magic loop.
Round 1 (RS) Ch1, 6dc into loop. [6 sts]
Round 2 2dc in each st around. [12 sts]
Round 3 Dc in each st around.
Fasten off.
Round 4 Join Yarn A in first st, dc in each st around. Fasten off.
Round 5 Join Yarn B in first st, (2dc in back loop only of next st) 12 times. [24 sts]
Round 6 (2dc in next st, 1dc) 12 times. [36 sts]
Round 7 Dc in each st around.
Round 8 (Dc2tog) 18 times. [18 sts]
Fasten off.
Round 9 Join Yarn A in first st, 2dc in each st around. [36 sts]
Fasten off.
Round 10 Join Yarn B in first st, (2dc in back loop only of next st, dc in back loop only of next st) 18 times. [54 sts]

Rounds 11-13 Dc in each st around.
Round 14 (Dc2tog) 27 times.
Fasten off. [27 sts]
Round 15 Join Yarn A in first st, 2dc in next 15 sts, dc in next 12 dc. [42 sts] Fasten off.
Round 16 Join Yarn B in first st, (2dc in back loop only of next dc, dc in back loop only of next 4 dc) 6 times, dc in back loop only of next 12 dc. [48 sts]
Round 17 (2dc in next st, 5dc) 6 times, dc in next 12 dc, do not fasten off. [54 sts]

TOP OF SHELL
The Top is worked in Rows.
Row 1 (RS) Dc in next 42 sts, turn. [42 dc]
Rows 2-7 Ch1, dc in next 42 sts, turn.
Row 8 (WS) Ch1, dc in next 42 sts, ch12, ss to first dc, turn, do not fasten off. [42 dc, 12 ch]

BACK OF SHELL
The Back is worked in Rounds.
Round 1 (RS) Dc in next 12 ch, dc in next 42 dc. [54 sts]
Round 2 (Dc2tog, 7dc) 6 times. [48 sts]
Round 3 (Dc2tog, 6dc) 6 times. [42 sts]
Round 4 (Dc2tog, 5dc) 6 times. [36 sts]
Round 5 (Dc2tog, 4dc) 6 times. [30 sts]
Round 6 (Dc2tog, 3dc) 6 times. [24 sts]
Round 7 (Dc2tog, 2dc) 6 times. [18 sts]
Round 8 (Dc2tog, 1dc) 6 times. [12 sts]
Round 9 (Dc2tog) 6 times. [6 sts]
Fasten off, leaving a long tail for sewing up.
Thread the yarn tail through the sts in Round 9, pulling tightly on the yarn to close.

DECORATIVE BANDS
Join Yarn A to the front loop of the first dc of Round 4 and ss into each st around, ss into the first st to join.
Fasten off.
Repeat on Rounds 9 and 15 to finish the Decorative Bands around the surface of the Shell.

HAT
CROWN
Using Yarn C, make a magic loop.

Rounds 1-6 Work as Rounds 1-6 of the Head. [36 sts]
Round 7 (2dc in next st, 5dc) 6 times. [42 sts]
Rounds 8-11 Dc in each st around.
Fasten off.
Round 12 Join Yarn A in first st, dc in each st around.
Round 13 Dc in each st around.
Fasten off.

BRIM
Round 14 Join Yarn C in first st, ss into next st, ch2 (counts as htr), htr in same st as ss, htr in next dc, (2htr in next st, htr in next st) 20 times, ss to top of beg ch-2 to join. [63 sts]
Round 15 Ch2 (counts as htr), htr in next 62 htr, ss to top of beg ch-2 to join.
Fasten off.

FLOWERS (MAKE 3)
Follow pattern for Lamb's Flower (p. 86), using Yarn A for the Flower Centre and Yarn B for the Petals.

RIBBON
Using Yarn A, *ch25.
Row 1 (RS) 1tr in the fourth ch from hook, tr in next ch, (2tr in next ch, tr in next ch) twice, (2htr in next ch, htr in next ch) 6 times, dc in next 3 ch, ss into next ch.
Repeat from * twice more. Fasten off, leaving a long tail of yarn at the end.

TO MAKE UP
BODY
Stuff the Body, keeping the base flat. Use the yarn tail to sew the edges together at the back of neck. Add more stuffing, filling to the top of the neck.

HEAD
Attach the safety eyes to the Head in Row 10, approximately 5 sts apart. Stuff the Head firmly.
Embroider the mouth using 3 strands of embroidery thread and the image as a guide.
Sew the Head to the Body, stitching all around the neck edge and inserting more stuffing into the neck before closing, if necessary.

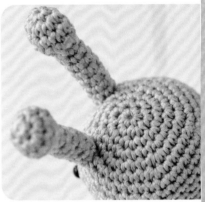

ANTENNAE
Use the end of the crochet hook to push a small amount of stuffing into the Antennae.
Sew the Antennae to the top of the Head at the front, stitching all around the edges.

SHELL
Stuff the Shell firmly.
Sew the Shell to the top of the Body, stitching all around the open edges

HAT
Using the yarn tail, sew the Ribbon and Flowers to the Hat.
Weave in all the yarn ends.

Sweet Rabbit

With her oversize buttoned shoes, dainty bloomers, Peter Pan collar and patch pockets, this rabbit is the picture of old-fashioned charm. This winsome bunny loves ice cream, riding her bicycle and sniffing freshly-cut grass, but her absolute favourite thing in the world is carrots, which she collects in her special carrot-gathering basket.

YOU WILL NEED

• DK weight cotton yarn, approximately two 50g balls of
- Yarn A Grey
• One 50g ball of each:
- Yarn B Dusky Pink
- Yarn C Cream
- Yarn D Berry
- Yarn E Plum
- Yarn F Taupe
- Yarn G Orange
- Yarn H Green

• A 2.5mm (US B/1 or C/2) hook

• A 3mm (US C/2 or D/3) hook

• A tapestry needle

• A pair of safety eyes, 6mm diameter

• Toy stuffing

• Embroidery thread in black

• Embroidery needle

• 20cm (8in) length of 5mm (¼in) wide elastic

• Four 1cm (3/8in) diameter buttons for the dress and shoes

• Sewing thread to match buttons or yarn, and elastic

• Sewing needle

MEASUREMENTS
25cm (10in) tall

NOTES
• The Dress, Bloomers and Shoes are all removable.

HEAD
Starting at Rabbit's nose, using a 2.5mm hook and Yarn A, make a magic loop.
Round 1 Ch1, 6dc into loop. [6 sts]
Round 2 (2dc in next st) 6 times. [12 sts]
Round 3 (2dc in next st, 1dc) 6 times. [18 sts]
Round 4 Dc in each st around.
Round 5 (2dc in next st, 2dc) 6 times. [24 sts]
Round 6 Dc in each st around.
Round 7 (2dc in next st, 3dc) 6 times. [30 sts]
Round 8 Dc in each st around.
Round 9 (2dc in next st, 4dc) 6 times. [36 sts]
Round 10 Dc in each st around.
Round 11 (2dc in next st, 5dc) 6 times. [42 sts]
Rounds 12-17 Dc in each st around.
Round 18 (Dc2tog, 5dc) 6 times. [36 sts]
Round 19 (Dc2tog, 4dc) 6 times. [30 sts]
Round 20 (Dc2tog, 3dc) 6 times. [24 sts]
Round 21 (Dc2tog, 2dc) 6 times. [18 sts]
Round 22 (Dc2tog, 1dc) 6 times, ss to first st to join. [12 sts]

Fasten off, leaving a long tail of yarn.

BODY
Starting at the base, using a 2.5mm hook and Yarn A, make a magic loop.
Round 1 Ch1, 6dc into loop. [6 sts]
Round 2 (2dc in next st) 6 times. [12 sts]
Round 3 (2dc in next st, 1dc) 6 times. [18 sts]
Round 4 (2dc in next st, 2dc) 6 times. [24 sts]
Round 5 (2dc in next st, 3dc) 6 times. [30 sts]
Round 6 (2dc in next st, 4dc) 6 times. [36 sts]
Round 7 (2dc in next st, 5dc) 6 times. [42 sts]
Round 8 (2dc in next st, 6dc) 6 times. [48 sts]

Embroider the nose by making a large stitch A to B then come up at C and down at D

Round 9 Dc in each st around.
Round 10 (2dc in next st, 7dc) 6 times. [54 sts]
Round 11 Dc in each st around.
Round 12 (2dc in next st, 8dc) 6 times. [60 sts]
Rounds 13-15 Dc in each st around.
Round 16 (Dc2tog, 8dc) 6 times. [54 sts]
Rounds 17-18 Dc in each st around.
Round 19 (Dc2tog, 7dc) 6 times. [48 sts]
Rounds 20-21 Dc in each st around.
Round 22 (Dc2tog, 6dc) 6 times. [42 sts]
Round 23 Dc in each st around.
Round 24 (Dc2tog, 5dc) 6 times. [36 sts]
Round 25 Dc in each st around.
Round 26 (Dc2tog, 4dc) 6 times. [30 sts]
Round 27 Dc in each st around.
Round 28 (Dc2tog, 3dc) 6 times. [24 sts]
Round 29 Dc in each st around.
Round 30 (Dc2tog, 2dc) 6 times. [18 sts]
Rounds 31-33 Dc in each st around, ss to first st to join. **Fasten off**, leaving a long tail of yarn.

EARS (MAKE 2)

INNER EAR

Using a 2.5mm hook and Yarn B, ch13.
Row 1 (WS) Dc into second ch from hook, dc into next 10 ch, 3dc in next ch, working along opposite side of starting ch, dc in next 11 ch. [25 sts]
Row 2 (RS) Ch1, dc in the first 12 dc, 3dc in next st, dc in the next 12 dc, turn. [27 sts]
Row 3 Ch1, dc in the first 13 dc, 3dc in next st, dc in the next 13 dc, turn. [29 sts]
Fasten off.

OUTER EAR

Using a 2.5mm hook and Yarn A, ch13.
Rows 1-3 Work as Rows 1-3 of Inner Ear.
Do not fasten off.

JOIN EAR PIECES

Place wrong sides of Inner and Outer Ear together, with the Inner Ear facing up.
Row 4 Using Yarn A, ch1, inserting the hook under both loops of each st of the Inner Ear first, then the Outer Ear to join, dc in each of the next 14 dc, 3dc in next st, dc into each of the next 14 dc. [31 sts]
Ss to the first dc to join the lower corners and shape the Ear.
Fasten off, leaving a long tail of yarn.

LEGS (MAKE 2)

The construction of the heel/ankle is the same as for the Puddle Duck. See diagram on p. 99. Using a 2.5mm hook and Yarn A, make a magic loop.
Rounds 1-2 Work as Rounds 1-2 of Head. [12 sts]
Round 3 Dc in each st around.
Round 4 (2dc in next st, 1dc) 6 times. [18 sts]
Round 5 Dc in each st around.
Round 6 (2dc in next st, 2dc) 6 times. [24 sts]
Round 7 (2dc in next st, 3dc) 6 times. [30 sts]

DIVIDE FOR LEG

Round 8 Dc in the next 6 dc, skip next 18 dc, dc in the next 6 dc. [12 dc]
Cont working on these 12 sts to finish Leg.
Rounds 9-20 Dc in each st around.
Fasten off, leaving a long tail of yarn.

FOOT

Rejoin Yarn A with a ss to the first skipped dc of Round 7. The join is a different place to that of the Duck. The gap on the front of the ankle will be sewn up later.
Round 1 Dc in the same st as the ss, dc in the next 17 dc. [18 sts]
Round 2 (2dc in next st, 2dc) 6 times. [24 sts]
Rounds 3-5 Dc in each st around.
Round 6 (2dc in next st, 3dc) 6 times. [30 sts]
Rounds 7-9 Dc in each st around.

Round 10 (Dc2tog, 3dc) 6 times. [24 sts]
Round 11 (Dc2tog, 2dc) 6 times. [18 sts]
Round 12 (Dc2tog, 1dc) 6 times, ss to first st to join. [12 sts]
Fasten off, leaving a long tail of yarn.

ARMS (MAKE 2)

Starting at Rabbit's paw, using a 2.5mm hook and Yarn A, make a magic loop.
Rounds 1-3 Work as Rounds 1-3 of Head. [18 sts]
Rounds 4-8 Dc in each st around.
Round 9 (Dc2tog, 1dc) 6 times. [12 sts]
Rounds 10-22 Dc in each st around.
Round 23 Dc in each st around, ss to first st to join.
Fasten off, leaving a long tail of yarn.

TAIL

The loops will appear at the back of the fabric as you work.
Using a 2.5mm hook and Yarn C, make a magic loop.
Round 1 Ch1, 6dc into loop, ss to first dc to join. [6 sts]
Round 2 Ch6, dc in back loop only of st at base of ch-6, (ch6, 1dc into back loop only of next st) 5 times. [6 loops]
Round 3 Working into front loops only of Round 1, (2dc in next dc, dc in next dc) 3 times, ss to the first dc to join. [9 sts]
Round 4 Ch6, dc in back loop only of st at base of ch-6, (ch6, dc into back loop only of next st) 8 times. [9 loops]
Round 5 Working into front loops only of Round 3, (2dc in next dc, 1dc in next 2 dc) 3 times, ss to the first dc to join. [12 sts]
Round 6 Ch6, dc in back loop only of st at base of ch-6, (ch6, dc into back loop only of next st) 11 times. [12 loops]
Round 7 Dc in the front loop only of each st of Round 5 around.
Fasten off, leaving a long tail of yarn.

DRESS

Starting at the neck, using a 3mm hook and Yarn D, ch23.
Row 1 (RS) Dc into the second ch

from hook, dc in the next 21 ch, turn. [22 sts]
Row 2 (WS) Ch1, (2dc in next st) 22 times. [44 sts]
Row 3 Ch1, dc in first 5 dc, 3dc in next st, (dc in next 10 dc, 3dc in next st) 3 times, dc in next 5 dc, turn. [52 sts]
Row 4 Ch1, dc in next 6 dc, 3dc in next st, (dc in next 12 dc, 3dc in next st) 3 times, dc in next 6 dc, turn. [60 sts]
Row 5 Ch1, dc in next 7 dc, 3dc in next st, (dc in next 14 dc, 3dc in next st) 3 times, dc in next 7 dc, turn. [68 sts]
Row 6 Ch1, dc in next 9 dc, skip next 16 dc, dc in next 18 dc, skip next 16 dc, dc in next 9 dc, turn.
Continue working on these 36 sts.
Rows 7-8 Ch1, dc in each dc across, turn.

SKIRT

Row 9 Ch1, (dc in next dc, ch2, skip 1 dc, dc in next dc, ch2) 11 times, dc in next dc, ch2, skip 1 dc, dc in next dc, turn. [23 ch-2 sps]
Row 10 Ch1, dc in first dc, *(dc, ch2, dc) in next ch-2 sp, skip next dc; repeat from * 21 more times, (dc, ch2, dc) in next ch-2 sp, dc in last dc, turn.
Rows 11-19 Ch1, dc in first dc, *skip next dc, (dc, ch2, dc) in next ch-2 sp, skip next dc; repeat from * 21 more times, (dc, ch2, dc) in next ch-2 sp, dc in last dc, turn.
Row 20 Ch1, dc in first dc, (skip 1 dc, 5tr in the next ch-2 sp, skip 2 dc, dc in next ch-2 sp, skip 1 dc) 11 times, skip 1 dc, 5tr in next ch-2 sp, skip 1 dc, dc in last dc, do not turn.

BUTTON BAND

Row 1 (RS) Work 10 dc evenly up the edge of the Skirt, work 8 dc evenly up the edge of the bodice, turn. [18 sts]
Row 2 (WS) Ch1, dc in each of the 18 dc, ss to the next st. **Fasten off.**

BUTTONHOLE BAND

Using a 3mm hook and RS facing, join Yarn D with a ss to the first st at the neck edge of the Dress.
Row 1 (RS) Working into Row ends, dc in the same st as the ss, work 7 dc evenly down the edge of the bodice,

work 10 dc evenly down the edge of the Skirt, ss into the first dc at the scalloped hem of the Skirt, turn. [18 sts]
Row 2 Ch1, dc in first 10 dc, (dc in next dc, ch2, skip 2 dc, dc in next dc) twice, ss to next dc at neckline.
Fasten off.

COLLAR

Using a 3mm hook and Yarn C, ch28.
Row 1 (RS) Dc in second ch from hook, htr in next ch, *5tr in next ch, (tr in next ch, 2tr in next ch) 3 times, tr in next ch, 5tr in next ch*, skip 2 ch, ss in next ch, skip 2 ch; repeat from * to *, htr in next ch, dc in next ch. **Fasten off,** leaving a long tail of yarn.

PATCH POCKETS (MAKE 2)

Using a 3mm hook and Yarn E, make a magic loop.
Round 1 Ch1, 8dc into loop, ss to the first dc to join. Fasten off. [8 sts]
Round 2 Join Yarn B in first st, ch1, (dc, ch2, dc) in same st, *dc in next dc, (dc, ch2, dc) in next dc; repeat from * twice more, dc in next dc, ss to first dc to join. **Fasten off.** [12 dc and 4 ch-2 sps]
Round 3 Join Yarn E in first st, ch1, dc in same st, *(dc, ch2, dc) in next ch-2 sp, dc in next 3 dc; repeat from * twice more, (dc, ch2, dc) in next ch-2 sp, dc in next 2 dc, ss to first dc to join.
Fasten off. [20 dc and 4 ch-2 sps]
Round 4 Join Yarn B in first st, ch1, dc in same st, dc in next dc, *(dc, ch2, dc) in next ch-2 sp, dc in next 5 dc; repeat from * twice more, (dc, ch2, dc) in next ch-2 sp, dc in next 3 dc, ss to first dc to join.
Fasten off. [28 dc and 4 ch-2 sps]

BLOOMERS

Using a 3mm hook and Yarn B, ch51.
Row 1 (RS) Htr in the third ch from hook, (ch1, skip 1 ch, htr in the next 2 ch) 16 times, turn. [34 htr, 16 ch-1 sps]
Row 2 (WS) Ch1, (dc in next 2 htr, dc in next ch-sp) 16 times, dc in next 2 htr, turn. [50 sts]
Rows 3-14 Ch1, dc in each dc across, turn.

FIRST LEG

Work each Bloomer Leg separately in Rounds.

Round 1 (RS) Ch1, dc in the first 25 dc, ch11, ss in first dc to join leaving rem sts unworked. [25 dc]

Round 2 Ch1, dc in first 25 sts, dc in next 11 ch, ss to first dc to join. [36 sts]

Round 3 Ch1, dc in each st around, ss to first st to join.

Round 4 Ch1, (dc2tog, 7dc) 4 times, ss to first st to join. [32 sts]

Rounds 5-6 Ch1, dc in each st around, ss to first st to join.

Round 7 Ch1, *dc in next dc, skip 1 dc, (dc, 3htr, dc) in next dc, skip 1 dc; repeat from * 7 more times, ss to first dc to join.

Fasten off.

SECOND LEG

With RS facing and a 3mm hook, rejoin Yarn B with a ss to the first skipped st of Round 14.

Round 1 (RS) Ch1, 1dc in same st, 1dc in the next 24 dc, 1dc in the reverse side of the ch-11, to form the second leg, ss to first dc to join. [25 dc]

Rounds 2-3 Ch1, dc in each st around, ss to first st to join.

Rounds 4-7 Work as Rounds 4-7 of the first leg.

Fasten off.

SECOND LEG

With RS facing and a 3mm hook, rejoin Yarn B with a ss to the first skipped st of Round 14.

Round 1 (RS) Ch1, dc in same st, dc in the next 24 dc, dc in each ch of the opposite side of the ch-11 to form the second leg, ss to first dc to join. [36 sts]

Rounds 2-3 Ch1, dc in each st around, ss to first st to join.

Rounds 4-7 Work as Rounds 4-7 of the first leg. **Fasten off.**

SHOES (MAKE 2)

UPPER

Using a 3mm hook and Yarn E, ch31.

Row 1 Dc in the second ch from hook, dc in next 29 ch, turn. [30 sts]

Row 2 Ch1, dc in first 9 dc, 2dc in each of next 2 dc, htr in next dc, tr in next 6 dc, htr in next dc, 2dc in each of next 2 dc, dc in next 9dc, turn. [34 sts]

Row 3 Ch1, dc in next 10 dc, 2dc in each of next 2 dc, htr in next 2 sts, tr in next 6 sts, htr in next 2 sts, 2dc in the next 2 dc, dc in next 10 dc, turn. [38 sts]

Row 4 Ch1, dc in next 11 dc, htr in each of next 3 dc, tr in next 10 sts, htr in each of next 3 dc, dc in next 11 dc, turn.

Row 5 Ch1, dc in each st across. Fasten off, leaving a long tail.

SOLE

Using a 3mm hook and Yarn C, ch10.

Round 1 Dc in second ch from hook, dc in next 7 ch, 3dc in next ch, working along opposite side of starting ch, dc in next 8 ch. [19 sts]

Round 2 2dc in next dc, dc in next 6 dc, 2htr in next dc, 2tr in next dc, 3tr in next dc, 2tr in next dc, 2htr in next dc, dc in next 6 dc, 2dc in next dc. [27 sts]

Round 3 2dc in next dc, dc in next 7 dc, htr in next htr, 2htr in next htr, 2tr in next 7 tr, 2htr in next htr, htr in next htr, dc in next 7 dc, 2dc in next dc. [38 sts]

Do not fasten off.

JOIN SOLE TO UPPER

Round 4 Place the Upper on top of the Sole of the Shoe.

Insert the hook under both loops of each stitch of the Upper first, then the Sole to join, dc in each of the next 38 dc, ss to the first dc to join. **Fasten off.**

RIGHT SHOE BUTTONHOLE STRAP

With the RS of the Shoe Upper facing, starting at the heel, join Yarn E with a ss to the opposite side of the first ch.

Row 1 Dc in the same st, dc in the opposite side of the next 4 ch, turn. [5 sts]

Row 2 Ch11, dc into seventh ch from hook to form a buttonhole, dc in next 4 ch, dc in the next 5 dc. [10dc and ch-6 loop]

Fasten off.

RIGHT SHOE BUTTON STAND

With WS of the Shoe Upper facing, join Yarn E with a ss to the opposite side of the first ch at the heel.

Row 1 Dc in the same st as the ss, dc in the opposite side of the next 4 ch, turn. [5 sts]

Row 2 Ch1, dc in each dc across. **Fasten off.**

LEFT SHOE BUTTONHOLE STRAP

With the WS of the Shoe Upper facing, starting at the heel, join Yarn E with a ss to the opposite side of the first ch.

Rows 1-2 Work as for Rows 1-2 of Right Shoe Buttonhole Strap.

LEFT SHOE BUTTONHOLE STRAP

With RS of the Shoe Upper facing, join Yarn E with a ss to the opposite side of the first ch at the heel.

Rows 1-2 Work as for Rows 1-2 of Right Shoe Button Stand.

BASKET

Starting at the base of the basket, using a 3mm hook and Yarn F, make a magic loop.

Rounds 1-8 As Rounds 1-8 of Body. [48 sts]

Round 9 (2dc in next st, 7dc) 6 times. [54 sts]

Round 10 (2dc in next st, 8dc) 6 times. [60 sts]

Rounds 11-22 Dc in each st around, do not fasten off.

HANDLES

Round 23 Dc in next 12 dc, ch8, skip 6 dc, dc in next 24 dc, ch8, skip 6 dc, dc in next 12 dc.

Round 24 Dc in next 12 dc, 12dc in the next ch-8 sp, dc in next 24 dc, 12dc in next ch-8 sp, dc in next 12 dc. [72 sts]

Round 25 Ss in both loops of each st around. **Fasten off.**

CARROT

Using a 2.5mm hook and Yarn G, make a magic loop.
Round 1 Ch1 (does not count as st), 6dc into loop. [6 sts]
Round 2 Dc in each st around.
Round 3 (2dc in next dc, dc in next dc) 3 times. [9 sts]
Rounds 4-6 Dc in each st around.
Round 7 (2dc in next dc, dc in next 2 dc) 3 times. [12 sts]
Rounds 8-10 Dc in each st around.
Round 11 (2dc in next dc, dc in next 3 dc) 3 times. [15 sts]
Rounds 12-14 Dc in each st around.
Round 15 (2dc in next dc, dc in next 4 dc) 3 times. [18 sts]
Rounds 16-18 Dc in each st around.
Round 19 (2dc in next dc, dc in next 5 dc) 3 times. [21 sts]
Rounds 20-22 Dc in each st around.
Round 23 (2dc in next dc, dc in next 6 dc) 3 times. [24 sts]
Rounds 24-26 Dc in each st around.
Round 27 (Dc2tog, 2dc) 6 times. [18 sts]
Round 28 (Dc2tog, 1dc) 6 times. **Fasten off.** [12 sts]
Stuff the Carrot firmly, using the end of the hook to push the stuffing right into the tip of the Carrot.

CARROT TOP
Round 28 Join in Yarn H in first st, dc in the back loop only of each st around.
Round 29 (Dc2tog) 6 times, do not fasten off. [6 sts]

LEAFY STALK
Row 1 Dc2tog, ch12 (stalk), *ch6, (ch5, ss in the 2nd ch from hook, ss in the next 3 ch) 3 times, ss down the next 6 ch to form the stem; rep from * twice more, ss down the next 4 ch of the stalk, 1dc in the next 8 ch to the top of the carrot.
Repeat Row 1 twice more to make 2 more Leafy Stalks, ss into the top of the Carrot.
Fasten off.

TO MAKE UP
HEAD
Attach the safety eyes to the crocheted Head between Rounds 7 and 8, approx 7 sts apart. Stuff the Head firmly. Thread the tail of the yarn onto a needle and run a gathering stitch around the last round of stitches, draw up to close.
Fasten off.
Embroider the nose in fly stitch, using 4 strands of embroidery thread.

BODY
Stuff the Body firmly, filling it right to the open end. Sew the Head to the Body, stitching all around the Neck edge and inserting more stuffing into the Neck before closing, if necessary.

ARMS AND LEGS
Stuff the Arms, keeping them soft. Stuff the feet firmly, pushing the stuffing to the end of the Foot and the heel. Stuff the Legs less firmly, filling them to the top. Run a gathering stitch around the last round of stitches at the end of the Foot, draw up to close. **Fasten off**. Sew tog the gap at the front of the ankle where the Leg was divided to form the foot. To finish each Arm and Leg, flatten the open end and, with the tail of yarn sew the sts tog from each side to form a straight edge. Sew an Arm to

each side of the Rabbit at the top of the Body using the image as a guide. Sew the Legs to the base of Body, slightly off centre towards the front.

EARS
With the tail of yarn sew each Ear neatly to the Head at approximately Round 17 and 5 sts apart, stitching all around the edges to attach them securely in place.

TAIL
With the tail of yarn run a gathering stitch around the last round of sts, draw up to close. **Fasten off**.
Sew the Tail to the lower end at the back of the Body.

DRESS
Pin the Collar to the neckline of the Dress with each end of the Collar at the back opening, but not overlapping the Button and Buttonhole Bands, and with the middle of the Collar at the centre front of the Dress. Use the tail of yarn to sew the Collar in place around the neckline. Stitch the pockets to the Skirt, using the tail of yarn.

BLOOMERS
Sew tog the back seam, leaving an opening for the Tail to poke through. Thread elastic through the eyelets in the waist. Overlap the ends of the elastic and stitch tog on the inside of the Bloomers, drawing the waistband in to fit. Trim away the excess elastic.

SHOES
Use the long tail of yarn to st tog the back seam of each Shoe Upper. Sew a button to the button stand at the side of each shoe. Weave in all the yarn ends.

Puddle Duck

This crocheted friend is definitely a puddle duck, as she's ready to go splashing through the farmyard wearing her brightly-coloured wellies.
We think you'd be quackers not to love her!

The Head and Neck are worked separately from the Body and need plenty of stuffing

When you stuff the beak, take care to leave the tip of it flat for the best possible shape

YOU WILL NEED

• DK weight cotton yarn, approximately two 50g balls of:
- Yarn A White
• Approximately one 50g ball of each:
- Yarn B Yellow
- Yarn C Purple

• A 2.5mm (US B/1 or C/2) hook

• A 3mm (US C/2 or D/3) hook

• A tapestry needle

• Safety eyes

• Toy stuffing

MEASUREMENTS

23cm (9in) tall

NOTE

• As with most other patterns in this book, where there is a ch-1 at the beginning of a dc round, it does not count as a st.

BODY

The Body starts at the chest and works down towards the tail. Using a 2.5mm hook and Yarn A, make a magic loop.

Round 1 Ch1, 6dc into loop. [6 sts]

Round 2 (2dc in the next st) 6 times. [12 sts]

Round 3 (2dc in the next st, 1dc) 6 times. [18 sts]

Round 4 (2dc in the next st, 2dc) 6 times. [24 sts]
Round 5 (2dc in the next st, 3dc) 6 times. [30 sts]
Round 6 (4dc, 2dc in the next st) 6 times. [36 sts]
Round 7 (5dc, 2dc in the next st) 6 times. [42 sts]
Round 8 (2dc in the next st, 6dc) 6 times. [48 sts]
Round 9 (2dc in the next st, 7dc) 6 times. [54 sts]
Round 10 (8dc, 2dc in the next st) 6 times. [60 sts]
Rounds 11-25 Dc in each st around.
Round 26 (Dc2tog, 8dc) 6 times. [54 sts]
Rounds 27-28 Dc in each st around.
Round 29 (Dc2tog, 7dc) 6 times. [48 sts]
Rounds 30-31 Dc in each st around.
Round 32 (Dc2tog, 6dc) 6 times. [42 sts]
Rounds 33-34 Dc in each st around.
Round 35 (Dc2tog, 5dc) 6 times. [36 sts]
Rounds 36-37 Dc in each st around. Do not fasten off.

Stuff the Body firmly, filling it to just a couple of rounds below the opening.
Round 38 (Dc2tog, 4dc) 6 times. [30 sts]
Rounds 39-40 Dc in each st around.
Round 41 (Dc2tog, 3dc) 6 times. [24 sts]
Rounds 42-43 Dc in each st around. Stuff the end of the Body.
Flatten the end to bring the 12 sts from each side of the last round together. Ss into the back loop only of one stitch from each side to join across, adding more stuffing if necessary before closing.
Do not fasten off.

TAIL
Round 1 Dc into the front loop of each st of Round 43 of the body. [24 sts]
Rounds 2-3 Dc in each st around.
Round 4 Dc in the next dc, (dc2tog, 2dc) 5 times, dc2tog, dc in the next dc. [18 sts]

Rounds 5-6 Dc in each st around.
Round 7 (1dc, dc2tog) 6 times. [12 sts]
Rounds 8-9 Dc in each st around.
Fasten off and thread yarn through the last round of stitches, pulling tightly.

HEAD
Starting at the top of the Head, using a 2.5mm hook and Yarn A, make a magic loop.
Rounds 1-7 As Rounds 1-7 of Body. [42 sts]
Rounds 8-15 Dc in each st around.
Round 16 (Dc2tog, 5dc) 6 times. [36 sts]
Round 17 (Dc2tog, 4dc) 6 times. [30 sts]
Round 18 (Dc2tog, 3dc) 6 times. [24 sts]
Round 19 (Dc2tog, 2dc) 6 times. [18 sts]
Round 20 (Dc2tog, 1dc) 6 times. [12 sts]

NECK
Round 21 Dc in each st around.
Round 22 (2dc in the next st, 1dc) 6 times. [18 sts]
Round 23 Dc in each st around.
Round 24 (2dc in the next st, 2dc) 6 times. [24 sts]
Round 25 Dc in each st around.
Round 26 (2dc in the next st, 3dc) 6 times. [30 sts]
Round 27 Dc in each st around, ss to first st to join.
Fasten off, leaving a long tail of yarn at the end.

BEAK
Using a 2.5mm hook and Yarn B, ch7.
Round 1 (RS) Dc into second ch from hook, dc into next 4 ch, 2dc in next ch, working along opposite side of starting ch, dc in next 5 ch. [12 sts]
Rounds 2-10 Dc in each st around.
Round 11 (2dc in next st, 1dc) 6 times. [18 sts]
Round 12 Dc in each st around. Ss to the next st.
Fasten off, leaving a long tail of yarn.

LEGS (MAKE 2)
Using a 2.5mm hook and Yarn B, make a magic loop. The centre of the following circle forms the heel; see the Diagram for the Heel on p. 99.
Round 1 Ch1, 6dc into loop. [6 sts]
Round 2 (2dc in the next st) 6 times. [12 sts]
Round 3 Dc in each st around.
Round 4 (2dc in next st, 1dc) 6 times. [18 sts]
Round 5 Dc in each st around.
Round 6 (2dc in next st, 2dc) 6 times. [24 sts]
Round 7 (2dc in next st, 3dc) 6 times. [30 sts]

DIVIDE FOR LEG
Round 8 Dc in the next 6 dc, skip the next 18 dc, 1dc in the next 6 dc. Continue on these 12 sts to finish the leg. The gap at the front of the ankle will be sewn together later.
Rounds 9-15 Dc in each st around.
Fasten off, leaving a long tail of yarn.

FOOT
Skip the first 9 stitches of the remaining 18 dc of Round 7, rejoin Yarn B with a ss to the next dc, which will be underneath the foot.
Rounds 1-9 Work as Rounds 1-9 of the instructions for Sweet Rabbit's Foot (see p. 93). [30 sts]
Fasten off.

JOIN END OF FOOT
Next stuff the Foot. Bring the 15 sts from each side of the last round together, flattening the Foot.
With the top of the Foot facing and a 2.5mm hook, join in Yarn B at one edge and ss into the back loop only of both stitches from each side to join, forming a straight edge.
Fasten off.

WINGS (MAKE 2)
Starting at the top of the Wing, using a 2.5mm hook and Yarn A, make a magic loop.
Rounds 1-6 Work as Rounds 1-6 of Body. [36 sts]
Rounds 7-9 Dc in each st around.

Round 10 (2dc in the next st, 5dc) 6 times. [42 sts]
Rounds 11-15 Dc in each st around.
Round 16 (Dc2tog, 5dc) 6 times. [36 sts]
Rounds 17-19 Dc in each st around.
Round 20 (Dc2tog, 4dc) 6 times. [30 sts]
Rounds 21-23 Dc in each st around.
Round 24 (Dc2tog, 3dc) 6 times. [24 sts]

SHAPE WING LOWER TIP
Round 25 Dc in the next 6 dc, skip next 12 dc, dc in the next 6 dc. Continue working on these 12 sts to finish the Lower Wing Tip shaping.
Round 26 Dc in each st around.
Round 27 (Dc2tog, 2dc) 3 times. [9 sts]
Round 28 Dc in each st around.
Round 29 (Dc2tog, 1dc) 3 times. [6 sts]
Fasten off and thread yarn through the back loops of the last round, pulling tightly to close.

SHAPE WING UPPER TIP
Round 25 With RS facing, rejoin Yarn A with a ss to first skipped st of Round 24, dc in same st, dc in the next 11 dc. [12 sts]
Rounds 26-28 Dc in each st around.
Rounds 29-31 Work as Rounds 27-29 of Lower Tip.
Fasten off and thread yarn through the back loops of the last round, pulling tightly to close.

WELLIES (MAKE 2)
UPPER
Using a 3mm hook and Yarn C, ch24, ss to first ch to join, being careful not to twist.
Round 1 Ch1, dc in each ch around. [24 sts]
Rounds 2-5 Dc in each st around.
The following is worked in rows:
Row 6 (WS) Dc in the next 9 dc, 2dc in the next dc, dc in the next 4 dc, 2dc in the next dc, dc in the next 9 dc, turn. [26 sts]
Row 7 (RS) Ch1, dc in first 8 sts, 2dc in the next 2 sts, htr in the next 6 sts, 2dc in the next 2 sts, dc in the next 8 sts, turn. [30 sts]

Row 8 Ch1, dc in the next 9 dc, 2dc in the next 2 dc, htr in the next 8 sts, 2dc in the next 2 dc, dc in the next 9 dc, turn. [34 sts]
Row 9 Ch1, dc in the next 10 dc, 2dc in the next 2 dc, htr in the next 2 sts, tr in the next 6 sts, htr in the next 2 sts, 2dc in the next 2 dc, dc in the next 10 dc, turn. [38 sts]
Row 10 Ch1, dc in the next 11 dc, htr in the next 3 dc, tr in the next 10 sts, htr in the next 3 dc, dc in the next 11 dc, turn.
Row 11 Ch1, dc in each st across.
Fasten off, leaving a long tail.

SOLE
Using a 3mm hook and Yarn A, ch10.
Rounds 1-3 Work as Rounds 1-3 of the instructions for the Sole of Rabbit's shoes. [38 sts]
Do not fasten off.

JOIN SOLE TO UPPER
Place the Upper on top of the Sole of the Welly. Insert the hook under both loops of each stitch of the Upper first, then the Sole to join, work 1dc in each of the next 38 dc, ss to the first dc.
Fasten off.

TO MAKE UP
HEAD
Attach the safety eyes to the Head between Rounds 10 and 11 approx 6 sts apart.
Stuff the Head and Neck firmly. Making sure the flat side of the tail is facing up, position the Head at the front of the Body using the image as a guide.
Sew the Head to the Body, stitching all around the Neck edge and inserting more stuffing into the Neck before closing, if necessary.

BEAK
Stuff the Beak, keeping the shape flat at the tip. Using the long tail stitch the Beak to the Head around the open edge and inserting more stuffing if needed.

Diagram for heel

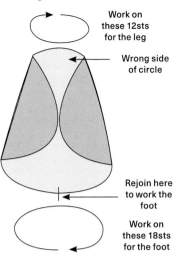

Work on these 12sts for the leg
Wrong side of circle
Rejoin here to work the foot
Work on these 18sts for the foot

LEGS
Push stuffing right into the end of the heel. Stuff the Legs less firmly, filling them to the top. Sew together the gap at the front of the ankle where the Leg was divided to form the Foot.

Flatten the open end at the top of the Leg and, sew across the top using the yarn tail. Position the Legs on the base of the Body so the Duck can sit down, with its feet sticking out at the front. Sew the Legs in place.

WINGS
Sew together the gap between the Wing tips. Flatten the Wings.
Sew a Wing to each side of the body, joining them at the curved front edge and halfway along the top using the image as a guide.

WELLIES
Use the long tail stitch to together the opening in the back of the heel.
Weave in all the yarn ends.

Dashing Donkey

This handsome donkey is all dressed up and ready to party! His delightful fluffy mane is fun and easy to create, while his colourful blanket is a great opportunity to use up oddments of yarn from your stash.

YOU WILL NEED

• Sport weight cotton yarn, approximately two 50g balls of:
- Yarn A Grey
• Approximately one 50g ball of each:
- Yarn B Turquoise
- Yarn C Yellow
- Yarn D Purple
- Yarn E Blue
- Yarn F Cerise
- Yarn G Orange

• A 2.5mm (US B/1 or C/2) hook

• 1 pair of 9mm safety eyes

• Black embroidery yarn

• Polyester toy filling

• Stitch markers

• Tapestry needle

MEASUREMENTS

17x22cm (6¾x8¾in)

ABBREVIATIONS

Spike st Work a standard dc stitch into the corresponding stitch that is 2 rows below

NOTES

• Body and Legs are worked in one piece starting from the Neck.
• Head, Ears, Tail and all the decorations are sewn to the main part.

HEAD

Using Yarn A, make a magic loop.
Round 1 (RS) Ch1 (does not count as st), 6dc into the loop. [6 sts]
Round 2 2dc in each st around. [12 sts]
Round 3 (2dc in next st, dc in next st) 6 times. [18 sts]
Round 4 (2dc in next st, dc in each of next 2 sts) 6 times. [24 sts]
Round 5 (2dc in next st, dc in each of next 3 sts) 6 times. [30 sts]
Rounds 6-11 Dc in each st around.
Round 12 (2dc in next st, dc in each of next 4 sts) 6 times. [36 sts]
Round 13 (2dc in next st, dc in each of next 5 sts) 6 times. [42 sts]
Round 14 Dc in each st around.
Round 15 (2dc in next st, dc in each of next 6 sts) 6 times. [48 sts]
Rounds 16-26 Dc in each st around.
Round 27 (Dc2tog, dc in each of next 6 sts) 6 times. [42 sts]
Round 28 (Dc2tog, dc in each of next 5 sts) 6 times. [36 sts]
Place the eyes between Rounds 15 and 16 of the Head, approx 16 sts apart.
Stuff the Head with toy filling and continue to stuff as you crochet.
Round 29 (Dc2tog, dc in each of next 4 sts) 6 times. [30 sts]
Round 30 (Dc2tog, dc in each of next 3 sts) 6 times. [24 sts]
Round 31 (Dc2tog, dc in each of next 2 sts) 6 times. [18 sts]
Round 32 (Dc2tog, dc in next st) 6 times. [12 sts]
Round 33 (Dc2tog) 6 times. [6 sts]
Fasten off. Thread tail end of yarn onto a tapestry needle; insert the needle into each front loop of the last round, pull tight to close the hole.
Fasten off and weave in end. Embroider the nose with 2 long stitches across Round 5 of the head.

EARS (MAKE 2)

Using Yarn A, make a magic loop.
Round 1 (RS) Ch1 (does not count as st), 6dc into the loop. [6 sts]
Round 2 2dc in next st, dc in each of next 5 sts. [7 sts]
Round 3 2dc in next st, dc in each of next 6 sts. [8 sts]
Round 4 Dc in each st around.
Round 5 (2dc in next st, dc in each of next 3 st) twice. [10 sts]
Round 6 Dc in each st around.
Round 7 (2dc in next st, dc in each of next 4 st) twice. [12 sts]
Round 8 Dc in each st around.
Round 9 (2dc in next st, dc in each of next 5 st) twice. [14 sts]
Rounds 10-15 Dc in each st around.
Round 16 (Dc2tog, dc in each of next 5 sts) twice. [12 sts]
Round 17 (Dc2tog, dc in each of next 4 sts) twice. [10 sts]

Fasten off leaving a long tail for sewing the Ears to the Head. Do not stuff.

Flatten the Ear and sew to Head between Rounds 25 and 27.

BODY (STARTING FROM NECK)

Leave a long piece of yarn before starting ch – you'll need it for sewing to Head later.

Using Yarn A, ch7.

Row 1 (RS) 2dc in 2nd ch from hook, dc in each of next 4 ch, 2dc in next ch, turn. [8 sts]

Row 2 Ch1 (does not count as st), 2dc in next st, dc in each of next 6 sts, 2dc in next st, ch8. [10 sts, 8 ch]

Ss to first dc of Row 2 to join into a ring.

Rounds 1-2 Dc in each st and in each ch around. [18 sts]

Round 3 Dc in each of next 6 sts (these are not included in the stitch count), ch19 (this is the spine of the donkey), 2dc in second ch from hook, dc in each of next 17 ch, dc in each of next 18 sts of the neck, continue working on the opposite side of the spine ch, dc in each of next 18 sts, place a stitch marker to indicate the end of the round. [55 sts]

Round 4 2dc in each of next 2 sts, dc in each of next 52 sts, 2dc in next st. [58 sts]

Round 5 (Dc in next st, 2dc in next st) twice, dc in each of next 24 sts, 2dc in next st, dc in each of next 3 sts, 2dc in next st, dc in each of next 24 sts, 2dc in next st. [63 sts]

Round 6 (Dc in each of next 2 sts, 2dc in next st) twice, dc in each of next 56 sts, 2dc in last st. [66 sts]

Round 7 (Dc in each of next 3 sts, 2dc in next st) twice, dc in each of next 24 sts, 2dc in next st, dc in each of next 5 sts, 2dc in next st, dc in each of next 26 sts, 2dc in next st. [71 sts]

Round 8 (Dc in each of next 4 sts, 2dc in next st) twice, dc in each of next 61 sts. [73 sts]

Round 9 Dc in each of next 36 sts, 2dc in next st, dc in each of next 7

The bright blanket is worked in rows of dc and finished off with little tassels

sts, 2dc in next st, dc in each of next 28 sts. [75 sts]

Rounds 10-18 Dc in each st around.

Round 19 (Dc in each of next 4 sts, dc2tog) twice, dc in each of next 23 sts, dc2tog, dc in each of next 11 sts, dc2tog, dc in each of next 23 sts, dc2tog. [70 sts]

Rounds 20 Dc in each st around. Next, work a dc into each st until you reach the middle back of the donkey (this is approx 4dc), dc in each of next 3 sts. Continue with Leg 1.

LEG 1

Round 1 (RS) Dc in each of next 9 sts of the Body, ch9, ss into the first dc on the leg to join into a ring. [9 sts, 9 ch]

Round 2 Dc in each of next 9 sts, dc

in each of next 9 ch. [18 sts]

Round 3 Dc in each st around.

Round 4 (Dc2tog, dc in each of next 7 sts) twice. [16 sts]

Rounds 5-6 Dc in each st around.

Round 7 (Dc2tog, dc in each of next 6 sts) twice. [14 sts]

Rounds 8-9 Dc in each st around.

Round 10 (Dc2tog, dc in each of next 5 sts) twice. [12 sts]

Rounds 11-12 Dc in each st around.

Round 13 (Dc2tog) 6 times. [6 sts]

Fasten off.

Thread tail end of yarn onto a tapestry needle; insert the needle into each front loop of the last round, pull tight to close the hole. Fasten off and weave in end.

Stuff the Leg from the open end.

LEG 2

Skip next 12 sts on Round 20 of the Body after Leg 1.
Start the second leg following the same instructions as Leg 1.

LEG 3

Skip next 5 sts on Round 20 of the Body after Leg 2.
Start the third leg following the same instructions as Leg 1.

LEG 4

Skip next 12 sts on Round 20 of the Body after Leg 3.
Start the fourth leg following the same instructions as Leg 1.

BELLY

Join Yarn A to Round 20, on the right-hand side of the 12 st space between Leg 1 and Leg 2.
Rows 1-5 (RS) Ch1 (does not count as st throughout), dc in each st to end, turn. [12 sts]
Row 6 Ch6, dc in second ch from hook, dc in each of next 4 ch, dc in each of next 12 sts, turn. [17 sts]
Row 7 Ch6, dc in second ch from hook, dc in each of next 4 ch, dc in each of next 17 sts, turn. [22 sts]
Rows 8-10 Ch1, dc in each st to end, turn.

Row 11 (partial row) Ch1, dc in each of next 17 sts, turn leaving the remaining sts unworked. [17 sts]
Row 12 (partial row) Ch1, dc in each of next 12 sts, turn leaving the remaining sts unworked. [12 sts]
Rows 13-16 Ch1, dc in each st to end, turn.
Fasten off leaving a long tail for sewing. Pin the Belly piece to Round 20 of the Body; sew it all around the Body and the Legs. Stuff the Body a few cm before ending the seam. Continue stuffing the Body from the Neck until it stands firm.
Place the Head on Rounds 16 to 22 of the Neck and sew all around.

TAIL

Using Yarn A, ch17.
Row 1 (RS) Htr in third ch from hook, htr in each of next 9 ch, dc in each of next 4 ch, ss in last ch. [15 sts]
Fasten off and tie a short piece of Yarn A to the end of the tail.

MANE

Cut lots of small strands of Yarn A by winding the yarn around a piece of cardboard approx 3.5cm tall to get strands of 7cm.
Fold the strands in half and tie each one (as if you are making a fringe for

a scarf), one by one, onto the head, starting from the middle of the forehead.

BLANKET

Each row of the blanket starts with a new colour. Do not turn the work, instead join the new yarn on top of the first st of the previous row. Leave a tail of yarn at the beginning and the end of every row for the tassels.
Using Yarn B, ch28.
Row 1 (RS) Skip the first ch from the hook, (dc in next ch, ch1, skip next ch) 13 times, dc in last ch. [27 sts]
Fasten off.
Row 2 Join Yarn C to first dc of previous row, ch1, dc in same st, (dc into next ch-1 sp, ch1, skip next st) 12 times, dc in each of next 2 sts.
Fasten off.
Row 3 Join Yarn D to first dc of previous row, ch1, dc in same st, (ch1, skip next st, dc in next ch-1 sp) 13 times.
Fasten off.
Repeat (Rows 2 and 3) another 6 times, ending in Yarn B.
Make a tassel at the beginning and the end of each row. Using the crochet hook, insert a strand of yarn into the edge sts of each row and make a loop. Make a knot close to the edge of the blanket, inserting the tail of yarn into the loop made.
Trim the tassels at the same lengths.

SADDLE

Using Yarn G, ch11, leaving a long tail of yarn before starting, to tie up the Saddle on the Donkey later.
Round 1 (RS) Dc in second ch from hook and in each of next 8 ch, 5dc in last ch, rotate to work along the opposite side of the foundation ch, dc in each of next 8 sts, 4dc in last st. [26 sts]
Round 2 (Dc in each of next 10 sts, 2dc in each of next 3 sts) twice. [32 sts]
Round 3 *Dc in each of next 10 sts, (2dc in next st, dc in next st) 3 times; rep from * once more. [38 sts]
Round 4 *Dc in each of next 10 sts, (2dc in next st, dc in each of next 2

Refer to this image when you're embroidering

sts) 3 times; rep from * once more. [44 sts]

Round 5 Ss in next st, dc in front loop only of each dc around, ss to top of first dc.

Round 6 Ch1, spike st, inserting the hook 1 row below in each dc around, ss to top of the first st.

Fasten off and weave in ends.

STRAP

Using Yarn G, ch36, dc in second ch from hook, dc in each of next 33 ch, 4dc in last ch, rotate to work along the opposite side of the foundation ch, dc in each of next 34 sts, ss to first st. [72 sts]

Fasten off. Sew the strap to the middle sts of the round side of the Saddle, opposite the beginning of the Saddle with the tail of yarn. **Fasten off** leaving a long tail of yarn. Use the tails of yarn at the end of the Strap and underneath the Saddle to tie the Saddle onto the Donkey.

NOSEBAND

Using Yarn F, ch30, ss into the first ch to join into a ring.

Round 1 (RS) Ch1, dc in same st, dc in each st around. [30 sts]

Fasten off and weave in ends.

REINS

Using Yarn B, ch37.

Row 1 (RS) Dc in second ch from hook, dc in next ch, (htr in next ch, ch3, ss into the third ch from hook) until last 2 ch, htr in next ch, dc in last ch. [36 sts]

Fasten off.

Embroider the Rein using Yarn C, D and F using long stitches and French knots.

Place the noseband on the muzzle, pin the Rein on both sides under the eyes, and sew it in place with a single stitch.

BROWBAND

Using Yarn G, ch50, ss into the first ch to join into a ring.

Round 1 Ch1, dc in same st, dc in each of next 24 ch, ch6, ss in second ch from hook, dc in next ch, htr in each of next 3 ch, continue along the main ch, dc in each of next 25 ch, ss to top of the first dc.

Fasten off and weave in ends.

Embroider the Browband using straight stitches in Yarn D and French knots in Yarn E, using the image as a guide.

Take your time to shape the ears before sewing them into position on your deer

Dapper Fox

With his shrewd but affable demeanour, we'd certainly sign up for an expedition with this friendly fox! He's crocheted almost in a single piece from head to toe and would make a perfect present for a well-travelled friend. To make his beautiful orange fur extra soft, choose a wool or wool-blend yarn.

YOU WILL NEED

• DK weight wool or wool-blend yarn, approximately two 50g balls of
- Yarn A Orange
• Approximately one 50g ball of each:
- Yarn B Cream
- Yarn C Light Green
- Yarn D Gold
- Yarn E Black

• A 2.75mm (US C/2) hook

• Toy stuffing

• 2 safety eyes, approx 8mm diameter

• Stitch markers

• Tapestry or yarn needle

MEASUREMENT

27cm (10½in) tall

ABBREVIATIONS

Bobble stitch Tr5tog in the same st as follows: (Yrh, insert hook in st indicated, yrh and pull up loop, yrh and draw through 2 loops) 5 times, inserting the hook in the same st each time, yrh and draw through all loops on hook
Jacquard Working with 2 colours, work 1 st in first colour and the next st in second colour and continue alternating colours with each st

NOTES

• Head, Body and Legs are worked in the amigurumi method as explained on p. 6.
• Carry unused yarns across the WS.
• There are images to guide you on the following pages. Each image is marked in the pattern by a corresponding number.

SNOUT

Using Yarn E, make a magic loop.
Round 1 (RS) Ch1 (does not count as st), 8dc in to loop. [8 sts]
Rounds 2-3 Dc in each st around. Change to Yarns B and A. Change colour during the round. When you change, make sure you twist the working ends around one another to avoid a hole in the fabric.
Round 4 4dc in Yarn B, 4dc in Yarn A.
Round 5 (Dc in next st, 2dc in next st) twice in Yarn B, repeat () twice in Yarn A. [12 sts]
Round 6 6dc in Yarn B, 6dc in Yarn A.
Round 7 (Dc in next st, 2dc in next st) 3 times in Yarn B, 3 times in Yarn A. [18 sts]
Round 8 9dc in Yarn B, 9dc in Yarn A.
Round 9 (Dc in next 2 sts, 2dc in next st) 3 times in Yarn B, 3 times in Yarn A. [24 sts]
Round 10 12dc in Yarn B, 12dc in Yarn A.
Round 11 (Dc in next 3 sts, 2dc in next st) 3 times in Yarn B, 3 times in Yarn A. [30 sts]
Round 12 15dc in Yarn B, 15dc in Yarn A.
Fasten off, leaving a long tail for sewing. Embroider the mouth with Yarn E using the images as a guide. Stuff the Snout.

HEAD

Head is worked from top down.
Using Yarn A, make a magic loop.
Round 1 (RS) Ch1 (does not count as st), 6dc in loop. [6 sts]
Round 2 2dc in each st around. [12 sts]
Round 3 (Dc in next st, 2dc in next st) 6 times. [18 sts]
Round 4 (Dc in next 2 sts, 2dc in next st) 6 times. [24 sts]
Round 5 (Dc in next 3 sts, 2dc in next st) 6 times. [30 sts]
Round 6 (Dc in next 4 sts, 2dc in next st) 6 times. [36 sts]
Round 7 (Dc in next 5 sts, 2dc in next st) 6 times. [42 sts]
Round 8 (Dc in next 6 sts, 2dc in next st) 6 times. [48 sts]
Round 9 (Dc in next 7 sts, 2dc in next st) 6 times. [54 sts]
Rounds 10-17 Dc in each st around.
Change to Yarn B.
Rounds 18-20 Dc in each st around.
Round 21 (Dc in next 7 sts, dc2tog) 6 times. [48 sts]
Round 22 (Dc in next 6 sts, dc2tog) 6 times. [42 sts]
Round 23 (Dc in next 5 sts, dc2tog) 6 times. [36 sts]
Round 24 (Dc in next 4 sts, dc2tog) 6 times. [30 sts]
Sew the Snout to the Head  and insert eyes, using the image as a guide.
Round 25 (Dc in next 3 sts, dc2tog) 6 times. [24 sts]
Round 26 (Dc in next 2 sts, dc2tog) 6 times. [18 sts]
Round 27 Dc in each st around.
Stuff the Head firmly.

VEST

Change to Yarn C.
Round 28 (Dc in next 2 sts, 2dc in next st) 6 times. [24 sts]
Change to Yarns B and C.
In the following row work in jacquard (see abbreviations) alternating colours with each st  :
Round 29 (Dc in next 3 sts, 2dc in next st) 6 times. [30 sts]
Round 30 In Yarn C, dc in each st around.
Round 31 In jacquard, dc in each st around.
Rounds 32-35 Repeat the last 2 rows twice more.
Round 36 In Yarn C, dc in each st around.
Stuff the Body.
Change to Yarn A.
Round 37 Working in bl of each st only, dc in each st around.

Rounds 38-39 Dc in each st around.

DIVIDE THE LEGS

FIRST LEG
To divide the work to make two Legs, identify the central stitch at the back of the Fox and place a stitch marker.  Dc in each st up to and including that marked st. There will be 15 sts on each Leg, and this marked st will be the 15th st of the First Leg. To join to first st of the Leg, count back from 15th st to find the first st which will be in the centre front. Now work a dc in first st, so that the sts of the First Leg are joined in the round.
Continue working the First Leg:
Rounds 40-62 Dc in each st around. Stuff the Body and Leg firmly.
Round 63 (Dc in next st, dc2tog) 5 times. [10 sts]
Round 64 (Dc2tog) 5 times. [5 sts]
Fasten off, leaving a long tail. Using a tapestry needle, weave the yarn tail through the front loop of each rem st and pull tight to close.

SECOND LEG
Rejoin Yarn A to the next unworked st of Round 39, which will be the first st of the Second Leg.
Round 40 Dc in each st of the Second Leg, and when you reach the 15th st of the Leg, dc in first st to join into the round.
Rounds 41-62 Repeat Rounds 41-62 of First Leg.
Stuff the Leg firmly.
Rounds 63-64 Repeat Rounds 63-64 of First Leg.
Fasten off, leaving a long tail. Using a tapestry needle, weave the yarn tail through the front loop of each rem st and pull tight to close.

EARS (MAKE 2)

Using Yarn E, make a magic loop.
Round 1 (RS) Ch1 (does not count as st), 5dc into loop. [5 sts]
Rounds 2-3 Dc in each st around. Change to Yarn A.
Round 4 2dc in each st around. [10 sts]
Rounds 5-6 Dc in each st around.

Round 7 (Dc in next st, 2dc in next st) 5 times. [15 sts]

Rounds 8-9 Dc in each st around.

Round 10 (Dc in next 2 sts, 2dc in next st) 5 times. [20 sts]

Rounds 11-12 Dc in each st around.

Fasten off, leaving a long tail for sewing. Do not stuff the Ears.

ARMS (MAKE 2)

Using Yarn A, make a magic loop.

Round 1 (RS) Ch1 (does not count as st), 5dc into loop. [5 sts]

Round 2 2dc in each st around. [10 sts]

Round 3 (Dc in next st, 2dc in next st) 5 times. [15 sts]

Round 4 Dc in each st around.

Round 5 Dc in next st, bobble st in next st, dc in next 13 sts.

Round 6 Dc in each st around.

Round 7 (Dc in next st, dc2tog) 5 times. [10 sts]

Rounds 8-20 Dc in each st around.

Round 21 (Dc in next st, dc2tog) 3 times, dc in last st. [7 sts]

Fasten off, leaving a long tail for sewing.

Stuff the Arm firmly.

TAIL

Using Yarn B, make a magic loop.

Round 1 (RS) Ch1 (does not count as st), 5dc into loop. [5 sts]

Round 2 Dc in each st around.

Round 3 2dc in each st around. [10 sts]

Round 4 Dc in each st around.

Round 5 (Dc in next st, 2dc in next st) 5 times. [15 sts]

Round 6 (Dc in next 2 sts, 2dc in next st) 5 times. [20 sts]

Round 7 (Dc in next 3 sts, 2dc in next st) 5 times. [25 sts]

Round 8 (Dc in next 4 sts, 2dc in next st) 5 times. [30 sts]

Round 9 (Dc in next 5 sts, 2dc in next st) 5 times. [35 sts]

Change to Yarn A.

Rounds 10-16 Dc in each st around.

Round 17 (Dc in next 5 sts, dc2tog) 5 times. [30 sts]

Rounds 18-19 Dc in each st around.

Round 20 (Dc in next 4 sts, dc2tog) 5 times. [25 sts]

Rounds 21-22 Dc in each st around.

Round 23 (Dc in next 3 sts, dc2tog) 5 times. [20 sts]

Rounds 24-25 Dc in each st around.

Round 26 (Dc in next 2 sts, dc2tog) 5 times. [15 sts]

Rounds 27-28 Dc in each st around.

Round 29 (Dc in next st, dc2tog) 5 times. [10 sts]

Round 30 Dc in each st around.

Fasten off, leaving a long tail for sewing.

Stuff the Tail.

BOW TIE

Using Yarn D, ch6.

Round 1 (RS) Dc in second ch from hook, dc in each ch to last ch, 3dc in the last ch, rotate to work on the other side of the foundation ch, dc in each st to last st, 2dc in last st. [12 sts]

Rounds 2-5 Dc in each st around.

Round 6 (Dc2tog) 6 times. [6 sts]

Round 7 2dc in each st around. [12 sts]

Round 8-12 Dc in each st around.

Fasten off, leaving a long tail for sewing. Do not stuff the Bowtie. Using a tapestry needle, close the open end of the Bow Tie and wrap yarn around the centre of the tie to pinch it in the middle.

Fasten off.

TO FINISH

Sew the Tail and the Arms to the Body. Sew the Ears to the Head, using the photo on p. 104 as a guide. Position the Bow Tie and sew it to the front of the Body.

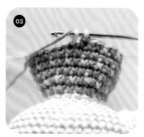

Adorable Axolotl

You've taken your child to the petting zoo, but how do you teach them about species further flung? This axolotl is the answer to your zoological concerns. Give to a little one to spark their curiosity; wait until they find out those 'pigtails' are gills!

The blue bow is a sweet nod to the axolotl's natural aquatic habitat

YOU WILL NEED

• 4ply weight cotton yarn, approximately one 50g ball of each:
- Yarn A Light Pink
- Yarn B Dark Pink
- Yarn C Powder Blue

• A 2.5mm (US B/1 or C/2) hook

• Black stranded cotton

• Toy stuffing

• 2 black safety eyes, 6mm

MEASUREMENTS

15cm (6in) tall

ABBREVIATIONS

picot Ch3, ss into last ch from hook

HEAD

Using Yarn A, make a magic loop.

Round 1 (RS) Ch1 (does not count as st throughout), 6dc into the loop. [6 sts]

Round 2 2dc in each dc around. [12 sts]

Round 3 (Dc in next dc, 2dc in next dc) 6 times. [18 sts]

Round 4 (Dc in next 2 dc, 2dc in next dc) 6 times. [24 sts]

Round 5 (Dc in next 3 dc, 2dc in next dc) 6 times. [30 sts]

Round 6 (Dc in next 4 dc, 2dc in next dc) 6 times. [36 sts]

Round 7 (Dc in next 5 dc, 2dc in next dc) 6 times. [42 sts]

Round 8 (Dc in next 6 dc, 2dc in next dc) 6 times. [48 sts]

Round 9 (Dc in next 7 dc, 2dc in next dc) 6 times. [54 sts]

Round 10 (Dc in next 8 dc, 2dc in next dc) 6 times. [60 sts]

Rounds 11-20 Dc in each st around.

Round 21 (Dc in next 8 dc, dc2tog) 6 times. [54 sts]

Round 22 (Dc in next 7 dc, dc2tog) 6 times. [48 sts]

Round 23 (Dc in next 6 dc, dc2tog) 6 times. [42 sts]

Round 24 (Dc in next 5 dc, dc2tog) 6 times. [36 sts]

Round 25 (Dc in next 4 dc, dc2tog) 6 times. [30 sts]

Round 26 (Dc in next 3 dc, dc2tog) 6 times. [24 sts]

Place the safety eyes between Rounds 17 and 18, 9 sts apart.

Use a single strand of black cotton to sew two eyelashes from each eye. You can use the image as a guide.

Round 27 (Dc in next 2 sts, dc2tog) 6 times. [18 sts]

Round 28 (Dc in next dc, dc2tog) 6 times. [12 sts]

Stuff the Head firmly with toy stuffing.

Round 29 (Dc2tog) 6 times, ss into next st to join. [6 sts]

Fasten off, thread the tail through the sts of Round 29, pull tight to close and weave in end.

LEFT LEG

Using Yarn A, ch7.

Round 1 (RS) Dc in the second ch from hook, dc in next 4 ch, 3dc in next ch, working into the back of the foundation ch, dc in next 4 ch, 2dc in next ch. [14 sts]

Round 2 (2dc in next dc, dc in next 4 dc, 2dc in next 2 sts) twice. [20 sts]

Round 3 Dc in each st around.

Round 4 Dc in next 19 sts, (mark the last st as new end of Round). [19 sts]

Round 5 (Dc2tog, dc in each of next 8 dc) twice. [18 sts]

Round 6 (Dc2tog, dc in each of next 7 dc) twice, dc in next st (marks new end of Round). [17 sts]

Round 7 (Dc in next 6 sts, dc2tog) twice. [14 sts]

Stuff the foot.

Flatten the top of the foot and work the next row through both sides to close.

Row 8 (The side facing you will be the front of the Left Leg), dc in next 6 sts, turn.

Round 9 Ch1, dc into the fl of next 6 sts, ch1, dc in the 6 unused bl loop. [12 sts]

Round 10 2dc in next st, dc in next 11 sts. [13 sts]

Round 11 2dc in next st, dc in next 12 sts. [14 sts]

Round 12 2dc in next 2 sts, dc in next 5 sts, (dc2tog), dc in next 5 sts. [15 sts]

Round 13 Dc in next 2 sts (mark last st), ss into next st to join. Fasten off. [2 sts]

RIGHT LEG

Repeat Rounds 1-12 of the Left Leg. On Row 8 the side facing away from you is the front of the Right Leg.

Round 13 (RS) Dc in next 2 sts, (mark last st). [2 sts]

Do not fasten off the Right Leg.

BODY

Continue from the Right Leg, using Yarn A.

Round 1 (RS) Ch3 (space between Legs), dc into the next dc after the marked st on Left Leg, dc in next 14 sts on Left Leg, dc into bl of each 3 ch, dc in next 15 sts of Right Leg. [33 sts]

Round 2 Dc into fl of 3 ch, dc in next 33 sts around. [36 sts]

Rounds 3-14 Dc in each st around. [36 sts]

Round 15 (Dc in next 10 sts, dc2tog) 3 times. [33 sts]

Round 16 (Dc in next 9 sts, dc2tog) 3 times. [30 sts]

Round 17 (Dc in next 8 sts, dc2tog) 3 times. [27 sts]

Round 18 (Dc in next 7 sts, dc2tog) 3 times. [24 sts]

Round 19 (Dc in next 6 sts, dc2tog) 3 times. [21 sts]

Round 20 (Dc in next 5 sts, dc2tog) 3 times. [18 sts]

Round 21 Dc in next 4 sts, ss into next st to join. [4 sts]

Fasten off, leaving a long tail. Stuff the Legs and Body. Sew the Body to the Head using the long tails. The opening of the Body should fall over Rounds 27-29 at the base of the Head. Tilt the Head slightly to one side to give a cute look.

ARMS (MAKE 2)

Using Yarn A, ch6.

Round 1 (RS) Dc in second ch from hook, dc in next 3 ch, 3dc into last ch, turn to work down the opposite side of the foundation ch, dc in next 3 ch, 2dc in last ch. [12 sts]

Round 2 Dc in each st around.

Round 3 Dc in next 11 sts, (mark last st as new end of Round). [11 sts]

Round 4 (Dc2tog, dc in next 4 sts) twice. [10 sts]

Round 5 (Dc2tog, dc in next 3 sts) twice. [8 sts]

Round 6 (Dc2tog, dc in next 2 sts) twice. [6 sts]

Round 7 (Dc in next 2 sts, 2dc in next st) twice. [8 sts]

Rounds 8-13 Dc in each st around.

Round 14 Dc in next 6 sts, (mark last st as new end of Round). [6 sts]
Stuff the Arm and flatten the top. Work the next row through both sides to close.
Row 15 Dc in 4 sts across. [4 sts]
Fasten off, leaving a long tail.
Sew the Arms to the Body between Rounds 19-20, 7 stitches apart at the front.

TAIL

Using Yarn A, make a magic loop.
Round 1 Ch1, 6dc into the loop. [6 sts]
Round 2 (Dc in next 2 sts, 2dc in next st) twice. [8 sts]
Round 3 Dc in each st around.
Round 4 (Dc in next 3 sts, 2dc in next st) twice. [10 sts]
Round 5 Dc in each st around.
Round 6 (Dc in next 4 sts, 2dc in next st) twice. [12 sts]
Round 7 Dc in each st around.
Round 8 Dc in next 5 sts, 2dc in next 2 sts, dc in next 5 sts. [14 sts]
Round 9 Dc in each st around.
Round 10 Dc in next 6 sts, 2dc in next 2 sts, dc in next 6 sts. [16 sts]
Round 11 Dc in next 7 sts, 2dc in next 2 sts, dc in next 7 sts. [18 sts]
Round 12 Dc in next 8 sts, 2dc next 2 sts, dc in next 8 sts. [20 sts]
Round 13 Dc in next 10 sts, 2dc in next 2 sts, (mark the 12th and 13th st of Round 13), dc in next 8 sts. [22 sts]
Round 14 (Dc2tog), dc in next 9 sts, 2dc in next 2 sts, dc in next 9 sts. [23 sts]
Round 15 Dc in each st around.
Round 16 (Dc2tog), dc in next 10 sts, 2dc in next st, dc in next 10 sts, ss into next st to close.
Fasten off, leaving a long tail. Stuff firmly.

TAIL FIN

Using Yarn A, ch32.
Row 1 Htr in third ch from hook, (htr in next ch, 2htr in next ch, htr in next ch) 9 times, htr in next ch, 2htr in last ch, turn. [40 sts]
Row 2 Ch2 (does not count as st), (htr in next st, 2htr in next st) 20 times.

Fasten off. [60 sts]
Sew the Tail Fin around the Tail. Start by attaching the Tail Fin to the bottom side of the Tail, and finish by sewing the end of the Tail Fin to the top side of the Tail.
Sew the Tail to the Body. The marked sts from Round 13 of the Tail indicates the top centre of the Tail. The opening of the Tail should be sewn over Rounds 4-11 of the Body.

GILL (MAKE 6)

Using Yarn B, make a magic loop.
Round 1 Ch1, 6dc into the loop. [6 sts]
Rounds 2-10 Dc in each st around.
Round 11 Dc in each st around, ss into next st to join. **Fasten off,** leaving a long tail.
Lightly stuff each Gill.

GILL EDGING (MAKE 6)

Using Yarn B, ch22.
Round 1 Ss into second ch from hook, (ss into next st, picot, ss into next st) 10 times. [10 picot]
Fasten off.

HEART

Using Yarn B, make a magic loop.
Round 1 Ch1, 6dc into the loop. [6 sts]
Round 2 Ch2, (3dtr, 4tr, dtr, 4tr, 3dtr, ch2, ss) into the loop. [16 sts]
Fasten off, and use the tail to sew the Heart onto the Body between Rounds 10 and 17.

BOW

Using Yarn C, ch21.
Row 1 (RS) Dc into second ch from hook, dc into each ch across, turn. [20 sts]
Rows 2-10 Ch1, dc into each st across, turn.
Work around Rows 1-10 for the next round.
Round 11 Ch1, dc into each st across, *2dc into first row end, dc into next 8 row ends, 2dc into last row end**, dc into the back of each foundation ch across; repeat from * to **, ss to first dc to join. Fasten off. [64 sts]

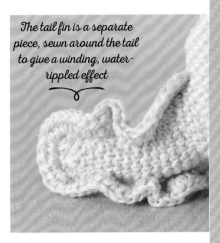

The tail fin is a separate piece, sewn around the tail to give a winding, water-rippled effect

Squeeze the centre of the Bow together and secure with a few sts of Yarn C.

MIDDLE OF BOW

Using Yarn C, ch10.
Row 1 (RS) Dc in second ch from hook, dc in each ch across, turn. [9 sts]
Rows 2-3 Ch1, dc into each st across.
Fasten off.
Wrap the Middle of the Bow around the centre of the Bow, then sew the ends together to make a loop.

TO FINISH

Sew each Gill Edging around the Gill with the start and end of each Edging attached between Rounds 10 and 11. Sew each Gill onto the Head; you can use the image as a guide. The top 2 Gills should fall over Rounds 9 and 10 of the Head, the middle Gills should fall over Rounds 13 and 14 of the Head, the bottom Gills should fall over Rounds 17 and 18 of the Head. Sew the Bow to the Head in front of the top right Gill. Weave in any remaining ends.

Party Pug

Some dogs fetch sticks and others bury bones, and a few don hats and frequent nightclubs. Party Pug falls into this latter camp. Make sure to keep on top of all his separate pieces to avoid an unpicking atrocity, and remember to stuff as you go.

YOU WILL NEED

• 4ply weight cotton yarn, approximately one 50g ball of each:
- Yarn A Beige
- Yarn B Brown
- Yarn C Blue
- Yarn D Yellow

• A 3mm (US C/2 or D/3) hook

• Toy stuffing

• 2 black safety eyes, 12mm

• Black stranded cotton

MEASUREMENTS

18cm (7in) tall

ABBREVIATIONS

inv dec (invisible decrease) Insert hook into the fl of the next st, insert hook into the fl of the next st, yrh and pull through the 2 sts, yrh and pull through the 2 loops on the hook (alternatively work a standard dc2tog)

bobble (Yrh, insert hook into st specified, yrh and pull up a loop, yrh and pull through 2 loops on the hook) 4 times working into the same st, yrh and pull through all loops on the hook

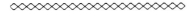

NOTES
• The Head is worked from the top down.

PUG
HEAD
Using Yarn A, make a magic loop.
Round 1 (RS) Ch1, 6dc into loop. [6 sts]
Round 2 2dc in each st around. [12 sts]
Round 3 (Dc in next st, 3dc in next st, dc in next st) 4 times. [20 sts]
Round 4 (Dc in next 2 sts, 3dc in next st, dc in next 2 sts) 4 times. [28 sts]
Round 5 (Dc in next 3 sts, 3dc in next st, dc in next 3 sts) 4 times. [36 sts]
Round 6 (Dc in next 5 sts, 2dc in next st) 6 times. [42 sts]
Round 7 (Dc in next 6 sts, 2dc in next st) 6 times. [48 sts]
Rounds 8-19 Dc in each st around.
Add safety eyes between Rounds 15-16, 10 sts apart.
Round 20 (Dc in next 4 sts, inv dec) 8 times. [40 sts]
Round 21 (Dc in next 3 sts, inv dec) 8 times. [32 sts]
Round 22 (Dc in next 2 sts, inv dec) 8 times. [24 sts]
Round 23 (Dc in next st, inv dec) 8 times.
[16 sts]
Add toy stuffing.
Round 24 (Inv dec) 8 times. [8 sts]
Fasten off, thread the tail through the fl of last 8 sts pulling tight to close.

MUZZLE
Using Yarn B, make a magic loop.
Rounds 1-2 (RS) As Rounds 1-2 of Head.
[12 sts]
Round 3 (Dc in next st, 2dc in next st) 6 times. [18 sts]
Round 4 (Dc in next 2 sts, 2dc in next st) 6 times. [24 sts]
Round 5 (Dc, 2dc in next st) 6 times, dc in next 12 sts. [30 sts]
Rounds 6-7 Dc in each st around.
Fasten off.
Using black stranded cotton, sew a

nose over Round 4 on the upper side of the Muzzle. We've used multiple whipstitches worked over 4 sts across.
Add some stuffing and sew to the front of the Head below the eyes. You can use the image as a guide.

MOUTH
Using Yarn B, make a magic loop.
Round 1 (RS) Ch1, 6dc into loop. [6 sts]
Round 2 (3dc in next st, dc in next st) 3 times. [12 sts]
Round 3 (Dc in next st, 3dc in next st, dc in next 2 sts) 3 times [18 sts]
Round 4 Dc in next 4 sts, 3dc in next st, dc in next 9 sts, 3dc in next st, dc in next 2 sts, ss in next st. **Fasten off.** [22 sts]
Sew the Mouth to back post of sts on the lower half of the Muzzle so that the top line of the Mouth protrudes slightly. You can use the image as a guide.

EARS (MAKE 2)
Using Yarn B, make a magic loop.
Rounds 1-3 (RS) Repeat Rounds 1-3 of Mouth. [18 sts]
Round 4 (Dc in next 2 sts, 3dc in next st, dc in next 3 sts) 3 times [24 sts]
Round 5 (Dc in next 3 sts, 3dc in next st, dc in next 4 sts) 3 times [30 sts]
Round 6 Dc in next 15 sts, ss in next st, leave rem sts unworked. **Fasten off.**

INNER EARS (MAKE 2)
Using Yarn A, make a magic loop.
Rounds 1-3 (RS) As Rounds 1-3 of Mouth.
[18 sts]
Fasten off.
Sew the Inner Ear onto the Ear, lining up at the bottom edge.
Sew the Ears onto the Head using the images as a guide.

COLLAR
Using Yarn C, ch30, ss into last ch from hook to form a loop.
Round 1 (RS) Ch1, dc in each ch around, ss to beg dc. [30 sts]

Rounds 2-3 Ch1, dc in each st around.
Fasten off.
Using Yarn D, sew the stud detail by working 2 small straight sts in the same position over Round 2. Repeat around the Collar.

BODY
Using Yarn A, make a magic loop.
Round 1 (RS) Ch1, 7dc into loop. [7 sts]
Round 2 2dc in each st around. [14 sts]
Round 3 (Dc in next st, 2dc in next st) 7 times. [21 sts]
Round 4 (Dc in next 2 sts, 2dc in next st) 7 times. [28 sts]
Round 5 (Dc in next 3 sts, 2dc in next st) 7 times. [35 sts]
Rounds 6-8 Dc in each st around.
Round 9 (Dc in next 4 sts, 2dc in next st) 3 times, dc in next 20 sts. [38 sts]

Add the eyes before stuffing the head, while you can still access the back of the fabric

Line up the ear and inner ear from the bottom edge so your pug doesn't end up cock-eared

Round 10 Dc in each st around.
Round 11 (Dc in next 4 sts, 2dc in next st) 3 times, dc in next 23 sts. [41 sts]
Rounds 12-15 Dc in each st around.
Round 16 Dc in next 30 sts, (inv dec) 3 times, dc last 5 sts. [38 sts]
Round 17 Dc in each st around.
Round 18 Dc in next 30 sts, dc3tog, dc in last 5 sts. [36 sts]
Round 19 Dc in next 29 sts, dc2tog, dc in last 4 sts. [34 sts]
Round 20 (Dc in next 4 sts, inv dec) 3 times, dc in next 10 sts, dc3tog, dc in last 3 sts. [29 sts]
Rounds 21-23 Dc in each st around. **Fasten off.**
Stuff the Body and place the Collar over the opening. Sew to the base of the Head. We've turned the Head slightly to give the pug a jaunty look.

FRONT RIGHT LEGS
Using Yarn A, make a magic loop.
Rounds 1-2 (RS) As Rounds 1-2 of Head. [12 sts]
Round 3 (Bobble in next st, dc in next st) 3 times, dc in next 6 sts.
Round 4 Dc in each st around.
Round 5 Dc in next 8 sts, inv dec, dc in last 2 sts. [11 sts]
Rounds 6-8 Dc in each st around.
Round 9 Dc in next 6 sts, ss in bl of next 5 sts.
Round 10 Dc in next 6 sts, ss in next st.
Fasten off.

FRONT LEFT LEG
Rounds 1-8 As Rounds 1-8 of Front Right Leg.
Round 9 Ss in bl of next 2 sts, dc in next 6 sts, ss in bl of next 3 sts.
Round 10 Ss in bl of next 2 sts, dc in next 6 sts, ss into next st. **Fasten off.**
Add stuffing to both the Legs. Position the Legs over Round 12 of the Body so that they can support the weight of the Body.

BACK LEGS
Using Yarn A, make a magic loop.
Round 1 (RS) Ch1, 6dc into loop. [6 sts]

Round 2 2dc in each st around [12 sts]
Round 3 (Dc in next st, 2dc in next st) 6 times [18 sts]
Round 4 Dc in each st around, turn.
Round 5 (WS) Ch1, bobble in each of next 3 sts, ch1, ss in next st. **Fasten off.**
Add a small amount of stuffing to Rounds 1-4 and sew to the Body with the bobbles pointing down. You can use the images as a guide.

TAIL
Using Yarn B, make a magic loop.
Round 1 (RS) Ch1, 6dc into loop. [6 sts]
Round 2 3dc in next st, dc in next 5 sts. [8 sts]
Round 3 Dc in each st around.
Round 4 Dc in next st, 3dc in next st, dc in next 6 sts. [10 sts]
Round 5 Dc in next 6 sts, inv dec, dc in last 2 sts. [9 sts]
Round 6 Dc in next 2 sts, 3dc in next st, dc in last 6 sts. [11 sts]
Rounds 7-11 Dc in each st around.
Fasten off, shape into a curl and sew to the back of the Body between Rounds 7 and 9.

HAT
Using Yarn C, make a magic loop.
Round 1 (RS) Ch1, 6dc into loop.

Round 2 Dc in each st around.
Round 3 (Dc in next st, 2dc in next st) 3 times. [9 sts]
Round 4 Dc in each st around.
Round 5 (Dc in next 2 sts, 2dc in next st) 3 times. [12 sts]
Round 6 Dc in each st around.
Round 7 (Dc in next 3 sts, 2dc in next st) 3 times. [15 sts]
Rounds 8-9 Dc in each st around.
Fasten off.
Sew stripes onto the Hat with Yarn D, then sew to the top of Head.

TO FINISH
Weave in any remaining ends.

You can add a piece of pipe cleaner inside the tail so that it's fully poseable

Otter Couple

Did you know that pairs or groups of otters hold hands (or paws) so they don't float away from each other while they sleep? It's called rafting. They're the original romantics. What could be a better gift for your sweetheart, then, than a pair of loved-up amigurumi otters? Otterly adorable!

YOU WILL NEED

• 4ply weight cotton yarn, approximately one 50g ball of each:
- Yarn A Beige
- Yarn B Light Brown

• A 2.5mm (US C/1 or B/2) hook

• 2 safety eyes, approx 5mm diameter

• Plastic nose, approx 1cm

• Black stranded cotton

• Pipe cleaners

• Stitch markers

• Toy stuffing

• PVA glue

MEASUREMENTS

Otter measures approx 12cm (4¾in) tall

NOTES

• Head and Body are worked as one piece starting from the top of the Head. All the other pieces are sewn to the Body. Choose either shade of yarn for your Otter; each piece for each Otter is made with the same colour.

HEAD AND BODY

Make a magic loop.
Round 1 (RS) Ch1 (does not count as st), 6dc into the loop. [6 sts]
Round 2 2dc in each st around. [12 sts]
Round 3 (2dc in next st, dc) 6 times. [18 sts]
Round 4 (2dc in next st, 2dc) 6 times. [24 sts]
Round 5 (2dc in next st, 3dc) 6 times. [30 sts]
Round 6 (2dc in next st, 4dc) 6 times. [36 sts]

Rounds 7-12 Dc in each dc around.
Round 13 (4dc, dc2tog) 6 times. [30 sts]
Round 14 (3dc, dc2tog) 6 times. [24 sts]
Round 15 (2dc, dc2tog) 6 times. [18 sts]
Secure the eyes between Rounds 9 and 10, approx 9 sts apart.
For the eyes, if you're using embroidery instead of safety eyes, you might like to wait until the Muzzle is attached before you sew them in place.

Stuff the Head with toy stuffing and continue stuffing as you go.
Rounds 16-18 Dc in each st around. [18 sts]
Round 19 (2dc in next st, 2dc) 6 times. [24 sts]
Rounds 20-21 Dc in each st around.
Round 22 (2dc in next st, 3dc) 6 times. [30 sts]
Rounds 23-24 Dc in each st around.
Round 25 (2dc in next st, 4dc) 6 times. [36 sts]
Rounds 26-28 Dc in each st around.
Round 29 (2dc in next st, 5dc) 6 times. [42 sts]
Rounds 30-34 Dc in each st around.
Round 35 (5dc, dc2tog) 6 times. [36 sts]
Round 36 (4dc, dc2tog) 6 times. [30 sts]
Round 37 (3dc, dc2tog) 6 times. [24 sts]
Round 38 (2dc, dc2tog) 6 times. [18 sts]
Round 39 (Dc, dc2tog) 6 times. [12 sts]
Round 40 (Dc2tog) 6 times. [6 sts]
Fasten off and weave in ends.

EARS (MAKE 2)
Make a magic loop.
Round 1 (RS) Ch1 (does not count as st), 4dc into the loop. [4 sts]
Round 2 Dc in each st around.
Fasten off, leaving a long tail.
Use the long tail to sew the Ears to the Head between Rounds 5 and 6.

MUZZLE
Make a magic loop.
Round 1 (RS) Ch1 (does not count as st), 6dc into the ring. [6 sts]
Round 2 2dc in each st around. [12 sts]
Round 3 (2dc in next st, dc) 6 times. [18 sts]
Round 4 Htr, 4tr, htr, 12dc. [18 sts]
Round 5 Htr, 4tr, htr, dc, ss in next st.
Fasten off, leaving a long tail.
Secure the plastic nose between Rounds 3 and 4 (in the middle of the tr sequence).
Embroider the mouth and stuff lightly with toy stuffing.

Use the long tail to sew the Muzzle to the Head, between Rounds 10 and 16.
If using black beads or embroidery for eyes, sew them on now.

WHISKERS
Split a strand of black embroidery thread, cut 3 pieces approx 20cm long for each otter.
Wet them in a solution of water and PVA glue. Place the soaked whiskers on a plastic sheet and let them dry.
Use these slightly stiffened threads to embroider the whiskers.

ARMS (MAKE 2)
Make a magic loop.
Round 1 (RS) Ch1 (does not count as st), 6dc into the loop. [6 sts]
Round 2 (2dc in next st, 2dc) twice. [8 sts]
Rounds 3-7 Dc in each st around.
Do not stuff, flatten the piece and start working in rows.
On the next row, work across the open top of the Arm, working each st through both layers to close the top.
Row 1 Ch1 (does not count as st), dc through both layers in each of 4 sts, turn. [4 sts]
Row 2 (Ch3, skip the first ch from hook, ss in each of next 2 ch, ss in next st, skipping the st at the base of the ch) 4 times to make paws.
Fasten off, leaving a long tail.
Use the long tail to sew the Arms to the Body, between Rounds 20 and 21.

FEET (MAKE 2)
Make a magic loop.
Round 1 (RS) Ch1 (does not count as st), 6dc into the loop. [6 sts]
Round 2 (2dc in next st, 2dc) twice. [8 sts]
Round 3 (2dc in next st, 3dc) twice. [10 sts]
Rounds 4-6 Dc in each st around.
Do not stuff, flatten the piece and start working in rows.
On the next row, work across the open top of the Foot, working each st through both layers to close and make the toes.

Row 7 Ch1 (does not count as st), dc through both layers in each of 5 sts, turn. [5 sts]
Row 8 Ch3, skip the first ch from the hook, dc in each of next 2 ch, ss in next st, skipping the st at base of ch, (ch4, skip the first ch from the hook, dc in each of next 3 ch, ss in the next st, skipping the st at the base of the ch) twice, ch3, skip the first ch from the hook, dc in each of next 2 ch, ss in the last st of the row.
Fasten off, leaving a long tail.
Use the long tail to sew the Feet to the Body, between Rounds 27 and 36.

TAIL
Make a magic loop.
Round 1 (RS) Ch1 (does not count as st), 4dc into the loop. [4 sts]
Round 2 Dc in each st around. [4 sts]
Round 3 2dc in next st, 3dc. [5 sts]
Rounds 4-5 Dc in each st around.
Round 6 2dc in next st, 4dc. [6 sts]
Rounds 7-8 Dc in each st around.
Round 9 2dc in next st, 5dc. [7 sts]
Rounds 10-11 Dc in each st around.
Round 12 2dc in next st, 6dc. [8 sts]
Rounds 13-14 Dc in each st around.
Round 15 2dc in next st, 7dc. [9 sts]
Rounds 16-17 Dc in each st around.
Round 18 2dc in next st, 8dc. [10 sts]
Rounds 19-20 Dc in each dc around.
Round 21 2dc in next st, 9dc. [11 sts]
Rounds 22-23 Dc in each dc around.
Round 24 2dc in next st, 10dc. [12 sts]
Rounds 25-32 Dc in each dc around.
Fasten off, leaving a long tail.
Insert a pipe cleaner into the tail and then stuff with toy stuffing.
Use the long tail of yarn to sew the Tail to the bottom of the Body.

Floppy–Eared Puppy

What's not to love about this big-pawed, floppy-eared cutie? You can personalise
your pup with different collar colours, or embroider his dog tag
for an extra-special bit of detail.

YOU WILL NEED

- Aran weight cotton yarn,
approximately two 50g balls
of each:
- Yarn A Orange
- Approximately one 50g ball
of each:
- Yarn B Cream
- Yarn C White
- Yarn D Dark Blue

- A 3.5mm (US E/4) hook

- 2 safety eyes, approx 15mm
diameter

- Toy stuffing

- Brown and black stranded
cotton

- Felt in blue, brown and yellow

- Fabric glue

- Red ribbon

MEASUREMENTS

20x18x15cm (8x7x6in)

NOTES

• The Head and Body are worked together as one piece. The Bone is made by making two circles and joining them to create each half of the finished Bone shape. Parts of this pattern are worked in the amigurumi method as explained on p. 6.

LEGS (MAKE 4)

Using Yarn A, make a magic loop.
Round 1 (RS) Ch1, 6dc into the loop. [6 sts]
Round 2 2dc in each st around. [12 sts]
Round 3 Dc in next 2 sts, 2dc in next st, dc in next 2 sts, 3htr in next st, htr in next 2 sts, 3htr in next st, dc in next 2 sts, 2dc in last st. [18 sts]
Round 4 Dc in each of next 3 sts, 2dc in next st, dc in each of next 2 sts, htr in next st, 2htr in next st, htr in each of next 4 sts, 2htr in next st, htr in next st, dc in next st, 2dc in next st, dc in each of next 2 sts. [22 sts]
Round 5 2dc in next st, dc in each of next 8 sts, 3htr in next st, htr in each of next 5 sts, 3htr in next st, dc in each of next 6 sts. [27 sts]
Round 6 Dc in each st around.
Round 7 Dc in next st, dc2tog, dc in each of next 8 sts, dc2tog, dc in each of next 6 sts, dc2tog, dc in each of next 6 sts. [24 sts]
Round 8 Dc in each of next 11 sts, htr3tog, htr in each of next 3 sts, htr3tog, dc in each of last 4 sts. [20 sts]
Round 9 Dc in each of next 3 sts, dc2tog, dc in each of next 4 sts, dc2tog, dc in next st, dc2tog, dc in next st, dc2tog, dc in each of next 3 sts. [16 sts]
Round 10 Dc in each of next 8 sts, dc2tog, dc in next st, dc2tog, dc in each of next 3 sts. [14 sts]
Round 11 Dc in each st around.
Round 12 Dc2tog, dc in each remaining st. [13 sts]
Rounds 13-23 Rep Rounds 11-12 another 5 times. [8 sts after Round 23]
Fasten off, leaving a long tail.
Stuff firmly with toy filling. Use the yarn tail to close the hole at the top of the Leg.

Using the image as a guide, cut paw pads out of brown felt and stick in place onto the base of the foot. Use brown stranded cotton to sew the detail on the paws. Anchor the thread to the base of the foot by sewing a few small stitches. Use the image as a guide to work long stitches, 1cm apart, 3 times over the paw to create the pads (pull the thread really tight as you do this, so it shapes the paw). Secure thread as before to keep paw shape in place, then weave in and cut off any loose ends.

EARS (MAKE 2)

Using Yarn A, make a magic loop.
Round 1 (RS) 6dc into the loop. [6 sts]
Round 2 2dc in each st around. [12 sts]
Round 3 (Dc in next st, 2dc in next st) 6 times. [18 sts]
Round 4 Dc in each st around.
Round 5 (Dc in each of next 2 sts, 2dc in next st) 6 times. [24 sts]
Round 6 Dc in each st around.
Round 7 (Dc in each of next 3 sts, 2dc in next st) 6 times. [30 sts]
Rounds 8-9 Dc in each st around.
Rounds 10-27 Dc2tog, dc in each remaining st. [12 sts at end of Round 27]
Fasten off and leave to one side until the Head and Body have been made.

EYE PATCH

Using Yarn B, make a magic loop.
Round 1 (RS) Ch1, 6dc into the loop. [6 sts]
Round 2 2dc in each st around. [12 sts]
Round 3 (Dc in next st, 2dc in next st) 6 times. [18 sts]
Round 4 Dc in each of next 4 sts, 2dc in next st, htr in each of next 2 sts, 2htr in next st, tr in each of next 2 sts, 2htr in next st, htr in each of next 2 sts, 2dc in next st, dc in each of next 4 sts, ss to first dc to join. [22 sts]
Fasten off. Insert a toy safety eye through the centre (do not fix washer yet) and leave to one side until the Head and Body have been created.

MUZZLE

Using Yarn A, ch5.
Round 1 (RS) Dc in second ch from hook, dc in each of next 2 ch, 3dc in last ch, turn and work along the opposite side of ch, dc in each of next 2 ch, 2dc in last ch. [10 sts]
Round 2 (Dc in next st, 2dc in next st) 5 times. [15 sts]
Round 3 (Dc in each of next 2 sts, 2dc in next st) 5 times. [20 sts]
Round 4 (Dc in each of next 3 sts, 2dc in next st) 5 times. [25 sts]
Round 5 (Dc in each of next 4 sts, 2dc in next st) 5 times. [30 sts]
Rounds 6-9 Dc in each st around.
Fasten off and leave to one side until the Head and Body have been created.

HEAD AND BODY

Using Yarn A, make a magic loop
Round 1 (RS) 6dc into the loop. [6 sts]
Round 2 2dc in each st around. [12 sts]
Round 3 (Dc in next st, 2dc in next st) 6 times. [18 sts]
Round 4 (Dc in each of next 2 sts, 2dc in next st) 6 times. [24 sts]
Round 5 (Dc in each of next 3 sts, 2dc in next st) 6 times. [30 sts]
Round 6 (Dc in each of next 9 sts, 2dc in next st) 3 times. [33 sts]
Round 7 (Dc in each of next 10 sts, 2dc in next st) 3 times. [36 sts]
Round 8 (Dc in each of next 11 sts, 2dc in next st) 3 times. [39 sts]
Round 9 (Dc in each of next 12 sts, 2dc in next st) 3 times. [42 sts]
Round 10 (Dc in each of next 13 sts, 2dc in next st) 3 times. [45 sts]
Round 11 (Dc in each of next 14 sts, 2dc in next st) 3 times. [48 sts]
Round 12 (Dc in each of next 15 sts, 2dc in next st) 3 times. [51 sts]
Round 13 (Dc in each of next 16 sts, 2dc in next st) 3 times. [54 sts]
Place 2 stitch markers on the next row, 15 sts apart, to mark where you will put the toy eyes.
Rounds 14-15 Dc in each st around.
Round 16 (Dc2tog, dc in each of next 7 sts) 6 times. [48 sts]
Round 17 (Dc2tog, dc in each of next 6 sts) 6 times. [42 sts]

Round 18 (Dc2tog, dc in each of next 5 sts) 6 times. [36 sts]
Round 19 (Dc2tog, dc in each of next 4 sts) 6 times. [30 sts]
Round 20 (Dc2tog) 15 times. [15 sts]

Put your working loop on a stitch holder and fix the toy safety eyes to your Head in the sts marked on Round 14 (one of the eyes will have the Eye Patch on it).
Stuff the Head. Put your working loop back onto your hook and continue:
Round 21 (Dc in each of next 4 sts, 2dc in the next st) 3 times. [18 sts]
Round 22 Dc in each st around.
Round 23 (Dc in each of next 5 sts, 2dc in the next st) 3 times. [21 sts]
Round 24 Dc in each st around.
Round 25 (Dc in each of next 6 sts, 2dc in the next st) 3 times. [24 sts]
Round 26 Dc in each st around.
Round 27 (Dc in each of next 7 sts, 2dc in the next st) 3 times. [27 sts]
Round 28 Dc in each st around.
Round 29 (Dc in each of next 8 sts, 2dc in the next st) 3 times. [30 sts]
Round 30 Dc in each st around.
Round 31 (Dc in next 9 sts, 2dc in next st) 3 times. [33 sts]
Round 32 Dc in each st around.
Round 33 (Dc in next 10 sts, 2dc in next st) 3 times. [36 sts]
Round 34 Dc in each st around.
Round 35 (Dc2tog, dc in next 10 sts) 3 times. [33 sts]
Round 36 (Dc2tog, dc in next 9 sts) 3 times. [30 sts]
Round 37 (Dc2tog, dc in each of next 3 sts) 6 times. [24 sts]
Round 38 (Dc2tog, dc in each of next 2 sts) 6 times. [18 sts]
Round 39 (Dc2tog, dc in next st) 6 times. [12 sts]
Stuff firmly.
Round 40 (Dc2tog) 6 times. [6 sts]
Fasten off, leaving a long tail. Sew the hole closed at base of Body.
Use the image as a guide to sew the Muzzle in place between the eyes, stuffing the Muzzle as you go. Weave in ends and trim.

TAIL
Using Yarn A, make a magic loop.
Round 1 (RS) 6dc into the loop. [6 sts]
Round 2 (Dc in next st, 2dc in next st) 3 times. [9 sts]
Round 3 (Dc in each of next 2 sts, 2dc in next st) 3 times. [12 sts]
Rounds 4-6 Dc in each st around.
Round 7 Dc2tog, dc in each remaining st. [11 sts]
Round 8 Dc in each st around.
Rounds 9-14 Rep Rounds 7-8 another 3 times. [8 sts after Round 14]
Rounds 15-21 Dc in each st around.
Fasten Off.
Stuff firmly and sew onto back of Body.

COLLAR
Using Yarn D, ch5.
Row 1 (RS) Dc in second ch from hook, dc in each ch to end, turn. [4 sts]
Rows 2-16 Ch1, dc in each stitch to end, ch42. [4 sts and 42 ch]
Fasten off and sew in place round the neck.

TO FINISH
Pin Legs in place so the Puppy is in a sitting position. When you are happy with the arrangement sew firmly in place. Sew Ears onto Head using the image as a guide for positioning. Sew the Eye Patch down onto the Head. Weave in ends and trim. Using the image as a guide, cut a nose out of brown felt and glue in place. Use black stranded cotton and long stitches to create the mouth. Using the image as a guide, cut the collar tag out of felt and glue in place.

BONE (MAKE 2)
CIRCLE 1
Using Yarn C, make a magic loop.
Round 1 (RS) Ch1, 6dc into the loop. [6 sts]
Round 2 2dc in each st around. [12 sts]
Rounds 3-5 Dc in each st around. [12 sts]
Ss in next st. **Fasten off.**

Finish off the puppy's little bone with a short length of brightly coloured ribbon

CIRCLE 2
Work as given for Circle 1 to the end of Round 5. Do not ss in next st or fasten off.

JOIN CIRCLES
Round 1 (RS) Dc in each of 12 sts of Circle 2, then dc in each of 12 sts of Circle 1. [24 sts]
Round 2 (Dc2tog, dc in each of next 6 sts) 3 times. [21 sts]
Round 3 (Dc2tog, dc in each of next 5 sts) 3 times. [18 sts]
Round 4 (Dc2tog, dc in each of next 4 sts) 3 times. [15 sts]
Round 5 (Dc2tog, dc in each of next 3 sts) 3 times. [12 sts]
Rounds 6-16 Dc in each st around.
Fasten off and stuff firmly.
Make second half of Bone then sew each end of Bone together to create the full Bone. Tie a piece of red ribbon around the join.

Tiny Deer

With his neatly coiffed hair and baby blue bow tie, this little deer's dressed to his best and ready to party! Embroider the eyes with black thread to be safe if you're planning to give this cute creature to a baby or small child.

YOU WILL NEED

• 4ply weight cotton yarn, approximately one ball of each:
- Yarn A White
- Yarn B Light Grey
- Yarn C Light Blue

• A 2.5mm (US C/2 or D/3) hook

• Toy stuffing

• Stitch markers

• 2 safety eyes, 6mm

• Stranded cotton in black and brown

• Blusher and make-up brush (optional)

MEASUREMENTS

12cm (4¾in) tall

BODY

Using Yarn A, make a magic loop.
Round 1 (RS) Ch1 (does not count as a st throughout), 6dc into loop. [6 sts]
Round 2 2dc in each dc around. [12 sts]
Round 3 (Dc in next dc, 2dc in next dc) 6 times. [18 sts]
Round 4 (Dc in next 2 dc, 2dc in next dc) 6 times. [24 sts]
Round 5 (Dc in next 3 dc, 2dc in next dc) 6 times. [30 sts]

Round 6 (Dc in next 4 dc, 2dc in next dc) 6 times. [36 sts]
Round 7 (Dc in next 5 dc, 2dc in next dc) 6 times. [42 sts]
Rounds 8-12 Dc in each dc around.
Round 13 Dc2tog, dc in next 40 dc. [41 sts]
Round 14 Dc2tog, dc in next 37 dc, dc2tog. [39 sts]
Rounds 15-17 Dc in each dc around. [39 sts]
Round 18 Dc in next dc, 2dc in next dc, dc in next 16 dc, dc2tog, dc in next dc, dc2tog, dc in next 16 dc. [38 sts]
Round 19 Dc in each dc around.
Round 20 Dc in next dc, 2dc in next dc, dc in next 16 dc, dc2tog, dc in next dc, dc2tog, dc in next 15 dc. [37 sts]
Round 21 Dc in each dc around. [37 sts]
Round 22 Dc in next dc, 2dc in next dc, dc in next 16 dc, (dc2tog) 2 times, dc in next 15 dc. [36 sts]
Round 23 Dc in each dc around.
Round 24 Dc in next 2 dc, 2dc in next dc, dc in next 15 dc, (dc2tog) 2 times, dc in next 14 dc, turn. [35 sts]
Start stuffing the Head firmly; continue on as you work.
Continue on in rows.
Row 25 (WS) Ch1, dc in next 12 dc, dc2tog, dc in next 2 dc, dc2tog, dc in next 11 dc, turn. [27 sts]
Row 26 (RS) Ch1, dc in next 10 dc, dc2tog, dc in next 2 dc, dc2tog, dc in next 11 dc, turn. [25 sts]

Row 27 Ch1, dc in next 10 dc, dc2tog, dc in next 2 dc, dc2tog, dc in next 9 dc, turn. [23 sts]
Row 28 Ch1, dc in next 9 dc, (dc2tog) 2 times, dc in next 10 dc, turn. [21 sts]
Row 29 Ch1, dc in next 9 dc, (dc2tog) 2 times, dc in next 8 dc, turn. [19 sts]
Flatten the two sides together and bring the front edges of the chest together. The first and last dc of Row 29 should meet.
Ss through the bl of each st across joining each side. You should have an opening for the Neck over the unworked sts from Round 24 and the row ends from Rows 25-29.
Fasten off and weave in tail.
Place marker in the first st on the Neck after the ss seam.

NECK

Join Yarn A into marked st on Neck.
Round 1 (RS) Dc in first 7 sts, dc in next 6 row-ends along the left side of the Neck, dc in next 6 row-ends along the right side of the Neck. [18 sts]
Round 2 (Dc in next 2 dc, 2dc in next dc) 6 times. [24 sts]
Ss in next st and **fasten off**.

HEAD

Using Yarn A, make a magic loop.
Rounds 1-3 (RS) As Rounds 1-3 of Body. [18 sts]
Round 4 Dc in next dc, 2dc in next dc, dc in next 14 dc, 2dc in next dc, dc in next dc. [20 sts]
Round 5 Dc in next dc, 2dc in next dc, dc in next 16 dc, 2dc in next dc, dc in next dc. [22 sts]

Round 6 Dc in next 8 dc, (2dc in next dc, dc in next dc) 3 times, dc in next 8 dc. [25 sts]
Mark the 12th and 13th sts of Round 6, which indicates the top centre of the Head.
Round 7 Dc in next 6 dc, (2dc in next dc, dc in next 3 dc) 4 times, dc in next 3 dc. [29 sts]
Round 8 Dc in next 7 dc, (2dc in next dc, dc in next 4 dc, 2dc in next dc, dc in next 3 dc) 2 times, dc in next 4 dc. [33 sts]
Round 9 Dc in next 8 dc, (2dc in next dc, dc in next 4 dc, 2dc in next dc, dc in next 5 dc) 2 times, dc in next 3 dc. [37 sts]
Round 10 Dc in next 9 dc, (2dc in next dc, dc in next 5 dc) 4 times, dc in next 4 dc. [41 sts]
Round 11 Dc in next 10 dc, (2dc in next dc, dc in next 6 dc, 2dc in next dc, dc in next 5 dc) 2 times, dc in next 5 dc. [45 sts]
Round 12 Dc in next 11 dc, (2dc in next dc, dc in next 6 dc, 2dc in next dc, dc in next 7 dc) 2 times, dc in next 4 dc. [49 sts]
Round 13 Dc in next 12 dc, (2dc in next dc, dc in next 7 dc) 4 times, dc in next 5 dc. [53 sts]
Round 14 Dc in next 13 dc, (2dc in next dc, dc in next 8 dc, 2dc in next dc, dc in next 7 dc) 2 times, dc in next 6 dc. [57 sts]
Rounds 15-22 Dc in each dc around.
Using brown stranded cotton, sew the nose over Rounds 1-3. The nose should be centred around the marked sts from Round 6. The base of the nose should go through the starting magic loop, while the top of the nose should be approx 5 sts wide.
Insert safety eyes between Rounds 10-11, 18 sts apart. Using black stranded cotton, sew eyebrows above each eye.
Round 23 (Dc in next 17 dc, dc2tog) 3 times. [54 sts]
Round 24 (Dc in next 7 dc, dc2tog) 6 times. [48 sts]
Round 25 (Dc in next 6 dc, dc2tog) 6 times. [42 sts]

Round 26 (Dc in next 5 dc, dc2tog) 6 times. [36 sts]
Start stuffing the Head firmly; continue on as you work.
Round 27 (Dc in next 4 dc, dc2tog) 6 times. [30 sts]
Round 28 (Dc in next 3 dc, dc2tog) 6 times. [24 sts]
Round 29 Dc in each dc around. [24 sts]
Round 30 (Dc in next 2 dc, dc2tog) 6 times. [18 sts]
Round 31 (Dc in next dc, dc2tog) 6 times. [12 sts]
Round 32 (Dc2tog) 6 times. [6 sts]
Ss in next stitch and fasten off.
Thread tail through final 6 sts, working from the centre and up through the fl of the st, pull tight to close hole and weave in ends.
Sew the Head to the opening of the Neck, making sure you stuff the Neck first.
The opening of the Neck should sit over Rounds 15-22 of base of Head.

Tilt the Head to the side slightly for an even cuter look.

LEFT BACK LEG
Using Yarn B, make a magic loop.
Rounds 1-4 As Rounds 1-4 of Body. [24 sts]
Rounds 5-8 Dc in each dc around. [24 sts]
Round 9 Dc in next 6 dc, (dc2tog) 6 times, dc in next 6 dc. [18 sts]
Mark the 9th and 10th st of Round 9, which indicate the top centre of Leg.
Change to Yarn A.
Round 10 Dc in next 4 dc, (dc2tog) 5 times, dc in next 4 dc. [13 sts]
Stuff base of Leg firmly, continuing to stuff as you work (the top of the leg needs less stuffing than the base).
Rounds 11-18 Dc in each dc around.
Round 19 Dc in next 2 dc only (final st marks end of round). [2 sts]
Flatten top of Leg and ss through sts on both sides to close.

RIGHT BACK LEG

Using Yarn B, make a magic loop.
Rounds 1-18 (RS) As Rounds 1-18 of Left Back Leg.
Round 19 Dc in next 9 dc only (final st marks new end of round). [9 sts]
Flatten top of Leg and ss through sts on both sides to close. **Fasten Off.**

LEFT FRONT LEG

Using Yarn B, make a magic loop.
Rounds 1-3 (RS) As Rounds 1-3 of Body. [18 sts]
Round 4 (Dc in next 5 dc, 2dc in next dc) 3 times. [21 sts]
Rounds 5-7 Dc in each dc around.
Round 8 Dc in next 4 dc, (dc2tog) 6 times, dc in next 5 dc. [15 sts]
Mark the 7th and 8th sts of Round 8 to indicate the top centre of Leg. Change to Yarn A.
Round 9 Dc in next 4 dc, (dc2tog) 3 times, dc in next 5 dc. [12 sts]
Rounds 10-17 Dc in each dc around.
Round 18 Dc in next 3 dc only (final st marks new end of round). [3 sts]
Flatten top of Leg and ss through sts on both sides to close. **Fasten Off.**

RIGHT FRONT LEG

Using Yarn B, make a magic loop.
Rounds 1-17 As Rounds 1-17 of Left Front Leg.
Round 18 Dc in next 8 dc only (final st marks new end of round). [8 sts]
Flatten top of Leg and ss through sts on both sides to close. **Fasten Off.**
Pin all the Legs to the Body and once happy with the position use the tails to sew in place.

EARS (MAKE 2)

Using Yarn A, make a magic loop.
Round 1 (RS) Ch1, 6dc into loop. [6 sts]
Round 2 (Dc in next dc, 2dc in next dc) 3 times. [9 sts]
Round 3 (Dc in next 2 dc, 2dc in next dc) 3 times. [12 sts]
Round 4 Dc in each dc around.
Round 5 (Dc in next 3 dc, 2dc in next dc) 3 times. [15 sts]
Round 6 Dc in each dc around.
Round 7 (Dc in next 4 dc, 2dc in next dc) 3 times. [18 sts]
Round 8 (Dc in next 2 dc, 2dc in next dc) 6 times. [24 sts]
Round 9 (Dc in next 5 dc, 2dc in next dc) 4 times. [28 sts]

Once the ears are attached, gently dab them with blusher, working from the inner ear

Rounds 10-12 Dc in each dc around.
Round 13 (Dc in next 5 dc, dc2tog) 4 times. [24 sts]
Round 14 (Dc in next 2 dc, dc2tog) 6 times. [18 sts]
Round 15 (Dc in next dc, dc2tog) 6 times. [12 sts]
Do not stuff Ear.
Flatten the sts from Round 15 and dc through both layers to close opening. **Fasten Off.**

Using the tail, sew Ears to Head. The front corners of each Ear should sit between Rounds 18-19 of the Head, 5 sts apart. The back bottom edge of each Ear should sit between Rounds 19-20 of the Head.

TAIL

Using Yarn A, make a magic loop.
Round 1 (RS) Ch1, 4dc into loop. [4 sts]
Round 2 (Dc in next dc, 2dc in next dc) 2 times. [6 sts]
Round 3 (Dc in next dc, 2dc in next dc) 3 times. [9 sts]
Round 4 (Dc in next 2 dc, 2dc in next dc) 3 times. [12 sts]
Round 5 Dc in each dc around.
Round 6 (Dc in next 3 dc, 2dc in next dc) 3 times. [15 sts]
Round 7 Dc in each dc around.
Round 8 (Dc in next 3 dc, dc2tog) 3 times. [12 sts]
Round 9 (Dc2tog) 6 times. [6 sts]
Do not stuff Ear.
Flatten the sts from Round 9 and dc through both layers to close opening.

The legs are made from the bottom up, with a colour change after round 8

Fasten Off.
Using the tail, sew the Tail to the Body.

TUFT
Using Yarn B, make a magic loop.
Round 1 (RS) Ch1, 6dc into loop. [6 sts]
Round 2 (Dc in next dc, 2dc in next dc) 3 times. [9 sts]
Round 3 Dc in each dc around.
Round 4 (Dc in next 2 dc, 2dc in next dc) 3 times. [12 sts]
Round 5 Dc in each dc around.
Round 6 2dc in next 2 dc, dc in next 4 dc, 2dc in next dc, dc in next 5 dc. [15 sts]
Round 7 Dc in next dc, 2dc in next 2 dc, dc in next 6 dc, 2dc in next dc, dc in next 5 dc. [18 sts]
Round 8 Dc in next dc, 2dc in next 4 dc, dc in next 5 dc, 2dc in next 2 dc, dc in next 6 dc. [24 sts]
Round 9 Dc in next 4 dc, 2dc in next 3 dc, dc in next 10 dc, 2dc in next dc, dc in next 6 dc. [28 sts]
Rounds 10-12 Dc in each dc around.
Round 13 Dc in next 7 dc, dc2tog, dc in next 12 dc, dc2tog, dc in next 5 dc. [26 sts]
Round 14 Dc in next 5 dc, (dc2tog) 2 times, dc in next 10 dc, (dc2tog) 2times, dc in next 3 dc. [22 sts]
Round 15 Dc in next 5 dc, (dc2tog) 2 times, dc in next 7 dc, (dc2tog) 2 times, dc in next 2 dc. [18 sts]
Round 16 (Dc in next 4 dc, dc2tog) 3 times. [15 sts]
Round 17 Dc in each dc around.
Round 18 (Dc in next 3 dc, dc2tog) 3 times. [12 sts]
Round 19 Dc in each dc around.
Round 20 (Dc in next 2 dc, dc2tog) 3 times. [9 sts]
Do not stuff Tuft.
Flatten the sts from Round 20 and dc through both layers to close opening.
Fasten Off.
Use black stranded cotton to sew small straight lines across the top of the Tuft. You should use the images for guidance.
Sew the Tuft to the top of the Head between the Ears. Sew along the underside of the Tuft to attach it to

The teardrop tail is stitched approximately 7-8 rounds in from the rear side of the body

the Head, ensuring that no stitches are seen on the upper side.

BOW
Using Yarn C, ch46.
Row 1 (RS) Dc in second ch from hook and each ch across, turn. [45 sts]
Rows 2-9 Ch1, dc in each st across, turn.
Fasten off leaving a long tail.
Sew the short edges of the Bow together and wind the yarn tails a few times around the middle to squeeze it together. Secure the ends and weave in all tails at the back near the seam.

BOW CENTRE
Using Yarn C, ch12.
Row 1 (RS) Dc in second ch from hook and each ch across, turn. [11 sts]
Rows 2-3 Ch1, dc in each st across, turn.
Fasten off leaving a long tail.

Wrap the Bow Centre around the main Bow over the wound yarn that squeezed the middle together. Sew the ends together at the back of the Bow. Work a few stitches through the Bow itself to prevent the centre of the Bow from sliding around.

NECK BAND
Using Yarn C, ch24.
Rows 1-3 As Rows 1-3 of Bow Centre. [23 sts]
Fasten off leaving a long tail.
Position around Neck and sew two short ends together. Sew the Bow into position onto the Neck Band.

TO FINISH
Weave in any remaining ends.
Apply cosmetic blusher to the inside of the Ears using a brush (optional).

Homey Hermit Crab

This happy hermit loves a day at the beach, but won't go without his home comforts – or even his home. We can all relate! This is a great time to master the invisible decrease – a simple adaptation that make decreases barely detectable on tightly curved shapes.

YOU WILL NEED

• 4ply weight cotton yarn, approximately one 50g ball of each:
- Yarn A Orange
- Yarn B White
- Yarn C Green
- Yarn D Pink
- Yarn E Light Blue

• A 2.75mm (US C/2) hook

• 2 black safety eyes, 11mm

• Toy stuffing

• Tapestry needle

• Brown stranded cotton

MEASUREMENTS

13cm (5in) tall

ABBREVIATIONS

inv dec (invisible decrease) Insert hook through fl of next 2 sts, yrh and pull through the two fl on hook, yrh and pull through two loops on hook (alternatively work standard dc2tog)
bobble Worked individually over surface of Shell, join yarn to st on Shell, ch2, tr3tog in same st, ch1, ss into Shell one round below

NOTES

• The Crab is made up of separate pieces, which are joined together at the end.
• Work standard decreases on Shell, and invisible decreases (inv dec – see Abbreviations) on all other pieces.

SHELL

Using Yarn B, make a magic loop.
Round 1 (RS) Ch1 (does not count as st throughout), 6dc into the loop. [6 dc]
Round 2 Dc in each st around.
Round 3 (1dc, 2dc in next st) 3 times. [9 dc]
Round 4 Change to Yarn C, (2dc, 2dc in next st) 3 times. [12 dc]
Round 5 Change to Yarn D, (3dc, 2dc in next st) 3 times. [15 dc]
Round 6 Change to Yarn B, (4dc, 2dc in next st) 3 times. [18 dc]
Rounds 7-8 As Round 2.
Round 9 (5dc, 2dc in next st) 3 times. [21 dc]
Round 10 As Round 2.
Round 11 Change to Yarn C, (6dc, 2dc in next st) 3 times. [24 dc]
Round 12 Change to Yarn D, as Round 2.
Round 13 Change to Yarn B, ss in each st around.
Round 14 Working into ss, (dc in next st, 2dc in next st) 12 times. [36 dc]
Round 15 As Round 2.
Round 16 Change to Yarn C, (5dc, 2dc in next st) 6 times. [42 dc]

Round 17 Change to Yarn D, (6dc, 2dc in next st) 6 times. [48 dc]
Rounds 18-21 Change to Yarn B, as Round 2.
Round 22 Change to Yarn D, (6dc, dc2tog) 6 times. [42 sts]
Round 23 Change to Yarn C, (5dc, dc2tog) 6 times. [36 sts]
Round 24 Change to Yarn B, as Round 13.
Round 25 Working into ss, (2dc, 2dc in next st) 12 times. [48 dc]
Round 26 Change to Yarn C, (7dc, 2dc in next st) 6 times. [54 dc]
Round 27 Change to Yarn D, (8dc, 2dc in next st) 6 times. [60 dc]
Rounds 28-32 Change to Yarn B, as Round 2.
Round 33 Change to Yarn D, (8dc, dc2tog) 6 times. [54 sts]
Round 34 Change to Yarn C, (7dc, dc2tog) 6 times. [48 sts]
Round 35 Change to Yarn B, (6dc, dc2tog) 6 times. [42 sts]
Fasten off, leaving a long tail for sewing Shell to Body.

BOBBLES

Using Yarn E, and using the image as a guide, add bobbles around the surface of the Shell over the Yarn B rounds, evenly spaced.
Fasten off and weave in ends.

BODY
Using Yarn A, make a magic loop.
Round 1 (RS) Ch1, 7dc into the loop.
[7dc]
Round 2 2dc in each st around. [14 dc]
Round 3 (Dc, 2dc in next st) 7 times.
[21 dc]
Round 4 (2dc, 2dc in next st) 7 times.
[28 dc]
Round 5 (3dc, 2dc in next st) 7 times.
[35 dc]
Round 6 (4dc, 2dc in next st) 7 times.
[42 dc]
Rounds 7-9 Dc in each st around.
Round 10 (4dc, inv dec) 7 times.
[35 sts]
Round 11 (3dc, inv dec) 7 times.
[28 sts]
Round 12 (2dc, inv dec) 7 times.
[21 sts]
Stuff firmly.
Round 13 (Dc, inv dec) 7 times. [14 sts]
Round 14 (Inv dec) 7 times. [7 sts]
Fasten off, thread tail through front
loop of each st of final round and pull
tight to close the hole. Weave in ends.

EYES (MAKE 2)
With Yarn A, make a magic loop.
Round 1 (RS) Ch1, 6dc into the loop.
[6 dc]
Round 2 2dc in each st around. [12 dc]
Rounds 3-7 Dc in each st around.
Add a safety eye between Rounds
4-5.
Rounds 8-11 As Round 3.
Round 12 2dc in next 3 sts, dc, (inv
dec) 3 times, 2dc. [12 sts]
Rounds 13-14 As Round 3.
Fasten off, leaving a long tail for
sewing Eyes to Body.

CLAWS (MAKE 2)
Snip off a 25cm length of Yarn A; this
will be used to sew the Claw into
shape before you stuff and finish the
Claw.
With Yarn A, make a magic loop.
Round 1 (RS) Ch1, 6dc into the loop.
[6 dc]
Round 2 2dc in each st around. [12 dc]
Round 3 Dc in each st around.
Round 4 (Dc, 2dc in next st) 6 times.
[18 dc]

Round 5 As Round 3.
Round 6 (2dc, 2dc in next st) 6 times.
[24 dc]
Round 7 As Round 3.
Round 8 (3dc, 2dc in next st) 6 times.
[30 dc]
Rounds 9-13 As Round 3.
Round 14 (3dc, inv dec) 6 times. [24
sts]
Round 15 (2dc, inv dec) 6 times. [18 sts]
Fold Claw flat and, using the strand
of Yarn A, backstitch a line from
Round 1 to Round 14, one-third from
side of Claw, to create claw shape.
Add stuffing to both sections.
Round 16 (Dc, inv dec) 6 times. [12 sts]
Rounds 17-22 As Round 3.
Fasten off, leaving a long tail for
sewing Claw to Body.

LEGS (make 6)
Using Yarn A, make a magic loop.
Round 1 (RS) Ch1, 7dc into the loop.
[7 dc]
Rounds 2-5 Dc in each st around.

Round 6 3dc in first st, 6dc. [9 dc]
Rounds 7-10 Dc around.
Fasten off leaving a long tail for
sewing Legs to Body.

TO MAKE UP
Stuff Shell. Place Shell over Body at
an angle so it covers more of one
side, then sew in place. For a tidy
seam, sew Shell around the posts,
rather than loops, of stitches from
final round.
Add stuffing to Eyes and sew to front
of Body, on opposite side from where
Shell is angled.
Top up stuffing in Claws and sew
them to sides of Body, close to, but
behind the Eyes.
Add a little stuffing to Legs and sew
to Body, 3 per side, behind the Claws.
Using Yarn D, embroider 2 cheeks
between Eyes and Claws. Using
brown stranded cotton, embroider
a smile below the Eyes.
Weave in all ends.

As you add stuffing inside the antennae, gently shape them so they curve upwards

Soft Seal

With his super-soft body and blue cotton muzzle, this lovely creature is sure to work his way into your heart. Seal the deal and hook up this fluffy bundle of joy!

YOU WILL NEED

• Super chunky weight yarn with a furry texture, such as Scheepjes Furry Tales; approximately one 50g ball of:
- Yarn A White

• 4ply weight cotton yarn, a small amount of:
- Yarn B Baby Blue

• A 4mm (G/6) hook

• A 3mm (C/2 or D/3) hook

• Toy stuffing

• 2 safety eyes, 9mm

• A small amount of dark grey stranded cotton

• Stitch markers

• Tapestry and embroidery needles

MEASUREMENTS

22cm (8½in) from nose to tail

NOTES

• When working with furry yarn, mark the last stitch of every pattern repeat at the very least or more if required. For example, for Round 3, mark the 6th, 12th and 18th stitches. For Round 14, mark the 4th, 8th, 12th, 16th, 20th, 24th, 28th and 32nd stitches. This will help you keep track of your stitches.
• The end of each round indicates the top side of the Head and Body. You can mark the top side to help orientate the assembly later if you wish.

HEAD AND BODY

Using a 4mm hook and Yarn A, make a magic loop.
Round 1 (RS) Ch1 (does not count as st throughout), 6dc into ring. [6 dc]
Round 2 2dc in each dc around. [12 dc]
Round 3 (Dc in next dc, 2dc in next dc) 6 times. [18 dc]
Round 4 (Dc in next 2 dc, 2dc in next dc) 6 times. [24 dc]
Round 5 (Dc in next 3 dc, 2dc in next dc) 6 times. [30 dc]
Round 6 (Dc in next 4 dc, 2dc in next dc) 6 times. [36 dc]
Leave the 6th and 30th stitches of Round 6 marked. This will indicate where the eyes will be inserted.
Rounds 7-11 Dc in each dc around. [36 dc]
Leave the 12th and 24th stitches of Round 11 marked. This will indicate where the Fore Flippers will be sewn. Insert the safety eyes at

approximately the 8th and 28th st between Rounds 6 and 7. Use the marked stitches from Round 6 as a guide.
Rounds 12-13 Dc in each dc around.
Round 14 (Dc in next 7 dc, dc2tog) 4 times.
[32 sts]
Round 15 Dc in each dc around.
Round 16 (Dc in next 6 dc, dc2og) 4 times.
[28 sts]
Round 17 Dc in each dc around.
Round 18 (Dc in next 5 dc, dc2tog) 4 times.
[24 sts]
Round 19 Dc in each dc around. Start stuffing the Head and Body firmly with toy stuffing and continue to do so as you crochet the rest of the Body.
Round 20 (Dc in next 4 dc, dc2tog) 4 times. [20 sts]
Round 21 Dc in each dc around.
Round 22 (Dc in next 3 dc, dc2tog) 4 times. [16 sts]
Round 23 (Dc in next 2 dc, dc2tog) 4 times. [12 sts]
Round 24 (Dc2tog) 6 times. [6 sts]
Slip stitch in next stitch and **fasten off**, leaving a long tail.
Thread the tail through a needle. Weave the needle through the front loop of each of the 6 dc, always going in the direction from the centre and under the front loop. Pull tail to close. Insert the needle through the middle of the hole and pull through the Body. Weave in the tail.

MUZZLE

Using a 3mm hook and Yarn B, make a magic ring.

Rounds 1-6 Work as Rounds 1-6 of Head and Body

Round 7 (Dc in next 5 dc, 2dc in next dc) 6 times. [42 dc]

Round 8 (Dc in next 6 dc, 2dc in next dc) 6 times. [48 dc]

Round 9 (Dc in next 7 dc, 2dc in next dc) 6 times. [54 dc]

Ss in next stitch and **fasten off**, leaving a long tail for sewing the Muzzle to the face.

Using dark grey stranded cotton and the image as a guide, embroider the nose over Rounds 1-3 of the Muzzle. The bottom of the nose should go through the start magic ring, while the top of the nose should be 6 sts wide.

FORE FLIPPERS (MAKE 2)

Using a 4mm hook and Yarn A, make a magic ring.

Round 1 (RS) Ch1, 6dc into ring. [6 dc]

Round 2 (Dc in next dc, 2dc in next dc) 3 times. [9 dc]

Round 3 (Dc in next 2 dc, 2dc in next dc) 3 times. [12 dc]

Rounds 4-5 Dc in each dc around. Flatten the opening of the Flipper and work 6dc through both layers to close the opening.

Fasten off, leaving a long yarn tail.

HIND FLIPPERS (MAKE 2)

Using a 4mm hook and Yarn A, make a magic ring.

Round 1 (RS) Ch1, 6dc into ring. [6 dc]

Round 2 (Dc in next 2 dc, 2dc in next dc) twice. [8 dc]

Round 3 (Dc in next 3 dc, 2dc in next dc) twice. [10 dc]

Rounds 4-8 Dc in each dc around.

Round 9 (Dc in next 3 dc, dc2tog) 2 times. [8 sts]

Flatten the opening of the Flipper and work 4dc through both layers to close the opening.

Fasten off, leaving a long yarn tail.

TO MAKE UP

Sew the Muzzle to the face between the eyes. The eyes should lie approximately in line with the top of the embroidered nose of the Muzzle. Stuff a little toy stuffing under the Muzzle as you join.

Sew the Fore Flippers to the Body.

The flat edge of each Flipper should be parallel to the plane of the Body. The front corner of the flat edge of each Flipper should be positioned above the marked stitches in Round 11 of the Body.

Sew the Hind Flippers to the back of the Body. The Hind Flippers should be in the same plane as the Fore Flippers. The inside corners of each Flipper should meet in the centre of the back end of the Body.

Make fore flippers separately, then sew them into the gap left in the body for them

Add the safety eyes before completing the head - between Rounds 6 and 7

Sleepy Lambkin

This sleepy lamb has tired itself out by gambolling in the fields!
Hook one up as a lovely gift, or just keep it for yourself.

YOU WILL NEED

- DK weight cotton yarn, approximately two 50g balls of:
  - Yarn A Off White
- Approximately one 50g ball of:
  - Yarn B Light Beige
- A small amount of yellow, pink, green and purple yarn
- Black stranded cotton
- A 2.5mm (US B/1 or C/2) hook
- A 3mm (US C/2 or D/3) hook
- Stitch marker

MEASUREMENTS

25cm (9¾in) long

NOTES

• All parts are made separately. You should refer to the images when joining the parts together.

FLEECE PATTERN

Throughout the pattern you will be asked to work in the Fleece pattern as follows:

Round 1 (Working in fl only) dc in next st, (ch6, dc in next st) rep to end.
Round 2 Working in unused bl 2 rounds below, dc in each st around.
Round 3 Dc in each st around.

BODY

Using a 3mm hook and Yarn A, make a magic loop.
Round 1 (RS) Ch1 (does not count as st throughout), 6dc in loop. [6 sts]
Round 2 (RS) As Round 1 of Fleece pattern.
Round 3 Working in unused bl from 2 rounds below, 2dc in each st around. [12 sts]
Round 4 (Dc in next st, 2dc in next st) 6 times. [18 sts]
Round 5 As Round 1 of Fleece pattern.
Round 6 Working in unused bl from 2 rounds below, (dc in next 2 sts, 2dc in next st) 6 times. [24 sts]
Round 7 (Dc in next 3 sts, 2dc in next st) 6 times. [30 sts]
Round 8 As Round 1 of Fleece pattern.
Round 9 Working in unused bl from 2 rounds below, (dc in next 4 sts, 2dc in next st) 6 times. [36 sts]
Round 10 (Dc in next 5 sts, 2dc in next st) 6 times. [42 sts]
Rounds 11-16 As Rounds 1-3 of Fleece pattern.
Rounds 17-18 As Rounds 1-2 of Fleece pattern.

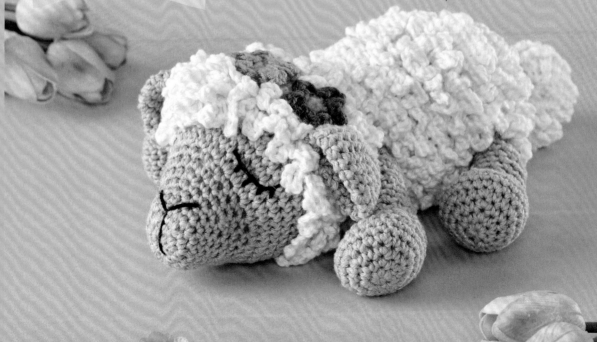

Round 19 (Dc in next 5 sts, dc2tog) 6 times. [36 sts]

Rounds 20-22 As Rounds 1-3 of Fleece pattern.

Round 23 As Round 1 of Fleece pattern.

Round 24 Working in unused bl from 2 rounds below, (dc in next 4 sts, dc2tog) 6 times. [30 sts]

Round 25 Dc in each st around.

Round 26 As Round 1 of Fleece pattern.

Round 27 Working in unused bl from 2 rounds below, dc in each st around.

Round 28 (Dc in next 3 sts, dc2tog) 6 times. [24 sts]

Stuff Body and cont stuffing as you work.

Round 29-31 As Rounds 1-3 of Fleece pattern.

Round 32 As Round 1 of Fleece pattern.

Round 33 Working in unused bl from 2 rounds below, (dc in next 2 sts, dc2tog) 6 times. [18 sts]

Round 34 Dc in each st around.

Fasten off.

HEAD

Using a 3mm hook and Yarn B, make a magic loop.

Round 1 (RS) Ch1, 6dc in loop. [6 sts]

Round 2 (RS) 2dc in each st around. [12 sts]

Round 3 (Dc in next st, 2dc in next st) 6 times. [18 sts]

Rounds 4-7 Dc in each st around.

Round 8 (Dc in next 2 sts, 2dc in next st) 6 times. [24 sts]

Rounds 9-10 Dc in each st around.

Round 11 Dc in next 3 sts, 2dc in next 18 sts, dc in final 3 sts. [42 sts]

Rounds 12-16 Dc in each st around. Change to Ecru.

Rounds 17-22 As Rounds 1-3 of Fleece pattern.

Round 23 As Round 1 of Fleece pattern.

Round 24 Working in unused bl from 2 rounds below, (dc in next 5 sts, dc2tog) 6 times. [36 sts]

Round 25 Dc in each st around.

Round 26 As Round 1 of Fleece pattern.

Round 27 Working in unused bl from 2 rounds below, (dc in next 4 sts, dc2tog) 6 times. [30 sts]

Round 28 (Dc in next 3 sts, dc2tog) 6 times.
[24 sts]

Stuff Head being careful not to stretch the stitches. Cont stuffing as you work.

Round 29 As Round 1 of Fleece pattern.

Round 30 Working in unused bl from 2 rounds below, (dc in next 2 sts, dc2tog) 6 times. [18 sts]

Round 31 (Dc in next st, dc2tog) 6 times.
[12 sts]

Round 32 As Round 1 of Fleece pattern.

Round 33 Working in unused bl from 2 rounds below, (dc2tog) 6 times.

Fasten off.

Thread tail through final 6 sts, pulling tight to close.

Using black stranded cotton, embroider a large straight line for each eye over Rounds 11-13. Then embroider a Y shape over the magic loop for the nose and mouth. You can use the images as a guide.
Sew the Head to the final round of Body.

TOP KNOT

Using a 3mm hook and Yarn A, make a magic loop.

Round 1 (RS) Ch1, 6dc in loop. [6 sts]

Round 2 (RS) As Round 1 of Fleece pattern.

Round 3 Working in unused bl from 2 rounds below, (dc in next 2 sts, 2dc in next st) twice.
[8 sts]

Round 4 (Dc in next 3 sts, 2dc in next st) twice. [10 sts]

Round 5 As Round 1 of Fleece pattern.

Round 6 Working in unused bl from 2 rounds below, (dc in next 4 sts, 2dc in next st) twice.
[12 sts]

Round 7 (Dc in next 5 sts, 2dc in next st) twice. [14 sts]

Fasten off.

Using the image as a guide, sew the Top Knot to the top of the Head.

EARS (MAKE 2)

Using a 3.5mm hook and Yarn B, make a magic loop.

Rounds 1-3 (RS) As Rounds 1-3 of Head. [18 sts]

Round 4 (Dc in next 2 sts, 2dc in next st) 6 times. [24 sts]

Rounds 5-8 Dc in each st around.

Round 9 (Dc in next 2 sts, dc2tog) 6 times.
[18 sts]

Round 10 (Dc in next st, dc2tog) 6 times. [12 sts]

Fasten off leaving a long tail.
Fold the Ears slightly to form the shape and sew the opening closed. Sew the Ears to the top of the Head.

FRONT LEGS (MAKE 2)

Using a 3mm hook and Yarn B make a magic loop.

Rounds 1-3 As Rounds 1-3 of Head. [18 sts]

Round 4 (Dc in next 2 sts, 2dc in next st) 6 times. [24 sts]

Rounds 5-6 Dc in each st around.

Round 7 Dc in next 5 sts, (dc2tog, dc in next 2 sts) 4 times, dc in final 3 sts. [20 sts]

Round 8 Dc in next 5 sts, (dc2tog, dc in next st) 4 times, dc in final 3 sts. [16 sts]

Round 9 (Dc2tog) first 2 sts, dc in each st to end. [15 sts]

Round 10 Dc in each st around.
Stuff Leg and cont stuffing as you work.

Round 11 (Dc in next 3 sts, dc2tog) 3 times.
[12 sts]

Rounds 12-13 Dc in each st around.

Round 14 Dc in next 5 sts, (dc2tog) next 2 sts, dc in final 5 sts. [11 sts]

Rounds 15-16 Dc in each st around.

Round 17 Dc in next 9 sts, (dc2tog) final 2 sts. [10 sts]

Rounds 18-19 Dc in each at around.

Round 20 Dc in next 4 sts, (dc2tog) next 2 sts, dc in final 4 sts. [9 sts]

Round 21 Dc in each st around.

Fasten off leaving a long tail.

BACK LEGS (MAKE 2)

Using a 3mm hook and Yarn B, make a magic loop.

Rounds 1-16 As Rounds 1-16 of Front Legs. [11 sts]

Round 18 (Dc in next 2 sts, dc2tog) twice, (dc2tog) next 2 sts, dc in final st. [8 sts]

Fasten off leaving a long tail.

Using the image as a guide, pin the Legs in place either side of the Body. Once happy with the position, use the tails to sew in place.

TAIL

Using a 3mm hook and Yarn A, make a magic loop.

Round 1 (RS) Ch1, 6dc in loop. [6 sts]

Round 2 (RS) As Round 1 of Fleece pattern.

Round 3 Working in unused bl 2 rounds below, 2dc in each st around. [12 sts]

Round 4 As Round 1 of Fleece pattern.

Round 5 Working in unused bl 2 rounds below, (dc in next st, 2dc in next st) 6 times. [18 sts]

Round 6 As Round 1 of Fleece pattern.

Round 7 Working in unused bl 2 rounds below, dc in each st around.

Round 8 As Round 1 of Fleece pattern.

Round 9 Working in unused bl 2 rounds below, (dc in next st, dc2tog) 6 times. [12 sts]

Round 10 As Round 1 of Fleece pattern.

Round 11 Working in unused bl 2 rounds below, (dc2tog) 6 times. [6 sts]

Change to Yarn B.

Rounds 12-17 Dc in each st around.

Fasten off.

Sew the Tail to the back of the Body.

HEADBAND (MAKE 3)

Using a 2.5mm hook and green yarn, ch19.

Row 1 Dc in second ch from hook and each ch across.

Fasten off.

Plait the 3 strands together to form the Headband.

FLOWERS (MAKE 3)

Using a 2.5mm hook and yellow yarn, make a magic loop.

Round 1 (RS) Ch1, 10dc in loop, ss to beg dc. [10 sts]

Fasten off.

Join pink or purple yarn into any st with a ss.

Round 2 *(Dc, htr, 2tr, htr, dc, ss) in same st as prev ss, ss in next 2 sts; rep from * 4 times more.

Fasten off.

Sew the Flowers over the centre of the Headband.

Sew the Headband to the top of the Head, between the Ears.

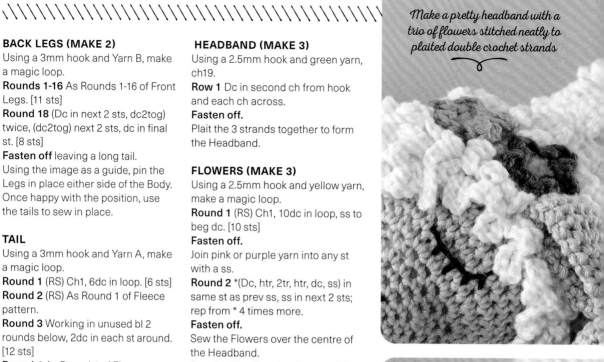

Make a pretty headband with a trio of flowers stitched neatly to plaited double crochet strands

Work about half of each leg, then stuff and continue to stuff as you work the remainder

The fleece pattern is made by chaining six stitches between each double crochet stitch

Handsome Highland Cow

Cuddle up with the most adorable friend on the farm! Complete with the iconic floppy Highland cow hair and distinctive red coat, this cutie can't wait to chew the cud with you.

YOU WILL NEED

- DK weight cotton yarn, approximately one 50g ball of each:
  - Yarn A Rust
  - Yarn B Grey
  - Yarn C Pink
  - Yarn D White

- Black stranded cotton

- A 3mm (US C/2 or D/3) hook

- 2 safety eyes, 10mm

- Toy stuffing

- Stitch markers

MEASUREMENTS

25cm (9¾in) tall

ABBREVIATIONS

inv dec Insert hook in front loop of first st to be decreased, insert hook into front loop of second st to be decreased, yrh and pull through both sts, yrh and pull through 2 loops on hook

NOTES

• Cow is made in separate pieces and sewn together as you go. Use the images as a guide when joining parts together.

HEAD

Using Yarn C, make a magic loop.
Round 1 (RS) Ch1 (does not count as a st throughout), 6dc in loop. [6 sts]
Round 2 (RS) 2dc in each st around. [12 sts]
Round 3 (Dc in next st, 2dc in next st) 6 times. [18 sts]
Round 4 (Dc in next 2 sts, 2dc in next st) 6 times. [24 sts]
Round 5 (Dc in next 3 sts, 2dc in next st) 6 times. [30 sts]
Round 6 (Dc in next 4 sts, 2dc in next st) 6 times. [36 sts]
Rounds 7-9 Dc in each st around. Change to Yarn A.
Round 10 Dc in next 6 sts, (dc in next 2 sts, inv dec) 6 times, dc in next 6 sts. [30 sts]
Round 11 Dc in the next 6 sts, (dc in the next 2 sts, 2dc in next st) 6 times, dc in the next 6 sts. [36 sts]
Round 12 Dc in each st around. Pm in the 15th and 25th st.
Rounds 13-14 Dc in each st around.
Round 15 (Dc in the next 5 sts, 2dc in next st) 6 times. [42 sts]
Rounds 16-20 Dc in each st around. Insert safety eyes between Rounds 15-16, 7 sts apart.
Round 21 (Dc in next 5 sts, inv dec) 6 times. [36 sts]
Stuff Head firmly.
Round 22 (Dc in next 4 sts, inv dec) 6 times. [30 sts]
Round 23 (Dc in next 3 sts, inv dec) 6 times. [24 sts]
Round 24 (Dc in next 2 sts, inv dec) 6 times. [18 sts]
Round 25 (Dc in next st, inv dec) 6 times. [12 sts]
Round 26 (inv dec) 6 times. [6 sts]
Fasten off.
Thread tail through fl of final 6 sts and pull tight to close.

Make indents at the eye sockets by sewing small stitches and pulling them very tight

EMBROIDER FACIAL FEATURES

Thread Yarn A onto a darning needle, pass through back of Head and bring out above one eye, make a small horizontal stitch and bring out above second eye, make another small horizontal stitch. Bring the needle out below first eye and make a small horizontal stitch, bring the needle out below second eye and make a final horizontal stitch. Pull yarn tight so the eyes sink into the Head.
Using Yarn D, embroider highlights at the side of both eyes. Using black stranded cotton, embroider the eyelashes and nostrils.

HORNS (MAKE 2)

Using Yarn D, make a magic loop.
Round 1 (RS) Ch1, 6dc in loop. [6 sts]
Round 2 (RS) Dc in each st around.
Round 3 2dc in first st, dc in each st around. [7 sts]
Rounds 4-7 Rep Rows 2-3 twice. [9 sts]
Round 8 Dc in each st around.
Fasten off, leaving a long tail.
Stuff Horns and sew 5 rounds above the eyes.

EARS (MAKE 4)

Make 2 each in Yarn A and Yarn C. Each Ear is made up of 2 pieces joined together.
Make a magic loop.
Round 1 (RS) Ch1, 6dc in a magic loop [6 sts]
Round 2 (RS) Dc in each st around.
Round 3 2dc in each st around. [12 sts]
Round 4 Dc in each st around.
Round 5 (Dc in next 3 sts, 2dc in next st) 3 times. [15 sts]
Rounds 6-7 Dc in each st around.
Round 8 (Dc in next 3 sts, inv dec) 3 times. [12 sts]
Round 9 Dc in each st around.
Round 10 (Inv dec) 6 times. [6 sts]
Fasten off Yarn C pieces only.
Place a Yarn A and C piece together with RS facing out. Dc through both pieces to join.
Fasten off, leaving a long tail.
Fold the Ear slightly to create the shape and use the tail to secure to the Head.

BODY

Using Yarn A, make a magic loop.

Rounds 1-6 (RS) As Rounds 1-6 of Head. [36 sts]

Round 7 (Dc in next 5 sts, 2dc in next st) 6 times. [42 sts]

Rounds 8-12 Dc in each st around. Stuff Body firmly as you work.

Round 13 (Dc in next 5 st, inv dec) 6 times. [36 sts]

Rounds 14-15 Dc in each st around.

Round 16 (Dc in next 4 sts, inv dec) 6 times. [30 sts]

Rounds 17-20 Dc in each st around.

Round 21 (Dc in next 3 sts, inv dec) 6 times. [24 sts]

Rounds 22-23 Dc in each st around.

Round 24 (Dc in next 2 sts, inv dec) 6 times. [18 sts]

Rounds 25-26 Dc in each st around.

Round 27 (Dc in next st, inv dec) 6 times. [12 sts]

Rounds 28-29 Dc in each st around.

Fasten off, leaving a long tail.
Sew the Head to the Body.

ARMS (MAKE 2)

Using Yarn B, make a magic loop leaving a 20cm beg tail.

Rounds 1-4 (RS) As Rounds 1-4 of Head. [24sts]

Round 5 Dc in bl of each st around.

Round 6 (Dc into next 2 sts, inv dec) 6 times. [18 sts]

Round 7 Dc in each st around.

Round 8 (Dc in next st, inv dec) 6 times. [12 sts]

Change to Yarn A.

Rounds 9-20 Dc in each st around.

Fasten off leaving a long tail.
Using the beg tail, embroider an indent on each Arm. Sew from the magic loop to the top of Round 5 on one side.
Sew the Arms to the Body.

LEGS (MAKE 2)

Using Yarn B, make a magic loop leaving a 20cm beg tail.

Rounds 1-5 (RS) As Rounds 1-5 of Head. [30 sts]

Round 6 Dc in bl of st around.

Round 7 (Dc in next 3 sts, inv dec) 6 times. [24 sts]

Ears are made with two pieces each, sewn together, folded and stitched to the head

Round 8 Dc in each st around.

Round 9 (Dc in next 2 sts, inv dec) 6 times. [18 sts]

Round 10 Dc in each st around.

Round 11 (Dc in next st, inv dec) 6 times. [12 sts]

Round 12 Dc in each st around. Change to Yarn A.

Rounds 13-18 Dc in each st around.

Fasten off, leaving a long tail.
Using the beg tail, embroider the indent as worked on the Arms.
Sew Legs to Body.

TAIL

Using Yarn A, ch21, ss in second ch from hook and each ch across.

Fasten off.
Cut 3 strands of Yarn A, 10cm long. Fold in half, insert hook in top of tail, place folded end on hook and pull through, thread tails through folded end and pull tight to secure.
Using a needle, separate strands of yarn and trim to desired length.
Sew the Tail to the back of the Body.

HAIR

Cut 9 strands of Yarn A, 15cm long. Attach to top of Head in the same way you attached strands to the Tail. Using a needle separate the strands and trim to desired length.

Create little cloven hooves at the end of all four limbs with long stitches pulled tightly

Baby Dragon

If there's one thing that connects most amigurumi characters, it's cuteness, and this little dragon is no exception. He's like a little baby dragon who's just popped out of his egg and hasn't yet learned how to breathe fire. Right now, he's just warm and cuddly and wants a hug.

Give your dragon a striped belly by wrapping stranded cotton around a piece of felt

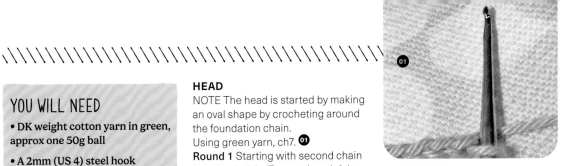

YOU WILL NEED

- DK weight cotton yarn in green, approx one 50g ball

- A 2mm (US 4) steel hook

- Yarn needle

- Toy stuffing

- Beige felt (for wings and scaled body), dark brown felt (for horns), and pink felt (for cheeks)

- 7.5mm safety eyes

- Stranded cotton:
Black for mouth
White for fang
Tan for scaled body

- Glue gun

- Fabric glue

NOTES

• He's made by stitching a few small pieces together and sticking on some felt – we love his little horns and wings, both of which are simple to make.

Create horns by rolling up small cones of black felt

HEAD

NOTE The head is started by making an oval shape by crocheting around the foundation chain.
Using green yarn, ch7. **01**

Round 1 Starting with second chain from hook, 6dc. Turn and work 6dc along the other side of the foundation ch. [12 sts] **02**

Round 2 (1dc, 2dc in next dc) 6 times. [18 sts]

Round 3 (2dc, 2dc in next dc) 6 times. [24 sts]

Round 4 (3dc, 2dc in next dc) 6 times. [30 sts]

Round 5 (4dc, 2dc in next dc) 6 times. [36 sts]

Rounds 6-8 Dc all round. [36 sts]

Round 9 (5dc, 2dc in next dc) 6 times. [42 sts]

Round 10 (6dc, 2dc in next dc) 6 times. [48 sts]

Round 11 (7dc, 2dc in next dc) 6 times. [54 sts]

Rounds 12-16 Dc all round. [54 sts] **03**

Round 17 (7dc, dc2tog) 6 times. [48 sts]

Round 18 Dc all round. [48 sts]

Round 19 (4dc, dc2tog) 8 times. [40 sts]

Round 20 (2dc, dc2tog) 10 times. [30 sts]

Position safety eyes and embroider mouth and fang.

Round 21 (1dc, dc2tog) 10 times. [20 sts]

Stuff head firmly. **04**

Round 22 (Dc2tog) 10 times. [10 sts]

Round 23 (Dc2tog) 5 times. [5 sts]

Fasten off and weave in end.
Cut 2 oval pieces of pink felt and glue onto face as cheeks.

WINGS (MAKE 2)

Cut out 2 isosceles triangles from beige felt. Using same yarn as head, cut 5 pieces of yarn for each wing and splay them outwards from the tip of the triangle. Using fabric glue, secure the yarn in place. **05**
Trim the felt, cutting from one piece of yarn to the next and then scallop

the edges between the yarn pieces.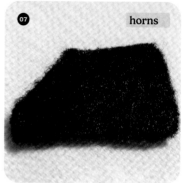
06
Secure wings onto the dragon's head using a glue gun.

HORNS (MAKE 4)
Make 2 small and 2 large horns. With dark brown felt, cut pieces into the shape shown in step **07** below. Make 2 larger cones for the back and 2 smaller cones for the front. Apply glue with a glue gun and roll into cone shapes. **08**
Glue them onto the dragon's head.

LEGS (MAKE 2) + BODY
Using green yarn, make a magic ring.
Round 1 6dc in magic ring. [6 sts]
Round 2 2dc in each dc around. [12 sts]
Round 3 Dc all round. [12 sts]
For the first leg, fasten off (no need to leave long end for sewing). For the second leg, do not cut off the yarn. Ch1 and join with ss to any dc on first leg. *Ss in next dc around on same leg, ch1, then ss to next dc on opposite leg; rep from * another 2 times. **09**
The leg joins should take up 4 stitches on each leg, leaving 8 dc on each leg remaining. For the next round, work one complete round around the joined leg pieces as follows:
Round 4 Work 8dc around the leg, 3dc evenly across the join, 8dc around the other leg, 3dc across the join. [22 sts]
Rounds 5-12 Dc all round. [22 sts]
Fasten off and leave long end for sewing. Sew body to head.

ARMS (MAKE 2)
Using green yarn, make a magic ring.
Round 1 6dc in magic ring. [6 sts]
Rounds 2-4 Dc all round. [6 sts]
Fasten off and leave long end for sewing.
Attach to the sides of the body.

TAIL
Using green yarn, make a magic ring.
Round 1 4dc in magic ring. [4 sts]

Rounds 2-3 Dc all round. [4 sts]
Round 4 (1dc, 2dc in next dc) 2 times. [6 sts]
Round 5 (2dc, 2dc in next dc) 2 times. [8 sts]
Fasten off and leave long end for sewing.
Attach tail to bottom-back of dragon to help give him balance. If you want your dragon to appear like he is leaning back and about to give out a puff of fire, angle the tail upwards.

TO FINISH
To add scaled detailing to the front of the body: cut out a shape to fit from beige felt. Wrap tan stranded cotton around the felt piece several times, applying glue dots on the back along the way to secure the stranded cotton in place. Glue the embroidered felt piece onto the body of the dragon when complete. **10**

horns

Cute Quokka

Quokkas are famous for their smiling faces and incredible friendliness towards humans. This amigurumi pal is just as cute, and will be a joy to have around!

YOU WILL NEED

• DK weight cotton yarn, approximately two 50g balls of:
- Yarn A Light Brown
• Approximately one 50g ball of each:
- Yarn B Dark Brown
- Yarn C Green

• A 3mm (US C/2 or D/3) hook

• 2 safety eyes, 9mm

• Toy stuffing

• Stitch markers

• Make-up blush (optional)

MEASUREMENTS

Quokka measures approx 25cm (9¾in) (16x16in) after joining

ABBREVIATIONS

invdec (Insert hook through fl on next st) twice, yrh and pull through both sts, yrh and pull through both loops on hook

NOTES

• Parts of the pattern are worked using the amigurumi method as explained on p. 6.
• Refer to images when joining pieces together.

• If you are making this toy for a child under 36 months, do not use safety eyes; instead, embroider eyes with black stranded cotton.

HEAD

Using Yarn A, make a magic loop.

Round 1 (RS) Ch1 (does not count as a st throughout), 6dc in loop. [6 sts]

Round 2 (RS) 2dc in each st around. [12 sts]

Round 3 (Dc in next st, 2dc in next st) 6 times. [18 sts]

Round 4 (Dc in next 2 sts, 2dc in next st) 6 times. [24 sts]

Round 5 (Dc in next 3 sts, 2dc in next st) 6 times. [30 sts]

Round 6 Dc in each st around.

Round 7 (Dc in next 4 sts, 2dc in next st) 6 times. [36 sts]

Round 8 Dc in each st around.

Round 9 (Dc in next 5 sts, 2dc in next st) 6 times. [42 sts]

Rounds 10-12 Dc in each st around.

Round 13 (Dc in next 6 sts, 2dc in next st) 6 times. [48 sts]

Round 14 (Dc in next 7 sts, 2dc in next st) 6 times. [54 sts]

Round 15 (Dc in next 8 sts, 2dc in next st) 6 times. [60 sts]

Rounds 16-23 Dc in each st around.

Round 24 (Dc in next 8 sts, invdec) 6 times. [54 sts]

Round 25 (Dc in next 7 sts, invdec) 6 times. [48 sts]

Insert safety eyes between Rounds 11-12, 9 sts apart.

Round 26 (Dc in next 6 sts, invdec) 6 times. [42 sts]

Stuff Head as you work.

Round 27 (Dc in next 5 sts, invdec) 6 times. [36 sts]

Round 28 (Dc in next 4 sts, invdec) 6 times. [30 sts]

Round 29 (Dc in next 13 sts, invdec) twice. [28 sts]

Fasten off.

EARS (MAKE 2)

Using Yarn A, make a magic loop.

Round 1 (RS) Ch1, 6dc in loop. [6 sts]

Round 2 (RS) 2dc in each st around. [12 sts]

Round 3 Dc in each st around.

Round 4 (Dc in next 3 sts, 2dc in next st) 3 times. [15 sts]

Round 5 Dc in each st around.

Round 6 (Dc in next 4 sts, 2dc in next st) 3 times. [18 sts]

Round 7 Dc in each st around.

Fasten off.

Flatten final round and sew the Ears either side of the Head, over Rounds 4-11.

SNOUT

Using Yarn B, make a magic loop.

Round 1 (RS) Ch1, 6dc in loop, ss to beg dc. [6 sts]

Round 2 Ch1, 2dc in each st around, ss to beg dc. [12 sts]

Round 3 Ch1, dc in each st around, ss to beg dc.

Change to Yarn A.

Round 4 Ch1, dc in next 3 sts, 2dc in next 6 sts, dc in next 3 sts, ss to beg dc. [18 sts]

Round 5 Ch1, dc in next 6 sts, 2dc in next 6 sts, dc in next 6 sts, ss to beg dc. [24 sts]

Round 6 As Round 3.

Fasten off.

Sew the Snout over Rounds 12-20 of Head, adding stuffing as you join.

DIMPLES

The Dimples are positioned between Rounds 21-22 and aligned with the side of the Snout.

Thread Yarn A onto a darning needle, bring the needle out from the back of the Head and out to where the first Dimple will be positioned. Make a small horizontal stitch and bring the needle out through the back of the Head. Pull the yarn tight and secure with a knot. Weave in ends.

Repeat for the second Dimple.

BODY

Using Yarn A, make a magic loop.

Rounds 1-5 (RS) As Rounds 1-5 of Head. [30 sts]

Round 6 (Dc in next 4 sts, 2dc in next st) 6 times. [36 sts]

Round 7 (Dc in next 5 sts, 2dc in next st) 6 times. [42 sts]

Round 8 (Dc in next 6 sts, 2dc in next st) 6 times. [48 sts]

Round 9 (Dc in next 7 sts, 2dc in next st) 6 times. [54 sts]

Round 10 (Dc in next 8 sts, 2dc in next st) 6 times. [60 sts]

Round 11 (Dc in next 9 sts, 2dc in next st) 6 times. [66 sts]

Rounds 12-19 Dc in each st around.

Round 20 (Dc in next 9 sts, invdec) 6 times. [60 sts]

Round 21 (Dc in next 13 sts, invdec) 4 times. [56 sts]

Round 22 Dc in each st around.

Round 23 (Dc in next 12 sts, invdec) 4 times. [52 sts]

Round 24 Dc in each st around.

Round 25 (Dc in next 11 sts, invdec) 4 times. [48 sts]

Round 26 Dc in each st around.

Round 27 (Dc in next 10 sts, invdec) 4 times. [44 sts]

Round 28 Dc in each st around.

Stuff Body as you work.

Round 29 (Dc in next 9 sts, invdec) 4 times. [40 sts]

Round 30 Dc in each st around.

Round 31 (Dc in next 8 sts, invdec) 4 times. [36 sts]

Round 32 Dc in each st around.

Round 33 (Dc in next 7 sts, invdec) 4 times. [32 sts]

Round 34 Dc in each st around.

Round 35 (Dc in next 6 sts, invdec) 4 times. [28 sts]

Rounds 36-39 Dc in each st around.

Fasten off.

ARMS (MAKE 2)

Using Yarn B, make a magic loop.

Round 1 (RS) Ch1, 6dc in loop. [6 sts]

Round 2 (RS) 2dc in each st around. [12 sts]

Round 3 (Dc in next 3 sts, 2dc in next st) 3 times. [15 sts]

Rounds 4-6 Dc in each st around. [15 sts]

Round 7 (Dc in next 3 sts, invdec) 3 times. [12 sts]

Round 8 Dc in each st around.

Stuff hand firmly.

Change to Yarn A.

Rounds 9-20 Dc in each st around. [12 sts]

Stuff the upper Arm lightly.

Flatten final round, work 6dc evenly to close.

Fasten off.

Sew the Arms either side of the Body over Rounds 33-38.

LEGS (MAKE 2)

Using Yarn B, ch6.

Round 1 Dc in second ch from hook, dc in next 3 ch, 3dc in next ch, turn to work in opposite side of foundation ch, dc in next 3 ch, 2dc in next ch. [12 sts]

Round 2 (2dc in next st, dc in next 3 sts, 2dc in next 2 sts) twice. [18 sts]

Round 3 Dc in next st, 2dc in next st, dc in next 4 sts, (2dc in next st, dc in next st) twice, 2dc in next st, dc in next 4 sts, 2dc in next st, dc in next st, 2dc in next st. [24 sts]

Change to Yarn A.

Rounds 4-6 Dc in each st around.

Round 7 Dc in next 6 sts, (invdec) 6 times, dc in next 6 sts. [18 sts]

Round 8 Dc in next 6 sts, (invdec) 3 times, dc in next 6 sts. [15 sts]

Rounds 9-13 Dc in each st around.

Round 14 (Dc in next 4 sts, 2dc in next st) 3 times. [18 sts]

Stuff Legs up to Round 13, leaving the remainder unstuffed.

Round 15 Dc in each st around.

Round 16 (Dc in next 2 sts, 2dc in next st) 6 times. [24 sts]

Round 17 (Dc in next 3 sts, 2dc in next st) 6 times. [30 sts]

Rounds 18-24 Dc in each st around.

Round 25 (Dc in next 3 sts, invdec) 6 times. [24 sts]

Round 26 Dc in each st around.

Round 27 (Dc in next 2 sts, invdec) 6 times. [18 sts]

Round 28 Dc in each st around.

Round 29 (Dc in next st, invdec) 6 times. [12 sts]

Round 30 (Invdec) 6 times.

Fasten off.

Finish by weaving the yarn tail through the fl of final 6 sts to close. Sew the Legs to the Body over Round 25.

TAIL

Using Yarn A, make a magic loop.

Round 1 (RS) Ch1, 6dc in loop. [6 sts]

Round 2 (RS) Dc in each st around.

Round 3 Dc in each st to final st, 2dc in final st. [7 sts]

Round 4 Dc in each st around.

Stuff the Tail as you work.

Rounds 5-26 Rep Rounds 3-4 another 11 times. [18 sts]

Fasten off.

LEAVES (MAKE 2)

Using Yarn C, ch14.

Round 1 (RS) 2tr in fourth ch from the hook, tr in next 3 ch, htr in next 3 ch, dc in next 3 ch, (dc, ch2, dc) in next ch, turn to work in opposite side of foundation chain, dc in next 3 ch, htr in next 3 ch, tr in next 3 ch, 3tr in next ch, ch5, ss in second ch from hook and next 3 ch, ss to top of beg tr.

Fasten off.

TO MAKE UP

Sew the Head to the Body, with the Head slightly tilted to one side.

Sew the Leaves to the inner part of one Arm, then sew the ends of the Arms together.

Sew the Tail to the back of the Body over Rounds 8-13.

Lightly apply a small amount of blush to the cheeks (optional).

Make dimples by working small stitches pulled in tight

Clutching Koala

Your post-it notes and pens will be safe in the arms of this cuddly koala. Why not make one for a friend who's starting a new job?

YOU WILL NEED

• DK weight cotton yarn, approximately one 50g ball of:
- Yarn A Light Grey
- Yarn C Black

• DK weight yarn with a fluffy texture, approximately one 50g ball of:
- Yarn B White

• A 3mm (C/2 or D/3) hook

• A 2mm (US B/1) hook

• A stitch marker

• Toy stuffing

• A snap band bracelet, 22cm long and up to 2.5cm wide

MEASUREMENTS

15cm (6in) tall

NOTES

• All parts are made separately. Use the images as a guide when joining parts together.

HARMS (MAKE 2)

Using a 3mm hook and Yarn A, make a magic loop.
Round 1 (RS) Ch1 (does not count as st throughout), 6dc in loop. [6 sts]
Round 2 2dc in each st around. [12 sts]
Round 3 (Dc in next st, 2dc in next st) 6 times. [18 sts]

Rounds 4-23 Dc in each st around. Fasten off.

BODY

Using a 3mm hook and Yarn A, ch5.
Round 1 (RS) Dc in second ch from hook, dc in next 2 ch, 3dc in last ch, turn to work across opposite side of foundation ch, dc in next 2 ch, 2dc in next ch. [10 sts]
Round 2 (2dc in next st, dc in next 2 sts, 2dc in next 2 sts) twice. [16 sts]
Round 3 *Dc in next st, 2dc in next st, dc in next 2 sts, (dc in next st, 2dc in next st) twice; rep from * once more. [22 sts]

Round 4 *Dc in next 2 sts, 2dc in next st, dc in next 2 sts, (dc in next 2 sts, 2dc in next st) twice; rep from * once more. [28 sts]
Round 5 *2dc in next st, dc in next 5 sts, (2dc in next st, dc in next 3 sts) twice; rep from * once more. [34 sts]
Round 6 *Dc in next 4 sts, 2dc in next st, dc in next 2 sts, (dc in next 4 sts, 2dc in next st) twice; rep from * once more. [40 sts]
Round 7 *2dc in next st, dc in next 7 sts, (2dc in next st, dc in next 5 sts) twice; rep from * once more. [46 sts]
Round 8 *Dc in next 6 sts, 2dc in next st, dc in next 2 sts, (dc in next 6 sts,

2dc in next st) twice; rep from * once more. [52 sts]
Round 9 *2dc in next st, dc in next 9 sts, (2dc in next st, dc in next 7 sts) twice; rep from * once more. [58 sts]
Round 10 *Dc in next 8 sts, 2dc in next st, dc in next 2 sts, (dc in next 8 sts, 2dc in next st) twice; rep from * once more. [64 sts]
Rounds 11-18 Dc in each st around. Arms are joined to Body over the next 2 rounds. On the first round you will join the inside of the Arm, meaning you will insert your hook from WS to RS on the Arm sts.
Round 19 Dc in next 10 sts, *place Arm next to Body, (dc through any st of Arm and next st on Body) 9 times, dc in next 17 sts of Body; rep from * once more, dc in final 2 sts.
Round 20 Dc in next 10 sts, *dc in next 9 unworked stitches of Arm, skip 9 joining sts of prev round, dc in next 17 sts of Body; rep from * once more, dc in next 2 sts of Body.
Round 21 (Dc in next 2 sts, invdec, dc in next 16 sts, invdec, dc in next 5 sts, invdec, dc in next 3 sts) twice. [58 sts]
Round 22 (Dc in next st, invdec, dc in next 15 sts, invdec, dc in next 4 sts, invdec, dc in next 3 sts) twice. [52 sts]
Round 23 (Dc in next st, invdec, dc in next 14 sts, invdec, dc in next 3 sts, invdec, dc in next 2 sts) twice. [46 sts]
Round 24 *Invdec, dc in next 13 sts, (invdec, dc in next 2 sts) twice; rep from * once more. [40 sts]
Fasten off and weave in ends.
Insert the snap band bracelet into the Arms and stuff the Body.

TUMMY
Using a 3mm hook and Yarn B, make a magic loop.
Round 1 (WS) Ch1, 6dc in loop. [6 sts]
Round 2 (2dc in next st, dc in next st, 2dc in next st) twice. [10 sts]
Rounds 3-7 Rep Rounds 2-6 of Body. [40 sts]
Fasten off leaving a long tail.
Sew the Tummy to final round of Body.

HEAD
Using a 3mm hook and Yarn A, make a magic loop.
Rounds 1-3 (RS) As Rounds 1-3 of Arms. [18 sts]
Round 4 (Dc in next 2 sts, 2dc in next st) 6 times. [24 sts]
Round 5 (Dc in next 3 sts, 2dc in next st) 6 times. [30 sts]
Round 6 (Dc in next 4 sts, 2dc in next st) 6 times. [36 sts]
Round 7 (Dc in next 5 sts, 2dc in next st) 6 times. [42 sts]
Round 8 (Dc in next 6 sts, 2dc in next st) 6 times. [48 sts]
Round 9 (Dc in next 7 sts, 2dc in next st) 6 times. [54 sts]
Round 10 (Dc in next 8 sts, 2dc in next st) 6 times. [60 sts]
Rounds 11-20 Dc in each st around.
Round 21 (Dc in next 8 sts, invdec) 6 times. [54 sts]
Round 22 (Dc in next 7 sts, invdec) 6 times. [48 sts]
Round 23 (Dc in next 6 sts, invdec) 6 times. [42 sts]
Round 24 (Dc in next 5 sts, invdec) 6 times. [36 sts]
Round 25 (Dc in next 4 sts, invdec) 6 times. [30 sts]
Fasten off leaving a long tail.
Secure safety eyes in the gap between Rounds 15-16, 13 stitches apart.
Stuff the Head and sew to the top of the Body.

EARS (MAKE 2)
Using a 3mm hook and Yarn A, make a magic loop.
Rounds 1-5 Rep Rounds 1-5 of Head.
Rounds 6-10 Dc in each st around. [30 sts]
Round 11 (Dc in next 3 sts, invdec) 6 times. [24 sts]
Fasten off leaving a long tail.

INNER EARS (MAKE 2)
Using a 3mm hook and Yarn B, make a magic loop.
Rounds 1-3 (RS) Rep Rounds 1-3 of Arms. [18 sts]
Fasten off leaving a long tail.

Flatten the Ears and Inner Ears. Sew the Inner Ears to one side of the Ears. Pinch into shape and sew to the Head.

NOSE
Using a 2mm hook and Yarn C, ch5.
Rounds 1-4 (RS) Rep Rounds 1-4 of Body.
[28 sts]
Round 5 Dc in each st around.
Fasten off leaving a long tail.
Sew the Nose to the Head, add a little stuffing as you join.

LEGS (MAKE 2)
Using a 3mm hook and Yarn A, ch5.
Rounds 1-4 (RS) Rep Rounds 1-4 of Body.
[28 sts]
Rounds 5-7 Dc in each st around.
Round 8 (Invdec) twice, dc in next 18 sts, (invdec) 3 times. [23 sts]
Round 9 (Invdec) twice, dc in next 13 sts, (invdec) 3 times. [18 sts]
Rounds 10-11 Dc in each st around.
Round 12 (2dc in next 2 sts, dc in next 5 sts, 2dc in next 2 sts) twice. [26 sts]
Round 13 Dc in each st around.
Round 14 2dc in next st, dc in next 24 sts, 2dc in next st. [28 sts]
Rounds 15-17 Dc in each st around.
Round 18 (Invdec, dc in next 10 sts, invdec) twice. [24 sts]
Round 19 (Invdec, dc in next 8 sts, invdec) twice. [20 sts]
Stuff the foot firmly, then lightly stuff the upper Leg.
Round 20 *(Invdec) twice, dc in next 2 sts, (invdec) twice; rep from * once more. [12 sts]
Round 21 (Invdec) 6 times. [6 sts]
Fasten off.
Thread the tail through the fl of final 6 sts, pulling tight to close.
Weave in ends.
Sew the Legs to the Body.

Playful Platypus

This peculiar pal is sure to win the hearts of your friends and family! Hook one up to give to a friend, or keep it to cuddle yourself – either way, this aquatic friend is a bound to be a real favourite.

YOU WILL NEED

- DK weight cotton yarn, approximately one 50g ball of each:
  - Yarn A Beige
  - Yarn B Brown
- A 2.75mm (US C/2) hook
- 2 safety eyes, 8mm
- Black stranded cotton
- Toy stuffing

MEASUREMENTS

20cm (7¾in) long

HEAD AND BODY

Using Yarn B, ch6.

Round 1 (RS) Dc in second ch from hook, dc in next 3 ch, 2dc in last ch, rotate and work along the opposite side of the ch, dc in next 4 ch. [10 sts]

Round 2 (2dc in first st, 3dc, 2dc in next st) twice. [14 sts]

Round 3 (2dc in next st, 1dc) 7 times. [21 sts]

Rounds 4-7 Dc in each st round.

Round 8 5dc, 2dc in next 4 sts, 12dc. [25 sts]

Round 9 8dc, 2dc in next 4 sts, 13dc. [29 sts]

Round 10 2dc first st, ss in next st.

Fasten off.

Join Yarn A in ss.

Round 11 2dc in the same st as join, 2dc in next st, dc in bl of next 3 sts, (dc in bl of next st, 2dc in bl of next st) 3 times, (2dc in bl of next st, dc in bl of next st) 3 times, dc in bl of next 3 sts, 2dc in next 2 sts, (2dc, 2dc in next st) twice, 2dc. [42 sts]

Round 12 2dc, 2dc in next st, 4dc, ch1, skip 1 st, 14dc, ch1, skip 1 st, 6dc, 2dc in next st, 12dc. [44 sts]

Rounds 13-16 Dc in each st and ch-sp around.

Round 17 Dc in next st, *(dc2tog) twice, 4dc, dc2tog, 4dc; rep from * once more, (dc2tog) twice, 11dc. [36 sts]

Rounds 18-19 Dc in each st around.

Round 20 Dc2tog, 4dc, dc2tog, 12dc, dc2tog, 4dc, dc2tog, 8dc. [32 sts]

Round 21 8dc, dc2tog, 6dc, dc2tog, 14dc. [30 sts]

Insert safety eyes in ch-sps from Round 12.

Round 22 Ch9, skip 3 sts, 16dc, ch9, skip 3 sts, 8dc. [24 sts, 2 ch-9 sps]

Rounds 23-35 Dc in each st and ch around. [42 sts]

Round 36 1dc, (1dc, dc2tog) 3 times, 16dc, (dc2tog, 1dc) 3 times, 7dc. [36 sts]

Rounds 37-40 Dc in each st and ch around.

Round 31 2dc, ch9, skip 3 sts, 21dc, ch9, skip 3 sts, 7dc. [30 sts, 2 ch-9 sps]

Round 32 Dc in each st and ch around. [48 sts]

Round 33 Dc in next 12 sts, (2dc, 2dc in next st) 3 times, 1dc, (2dc in next st, 2dc) 3 times, 17dc. [54 sts]

Rounds 34-35 Dc in each st round. Stuff Head and Body as you work.

Round 36 (Dc2tog, 4dc) 9 times. [45 sts]

Round 37 Dc in each st round.

Round 38 5dc, (2dc, dc2tog) 4 times, (dc2tog, 2dc) 4 times, 8dc. [37 sts]

Round 39 5dc, (dc2tog, 3dc) 5 times, 7dc. [32 sts]

Round 40 2dc, (dc2tog, 1dc) 4 times, (1dc, dc2tog) 4 times, 6dc. [24 sts]

Rounds 41-48 Dc in each st round. [24 sts]

Round 49 5dc, dc2tog, 11dc, dc2tog, 4dc. [22 sts]

Round 50 5dc, dc2tog, 11dc, dc2tog, 2dc. [20 sts]

Round 51 Dc in each st round.

Round 52 (Dc2tog, 2dc) twice, 4dc, (2dc, dc2tog) twice. [16 sts]

Round 53 (Dc2tog, 2dc) 4 times. [12 sts]

Round 54 (Dc2tog) 6 times. [6 sts]

Fasten off.

Thread tail through final 6 sts, pulling tight to close.

FRONT LEGS

Work Front Legs around ch-sps from Round 22.

Join Yarn A in first skipped st from Round 22.

Round 1 (RS) Dc in 3 skipped sts, dc in each ch across. [12 sts]

Rounds 2-3 (RS) Dc in each st around.

Change to Yarn B.

Round 4 2dc, 2dc in next st, 5dc, 2htr in next 2 sts, 2dc. [15 sts]

Round 5 Dc in next 3 sts, leave rem sts unworked.

Stuff Front Leg and Body.

Flatten final round and work next row through both layers to close.

Row 6 Dc in next 4 sts, htr in next 3 sts.

Fasten off and use the tail to close any gaps.

Repeat Front Leg on second ch-sp from Round 22.

HIND LEGS

Hind Legs are worked around the ch-sps from Round 31.

Join Yarn A in first skipped st from Round 31.

Round 1 Dc in 3 skipped sts, (2dc in next ch, dc in next 2 ch) 3 times. [15 sts]

Rounds 2-3 Dc in each st round.

Round 4 Dc in next 2 sts, change to Yarn B, (dc2tog, 2dc) 3 times, 1dc. [12 sts]

Round 5 Dc in next 3 sts, leave rem sts unworked.

Stuff Hind Leg and Body.

Flatten final round and work next row through both layers to close.

Row 6 Dc in next 3 sts, htr in next 3 sts.

Fasten off and use the tail to close any gaps.

Repeat Hind Leg on second ch-sp from Round 31.

TO FINISH

Using black stranded cotton, embroider nostrils at the tip of the beak.

Using Yarn A, embroider the eyelids to create a sleepy eye effect.

Circus Bear

For a birthday celebration or just because, this adorable little bear is just the right amount of quirky and cute. He has so much character with his dark eyes and shiny black nose, and his hat and ruff make him look like he's about to jump up and dance!

YOU WILL NEED

- DK weight tweed yarn, approximately one 50g ball of:
  - Yarn B Brown
- Small amounts of each:
  - Yarn A Cream
  - Yarn C Light Blue
  - Yarn D Red

- A 3.5mm (US E/4) hook

- A 4mm (US G/6) hook

- Stitch markers

- Toy stuffing

- A pair of 9mm safety eyes

- A 15mm safety nose

- 4 sets of 16mm safety joints

MEASUREMENTS

22cm (8½in) tall

NOTES
- Any brown DK yarn will do but we used one with a tweedy slub to mimic the different shades that naturally occur in a bear's fur.
- His head, body, arms, legs and accessories are all worked separately then sewn together.
- This bear has been made with posable limbs – just like a traditional teddy – but you don't have to do this. If it's too complicated you can simply stitch his limbs in place.

HEAD
NOTE Before starting to make the head, cut a 40cm (16in) length of Yarn B. This will be used to stitch up the head before you begin Round 22.

Round 1 Using Yarn A and a 4mm hook, ch2, 6dc into second ch from hook, ss to first dc to join. [6 sts]
Round 2 *1dc, 2dc into next st; repeat from * around. [9 sts]
Round 3 *2dc, 2dc into next st; repeat from * around. [12 sts]
Round 4 *3dc, 2dc into next st; repeat from * around. [15 sts]
Rounds 5 and 6 Dc into each st around.
Round 7 Change to Yarn B, 5dc, 2dc into each of next 5 sts, 5 dc. [20 sts]
Round 8 5dc, 2dc into each of next 10 sts, 5dc. [30 sts]
Round 9 Dc into each st around.
Round 10 10dc, 2dc into each of next 10 sts, 10dc. [40 sts]
Round 11 Dc into each st around.
Round 12 15dc, 2dc into each of next 10 sts, 15dc. [50 sts]
Rounds 13-15 Dc into each st around.
The following round creates a hole that is sewn up later.
Round 16 13dc, ch12, skip the next 24 sts, 13dc. [26 dc and ch12-sp]

Round 17 13dc, dc in ch12-sp, 13dc. [38 sts] ❶
Round 18 Dc into each st around.
Round 19 7dc, skip the next st, *5dc, skip the next st; repeat from * 4 times more. [32 sts]
Round 20 6dc, skip the next st, *4dc, skip the next st; repeat from * 4 times more. [26 sts]
Round 21 5dc, skip the next st, *3dc, skip the next st; repeat from * 4 times more. [20 sts]

Using the pre-cut length of Yarn B, sew up the hole left between Rounds 16 and 17. Curve the longer edge (the 24-st side) of the hole around the shorter edge (the 12-ch side) so that both sides join up. Sew together. This forms two equal bumps on the bear's head. ❷
Round 22 2dc, *skip the next st, 2dc; repeat from * 5 times more. [14 sts]

Before inserting the eyes and nose, stuff the head firmly as this helps to get them into the perfect position. Place the eyes and nose into position using the image as a guide, remove stuffing then attach the safety backs to the eyes and nose and re-stuff ❸. Stuff the forehead so that the bumps are even, leaving a little cleft between the two. ❹

Round 23 (2dc, skip next st) twice, *1dc, skip next st; repeat from * 3 times more. [8 sts]

Round 24 *1dc, skip next st; repeat from * 3 times more. [4 sts]
Fasten off, leaving a long tail.

EARS (MAKE 2)
Round 1 Using Yarn B and a 4mm hook, ch2, 6dc into the second ch from the hook, ss to the first dc to join. [6 sts]
Round 2 2dc in each st around. [12 sts]
Round 3 *1dc, 2dc into next st; repeat from * around. [18 sts]
Round 4 Dc into each st around.
Round 5 *5dc, skip next st; repeat from * around. [15 sts]
Fasten off, leaving a long tail.

Position the 2 ears on the bear's head, using the image as a guide, and sew them securely in place using long tail and a needle.

ARMS (MAKE 2)
Round 1 Using Yarn B and a 4mm hook, ch2, 6dc into the second ch from the hook, ss to the first dc to join. [6 sts]
Round 2 2dc in each st around. [12 sts]
Round 3 *3dc, 2dc into the next st; repeat from * around. [15 sts]
Rounds 4-7 Dc into each st around.
Round 8 *4dc, skip the next st; repeat from * around. [12 sts]
Rounds 9-11 Dc into each st around.

The elbow is worked back and forth in rows but counted as Round 12:
Round 12 2dc, place marker in the next st, turn, ch1 (does not count as st), dc in the same st, 3dc, turn, ch1 (does not count as st), skip same st, dc into the next st.
Round 13 2dc, dc into the side of the elbow, dc into marked st, skip the next st, 6dc, dc into the other side of the elbow, dc into the next st. [12 sts]
Round 14 *3dc, skip next st; repeat from * around. [9 sts]

If you are adding joints to your bear, position the spindle disc into the inward-facing side of the shoulder with the disc plate inside the arm,

spindle poking out.
Stuff the arm.
Rounds 15-18 Dc into each st around. [9 sts]
Add a little more stuffing.
Round 19 *2dc, skip next st; repeat from * around.
Fasten off. [6 sts]

LEGS (MAKE 2)
Round 1 Using Yarn B and a 4mm hook, ch2, 6dc into the second ch from the hook, ss to the first dc to join. [6 sts]
Round 2 2dc in each st around. [12 sts]
Round 3 *1dc into the next st, 2dc into the next st; rep from * around. [18 sts]
Rounds 4-9 Dc into each st around.

Round 10 *5dc, skip next st; repeat from * around. [15 sts]
Rounds 11 and 12 Dc into each st around.
Round 13 *4dc, skip next st; repeat from * around. [12 sts]
Rounds 14-16 Dc into each st around.
Round 17 *3dc, 2dc into next st; repeat from * around. [15 sts]

The foot is worked back and forth in rows but counted as Round 18:
Round 18 3dc, place marker in next st, turn, ch1 (does not count as st), dc in same st, 3dc, turn, ch1 (does not count as st), skip same st, 3dc, dc into marked st, dc into next st, turn, ch1 (does not count as st), skip same st,

4dc, turn, ch1 (does not count as st), skip same st, 3dc, turn, ch1 (does not count as st), skip same st, 2dc, turn.

Round 19 Ch1 (does not count as st), skip the same st, dc into the next st, work 5dc into the side of the foot, dc into each of the next 9 sts around the back of the foot, work 5dc into the other side of the foot. [20 sts]

If you are adding joints to your bear, position the spindle disc into the inward facing side of the shoulder with the disc plate inside the arm, spindle poking out. **05**

Round 20 *3dc, skip the next st; repeat from * around. [15 sts]

Round 21 *2dc, skip the next st; repeat from * around. [10 sts]

Fasten off, leaving a tail.

Stuff the leg and use the tail to close up the hole.

BODY

Round 1 Using Yarn B and a 4mm hook, ch2, 6dc into the second ch from the hook, ss to first dc to join. [6 sts]

Round 2 2dc into each st around. [12 sts]

Round 3 *1dc, 2dc into the next st; repeat from * around. [18 sts]

Round 4 *2dc, 2dc into the next st; repeat from * around. [24 sts]

Round 5 Dc into each st around.

Round 6 *3dc, 2dc into the next st; repeat from * around. [30 sts]

Round 7 Dc into each st around.

Round 8 *4dc, 2dc into the next st; repeat from * around. [36 sts]

Round 9 *5dc, 2dc into the next st; repeat from * around. [42 sts]

Rounds 10-12 Dc into each st around. [42 sts]

Round 13 *6dc, skip the next st; repeat from * around. [36 sts]

Rounds 14-16 Dc into each st around.

Round 17 *5dc, skip the next st; repeat from * around. [30 sts]

Round 18 Dc into each st around.

Round 19 *4dc, skip the next st; repeat from * around. [24 sts]

Round 20 Dc into each st around.

Round 21 *3dc, skip the next st; repeat from * around. [18 sts]

Round 22 Dc into each st around.

If you are using joints, stuff the body firmly for shape and then attach the arms and legs, inserting the protruding spindle through the body.

Take out the stuffing and then fix the washer and locking disc onto the spindle inside the body.

Round 23 *2dc, skip the next st; repeat from * around. [12 sts]

Stuff firmly.

Round 24 *Dc, skip the next st; repeat from * around.

Fasten off. [6 sts]

HAT

Round 1 Using Yarn C and a 3.5mm hook, ch2, 4dc into the second ch from the hook, ss to the first dc to join. [4 sts]

Round 2 *1dc, 2dc into the next st; repeat from * around. [6 sts]

Round 3 Dc into each st around.

Round 4 *1dc, 2dc into the next st; repeat from * around. [9 sts]

Round 5 Dc into each st around.

Round 6 *2dc, 2dc into the next st; repeat from * around. [12 sts]

Round 7 Dc into each st around.

Round 8 *3dc, 2dc into the next st; repeat from * around. [15 sts]

Round 9 Dc into each st around.

Round 10 *4dc, 2dc into the next st; repeat from * around. [18 sts]

Round 11 Change to Yarn D, dc into each st around.

Fasten off.

Using Yarn D, embroider 3 polka dots up the hat in a line and one on top. Stuff the hat and then stitch it onto the bear's head at a jaunty angle using the image as a guide.

RUFF

Round 1 Using Yarn C and a 3.5mm hook, ch10, ss to first ch to join in a loop.

Round 2 Ch2 (counts as htr), 29htr into the loop, ss to first htr to join. [30 htr]

Round 3 2htr in each st around. [60 htr]

Round 4 2htr in each st around. [120 htr]

Round 5 Change to Yarn D, dc into each st around. [120 sts]

TO FINISH

Sew the ruff to the body taking care to pleat it evenly. **05**

Sew the head to the body using tail of yarn and a needle.-

Snug Penguin

Heartwarming, wholesome and huggable, this penguin chick is the ultimate crochet pick-me-up. Bringing you all the joy in so many ways, he's a must-make for last minute winter gifts or just because. Our favourite part has to be the fluffy fur, which you can create by brushing up super-soft alpaca-blend yarn.

YOU WILL NEED

• DK weight alpaca-blend yarn, approximately one 50g ball of each:
- Yarn A Black
- Yarn B Grey
- Yarn C White
- Yarn D Red

• 4.5mm (US 7) crochet hook

• 3mm (US C/2 or D/3) hook

• Pair of black safety eyes, 9mm (3/8 ")

• Stitch marker

• Yarn needle

• Soft toy stuffing

• Wire brush

ABBREVIATIONS

inv dc2tog invisible double crochet 2 together – insert hook in front loop of next st, yrh and draw loop through, insert hook in both loops of next st, yrh and draw loop through, yrh and draw through all 3 loops on hook decrease

inv dc3tog invisible double crochet 3 together – (insert hook in front loop of next st, yrh and draw loop through) twice, insert hook in both loops of next st, yrh and draw loop through, yrh and draw through all 4 loops on hook decrease

FPdc front post double crochet – work a double crochet around the front post of the st rather than into the top 2 loops of the st, insert hook from the front of your work to the back, around the back of the indicated st and back through to the front, yrh and draw round the back of the post of the indicated st, yrh and complete double crochet as normal

magic ring to make a magic ring, hold the yarn in your hand and wrap the working yarn around your forefinger twice to create a ring, slip the ring off your finger and insert hook to pick up first st, ch1, then work the necessary sts for Round 1 and close the ring tightly by pulling the loose end

MEASUREMENTS

23cm (91/8") tall

NOTES

• The pattern below is for a penguin with a stripy jumper worked as part of the body. To make a separate jumper, work the rounds in Yarns C and D in Yarn B to crochet the penguin, then work the rounds in Yarns C and D on their own, starting with ch40.
• The pattern uses concise crochet terms, for example 6 dc means work 1 dc in each of next 6 sts.
• Most parts of the pattern are worked using the amigurumi method as explained on p. 6.

PENGUIN
Work using yarn held double throughout unless stated otherwise

HEAD AND BODY
Worked from the head downward
Round 1 Using Yarn A and 4.5mm hook, start with 6 dc in a magic ring, pull ring tight. [6 sts]
Round 2 2 dc in each st around. [12 sts]
Round 3 *3 dc, 2 dc in each of next 3 sts; repeat from * to end of round. [18 sts]
Round 4 *3 dc, (2 dc in next st, 1 dc) 3 times; repeat from * to end of round. [24 sts]
Round 5 *3 dc, (2 dc, 2 dc in next st) 3 times; repeat from * to end of round. [30 sts]
Round 6 *3 dc, (2 dc in next st, 3 dc) 3 times; repeat from * to end of round. [36 sts]
Rounds 7-12 1 dc in each st around
Round 13 Change to Yarn B, 1 dc in each st around
Round 14 12 dc, 2 dc in next st, 17 dc, 2 dc in next st, 5 dc. [38 sts]
Round 15 1 dc in each st around
Round 16 12 dc, 2 dc in next st, 18 dc, 2 dc in next st, 6 dc. [40 sts]
Round 17 1 dc in each st around
Round 18 Change to Yarn C, 1 dc in each st around
Round 19 Working in back loops only, 1 dc in each st around
Round 20 12 dc, 2 dc in next st, 19 dc, 2 dc in next st, 7 dc. [42 sts]
In Round 21, gaps are created for adding in wings
Round 21 Change to Yarn D, 9 dc, ch9, miss 9 sts, 12 dc, ch9, miss 9 sts, 3 dc. [42 sts]
Rounds 22-23 1 dc in each st around
Round 24 Change to Yarn C, 12 dc, 2 dc in next st, 20 dc, 2 dc in next st, 8 dc. [44 sts]
Rounds 25-26 1 dc in each st around
Round 27 Change to Yarn D, 12 dc, 2 dc in next st, 21 dc, 2 dc in next st, 9 dc. [46 sts]
Rounds 28-29 1 dc in each st around
Rounds 30-32 Change to Yarn C, 1 dc in each st around
Rounds 33-35 Change to Yarn D, 1 dc in each st around
Rounds 36-38 Change to Yarn C, 1 dc in each st around
Round 39 Change to Yarn B, working in back loops only, 1 dc in each st around
In Round 40, the pattern starts increasing for the tail. Check the placement of the increase is at the centre back – if not, move the beginning of the round by working a few extra sts
Round 40 7 dc, 3 dc in next st, 38 dc. [48 sts]
Round 41 8 dc, 3 dc in next st, 39 dc. [50 sts]
Round 42 9 dc, 3 dc in next st, 40 dc. [52 sts]

Rounds 43-45 1 dc in each st around
Round 46 (7dc, inv dc2tog) 4 times.. [48 sts]
Round 47 (6 dc, inv dc2tog) 6 times. [42 sts]
Round 48 (4 dc, inv dc2tog) 7 times. [35 sts]
Round 49 (3 dc, inv dc2tog) 7 times. [28 sts]
Round 50 (2 dc, inv dc2tog) 7 times. [21 sts]
Round 51 (1 dc, inv dc2tog) 7 times. [14 sts]
Round 52 (Inv dc2tog) 7 times.. [7 sts]
Fasten off, thread tail through all front loops and pull tight to close

WINGS (MAKE TWO)

These are worked from the body in the gaps left on Round 21
Round 1 Using Yarn D and 4.5mm hook, attach yarn to middle st of the underarm, 1 dc in each st around [18 sts]
Rounds 2-3 1 dc in each st around
Rounds 4-6 Change to Yarn C, 1 dc in each st around
Rounds 7-9 Change to Yarn D, 1 dc in each st around
Rounds 10-12 Change to Yarn C, 1 dc in each st around
Round 13 Change to Yarn B, working in back loops only, 1 dc in each st around
Round 14 1 dc in each st around
Round 15 (Inv dc2tog, 4 dc) 3 times. [15 sts]
Round 16 1 dc in each st around
Round 17 (Inv dc2tog, 3 dc) 3 times. [12 sts]
Round 18 1 dc in each st around
Round 19 (Inv dc2tog, 2 dc) 3 times. [9 sts]
Round 20 1 dc in each st around
Round 21 (Inv dc2tog, 1 dc) 3 times. [6 sts]
Fasten off, then thread the tail up through all the front loops and pull tight to close
Stuff the body after making the first wing, stuffing the wing section lightly, then stuff the second wing as you go

BEAK

Round 1 Using Yarn A and 4.5mm hook, start with 5 dc in a magic ring, pull ring tight. [5 sts]
Round 2 1 dc in each st around
Round 3 2 dc in next st, 4 dc. [6 sts]
Fasten off, leaving a tail for sewing

CHEEKS (MAKE TWO)

Worked in rows, turning at the end of each row
Row 1 Using a single strand of Yarn C and 3mm hook, start with 5 dc in a magic ring, pull ring tight, turn. [5 sts]
Row 2 Ch1 (does not count as st here and throughout), 1 dc, 2 dc in each of next 3 sts, 1 dc, turn. [8 sts]
Row 3 Ch1, 1 dc, (2 dc in next st, 1 dc) 3 times, 1 dc, turn. [11 sts]
Row 4 Ch1, 1 dc, (2 dc in next st, 2 dc) 3 times, 1 dc, turn. [14 sts]
Row 5 Ch1, 1 dc, (2 dc in next st, 3 dc) 3 times, 1 dc. [17 sts]
Row 6 Turn sideways and work along the long edge, ch1, 10 dc. [10 sts]
Fasten off, leaving a tail for sewing

CUFFS AND RIBBING

Work in front loops on the sleeve cuffs, neck and bottom edge of jumper
Round 1 Using a single strand of Yarn D and 4.5mm hook, attach yarn to any st, 1 dc in each st around
Round 2 (1 FPdc, 1 dc) repeat around
Round 3 (1 FPdc, 1 dc) repeat around until last st, 1 ss in last st
Fasten off, sewing the last st join to close, weave in loose ends

FEET (MAKE TWO)

Round 1 Using Yarn A and 4.5mm hook, start with 6 dc in a magic ring, pull ring tight. [6 sts]
Round 2 (2 dc in next st) 6 times. [12 sts]
Round 3 (2 dc in next st, 1 dc) 6 times. [18 sts]
Round 4 6 dc, (3 dc in next st, 1 dc) 3 times, 6 dc. [24 sts]
Round 5 7 dc, (3 dc in next st, 3 dc) 3 times, 5 dc. [30 sts]
Round 6 7 dc, (inv dc3tog, 3 dc) 3 times, 5 dc. [24 sts]
Round 7 6 ss, (inv dc3tog, 1 ss) 3 times, 6 ss. [18 sts]
Fasten off, leaving a tail for sewing

FINISHING

Brush out all the grey sections with a wire brush to create a fluffy coat. Place safety eyes through the cheeks, between Rows 2-3, off to the sides. Sew the cheeks onto the body, then sew the beak in the middle of the cheeks.
For the feet, poke out each toe from the inside to encourage the shape. Sew the feet to the base of the body, stuffing each foot.
Re-brush the grey sections to hide the seams, then weave in all ends.

Go
Pro!

Gorgeous Guinea Pig

If you need another pet in your life then this fluffy guinea pig could be the answer. Easy to care for and with gorgeous shed-free fur, this little cutie is just waiting to be hooked and loved. Make sure you keep track of your stitches when working with the furry yarn – light up hook might help!

YOU WILL NEED
- **Super chunky weight yarn with a furry texture (such as Scheepjes Furry Tales),** approximately one 50g ball of each:
  - Yarn A Brown
  - Yarn B White
- **Sport weight cotton yarn,** approximately one 50g ball of each:
  - Yarn C Cream
  - Yarn D Brown
  - Yarn E Pink
- **A 4mm (US G/6) hook**
- **A 3mm (US C/2 or D/3) hook**
- **Toy stuffing**
- **2 black safety eyes, 9mm**
- **Pink stranded cotton**
- **Stitch markers**

MEASUREMENTS
17cm (6¾in) long

NOTES
- To help you keep track of your stitches when using furry yarn we suggest marking all increase/decrease sts.
- The Head and Body are made in one piece. The Muzzle, Feet, Ears and Bow are made separately and joined at the end.

HEAD AND BODY
Using a 4mm hook and Yarn A, make a magic loop.
Round 1 (RS) Ch1 (does not count as a st throughout), 6dc into loop. [6 sts]
Round 2 2dc in each dc around. [12 sts]
Round 3 *Dc in next st, 2dc in next st (pm in last st); rep from * 5 times more. [18 sts]
Round 4 *Dc in each st to marker, 2dc in marked st (pm in last st); rep from * 5 times more. [24 sts]
Rounds 5-6 As Round 4. [36 sts]
Leave the 6th and 30th sts marked, remove all other markers.
Rounds 7-12 Dc in each dc around. Insert safety eyes at markers, between Rounds 6-7.
Change to Yarn B.
Rounds 13-19 Dc in each dc around.
Round 20 Dc in next 3 sts, change to Yarn A, dc in next 33 sts.
Rounds 21-25 Dc in each dc around.
Round 26 *Dc in next 4 dc, dc2tog (pm in st before dc2tog); rep from * 5 times more. [30 sts]

Round 27 *Dc in each st to marker, dc2tog (pm in st before dc2tog); rep from * 5 times more. [24 sts]
Stuff Head and Body, continuing to stuff as you work.
Rounds 28-29 As Round 27. [12 sts]
Round 30 (Dc2tog) 6 times. [6 sts]
Ss in next st and **fasten off**.
Thread tail through final 6 sts, pulling tight to close.

MUZZLE
Using a 3mm hook and Yarn C, make a magic loop.
Rounds 1-6 As Round 1-6 of Head and Body. [36 sts]
Round 7 (Dc in next 5 dc, 2dc in next dc) 6 times. [42 sts]
Round 8 (Dc in next 6 dc, 2dc in next dc) 6 times. [48 sts]
Work on in rows.
Row 9 (RS) Dc in next 11 dc, turn. [11 sts]
Row 10 (WS) Ch1, 11dc across, turn.
Row 11 Ch1, dc2tog first 2 sts, dc in each st to final 2 sts, dc2tog, turn. [9 sts]
Row 12 Ch1, dc in each st across turn.
Rows 13-18 Repeat Rows 11-12 three times more. [3 sts]
Row 19 Ch1, dc3tog, do not turn.
Work a round of dc around the Muzzle as follows:
Round 20 Dc in each row end down to Round 8, dc in 37 unworked sts from Round 8, dc in each row ends up to Row 19, ss to top of dc3tog.
Fasten off.

Using pink stranded cotton, sew a triangular nose onto the Muzzle, working the base of the triangle through the beg magic loop. You can use the images as a guide.

EARS (MAKE 2)
Using a 3mm hook and Yarn D, make a magic loop.
Rounds 1-5 (RS) As Rounds 1-5 of Head and Body. [30 sts]
Fold the Ear in half so WS are facing in and work a two dc sts through both layers to join the sides of the Ear at the base.
Fasten off.

FRONT LEG (MAKE 2)
Using a 3mm hook and Yarn D, make a magic loop.
Rounds 1-2 As Rounds 1-2 of Head and Body. [12 sts]
Round 3 (Dc in next 3 dc, 2dc in next dc) 3 times. [15 sts]
Rounds 4-8 Dc in each dc around.
Stuff the Leg lightly.
Flatten the final round and work 7 dc through both layers to join.
Fasten off.

BACK LEG (MAKE 2)
Using a 3mm hook and Yarn D, make a magic loop.
Rounds 1-3 As Rounds 1-3 of Head and Body. [18 sts]
Rounds 4-9 Dc in each dc around.
Stuff the Leg lightly.
Flatten the final round and work 9 dc through both layers to join.
Fasten off.

BOW
Using a 3mm hook and Yarn E, ch47.
Row 1 (RS) Dc in second ch from hook and next 45 ch, turn. [46 sts]
Rows 2-9 Ch1, dc in each st across, turn.
Fasten off.
Sew the short ends of the Bow together to form a loop.

CENTRE OF BOW
Using a 3mm hook and Yarn E, ch13.
Rows 1-3 As Rows 1-3 of Bow. [12 sts]

Fasten off.
Wrap the Centre of Bow around the Bow and secure with a few sts.

TO MAKE UP
Use the images as a guide when assembling your Guinea Pig.
Sew the Muzzle to the face, centred between the eyes. Stuff a little toy stuffing under the Muzzle as you join it.
Sew the Ears to the Head, keeping them in line with the eyes.
Sew the Legs to the underside of the Body so that the closed edge runs lengthways down the Body.
Sew the Bow to the top of the Head.

For the ears, make circles, then fold them in half and secure with a few dc stitches

The pretty pink bow is created from a looped rectangle, cinched tightly in the middle

Happy Hedgehog

Fine food, warm weather and stunning vistas: no wonder this happy hedgehog is wearing a smile. Ensure you stuff her legs firmly, and take special care to position the legs so that she can stand up independently. To make her spiny back soft and fluffly, choose a boucle yarn for Yarns D and E.

YOU WILL NEED

• DK weight wool or wool and alpaca blend yarn, approximately one 50g ball of each:
- Yarn A Light Beige
• A small amount of each:
- Yarn B Brown
- Yarn C Rust

• Aran weight boucle yarn, approximately one 50g ball of each:
- Yarn D Light Beige
- Yarn E Brown

• A 4mm (US G/6) hook

• A 2.75mm (US C/2) hook

• 2 safety eyes, 10mm

• Toy stuffing

• Stitch markers

MEASUREMENTS

18cm (7in) tall

ABBREVIATIONS

loop st Wrap yarn from front to back over the index finger of hand holding yarn, insert hook into st indicated, pick up yarn with hook from behind your index finger, draw it through the st, with the loop still on your finger, yrh using the working yarn and draw it through the two loops on the hook, remove loop from finger
dc3tog (Insert hook into next st, yrh and pull up a loop) 3 times, yrh and pull through all loops on the hook

NOTES

• The Spikes are made by using Yarns D and E held together and worked as a single strand.

NOSE

Using a 4mm hook and Yarn B, make a magic loop.
Round 1 Ch1 (doesn't count as st throughout), 8dc into loop. [8 sts]
Round 2 Dc in each st around.
Fasten off, leaving a long tail.

The nose is made bulbous and snubby from two rounds of eight double crochet stitches

For the body of the picnic basket, work double crochet stitches into the back loops

BODY
Using a 4mm hook and Yarn A, make a magic loop.
Round 1 Ch1, 6dc into loop. [6 sts]
Round 2 2dc in each st around. [12 sts]
Round 3 (Dc in next st, 2dc in next st) 6 times. [18 sts]
Round 4 (Dc in next 2 sts, 2dc in next st) 6 times. [24 sts]
Round 5 (Dc in next 3 sts, 2dc in next st) 6 times. [30 sts]
Round 6 (Dc in next 4 sts, 2dc in next st) 6 times. [36 sts]
Round 7 Dc in each st around.
Round 8 3dc in next st (mark 2nd st), dc in next 35 sts. [38 sts]
Round 9 Dc, 3dc in marked st (mark 2nd st), dc in next 36 sts. [40 sts]
Round 10 Dc in each st to marked st, 3dc in marked st (place marker in 2nd st), dc in each st to end. [42 sts]
Rounds 11-12 As Round 10. [46 sts]
Rounds 13-15 As Round 7.
Round 16 Dc in next 3 sts, (dc2tog) 3 times, dc in next 37 sts. [43 sts]
Round 17 As Round 7.
Round 18 Dc in next 2 sts, (dc2tog), dc in next st, (dc2tog), dc in next 36 sts. [41 sts]
Round 19 As Round 7.
Round 20 Dc in next st, (dc2tog) 3 times, dc in next 34 sts. [38 sts]
Round 21 Dc in next st, (dc3tog), dc in next 34 sts. [36 sts]
Rounds 22-31 As Round 7.
Add safety eyes over Rounds 11-12, approx 17 sts apart.
Round 32 (Dc in next 4 sts, dc2tog) 6 times. [30 sts]
Round 33 (Dc in next 3 sts, dc2tog) 6 times. [24 sts]
Round 34 (Dc in next 2 sts, dc2tog) 6 times. [18 sts]
Stuff the Hedgehog firmly.
Round 35 (Dc in next st, dc2tog) 6 times. [12 sts]
Round 36 (Dc2tog) 6 times. [6 sts]
Fasten off.
Pull tail through last 6 sts, pulling tight to close, weave in ends.

ARMS (MAKE 2)
Using a 4mm hook and Yarn A, make a magic loop.

Round 1 Ch1, 6dc into loop. [6 sts]
Round 2 (Dc in next 2 sts, 2dc in next st) twice. [8 sts]
Rounds 3-9 Dc in each st around.
Fasten off.
Stuff the Arms.

LEGS (MAKE 2)
Using a 4mm hook and Yarn A, make a magic loop.
Round 1 Ch1, 6dc into loop. [6 sts]
Round 2 3dc in next st, dc in next 5 sts. [8 sts]
Round 3 2dc in next 3 sts, dc in next 5 sts. [11 sts]
Round 4 Dc in next 2 sts, 2dc in next 3 sts, dc in next 6 sts. [14 sts]
Rounds 5-6 Dc in each st around.
Round 7 Dc in next 2 sts, (dc2tog) 5 times, dc in last 2 sts. [9 sts]
Rounds 8-11 Dc in each st around.
Fasten off.
Stuff the Legs.

SPIKES
Using a 4mm hook and Yarns D and E as 1 strand held together, ch10.
Round 1 (WS) Dc in 2nd ch from hook, dc in next 8 ch, (working across opposite side of foundation ch) loop st in each ch across.
[18 sts]
Round 2 (WS) (3 loop st in next st, loop st in next 8 sts) twice. [22 sts]
Round 3 (2 loop st in next 3 sts, loop st in next 8 sts) twice. [28 sts]
Round 4 *(2 loop st in next st, loop st in next st) 3 times, loop st in next 8 sts; rep from * once more. [34 sts]
Round 5 *(2 loop st in next st, loop st in next 2 sts) 3 times, loop st in next 8 sts; rep from * once more. [40 sts]
Round 6 *(2 loop st in next st, loop st in next 3 sts) 3 times, loop st in next 8 sts; rep from * once more. [46 sts]
Round 7 *(2 loop st in next st, loop st in next 4 sts) 3 times, loop st in next 8 sts; rep from * once more. [52 sts]
Round 8 *(2 loop st in next st, loop st in next 5 sts) 3 times, loop st in next 8 sts; rep from * once more. [58 sts]
Round 9 *(2 loop st in next st, loop st in next 6 sts) 3 times, loop st in next 8 sts; rep from * once more. [64 sts]

Rounds 10-11 Loop st in each st around.
Fasten off.

PICNIC BASKET
Using a 2.75mm hook and Yarn B, make a magic loop.
Round 1 (RS) Ch1, 6dc into loop. [6 sts]
Round 2 2dc in each st around. [12 sts]
Round 3 As Round 2. [24 sts]
Round 4 (2dc in next st, dc in next 3 sts) 6 times. [30 sts]
Rounds 5-10 (Working in bl only) Dc in each st around.
Row 11 Ss in next st, ch18, skip 14 sts, ss in next 2 sts, turn.
Row 12 Dc in each ch across, ss in next st from Round 10 to secure the Handle.
Fasten off and weave in ends.

PICNIC BLANKET
Using a 2.75mm hook and Yarn C, ch16.
Row 1 Dc in second ch from hook, dc in next 14 ch, turn. [15 sts]
Row 2 Ch1, dc in each st across, turn.
Rows 3-15 As Row 2.
Fasten off and weave in the ends.
Using Yarn A, make small sts over the Blanket to create a polka dot effect.

TO FINISH
Use the image as a guide and sew the Arms, Legs and Nose in place.
Using Yarn B, sew a straight line approx 2 sts long to create the mouth.
Sew the Spikes on to the back of the Hedgehog.
Sew the handle of the Basket to one of the hands, placing the Picnic Blanket inside.

Socktopus

Octopuses aren't known for wearing socks but we're sure they'd love a few pairs to put on when the water's a bit chilly. And what fun for us humans to decide which sock goes on which tentacle. We'd be ten-tickled all over to receive this socktopus!

YOU WILL NEED

• Sport weight cotton yarn, approximately two 50g balls of:
- Yarn A Orange
• Approximately one ball of each:
- Yarn B Turquoise
- Yarn C Off White
- Yarn D Red

• Scrap of black yarn

• A 3mm (US C/2 or D/3) hook

• Stitch markers

• Polyester toy stuffing

• Small bead (optional)

MEASUREMENTS

16cm (6¼in) tall

NOTES

• The Socktopus is worked from the top down, in one piece. Eight Tentacles are worked off the sts of the final round of Body. The Base is worked into the opposite side of the Tentacles, in decreasing rounds to close.

• Parts of the pattern are worked using the amigurumi method as explained on p. 6.

• You will alternate between two colours when working the Socks. Change colour on the final yrh of st before colour change is indicated and carry the unused colours across the top of the sts, enclosing them as you work.

• The small hook shown here was created using a 3D printer, but you could use a pipe cleaner or some craft wire to create your own.

This Socktopus's work in progrerss is Round 1 of a sock worked around a bead

HEAD AND BODY

Using Yarn A, make a magic loop.
Round 1 Ch1 (does not count as a st), 6dc into loop. [6 sts]
Round 2 2dc in each st around. [12 sts]
Round 3 (2dc in next st, 1dc) 6 times. [18 sts]
Round 4 (2dc in next st, 2dc) 6 times. [24 sts]
Round 5-12 Continue in patt, increasing 6 sts each round. [72 sts at end of Round 12]
Rounds 13-27 Dc in each st around.
Round 28 (Dc2tog, 22dc) 3 times. [69 sts]
Round 29 Dc in each st around.
Round 30 (Dc2tog, 21dc) 3 times. [66 sts]
Round 31 Dc in each st around.
Round 32 (Dc2tog, 20dc) 3 times. [63 sts]
Round 33 Dc in each st around.
Round 34 (Dc2tog, 19dc) 3 times. [60 sts]
Round 35 Dc in each st around.
Round 36 (Dc2tog, 13dc) 4 times. [56 sts]
Round 37 Dc in each st around.
Do not fasten off.

TENTACLES

Tentacles are made as you work the next round from the Body. Tentacle pattern is written first; work from Round 38 referring back to the Tentacle pattern where 'make Tentacle' is stated.

TENTACLE STITCH PATTERN
Begin in first marked st of repeat.
Round 1 Dc in first 7 sts, dc in next 11 ch. [18 sts]
Round 2 (2dc in next st, 5dc) 3 times. [21 sts]
Rounds 3-8 Dc in each st around.
Round 9 15dc, (dc2tog) 3 times. [18 sts]
Round 10 Dc in next 6 sts, 2dc in next st, dc in next 7 sts, (dc2tog) twice. [17 sts]
Round 11 Dc in next 7 sts, 2dc in next st, dc in next 5 sts, (dc2tog) twice. [16 sts]

Round 12 Dc in each st around.
Round 13 (Dc2tog), dc in next 6 sts, 2dc in next st, dc in next 5 sts, (dc2tog). [15 sts]
Round 14 (Dc2tog), dc in next 11 sts, (dc2tog). [13 sts]
Round 15 (Dc2tog), dc in next 4 sts, 2dc in next st, dc in next 4 sts, (dc2tog). [12 sts]
Round 16 (Dc2tog, dc in next 2 sts) 3 times. [9 sts]
Round 17 (Dc2tog, dc in next st) 3 times. [6 sts]
Fasten off and rejoin yarn into second marked st.

Round 38 *Dc in next st, pm, dc in next 6 sts, pm, ch11, make tentacle; rep from * 7 times more referring back to the Tentacle pattern as instructed.
Using the tails, sew the opening between the Tentacles closed over 3 ch on each. This will leave ch-5 at the base of each Tentacle which you will work over the next round.

BASE
Join Yarn A in any st on open side of Tentacles.
Round 39 Dc in each ch around. [40 sts]
Round 40 (Dc2tog, 6dc) 5 times. [35 sts]
Round 41 (Dc2tog, 5dc) 5 times. [30 sts]
Stuff Body and Tentacles.
Round 42 (Dc2tog, 4dc) 5 times. [25 sts]
Round 43 (Dc2tog, 3dc) 5 times. [20 sts]
Round 44 (Dc2tog, 2dc) 5 times. [15 sts]
Round 45 (Dc2tog, 1dc) 5 times. [10 sts]
Fasten off and thread tail through final five sts, pulling tight to close.

CHEEKS (MAKE 2)

Using Yarn D, make a magic loop.
Rounds 1-2 (RS) As Rounds 1-2 of Head and Body. [12 sts]
Round 3 Ss in each st around.

Fasten off.
Using the image as a guide, sew to the Socktopus.

HAT

Using Yarn B, ch16.
Row 1 (RS) Dc in second ch from hook and each ch across, turn. [15 sts]
Row 2 Ch1, dc fl of each st around, turn.
Row 3 Ch1, dc in bl of each st around, turn.
Rep Rows 2-3 another 12 times.
Fasten off leaving a 25cm tail.
Using the tail, sew short ends of Hat together. Thread yarn in and out of one open side and pull tight to gather fabric and create the Hat shape. Secure with a sew small stitches.
Using Yarn C, make a small pompom and attach to top of the Hat.

SOCKS (MAKE 6)

SINGLE-SPOT SOCK (MAKE 2)
Make one using Yarn B as main colour and one using Yarn D as main colour.
Make a magic loop.
Round 1 (RS) Ch1, 6dc into loop. [6 sts]
Round 2 (2dc in next st, 1dc) 3 times. [9 sts]
Round 3 (2dc in next st, 2dc) 3 times. [12 sts]
Change to Yarn C.
Round 4 Dc in each st around.
Round 5 (2dc in next st, 3dc) 3 times. [15 sts]
Round 6 (2dc in next st, 4dc) 3 times. [18 sts]
Rounds 7-8 Dc in each st around.
Change to Yarn B or D.
Round 9 2dc in next 3 sts, change to Yarn C dc in next 15 sts. [21 sts]
Change to Yarn B or D.
Round 10 Dc in next 6 sts, change to Yarn C dc in next 15 sts.
Round 11 Dc in next st, change to Yarn B or D, dc in next 4 sts, change to Yarn C, dc in next 16 sts.
Rounds 12-13 Dc in each st around.
Change to Yarn B or D.
Round 14 Ch1, htr in each st around, ss in beg htr.

Round 15 Ss in each st around.
Fasten off and weave in ends.

STRIPED SOCK (MAKE 2)
Make one using Yarn B and one using Yarn D.
Make a magic loop.
Rounds 1-5 (RS) As Rounds 1-5 of Single-Spot Sock, changing to Yarn C for Rounds 4-5. [15 sts]
Change to Yarn B or D.
Round 6 (2dc in next st, 4dc) 3 times. [18 sts]
Round 7 Dc in each st around.
Change to Yarn C.
Round 8 Dc in each st around.
Round 9 2dc in next 3 sts, dc in next 15 sts.
[21 sts]
Change to Yarn B or D.
Rounds 10-11 Dc in each st around.
Change to Yarn C.
Rounds 12-13 Dc in each st around.
Change to Yarn B or D.
Rounds 14-15 As Rounds 14-15 of Single-Spot Sock.
Fasten off and weave in ends.

POLKA DOT SOCK (MAKE 2)
Make one using Yarn B and one using Yarn D.
Rounds 1-5 (RS) As Rounds 1-5 of Single-Spot Sock, changing to Yarn C

The Socktopus has six socks in three designs but you could make him the full set of eight!

for Rounds 4-5. [15 sts]
Continue with Yarn C.
Round 6 *2dc in next st, change to Yarn B or D, dc in next st, change to Yarn C, dc in next 2 sts, change to Yarn B or D, dc in next st, change to Yarn C; rep from * twice more. [18 sts]
Change to Yarn B or D.
Rounds 7-8 Dc in each st around.
Round 9 2dc in next st, change to Yarn C, dc in next st, change to Yarn B or D, dc in same st as last dc, 2dc in next st, *change to Yarn C, dc in next 2 sts, change to Yarn B or D, dc in next st; rep from * four times more.

[21 sts]
Change to Yarn C.
Rounds 10-11 Dc in each st around.
Round 12 Dc in next st, change to Yarn B or D, dc in next st, *change to Yarn C, dc in next 3 sts, change to Yarn B or D, dc in next st; rep from * once more, **change to Yarn C, dc in next 2 sts, change to Yarn B or D, dc in next st; rep from ** twice more, change to Yarn C, dc in next 2 sts.
Round 13 Dc in each st around.
Change to Yarn B or D.
Rounds 14-15 As Rounds 14-15 of Single-Spot Sock.
Fasten off and weave in ends.

TO FINISH
Using any black yarn, sew the eyes with small straight sts.
Leaving a long starting tail, wrap any colour yarn around your bead. Using the tail, work Round 1 of Single-Spot Sock.
Fasten off and weave in ends.

Embroider the Socktopus's sleepy eyes with straight stitches using scraps of black yarn

Busy Bees

Get everyone buzzing around with this fun beehive, which also works as a family-friendly table decoration. Give the bees their own personalities with different expressions, perhaps representing those in your hive!

YOU WILL NEED

• DK weight cotton yarn, approximately two 50g balls of each:
- Yarn A Yellow
- Yarn B Brown
• Approximately one 50g ball of each:
- Yarn C Black
- Yarn D White
- Yarn E Dark Yellow

• A 3mm (US C/2 or D/3) hook

• 10 safety eyes, 6mm

• Stitch markers

• Toy stuffing

• Black stranded cotton

• Tapestry needle

MEASUREMENTS

Beehive Flower measures approx 29cm (11½in) wide and 5cm (2in) tall
Bee measures approx 11cm (4¼in) tall

ABBREVIATIONS

popcorn 3TR in same st, drop the loop from hook, insert the hook in top of first tr, place loop back on hook and pull through the first st

BEE (MAKE 7)

When making the Bees you can use any combination of yarns A, B, C, D and E. The pattern will refer to light colour or dark colour for colour changes.
Using a light colour, make a magic loop.
Round 1 (RS) Ch1 (does not count as st throughout), 6dc in the loop. [6 sts]
Round 2 2dc in each st around. [12 sts]
Round 3 (Dc in next st, 2dc in next st) 6 times. [18 sts]
Round 4 (Dc in next 2 sts, 2dc in next st) 6 times. [24 sts]
Round 5 (Dc in next 3 sts, 2dc in next st) 6 times. [30 sts]
Rounds 6-9 Dc in each st around.
Round 10 (Dc in next 8 sts, invdec) 3 times. [27 sts]
Round 11 Dc in each st around. Change colour to dark colour.
Round 12 (Dc in next 8 sts, 2dc in next st) 3 times. [30 sts]
Rounds 13-14 Dc in each st around. Change to light colour.

Rounds 15-17 Dc in each st around. Change to dark colour.
Round 18 Dc in each st around.
Round 19 (Dc in next 3 sts, invdec) 6 times. [24 sts]
Round 20 Dc in each st around. Change to light colour.
Round 21 (Dc in next 2 sts, invdec) 6 times. [18 sts]
Use safety eye on 5 of the Bees. Position safety eyes between Rounds 8-9, approx 7 sts apart.
Round 22 (Dc in next st, invdec) 6 times. [12 sts]
Stuff the Bee.
Round 23 Dc in each st around.
Round 24 (Invdec) 6 times. [6 sts]
Fasten off.
Thread tail through final 6 sts, pulling tight to close.
Using black stranded cotton, embroider eyelashes around the safety eyes. For the Bees without safety eyes, embroider the eyes with black stranded cotton. Embroider mouths on all the Bees. You can use the images as a guide.

WINGS (MAKE 2 PER BEE)
Using Yarn D, make a magic loop.
Rounds 1-3 (RS) As Rounds 1-3 of Bee Body. [18 sts]
Rounds 4-5 Dc in each st around.
Round 6 (Invdec, dc in next 5 sts, invdec) twice. [14 sts]
Round 7 (Invdec, dc in next 3 sts, invdec) twice. [10 sts]
Round 8 Invdec, dc in next 6 sts, invdec, ss to beg dc. [8 sts]
Fasten off leaving a long tail.
Sew the Wings side by side to the back of the Bee along Round 11 (just above the first stripe).

ANTENNAE (MAKE 2 PER BEE)
Using Yarn C, ch5.
Row 1 Popcorn in second ch from hook, ss in next 3 ch.
Fasten off leaving a long tail.
Sew over Round 3 of Bee.

CROWN
Using Bumblebee, ch10, ss in first ch being careful not to twist the chain.

Round 1 Ch1, dc in each ch around. [10 sts]
Round 2 (Ss in next st, ch2, ss in second ch from hook, ss in next st) 5 times, ss in beg ss.
Fasten off leaving a long tail.
Sew to one of the Bees, between the Antennae.

BOW (MAKE 4)
Make 3 using Yarn B and 1 using Yarn D.
Make a magic loop.
Round 1 (Ch2, 2tr in loop, ch2, ss in loop) twice.
Fasten off leaving a long tail.
Place the bow made from Yarn D on one Bee by wrapping the tails around the neck and securing with a small knot.
Sew one Bow to the top of any Bee's head.
Sew the rem 2 Bows to the base of the Antennae on any Bee.

BEEHIVE FLOWER
HONEYCOMB (MAKE 7)
Using Yarn B, make a magic loop.
Rounds 1-5 (RS) As Rounds 1-5 of Bee Body. [30 sts]
Round 6 (Dc in next 4 sts, 2dc in next st) 6 times. [36 sts]
Round 7 *Dc in next 5 sts, (dc, ch2, dc) in next st; rep from * 5 times more, turn. [42 sts, 6 ch-2 sps]
Round 8 (WS) Ch1, dc in bl of next st, skip ch-2 sp, (dc in bl of next 7 sts, skip ch-2 sp) 5 times, dc in bl of next 6 sts. [42 sts]
Rounds 9-13 (FPdc around next st, dc in next 6 sts) 6 times.
Round 14 Dc in next st, ch1, (dc in next 7 sts, ch1) 5 times, dc in next 6 sts, ss to beg dc. [42 sts, 6 ch-sps]
Fasten off and weave in ends.

FLOWER PETALS (MAKE 8)
Using Bumblebee, make a magic loop
Round 1 (RS) Ch1, 6dc in the loop. [6 sts]
Round 2 (Dc in next 2 sts, 2dc in next st) twice. [8 sts]
Round 3 (Dc in next 2 sts, 2dc in next 2 sts) twice. [12 sts]

Work the wings in the round, then sew the open end, flat, to the bees' bodies

Work each of the eight petals separately, then join them to the flower centre one by one

Round 4 (Dc in next 5 sts, 2dc in next st) twice. [14 sts]
Round 5 (Dc in next 6 sts, 2dc in next st) twice. [16 sts]
Round 6 (Dc in next 6 sts, 2dc in next 2 sts) twice. [20 sts]
Round 7 (Dc in next 9 sts, 2dc in next st) twice. [22 sts]
Round 8 (Dc in next 10 sts, 2dc in next st) twice. [24 sts]

Round 9 (Dc in next 11 sts, 2dc in next st) twice. [26 sts]
Round 10 (Dc in next 12 sts, 2dc in next st) twice. [28 sts]
Round 11 (Dc in next 13 sts, 2dc in next st) twice. [30 sts]
Round 12 (Dc in next 14 sts, 2dc in next st) twice. [32 sts]
Rounds 13-16 Dc in each st around.
Round 17 (Dc in next 14 sts, invdec) twice.
[30 sts]
Rounds 18-20 Dc in each st around.
Round 21 (Dc in next 13 sts, invdec) twice.
[28 sts]
Rounds 22-23 Dc in each st around.
Round 24 (Dc in next 12 sts, invdec) twice.
[26 sts]
Fasten off.
Flatten the Petal. When the Petal is joined to the flower centre you will work through both the front and the back layers, beginning in the first and last stitch of Round 24.

FLOWER CENTRE
Using Yarn B, make a magic loop.
Rounds 1-5 (RS) As Rounds 1-5 of Bee Body. [30 sts]
Round 6 (Dc in next 4 sts, 2dc in next st) 6 times. [36 sts]
Round 7 (Dc in next 5 sts, 2dc in next st) 6 times. [42 sts]
Round 8 Dc in next 3 sts, 2dc in next st, (dc in next 6 sts, 2dc in next st) 5 times, dc in next 3 sts. [48 sts]
Round 9 (Dc in next 7 sts, 2dc in next st) 6 times. [54 sts]
Round 10 Dc in next 4 sts, 2dc in next st, (dc in next 8 sts, 2dc in next st) 5 times, dc in next 4 sts. [60 sts]
Round 11 (Dc in next 9 sts, 2dc in next st) 6 times. [66 sts]
Change to Bumblebee.
Round 12 Dc in next 5 sts, 2dc in next st, (dc in next 10 sts, 2dc in next st) 5 times, dc in next 5 sts. [72 sts]
Over the next round, 4 Petals are joined to the Flower Centre. When indicated, work stitches through both layers of a flattened Petal and the stitches from Round 12. At the end of

one Petal you may be directed to join a second Petal. In this instance work stitches through 5 layers (4 layers of Petals and 1 layer of Base).
Round 13 *Dc in next 2 sts, 2dc in next st, dc in next 2 sts, working through Petal to join, dc in next 13 sts: rep from * twice more, dc in next 2 sts, 2dc in next st, dc in next 2 sts, working through Petal to join, dc in next 10 sts, begin joining next Petal, dc in next 3 sts (through 5 layers). [76 sts]
Remaining Petals are joined over the next round in the same way.
Round 14 Dc through current Petal and next 10 sts of prev round, *dc in next 2 sts, 2dc in next st, dc in next 3 sts, working through Petal to join, dc in next 13 sts; rep from * twice more, dc in next 2 sts, 2dc in next st, dc in next 6 sts, ss in beg dc. [80 sts]
Fasten off and weave in ends.

TO MAKE UP
Sew the Honeycomb together; you can use the image as a guide.
Using Yarn B, sew the joined Honeycomb to the centre of the Flower Centre.
Weave in any rem ends.

Join the honeycomb sections together along the top edges

Dinosaur Family

Four patterns in one, this dinosaur family has something for everyone! A real diplodocus may have measured up to a whopping 24 metres long – thankfully this is much smaller and easier to cuddle.

YOU WILL NEED

SMALL DIPLODOCUS

• 4ply weight cotton yarn, approximately two 50g balls of:
- Yarn A Blue
• Approximately one 50g ball of each:
- Yarn B White
- Yarn C Coral
- Yarn D Green

• A 2.5mm (US B/1 or C/2) hook

• 2 safety eyes, 8mm

• Toy stuffing

LARGE DIPLODOCUS

• Aran weight cotton yarn, approximately three 50g balls of:
- Yarn A Green
• Approximately one 50g ball of each:
- Yarn B White
- Yarn C Pink
- Yarn D Yellow

• A 4.5mm (US 7) hook

• 2 safety eyes, 9mm

• Toy stuffing

MEASUREMENTS

Small diplodocus measures approx 24cm (9½in) tall
Large diplodocus measures approx 36cm (14¼in) tall

ABBREVIATIONS

invdec Insert hook in front loop of first st to be decreased, insert hook into front loop of second st to be decreased, yrh and pull through 2 sts, yrh and pull through 2 loops on hook

This pattern shows how much your yarn weight and hook size can affect the measurements of your finished project!

Diplodocus

NOTES

• The pattern for the Small and Large Diplodocus is the same. The size is achieved through the yarn and hook size used.
• Parts of this pattern are worked using the amigurumi method as explained on p. 6.
• Where the pattern specifies the right or left leg, it refers to the dinosaur's perspective.

HEAD

Using Yarn A, ch5.
Round 1 (RS) Dc in second ch from hook and next 2 ch, 3dc in next ch, turn to work in opposite side of foundation ch, dc in next 2 ch, 2dc in next ch. [10 sts]
Round 2 (2dc in next st, dc in next 2 sts, 2dc in next st, dc in next st) twice. [14 sts]
Round 3 (Dc in next st, 2dc in next st, dc in next 2 sts, 2dc in next st, dc in next 2 sts) twice. [18 sts]
Round 4 (Dc in next 2 sts, 2dc in next st) 6 times. [24 sts]
Round 5 (Dc in next 3 sts, 2dc in next st) 6 times. [30 sts]
Round 6 (Dc in next 4 sts, 2dc in next st) 6 times. [36 sts]
Round 7 (Dc in next 5 sts, 2dc in next st) 6 times. [42 sts]
Round 8 (Dc in next 6 sts, 2dc in next st) 6 times. [48 sts]
Round 9 Dc in each st around.

Round 10 Dc in next 13 sts, 2dc in next st, (dc in next 7 sts, 2dc in next st) twice, dc in next 18 sts. [51 sts]

Round 11 Dc in each st around.

Round 12 Dc in next 13 sts, 2dc in next st, (dc in next 8 sts, 2dc in next st) twice, dc in next 19 sts. [54 sts]

Round 13 Dc in each st around.

Round 14 Dc in next 13 sts, 2dc in next st, (dc in next 9 sts, 2dc in next st) twice, dc in next 20 sts. [57 sts]

Round 15 Dc in each st around.

Round 16 Dc in next 13 sts, 2dc in next st, (dc in next 10 sts, 2dc in next st) twice, dc in next 21 sts. [60 sts]

Round 17 Dc in each st around.

Round 18 Dc in next 43 sts, ch12, leave rem sts unworked. [43 sts]

A space is created over the next round. The Body will be worked from these skipped sts once the Head is complete.

Round 19 Skip first 11 sts from Round 18, dc in 12th st and each st to ch-12 sp, dc in next 12 ch. [44 sts]

Round 20 Dc in each st around.

Round 21 Invdec, (dc in next 8 sts, invdec) 3 times, dc in next 12 sts. [40 sts]

Round 22 (Dc in next 4 sts, invdec) 4 times, dc in next 16 sts. [36 sts]

Round 23 Dc in each st around.

Round 24 (Dc in next 4 sts, invdec) 6 times. [30 sts]

Round 25 (Dc in next 3 sts, invdec) 6 times. [24 sts]

Round 26 (Dc in next 2 sts, invdec) 6 times. [18 sts]

Round 27 (Dc in next st, invdec) 6 times. [12 sts]

Round 28 (Invdec) 6 times. [6 sts]

Fasten off.

Thread tail through the front loop of each st and pull tight to close.

Place the safety eyes between Rounds 15-16, approx 22 sts apart.

NECK AND BODY

Join Yarn A in first unworked st of Round 17 of Head.

Round 1 (RS) Dc in each skipped st from Round 17, 12dc in opposite edge of ch-12 from Round 18. [40 sts]

Round 2 Dc in each st around.

Round 3 Invdec, dc in next 24 sts, (invdec) twice, dc in next 8 sts, invdec. [36 sts]

Stuff Head, Neck and Body and cont stuffing as you work

Rounds 4-19 Dc in each st around.

Round 20 Dc in next 9 sts, (2dc in next st, dc in next 4 sts) 4 times, dc in next 7 sts. [40 sts]

Round 21 Dc in next 18 sts, 2dc in next 2 sts, dc in next 20 sts. [42 sts]

Round 22 Dc in next 20 sts, ch9, dc in second ch from hook and next 7 ch, dc in same st as dc before ch-9, dc in next 22 sts. [51 sts]

Round 23 Dc in next 20 sts, work into opposite side of ch-9 from Round 22, dc in next 5 ch, 2dc in next 3 ch, turn to work in sts in opposite side of ch, 2dc in next 3 sts, dc in next 28 sts. [65 sts]

Round 24 Dc in next 7 sts, 2dc in next st, dc in next 11 sts, invdec, dc in next 5 sts, 2dc in next st, dc in next st, 2dc in next st, dc in next 4 sts, 2dc in next st, dc in next st, 2dc in next st, dc in next 5 sts, invdec, dc in next 11 sts, 2dc in next st, dc in next 10 sts. [69 sts]

Round 25 Dc in next 25 sts, (2dc in next st, dc in next 3 sts) twice, (dc in next 3 sts, 2dc in next st) twice, dc in next 28 sts. [73 sts]

Round 26 Dc in each st around.

Begin working the diplodocus at the head and add eyes before moving on to the neck

Make a row of toenails for each leg by working treble stitches in white yarn

Round 27 Dc in next 25 sts, (2dc in next st, dc in next 4 sts) twice, (dc in next 4 sts, 2dc in next st) twice, dc in next 28 sts. [77 sts]

Round 28 Dc in each st around.

Round 29 Dc in next 8 sts, 2dc in next st, dc in next 16 sts, 2dc in next st, dc in next 5 sts, 2dc in next st, dc in next 10 sts, 2dc in next st, dc in next 5 sts, 2dc in next st, dc in next 16 sts, 2dc in next st, dc in next 11 sts. [83 sts]

Rounds 30-34 Dc in each st around.

Round 35 Dc in next 13 sts, invdec, dc in next 9 sts, invdec, dc in next 28 sts, invdec, dc in next 9 sts, invdec, dc in next 16 sts. [79 sts]

Rounds 36-37 Dc in each st around.

Round 38 Dc in next 77 sts, invdec, pm in last st. [78 sts]
Do not fasten off.
Legs are worked off the Body.

LEGS
FRONT LEFT LEG
Cont with Yarn A.

Round 1 Dc in next 16 sts, ch13. [16 sts]

Round 2 Being careful not to twist the chain, dc in marked st, dc in next 16 sts, dc in next 13 ch. [30 sts]

Round 3 Dc in next 15 sts, (invdec) twice, dc in next 11 sts. [28 sts]

Rounds 4-12 Dc in each st around.

Round 13 (Working in bl only), (dc in next 5 sts, invdec) 4 times. [24 sts]

Round 14 (Dc in next 2 sts, invdec) 6 times. [18 sts]

Round 15 (Dc in next st, invdec) 6 times. [12 sts]

Round 16 (Invdec) 6 times. [6 sts]
Fasten off.
Thread tail through the front loop of each st and pull tight to close.

BACK LEFT LEG
Skip 5 sts from final round of Body after Front Left Leg. Join Yarn A in 6th st.

Round 1 (RS) Dc in same st as join and next 16 sts, ch13. [17 sts]

Round 2 Dc in first 17 sts, dc in next 13 ch. [30 sts]

Round 3 Invdec, dc in next 26 sts, invdec. [28 sts]

Rounds 4-16 Repeat Rounds 4-16 of Front Left Leg.
Fasten off.
Thread tail through the front loop of each st and pull tight to close.

BACK RIGHT LEG
Join Yarn A in next unworked st from Round 38 of Body after Back Left leg.

Rounds 1-2 (RS) As Rounds 1-2 of Back Left Leg. [30 sts]

Round 3 Dc in next 15 sts, (invdec) twice, dc in next 11 sts. [28 sts]

Rounds 4-16 As Rounds 4-16 of Front Left Leg.
Fasten off.
Thread tail through the front loop of each st and pull tight to close.

FRONT RIGHT LEG
Skip next 5 sts from Round 38 of Body after Back Right Leg. Join Yarn A in next st.

Rounds 1-16 As Rounds 1-16 of Back Left Leg.
Fasten off.
Thread tail through the front loop of each st and pull tight to close.

BELLY
LEFT BELLY FLAP
Join Yarn A in same st as final dc from Round 1 of Front Left Leg.

Row 1 (RS) Dc in same st as join and next 6 skipped sts, turn. [7 sts]

Row 2 Ch1, dc in each st across, turn.

Row 3 Ch1, dc in each st to final st, 2dc in next st, turn. [8 sts]

Rows 4-5 As Row 2.

Row 6 Ch1, 2dc in first st, dc in each st to final st, 2dc in final st, turn. [10 sts]

Row 7 As Row 6. [12 sts]

Row 8 Ch1, dc in each st across in next st.
Fasten off.

RIGHT BELLY FLAP
Join Yarn A in same st as final dc from Round 1 of Back Right Leg.

Rows 1-2 As Rows 1-2 of Left Belly Flap.

Row 3 Ch1, 2dc in first st, dc in each st to end, turn. [8 sts]

Rows 4-7 As Rows 4-7 of Left Belly Flap. [12 sts]

Fasten off leaving a long tail.

Sew the final rows of each Belly Flap together, stuffing the Legs and Belly as you join.

Sew the ch-sps from Round 1 of each Leg to the Belly Flap.

TAIL

Using Yarn A, make a magic loop.

Round 1 (RS) Ch1, 6dc in the loop. [6 sts]

Round 2 (Dc in next st, 2dc in next st) 3 times. [9 sts]

Round 3 (Dc in next 2 sts, 2dc in next st) 3 times. [12 sts]

Round 4 Dc in each st around.

Round 5 (Dc in next st, 2dc in next st) 4 times, dc in next 4 sts. [16 sts]

Round 6 Dc in each st around.

Round 7 (Dc in next 2 sts, 2dc in next st) 4 times, dc in next 4 sts. [20 sts]

Round 8 Dc in each st around.

Round 9 (Dc in next 3 sts, 2dc in next st) 4 times, dc in next 4 sts. [24 sts]

Round 10 Dc in each st around.

Round 11 (Dc in next 4 sts, 2dc in next st) 4 times, dc in next 4 sts. [28 sts]

Round 12 Dc in next st, invdec, dc in next 3 sts, 2dc in next st, (dc in next 2 sts, 2dc in next st) 5 times, dc in next 3 sts, invdec, dc in next st. [32 sts]

Round 13 Dc in next 2 sts, invdec, dc in next 4 sts, 2dc in next st, dc in next 5 sts, 2dc in next st, dc in next 2 sts, 2dc in next st, dc in next 5 sts, 2dc in next st, dc in next 4 sts, invdec, dc in next 2 sts. [34 sts]

Round 14 Dc in each st around.

Round 15 Dc in next 14 sts, (2dc in next st, dc in next 4 sts) twice, dc in next 10 sts. [36 sts]

Round 16 Dc in next 2 sts, invdec, dc in next 28 sts, invdec, dc in next 2 sts. [34 sts]

Round 17 Dc in next st, invdec, dc in next 7 sts, (dc in next 2 sts, 2dc in next st) 4 times, dc in next 9 sts, invdec, dc in next st. [36 sts]

Round 18 Dc in each st around.

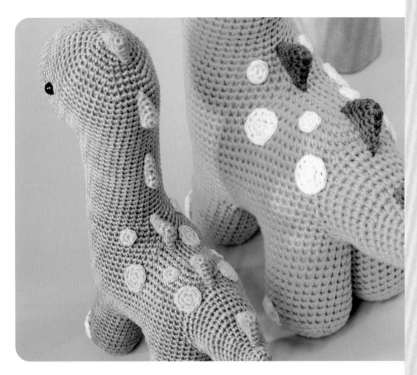

Fasten off leaving a long tail.

Stuff the Tail and then sew it to the back.

TOENAILS (MAKE 4)

Using Yarn B, ch10.

Row 1 (WS) Dc in second ch from hook and each ch across, turn. [9 sts]

Row 2 (RS) Ch1, (skip next st, 3tr in next st, ss in next st) 3 times. [12 sts]

Fasten off leaving a long tail.

Sew the Toenails to the Feet with the flat edge of the Toenails sewn to the fl from Round 13 of Legs. Use the image as a guide.

SPIKES (MAKE 6)

Using Yarn C, make a magic loop.

Round 1 Ch1, 6dc in the loop. [6 sts]

Round 2 (Dc in next 2 sts, 2dc in next st) twice. [8 sts]

Round 3 (Dc in next 3 sts, 2dc in next st) twice. [10 sts]

Round 4 (Dc in next 4 sts, 2dc in next st) twice. [12 sts]

Round 5 (Dc in next 5 sts, 2dc in next st) twice. [14 sts]

Fasten off leaving a long tail.

Flatten Spikes and pin them evenly along the neck, back and Tail. Once happy with the position, sew in place.

SPOTS

BIG SPOT (MAKE 4)

Using Yarn D, make a magic loop.

Round 1 Ch1, 5dc in the loop. [5 sts]

Round 2 2dc in each st around, ss to beg dc. [10 sts]

Fasten off leaving a long tail.

SMALL SPOT (MAKE 4)

Using Yarn D, make a magic loop.

Round 1 Ch1, 6dc in the loop, ss to beg dc. [6 sts]

Fasten off with a long tail.

TO FINISH

Sew the Spots to the Body, using the image as a guide.

Triceratops

YOU WILL NEED

SMALL TRICERATOPS

• 4ply weight cotton yarn, approximately two 50g balls of each:
 - Yarn A Coral
 - Yarn D Green

• Approximately one 50g ball of each:
 - Yarn B White
 - Yarn C Blue

• A 2.5mm (US B/1 or C/2) hook

• 2 safety eyes, 8mm

• Toy stuffing

LARGE TRICERATOPS

• Aran weight cotton yarn, approximately three 50g balls of
 - Yarn A Yellow

• Approximately one 50g ball of each:
 - Yarn B White
 - Yarn C Green
 - Yarn D Pink

• A 4.5mm (US 7) hook

• 2 safety eyes, 9mm

• Toy stuffing

MEASUREMENTS

Small Triceratops measures approx 19cm (7½in) tall
Large Triceratops measures approx 28cm (11in) tall

ABBREVIATIONS

invdec Insert hook in front loop of first st to be decreased, insert hook into front loop of second st to be decreased, yrh and pull through 2 sts, yrh and pull through 2 loops on hook

NOTES

• The pattern for the Small and Large Triceratops is the same. The size is achieved through the yarn and hook size used.
• Parts of this pattern are worked using the amigurumi method.
• Where the pattern specifies the right or left leg, it refers to the dinosaur's perspective.

HEAD

Using Yarn A, make a magic loop.
Round 1 (RS) Ch1 (does not count as st throughout), 6dc in the loop. [6 sts]
Round 2 2dc in each st around. [12 sts]
Round 3 (Dc in next st, 2dc in next st) 6 times. [18 sts]
Round 4 (Dc in next 2 sts, 2dc in next st) 6 times. [24 sts]
Round 5 (Dc in next 3 sts, 2dc in next st) 6 times. [30 sts]
Round 6 (Dc in next 4 sts, 2dc in next st) 6 times. [36 sts]
Round 7 (Dc in next 5 sts, 2dc in next st) 6 times. [42 sts]
Round 8 (Dc in next 6 sts, 2dc in next st) 6 times. [48 sts]
Rounds 9-15 Dc in each st around.
Round 16 Dc in next 4 sts, (dc in next 7 sts, 2dc in next st) 4 times, dc in next 12 sts. [52 sts]
Round 17 Dc in next 4 sts, (dc in next 8 sts, 2dc in next st) 4 times, dc in next 12 sts. [56 sts]
Rounds 18-19 Dc in each st around.
Round 20 Dc in next 4 sts, (dc in next 9 sts, 2dc in next st) 4 times, dc in next 12 sts. [60 sts]
The top of the Head is sloped while the bottom is flat. Mark the top of the Head (30th st) with a marker so you can identify which way up the Head should go when stuffed.
Rounds 21-25 Dc in each st around.
Round 26 (Dc in next 8 sts, invdec) 6 times. [54 sts]
Round 27 (Dc in next 7 sts, invdec) 6 times. [48 sts]
Round 28 (Dc in next 6 sts, invdec) 6 times. [42 sts]
Round 29 (Dc in next 5 sts, invdec) 6 times. [36 sts]

Round 30 (Dc in next 4 sts, invdec) 6 times. [30 sts]
Round 31 (Dc in next 3 sts, invdec) 6 times. [24 sts]
Round 32 (Dc in next 2 sts, invdec) 6 times. [18 sts]
Position safety eyes between Rounds 14-15, approx 16 sts apart.
Stuff the Head.
Round 33 (Dc in next st, invdec) 6 times. [12 sts]
Round 34 (Invdec) 6 times. [6 sts]
Fasten off.
Thread tail through final 6 sts, pulling tight to close.

BODY

The beginning of the Body is made in short rows which will be connected into rounds later in the pattern.
Using Yarn A, ch40 and ss in first ch to make a ring (being careful not to twist the ch).
Row 1 (RS) Dc in next 28 ch, ss in next ch, turn leaving rem ch unworked. [29 sts]
Row 2 (WS) Ch1, ss in first ss, dc in next 18 sts, ss in next st, turn. [20 sts]
Row 3 Ch1, ss in first ss, dc in next 15 sts, ss in next st, turn. [17 sts]
Row 4 Ch1, ss in first ss, dc in next 6 sts, 2dc in next 2 sts, dc in next 4 sts, ss in next st, turn. [16 sts]
Row 5 Ch1, ss in first ss, dc in next 7 sts, ch9, dc in second ch from hook and next 7 ch, dc in same st at base of ch-8, dc in next 8 sts, dc in next 3 sts from Row 2, dc in next 11 ch of the foundation ch, do not turn. [39 sts]
Round 6 (RS) Dc in next 9 sts, dc in next 3 sts from Row 3, dc in next 8 sts from Row 5, working in opposite side of ch-8 from Row 5, dc in next 5 ch, 2dc in next 3 ch, turn to work in sts on opposite side of ch, 2dc in next 3 sts, dc in each st to end. [65 sts]
Round 7 Dc in next 7 sts, 2dc in next st, dc in next 11 sts, invdec, dc in next 5 sts, 2dc in next st, dc in next st, 2dc in next st, dc in next 4 sts, 2dc in next st, dc in next st, 2dc in next st, dc in next 5 sts, invdec, dc in next 11 sts, 2dc in next st, dc in next 10 sts. [69 sts]

Round 8 Dc in next 25 sts, (2dc in next st, dc in next 3 sts) twice, (dc in next 3 sts, 2dc in next st) twice, dc in next 28 sts. [73 sts]
Round 9 Dc in each st around.
Round 10 Dc in next 25 sts, (2dc in next st, dc in next 4 sts) twice, (dc in next 4 sts, 2dc in next st) twice, dc in next 28 sts. [77 sts]
Round 11 Dc in each st around.
Round 12 Dc in next 8 sts, 2dc in next st, dc in next 16 sts, 2dc in next st, dc in next 5 sts, 2dc in next st, dc in next 10 sts, 2dc in next st, dc in next 5 sts, 2dc in next st, dc in next 16 sts, 2dc in next st, dc in next 11 sts. [83 sts]
Rounds 13-17 Dc in each st around.
Round 18 Dc in next 13 sts, invdec, dc in next 9 sts, invdec, dc in next 28 sts, invdec, dc in next 9 sts, invdec, dc in next 16 sts. [79 sts]
Rounds 19-20 Dc in each st around.
Round 21 Dc in next 77 sts, invdec. [78 sts]
Do not fasten off.

LEGS

FRONT LEFT LEG
Cont on from Body using Yarn A.
Round 1 (RS) Dc in next 16 sts, ch13. [16 sts]
Round 2 Being careful not to twist ch, dc in last st from Round 21 of Body, dc in next 16 sts, dc in next 13 ch. [30 sts]
Round 3 Dc in next 15 sts, (invdec) twice, dc in next 11 sts. [28 sts]
Rounds 4-12 Dc in each st around.
Round 13 (Working in bl only), (dc in next 5 sts, invdec) 4 times. [24 sts]

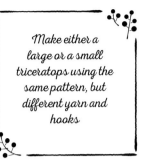

Make either a large or a small triceratops using the same pattern, but different yarn and hooks

Round 14 (Dc in next 2 sts, invdec) 6 times. [18 sts]

Round 15 (Dc in next st, invdec) 6 times. [12 sts]

Round 16 (Invdec) 6 times. [6 sts]

Fasten off.

Thread tail through final 6 sts, pulling tight to close.

BACK LEFT LEG

Skip 5 sts from Round 21 of Body after Front Left Leg, join Yarn A in next st.

Round 1 (RS) Dc in same st as join and next 16 sts, ch13. [17 sts]

Round 2 Being careful not to twist the ch, dc in first st from Round 1, dc in next 16 sts, dc in next 13 ch. [30 sts]

Round 3 (Invdec), dc in next 26 sts, (invdec). [28 sts]

Rounds 4-16 Repeat Rounds 4-16 of Front Left Leg.

Fasten off.

Thread tail through final 6 sts, pulling tight to close.

BACK RIGHT LEG

Join Yarn A in next unworked st from final round of Body, after Back Left Leg.

Round 1 (RS) Dc in same st as join and next 16 sts, ch13. [17 sts]

Round 2 Being careful not to twist the ch, dc in first st from Round 1, dc in next 16 sts, dc in next 13 ch. [30 sts]

Rounds 3-16 Rep Rounds 3-16 of Front Left Leg.

Fasten off.

Thread tail through final 6 sts, pulling tight to close.

FRONT RIGHT LEG

Skip the next 5 sts from final round of Body after Back Right Leg, join Yarn A in next st.

Rounds 1-16 Rep Rounds 1-16 of Back Left Leg.

Fasten off.

Thread tail through final 6 sts, pulling tight to close.

BELLY

LEFT BELLY FLAP

Join Yarn A in same st as last dc from Round 1 of Front Left Leg.

Row 1 (RS) Dc in same st as join and next 6 sts, turn. [7 sts]

Row 2 Ch1, dc in each st across, turn.

Row 3 Ch1, dc in next 6 sts, 2dc in next st, turn. [8 sts]

Rows 4-5 As Row 2.

Rows 6-7 Ch1, 2dc in first st, dc in each st to final st, 2dc in final st, turn. [12 sts]

Row 8 Ch1, dc in each st across in next st.

Fasten off.

RIGHT BELLY FLAP

Join Yarn A in same st as last dc from Round 1 of Back Right Leg.

Row 1 (RS) Dc in same st as join and next 6 sts, turn. [7 sts]

Row 2 Ch1, dc in each st across, turn.

Row 3 Ch1, 2dc in first st, dc in next 6 sts, turn. [8 sts]

Rows 4-7 As Rows 4-7 of Left Belly Flap. [12 sts]

Fasten off leaving a long tail.

Sew the final rows of each Belly Flap together, stuffing the Legs and Belly as you join.

Sew the ch-sps from Round 1 of each Leg to the Belly Flap.

TAIL

Using Yarn A, make a magic loop.

Round 1 (RS) Ch1, 6dc in the loop. [6 sts]

Round 2 2dc in next 3 sts, dc in next 3 sts. [9 sts]

Round 3 (Dc in next st, 2dc in next st) 3 times, dc in next 3 sts. [12 sts]

Round 4 Dc in each st around.

Round 5 (Dc in next st, 2dc in next st) 4 times, dc in next 4 sts. [16 sts]

Round 6 (Dc in next 2 sts, 2dc in next st) 4 times, dc in next 4 sts. [20 sts]

Round 7 (Dc in next 3 sts, 2dc in next st) 4 times, dc in next 4 sts. [24 sts]

Round 8 (Dc in next 4 sts, 2dc in next st) 4 times, dc in next 4 sts. [28 sts]

Round 9 Dc in next st, invdec, dc in next 3 sts, 2dc in next st, (dc in next 2 sts, 2dc in next st) 5 times, dc in next 3 sts, invdec, dc in next st. [32 sts]

Round 10 Dc in next 2 sts, invdec, dc in next 4 sts, 2dc in next st, dc in next 5 sts, 2dc in next st, dc in next 2 sts, 2dc in next st, dc in next 5 sts, 2dc in next st, dc in next 4 sts, invdec, dc in next 2 sts. [34 sts]

Before sewing, pin on the bony frill and adjust until you're happy with the positioning

Round 11 Dc in each st around.
Round 12 Dc in next 14 sts, (2dc in next st, dc in next 4 sts) twice, dc in next 10 sts. [36 sts]
Round 13 Dc in next 2 sts, invdec, dc in next 28 sts, invdec, dc in next 2 sts. [34 sts]
Round 14 Dc in next st, invdec, dc in next 7 sts, (dc in next 2 sts, 2dc in next st) 4 times, dc in next 9 sts, invdec, dc in next st. [36 sts]
Round 15 Dc in each st around.
Fasten off leaving a long tail.
Stuff the Tail and sew it to the back of the Triceratops.

BONY FRILL (MAKE 2)
Using Yarn D, ch47.
Row 1 (RS) Dc in second ch from hook and each ch across, turn. [46 sts]
Row 2 Ch1, dc in next st, (dc in next 8 sts, 2dc in next st) 5 times, turn. [51 sts]
Row 3 Ch1, dc in next st, (dc in next 9 sts, 2dc in next st) 5 times, turn. [56 sts]
Row 4 Ch1, dc in next st, (dc in next 10 sts, 3dc in next st) 4 times, dc in next 11 sts, turn. [64 sts]
Row 5 Ch1, (dc in next 12 sts, 3dc in next st) 4 times, dc in next 12 sts. [72 sts]
Fasten off the first Frill only.
Frills are joined together over the next row. Place Frills together with RS facing out. Work through sts on both pieces to join.
Row 6 Ch1, 2dc in first st, dc in next 12 sts, 2dc in next st, (dc in next 14 sts, 2dc in next st) 3 times, dc in next 12 sts, 2dc in next st. [78 sts]
Fasten off leaving a long tail.

HORNS
NOSE HORN
Using Yarn B, make a magic loop.
Round 1 Ch1, 4dc in the loop. [4 sts]
Round 2 (Dc in next st, 2dc in next st) twice. [6 sts]
Round 3 (Dc in next st, 2dc in next st) 3 times. [9 sts]
Round 4 Dc in each st around.
Round 5 (Dc in next 2 sts, 2dc in next st) 3 times. [12 sts]
Rounds 6-7 Dc in each st around.
Fasten off leaving a long tail.

Attach the horns after you have completed, and stuffed, the head and body

HEAD HORNS (MAKE 2)
Using Yarn B, make a magic loop.
Rounds 1-7 As Rounds 1-7 of Nose Horn. [12 sts]
Round 8 (Dc in next 3 sts, 2dc in next st) 3 times. [15 sts]
Rounds 9-10 Dc in each st around.
Fasten off leaving a long tail.

TOENAILS (MAKE 4)
Using Yarn B, ch10.
Row 1 (WS) Dc in second ch from hook and each ch across, turn. [9 sts]
Row 2 (RS) Ch1, (skip next st, 3tr in next st, ss in next st) 3 times. [12 sts]
Fasten off leaving a long tail.
Sew the Toenails to the Feet with the flat edge of the Toenails sewn to the fl from Round 13 of Legs. Use the image as a guide.

SPOTS
BIG SPOT (MAKE 4)
Using Yarn C, make a magic loop.
Round 1 (RS) Ch1, 5dc in the loop. [5 sts]
Round 2 2dc in each st around, ss to beg dc. [10 sts]
Fasten off leqaving a long tail.

SMALL SPOT (MAKE 4)
Using Yarn C, make a magic loop.

Round 1 Ch1, 6dc in the loop, ss to beg dc. [6 sts]
Fasten off leaving a long tail.

TO FINISH
Stuff the Horns.
Pin the Horns and Bony Frill to the Head. Once happy with the position, sew in place.
Sew the Spots to the Body, using the image as a guide.
Weave in all ends.

Crafty Crocodile

With his sweet embroidered face, nifty hat and colourful scales, this adorable pot-bellied croc is the snazziest reptile we've ever met.

YOU WILL NEED

• 4ply weight cotton yarn, approximately two 50g balls of:
- Yarn A Light Green
• One 50g ball of:
- Yarn B Beige
• A small amount of each:
- Yarn C Blue
- Yarn D White
- Yarn E Pink
- Yarn F Dark Yellow
- Yarn G Dark Green
- Yarn H Light Blue

• A 2.5mm (US B/1 or C/2) hook

• 2 safety eyes, 12mm

• Toy stuffing

• Stitch markers

MEASUREMENTS

21cm (8¼in) tall

ABBREVIATIONS

split tr-cl *Yrh, insert hook in st 2 rounds below, yrh and pull up a loop, yrh and pull through 2 loops on hook; rep from * once more, **yrh, insert hook in next st 2 rounds below, yrh and pull up a loop, yrh and pull through 2 loops on hook; rep from ** once more, yrh and pull through all loops on hook

NOTES

• Parts of this pattern are worked in the amigurumi style as explained on p. 6..
• Stitch markers are used throughout the pattern to show the orientation of parts. Use this along with the images when joining the pieces together.

HEAD

Using Yarn A, make a magic loop.
Round 1 (RS) Ch1 (does not count as st throughout), 6dc in loop. [6 sts]
Round 2 (RS) 2dc in each st around. [12 sts]
Round 3 (Dc in next st, 2dc in next st) 6 times. [18 sts]
Round 4 Dc in each st around.
Round 5 2dc in next st, dc in next 17 sts. [19 sts]
Round 6 Dc in next st, 2dc in next st, dc in next 6 sts, split tr-cl, skip 2 sts on current round, dc in next 8 sts, 2dc in next st. [20 sts]
Round 7 Dc in each st around.
Round 8 Dc in next st, 2dc in next st, dc in next 18 sts. [21 sts]
Round 9 Dc in each st around.
Round 10 Dc in next st, 2dc in next st, dc in next 19 sts. [22 sts]
Round 11 Dc in each st around.
Round 12 Dc in next st, 2dc in next st, dc in next 20 sts. [23 sts]
Round 13 Dc in each st around.
Round 14 Dc in next st, 2dc in next st, dc in next 8 sts, 2dc in next st, dc in next 3 sts, 2dc in next st, dc in next 8 sts. [26 sts]
Round 15 Dc in next 12 sts, 2dc in next st, dc in next 3 sts, 2dc in next st, dc in next 9 sts. [28 sts]

Round 16 Dc in next 10 sts, (2dc in next st, dc in next 4 sts) 3 times, dc in next 3 sts. [31 sts]
Round 17 Dc in next 3 sts, 2dc in next st, dc in next 9 sts, (2dc in next st, dc in next 3 sts,) 3 times, dc in next 5 sts, 2dc in next st. [36 sts]
Round 18 Dc in next 16 sts, (2dc in next st, dc in next 3 sts) 3 times, dc in next 8 sts. [39 sts]
Round 19 Dc in next 18 sts, (2dc in next st, dc in next 2 sts) 3 times, dc in next 12 sts. [42 sts]
Round 20 Dc in next 20 sts, (2dc in next st, dc in next 2 sts) 3 times, dc in next 13 sts. [45 sts]
Round 21 Dc in next 22 sts, (2dc in next st, dc in next 2 sts) 3 times, dc in next 14 sts. [48 sts]
Round 22 (Dc in next 11 sts, 2dc in next st) 4 times. [52 sts]
Rounds 23-34 Dc in each st around. Mark the 29th and 30th sts of Round 23 – this marks the top centre of the Head. Insert safety eyes between Rounds 24-25, approx 26 sts apart.
Round 35 (Dc in next 11 sts, invdec) 4 times. [48 sts]
Round 36 (Dc in next 6 sts, invdec) 6 times. [42 sts]
Round 37 (Dc in next 5 sts, invdec) 6 times. [36 sts]
Round 38 Dc in next 2 sts, invdec, (dc in next 4 sts, invdec) 5 times, dc in next 2 sts. [30 sts]
Round 39 (Dc in next 3 sts, invdec) 6 times. [24 sts]
Round 40 (Dc in next 2 sts, invdec) 6 times. [18 sts]
Stuff the Head.
Round 41 (Dc in next st, invdec) 6 times. [12 sts]

Round 42 (Invdec) 6 times. [6 sts]
Fasten off.
Thread tail through final 6 sts and pull tight to close.

BODY

Using Yarn A, make a magic loop.
Rounds 1-3 (RS) As Rounds 1-3 of Head. [18 sts]
Round 4 (Dc in next 2 sts, 2dc in next st) 6 times. [24 sts]
Round 5 (Dc in next 3 sts, 2dc in next st) 6 times. [30 sts]
Round 6 (Dc in next 2 sts, 2dc in next st, dc in next 2 sts) 6 times. [36 sts]
Round 7 (Dc in next 5 sts, 2dc in next st) 6 times. [42 sts]
Round 8 (Dc in next 3 sts, 2dc in next st, dc in next 3 sts) 6 times. [48 sts]
Round 9 (Dc in next 7 sts, 2dc in next st) 6 times. [54 sts]
Round 10 (Dc in next 4 sts, 2dc in next st, dc in next 4 sts) 6 times. [60 sts]
Rounds 11-22 Dc in each st around.
Round 23 (Dc in next 13 sts, invdec) 4 times. [56 sts]
Round 24 (Dc in next 12 sts, invdec) 4 times. [52 sts]
Round 25 Dc in next 18 sts, (dc in next 3 sts, invdec) 3 times, dc in next 19 sts. [49 sts]
Round 26 Dc in next 17 sts, (invdec, dc in next 3 sts) 3 times, dc in next 17 sts. [46 sts]
Round 27 Dc in next 15 sts, (dc in next 3 sts, invdec) 3 times, dc in next 16 sts. [43 sts]
Mark the 22nd st to indicate the front centre of the Body.
Round 28 Dc in each st around.
Round 29 Dc in next 12 sts, (dc in next 5 sts, invdec) twice, dc in next 17 sts. [41 sts]
Round 30 Dc in each st around.
Round 31 Dc in next 11 sts, (dc in next 5 sts, invdec) twice, dc in next 16 sts. [39 sts]
Stuff Body as you work.
Round 32 Dc in each st around.
Round 33 Dc in next 10 sts, (dc in next 5 sts, invdec) twice, dc in next 15 sts. [37 sts]

Round 34 Dc in next 9 sts, (dc in next 5 sts, invdec) twice, dc in next 14 sts. [35 sts]
Mark the 18th st to indicate the front centre of the Body.
Round 35 Dc in next 8 sts, (dc in next 5 sts, invdec) twice, dc in next 13 sts. [33 sts]
Round 36 Dc in next 7 sts, (dc in next 5 sts, invdec) twice, dc in next 12 sts. [31 sts]
Round 37 Dc in next 6 sts, (dc in next 5 sts, invdec) twice, dc in next 11 sts. [29 sts]
Round 38 Dc in next 5 sts, (dc in next 5 sts, invdec) twice, dc in next 10 sts. [27 sts]
Round 39 Dc in next 4 sts, (dc in next 5 sts, invdec) twice, dc in next 9 sts. [25 sts]

Round 40 Dc in next 3 sts, (dc in next 5 sts, invdec) twice, dc in next 8 sts. [23 sts]
Round 41 Dc in each st around.
Fasten off, leaving a long tail.

TAIL

Using Yarn A, make a magic loop.
Round 1 (RS) Ch1, 6dc in the loop. [6 sts]
Round 2 Dc in each st around.
Round 3 (Dc in next 2 sts, 2dc in next st) twice. [8 sts]
Round 4 Dc in each st around.
Round 5 (Dc in next 3 sts, 2dc in next st) twice. [10 sts]
Round 6 Dc in each st around.
Round 7 (Dc in next 4 sts, 2dc in next st) twice. [12 sts]
Round 8 Dc in each st around.

Round 9 (Dc in next 5 sts, 2dc in next st) twice. [14 sts]
Round 10 Dc in each st around.
Round 11 (Dc in next 6 sts, 2dc in next st) twice. [16 sts]
Round 12 Dc in each st around.
Round 13 (Dc in next 7 sts, 2dc in next st) twice. [18 sts]
Round 14 Dc in each st around.
Round 15 Invdec, dc in next 5 sts, 2dc in next 4 sts, dc in next 5 sts, invdec. [20 sts]
Rounds 16-17 Dc in each st around.
Round 18 Invdec, dc in next 6 sts, 2dc in next 4 sts, dc in next 6 sts, invdec. [22 sts]
Rounds 19-20 Dc in each st around.
Round 21 Invdec, dc in next 7 sts, 2dc in next 4 sts, dc in next 7 sts, invdec. [24 sts]
Rounds 22-23 Dc in each st around.
Round 24 Invdec, dc in next 8 sts, 2dc in next 4 sts, dc in next 8 sts, invdec. [26 sts]
Rounds 25-26 Dc in each st around.
Round 27 Invdec, dc in next 9 sts, 2dc in next 4 sts, dc in next 9 sts, invdec. [28 sts]

Rounds 28-29 Dc in each st around.
Round 30 2dc in next st, dc in next 26 sts, 2dc in next st. [30 sts]
Round 31 Dc in each st around.
Round 32 Dc in next 23 sts, 2dc in next 2 sts, dc in next 5 sts. [32 sts]
Round 33 Dc in each st around.
Round 34 Dc in next 23 sts, 2dc in next st (pm to indicate top centre of tail), dc in next 2 sts, 2dc in next st, dc in next 5 sts. [34 sts]
Round 35 Dc in each st around.
Round 36 Dc in next 18 sts, (2dc in next st, dc in next 4 sts) 3 times, 2dc in next st. [38 sts]
Round 37 Dc in next 12 sts, (dc in next 6 sts, 2dc in next st, dc in next 5 sts, 2dc in next st) twice. [42 sts]
Round 38 Dc in next 12 sts, (dc in next 6 sts, 2dc in next st, dc in next 7 sts, 2dc in next st) twice. [46 sts]
Round 39 Dc in next 18 sts, (2dc in next st, dc in next 8 sts) 3 times, 2dc in next st. [50 sts]
Round 40 Dc in next 8 sts, (dc in next 10 sts, 2dc in next st, dc in next 9 sts, 2dc in next st) twice. [54 sts]
Fasten off, leaving a long tail.

ARMS (MAKE 2)

Using Yarn A, make a magic loop.
Rounds 1-3 (RS) As Rounds 1-3 of Head. [18 sts]
Round 4 (Dc in next 5 sts, 2dc in next st) 3 times. [21 sts]
Rounds 5-6 Dc in each st around.
Round 7 (Invdec) twice, dc in next 15 sts, invdec. [18 sts]
Round 8 (Invdec) twice, dc in next 10 sts, (invdec) twice. [14 sts]
Rounds 9-24 Dc in each st around.
Stuff Arm lightly.
Round 25 Dc in next 2 sts, leave remaining sts unworked. [2 sts]
Flatten the final round and work 7dc evenly across to close.
Fasten off, leaving a long tail.

LEGS (MAKE 2)

Using Yarn A, make a magic loop.
Rounds 1-3 (RS) As Rounds 1-3 of Head. [18 sts]
Round 4 (Dc in next 2 sts, 2dc in next st) 6 times. [24 sts]
Round 5 (Dc in next 3 sts, 2dc in next st) 6 times. [30 sts]
Round 6 (Dc in next 9 sts, 2dc in next st) 3 times. [33 sts]
Round 7 (Working in bl only) Dc in each st around.
Round 8 Dc in next 2 sts, invdec, dc in next 25 sts, invdec, dc in next 2 sts. [31 sts]
Round 9 (Dc in next 8 sts, invdec) twice, dc in next 9 sts, invdec. [28 sts]
Round 10 Dc in each st around.
Round 11 Dc in next 10 sts, (invdec) 4 times, dc in next 10 sts. [24 sts]
Mark the 2nd and 3rd decreases to show the top centre of the foot.
Round 12 (Dc in next 4 sts, invdec) 4 times. [20 sts]
Round 13 Dc in each st around.
Round 14 Dc in next 8 sts, (invdec) twice, dc in next 8 sts. [18 sts]
Round 15 Dc in each st around.
Round 16 (Dc in next 2 sts, 2dc in next st) 6 times. [24 sts]
Rounds 17-22 Dc in each st around.
Round 23 Dc in next st, leave remaining sts unworked. [1 st]
Stuff the foot firmly, then lightly stuff the Leg.

Flatten the final round and work 12dc evenly across to close.
Fasten off, leaving a long tail.

EYELID (MAKE 2)
Using Yarn A, make a magic loop.
Row 1 (RS) Ch1, 3dc in loop, turn. [3 sts]
Row 2 (WS) Ch1, 2dc in each st across, turn. [6 sts]
Row 3 Ch1, (dc in next st, 2dc in next st) 3 times. [9 sts]
Fasten off, leaving a long tail.

SPIKES (MAKE 16)
Make 3 each using Yarns E, F G and H.
Make 2 each using Yarn B and C.
Make a magic loop.
Round 1 (RS) Ch1, 6dc in loop. [6 sts]
Round 2 (Dc in next st, 2dc in next st) 3 times. [9 sts]
Round 3 (Dc in next 2 sts, 2dc in next st) 3 times. [12 sts]
Round 4 (Dc in next 4 sts, invdec) twice. [10 sts]
Fasten off, leaving a long tail.

BERET
Using Yarn B and leaving a long tail, make a magic loop.
Round 1 (RS) Ch1, 8htr in loop. [8 sts]
Round 2 2htr in each st around. [16 sts]
Round 3 (Htr in next st, 2htr in next st) 8 times. [24 sts]
Round 4 (Htr in next 2 sts, 2htr in next st) 8 times. [32 sts]
Round 5 (Htr in next 3 sts, 2htr in next st) 8 times. [40 sts]
Round 6 (Htr in next 2 sts, 2htr in next st, htr in next 2 sts) 8 times. [48 sts]
Round 7 (Htr in next 5 sts, 2htr in next st) 8 times. [56 sts]
Round 8 (Htr in next 3 sts, 2htr in next st, htr in next 3 sts) 8 times. [64 sts]
Round 9 Htr in each st around.
Round 10 (Htr in next 3 sts, htr2tog, htr in next 3 sts) 8 times. [56 sts]
Round 11 (Dc in next 5 sts, invdec) 8 times. [48 sts]
Rounds 12-15 Dc in each st around.

Fasten off.
Use the starting yarn tail to create a loop at the top of the Beret.

TO MAKE UP
Using Yarn D, add a waterline detail to both eyes.
Using Yarn E, make small straight sts across each cheek.
Sew the Eyelids above each eye.
Using Yarn C, embroider the mouth and snout details.
Using Yarn D, embroider the teeth.
Sew the Head to the Body, topping up with stuffing as you join. Use the marked stitches to position the Head so that the snout is centred.
The opening of the Body should sit over Rounds 26-32 at the bottom of the Head.
Sew the Tail to the Body, topping up with stuffing as you join. Position the Tail so that the marked stitch is centred to the top. The opening of the Tail should sit over Rounds 8-28 of the Body.
Sew the Legs and Arms to the Body. The Legs should be positioned so that the closing seam sits in front of the Tail and Body join. The Arms should be joined so the closing seam sits diagonally across Rounds 38-40 of the Body (approx 7 sts apart).
Sew the Spikes to the back of the Body and Tail.
Weave in all ends.

The main part of the beret is worked in half trebles and the brim in double crochet

Embroider teeth, mouth and eye details on the face, then sew the croc's head to the body

The croc has been designed to sit upright when the parts are assembled

Snuggly Red Panda

With his rosy cheeks and round belly, this unusual crocheted companion is too cute to resist! The finishing details make him look very impressive – perfect for someone looking to try some new skills.

YOU WILL NEED

- DK weight cotton yarn, approximately two 50g balls of each:
  - Yarn A Orange
  - Yarn C Brown
- A small amount of each:
  - Yarn B White
  - Yarn D Pink
- A 3mm (US C/2 or D/3) hook
- 2 safety eyes, 12mm
- 1 safety nose, 18mm
- Toy stuffing
- Black stranded cotton

MEASUREMENTS

25cm (9¾in) tall

HEAD

Using Yarn B, make a magic loop.
Round 1 (RS) Ch1 (does not count as st throughout), 6dc in loop. [6 sts]
Round 2 (RS) 2dc in each st around. [12 sts]
Round 3 (1dc, 2dc in next st) 6 times. [18 sts]
Round 4 (2dc, 2dc in next st) 6 times. [24 sts]
Round 5 (3dc, 2dc in next st) 6 times. [30 sts]
Round 6 (4dc, 2dc in next st) 6 times. [36 sts]

Rounds 7-12 Dc in each st around. Change to Yarn C.
Round 13 (5dc, 2dc in next st) twice, change to Yarn A, (5dc, 2dc in next st) twice, change to Yarn C, (5dc, 2dc in next st) twice. [42 sts]
For Rounds 14-15 use Yarn C when working in all Yarn C sts and Yarn A in all Yarn A sts.
Round 14 (6dc, 2dc in next st) 6 times. [48 sts]
Round 15 (7dc, 2dc in next st) 6 timed. [54 sts]
Change to Yarn B.
Round 16 (8dc, 2dc in next st) twice, change to Yarn A, (8dc, 2dc in next st) twice, change to Yarn B, (8dc, 2dc in next st) twice. [60 sts]
For Rounds 17-18 use Yarn B when working in all Yarn B sts and Yarn A in all Yarn A sts.
Round 17 (9dc, 2dc in next st) 6 times. [66 sts]
Round 18 Dc in each st around. Cont with Yarn A.
Rounds 19-26 Dc in each st around. Position safety nose between Rounds 4-5 and safety eyes between Rounds 15-16,13 sts apart.
Round 27 (9dc, dc2tog) 6 times. [60 sts]
Round 28 (8dc, dc2tog) 6 times. [54 sts]
Round 29 (7dc, dc2tog) 6 times. [48 sts]
Round 30 (6dc, dc2tog) 6 times. [42 sts]
Round 31 (5dc, dc2tog) 6 times. [36 sts]
Stuff the Head.

Round 32 (4dc, dc2tog) 6 times. [30 sts]
Round 33 (3dc, dc2tog) 6 times. [24 sts]
Round 34 (2dc, dc2tog) 6 times. [18 sts]
Round 35 (1dc, dc2tog) 6 times. [12 sts]
Round 36 (Dc2tog) 6 times.
Fasten off.
Thread tail through final 6 sts, pulling tight to close.

BODY

Using Yarn A, make a magic loop.
Rounds 1-6 (RS) As Rounds 1-6 of Head. [36 sts]
Round 7 (5dc, 2dc in next st) 6 times. [42 sts]
Rounds 8-9 As Rounds 14-15 of Head. [54 sts]
Rounds 10-16 Dc in each st around.
Round 17 (7dc, dc2tog) 6 times. [48 sts]
Rounds 18-19 Dc in each st around.
Round 20 (6dc, dc2tog) 6 times. [42 sts]
Rounds 21-22 Dc in each st around.
Round 23 (5dc, dc2tog) 6 times. [36 sts]
Rounds 24-25 Dc in each st around.
Round 26 (4dc, dc2tog) 6 times. [30 sts]
Rounds 27-28 Dc in each st around.
Round 29 (3dc, dc2tog) 6 times. [24 sts]
Stuff the Body.
Round 30 Dc in each st around.
Fasten off, leaving a long tail.

ARMS (MAKE 2)

Using Yarn C, make a magic loop.
Rounds 1-4 (RS) As Rounds 1-4 of Head. [24 sts]
Rounds 5-8 Dc in each st around. [24 sts]
Round 9 Dc2tog, dc in each st to end. [23 sts]
Rounds 10-20 As Round 9. [12 sts]
Stuff the Arms.
Round 21-26 Dc in each st around.
Fasten off, leaving a long tail.

LEGS (MAKE 2)

Using Yarn C, make a magic loop.
Rounds 1-5 (RS) As Rounds 1-5 of Head. [30 sts]
Rounds 6-9 Dc in each st around. [30 sts]
Round 10 7dc, (2dc, dc2tog) 4 times, 7dc. [26 sts]
Round 11 7dc, (1dc, dc2tog) 4 times, 7dc. [22 sts]
Round 12 7dc, (dc2tog) 4 times, 7dc. [18 sts]
Round 13 (7dc, dc2tog) twice. [16 sts]
Round 14 Dc in each st around.
Round 15 (6dc, dc2tog) twice. [14 sts]
Round 16 Dc in each st around.
Stuff the Legs as you go.
Round 17 (5dc, dc2tog) twice. [12 sts]
Rounds 18-25 Dc in each st around.
Fasten off, leaving a long tail.

EARS (MAKE 2)

Using Yarn B, make a magic loop.
Round 1 (RS) Ch1, 6dc in a loop. [6 sts]
Round 2 Dc in each st around.
Round 3 2dc in each st around. [12 sts]
Round 4 Dc in each st around.
Round 5 (3dc, 2dc in the next st) 3 times [15 sts]
Round 6 (4dc, 2dc in the next st) 3 times [18 sts]
Round 7 (5dc, 2dc in the next st) 3 times [21 sts]
Round 8 (6dc, 2dc in the next st) 3 times [24 sts]
Rounds 9-10 Dc in each st around.
Round 11 (2dc, dc2tog) 6 times. [18 sts]
Fasten off, leaving a long tail.

INNER EAR (MAKE 2)

Using Yarn C, make a magic loop.
Rounds 1-2 (RS) As Rounds 1-2 of Head. [12 sts]
Fasten off, leaving a long tail.

BLUSH (MAKE 2)

Using Yarn D, work as for Inner Ear.

TUMMY PATCH

Using Yarn C, make a magic loop.
Rounds 1-6 (RS) As Rounds 1-6 of Head. [36 sts]
Fasten off, leaving a long tail.

TAIL

Using Yarn C, make a magic loop.
Rounds 1-5 (RS) As Rounds 1-5 of Head. [30 sts]
Rounds 6-7 Dc in each st around.
Change to Yarn A.
Rounds 8-10 Dc in each st around.
Change to Yarn B.
Round 11 (13dc, dc2tog) twice. [28 sts]
Round 12 Dc in each st around.
Round 13 (12dc, dc2tog) twice. [26 sts]
Change to Yarn A.
Round 14 Dc in each st around.
Round 15 (11dc, dc2tog) twice. [24 sts]
Round 16 Dc in each st around.
Change to Yarn B.
Round 17 (10dc, dc2tog) twice. [22 sts]

Round 18 Dc in each st around.
Round 19 (9dc, dc2tog) twice. [20 sts]
Change to Yarn A.
Round 20 Dc in each st around.
Round 21 (8dc, dc2tog) twice. [18 sts]
Round 22 Dc in each st around.
Change to Yarn B.
Round 23 (7dc, dc2tog) twice. [16 sts]
Round 24 Dc in each st around.
Round 25 (6dc, dc2tog) twice. [14 sts]
Change to Yarn A.
Round 26 Dc in each st around.
Stuff the Tail as you go.
Round 27 (5dc, dc2tog) twice. [12 sts]
Rounds 28-30 Dc in each st around.
Fasten off, leaving a long tail.

TO MAKE UP

Use the images as a guide when making up.
Sew the Head to the Body.
Sew the Inner Ears to the Ears, then sew the Ears to the Head.
Sew the Blush to the cheek area of the Head, and the Tummy to the front of the Body.
Sew the Arms, Legs and Tail in place.
Using Yarn C, embroider the eyebrows and belly button.
Using black stranded cotton, embroider
a mouth.
Weave in any remaining ends.

Beautiful Butterfly

This stunning butterfly is sure to elicit plenty of compliments from your family and friends. Tricky but rewarding, this lovely creature makes a stunning decoration for a child's bedroom, or simply a pretty new friend for a loved one to cherish. Grab an array of blue yarns and get to work!

YOU WILL NEED

• DK weight cotton yarn, a small amount of each:
- Yarn A Light Blue
- Yarn B Dark Navy
- Yarn C Orange
- Yarn D Turquoise Blue
- Yarn E Navy

• A 3.5mm (US E/4) hook

• A 2mm (US B/1) hook

• Metal wire, 0.5mm thick

• Metal wire, 1mm thick

• Stitch markers

MEASUREMENTS

19.5x14cm (7¾x5½in)

LOWER WINGS

Using a 3.5mm hook and Yarn A, ch17.
Row 1 (RS) Dc in second ch from hook and each ch across, turn. [16 sts] Place live loop on marker.
With RS facing, join Yarn B in second dc.
Row 2 (RS) Ch1 (does not count as st), *insert hook in next st, yrh and pull up loop, yrh and pull through 1 loop on hook, skip 1 st, insert hook in next st, yrh and pull up a loop, yrh and pull through 1 loop on hook; rep from * 3 times more, insert hook in next st, yrh and pull up loop (10 loops on hook), place all 10 loops onto your 2mm hook.
Do not fasten off.
With RS facing, join Yarn C in first st from Row 1.
Row 3 Ch1 (counts as dc), dc in first loop on hook, remove loop from 2mm hook, *dc in next loop on 2mm hook, remove loop from 2mm hook, dc in skipped st from Row 1, dc in next loop on hook; rep from * 3 times more, dc in next loop on hook, dc in final st from Row 1, turn. [16 sts]
Row 4 Ch1 (counts as dc), dc in next 2 sts, (ss in centre of next dc, dc in next 2 sts) 4 times, dc in final st, turn. Change to Yarn D.
Row 5 Ch1 (counts as dc), (2dc, skip 1 st) 4 times, 3dc, turn. [12 sts]
Rows 6-7 Ch1 (counts as dc), dc in each st across, turn.
Row 8 Ch1 (counts as dc), dc in next 9 sts, skip 1 st, dc in final st, turn. [11 sts]
Row 9 Ch1 (counts as dc), dc in each st across, turn.
Row 10 Ch1 (counts as dc), dc in each st to final 2 sts, skip 1 st, dc in final st, turn. [10 sts]
Rows 11-12 As Row 10. [8 sts]
Row 13 Ch1 (counts as dc), (dc in next 2 sts, skip 1 st) twice, dc in final st, turn. [6 sts]
Row 14 Ch1 (counts as dc), (dc in next st, skip 1 st) twice, dc in final st.
Fasten off.

EDGING

With RS facing, insert hook into live loop of Yarn A from Row 1.
Work the next round around the 0.5mm wire so the Wings maintain their shape.
Work 17dc around base of Wing, change to Yarn E, 27dc around rem Wing, ss to beg dc.
Fasten off.
Weave in the tails and wire.
Using Yarn E, embroider straight lines down each Wing. You can use the image as a guide.

UPPER LEFT WING

Using a 3.5mm hook and Yarn A, ch17.
Rows 1-4 As Rows 1-4 of Lower Wings. [16 sts]
Change to Yarn D.
Row 5 Ch1 (counts as dc from here to end), dc in st at base of ch-1, dc in next st, (dc in next st, skip 1 st, dc in next st) 4 times, 2dc in next st, dc in final st, turn. [14 sts]
Row 6 Ch1, dc in each st across, turn.
Row 7 Ch1, 2dc in next st, dc in each st across, turn. [15 sts]
Row 8 Ch1, skip next st, dc in next 12 sts, 2dc in next st, turn. [15 sts]
Row 9 Ch1, dc in next 13 sts, ss in next st, turn.
Row 10 Ch1, skip next st, dc in next 13 sts, turn. [14 sts]
Row 11 Ch1, dc in next 11 sts, ss in next st, turn leaving rem st unworked. [13 sts]
Row 12 Ch1, skip next st, dc in next 9 sts, 2dc in next st, turn leaving rem st unworked. [12 sts]
Row 13 Ch1, dc in next 8 sts, ss in next st, turn leaving rem sts unworked. [10 sts]

Row 14 Ch1, skip next st, dc in next 6 sts, 2dc in next st, turn leaving rem st unworked. [9 sts]
Row 15 Ch1, skip next st, dc in next 4 sts, ss in next st, turn leaving rem sts unworked. [6 sts]
Row 16 Ch1, skip next st, dc in next 4 sts, turn. [5 sts]
Row 17 Ch1, skip next st, dc in next st, ss in next st.
Fasten off.

EDGING

With RS facing, insert hook into live loop of Yarn A from Row 1.
Work the next round around the 0.5mm wire so that the Wing maintains it shape.
Work 17dc around base of Wing using Yarn A, change to Yarn E, 34dc around rem Wing, ss to beg dc.
Fasten off.
Weave in the tails and wire.
Using Yarn E, embroider straight lines down each Wing. You can use the image as a guide.

UPPER RIGHT WING

Using a 3.5mm hook and Yarn A, ch17.
Rows 1-4 As Rows 1-4 of Lower Wings. [16 sts]
Change to Yarn D.
Row 5 Ch1 (counts as dc from here to end), dc in st at base of ch-1, dc in next st, (dc in next st, skip 1 st, dc in next st) 4 times, 2dc in next st, dc in final st, turn. [14 sts]
Row 6 Ch1, dc in each st across, turn.
Row 7 Ch1, dc in each st across to final st, 2dc in final st, turn. [15 sts]
Row 8 Ch1, 2dc in next st, dc in next 12 sts, ss in next st, turn. [15 sts]
Row 9 Ch1, skip next st, dc in next 12 sts, 2dc in final, turn.
Row 10 Ch1, dc in next 12 sts, skip 1 st, ss in next st, turn. [14 sts]
Row 11 Ch1, skip next st, dc in next 11 sts, turn leaving rem st unworked. [12 sts]
Row 12 Ch1, 2dc in next st, dc in next 8 sts, ss in next st, turn leaving rem st unworked. [12 sts]

Row 13 Ch1, skip next st, dc in next 9 sts, turn leaving rem sts unworked. [10 sts]
Row 14 Ch1, dc in next 7 sts, ss in next st, turn leaving rem st unworked. [9 sts]
Row 15 Ch1, skip next st, dc in next 4 sts, skip 1 st, dc in next st, turn leaving rem st unworked. [6 sts]
Row 16 Ch1, dc in next 3 sts, ss in next st, turn leaving rem st unworked. [5 sts]
Row 17 Ch1, ss in next st, dc in next st, ss in next st.
Fasten off.
Work Edging and embroidery as Upper Left Wing.

BODY

Using approx 40cm of 0.5mm wire, create a frame for the Body as shown in images on the right. The wire should be threaded over 4 sts on both Upper Wings and 7 sts on both Lower Wings. The base of the Body should measure approx 1cm shorter than the Lower Wings and the antennae approx 2cm.
Cut the same amount of 1mm wire, approx 40cm and work the next round around the 1mm wire.
Using a 2mm hook and Yarn B, join yarn with a dc in first st on Upper Right Wing threaded with wire.

Dc in next 3 sts, dc in next 7 sts on Lower Wing, 20dc around wire at base of Body, 7dc in next Wing, 4dc in next Wing, 3dc in sp before first antennae, place live loop on hook and fasten off leaving approx 4m of yarn to finish the Body.
Wrap Yarn B around the antennae from bottom to top to bottom, so both are covered, and the tails are at the base. Make sure you work around the 1mm wire as well as the 0.5mm frame.
Place live loop of Yarn B back on hook and work over the tails from the antennae.
2dc between antennae, 3dc in sp after antennae. [48 sts around Body]
Round 2 (RS) Dc in next st, (dc2tog) twice, dc in next 5 sts, (dc2tog, dc in next 2 sts) twice, skip 4 sts, (dc in next 2 sts, dc2tog) twice, dc in next 5 sts, (dc2tog) twice, dc in next st, (dc2tog, dc in next 2 st) twice. [38 sts]
Round 3 (Dc in next st, dc2tog) twice, dc in next st, skip 16 sts, (dc in next st, dc2tog) twice, dc in next st, (dc2tog) 4 times. [14 sts]
Fasten off.
Using Yarn B, wrap yarn around the Body.
Weave in all ends.

Sea Turtle

This charming turtle is sure to be a showstopper – with his expressive, wide-set eyes and detailed shell, he's guaranteed to impress!

YOU WILL NEED

• DK weight cotton yarn, approximately one 50g ball of each:
- Yarn A Green
- Yarn B Beige
- Yarn C Brown

• A 2.75mm (C/2) hook

• 2 safety eyes, 9mm

• Stitch marker

• Toy stuffing

MEASUREMENTS

18cm (7in) long

ABBREVIATIONS

fldtr3d Work double treble stitch in front loop 3 rounds below, skip next st on current round

HEAD

Using Yarn A, make a magic loop.
Round 1 (RS) Ch1 (does not count as st throughout), 6dc in loop. [6 sts]
Round 2 (RS) 2dc in each st around. [12 sts]
Round 3 (1dc, 2dc in next st) 6 times. [18 sts]
Round 4 Dc in each st around.
Round 5 (2dc, 2dc in next st) 6 times. [24 sts]
Round 6 (3dc, 2dc in next st) 6 times. [30 sts]
Round 7 (4dc, 2dc in next st) 6 times. [36 sts]
Round 8 Dc in each st around.
Round 9 (5dc, 2dc in next st) 6 times. [42 sts]
Rounds 10-12 Dc in each st around.
Round 13 *(5dc, invdec) twice, 7dc; rep from * once more. [38 sts]
Round 14 *(4dc, invdec) twice, 7dc; rep from * once more. [34 sts]
Rounds 15-16 Dc in each st around.
Round 17 *(3dc, invdec) twice, 7dc; rep from * once more. [30 sts]
Round 18 *(2dc, invdec) twice, 7dc; rep from * once more. [26 sts]
Round 19 *(1dc, invdec) twice, 7dc; rep from * once more. [22 sts]
Round 20 *(Invdec) twice, 7dc; rep from * once more. [18 sts]
Round 21 Dc in each st around.
Fasten off.
Place eyes between Rounds 10-11, 18 sts apart.
The Head should be flatter on the top and the bottom, stuff the Head.

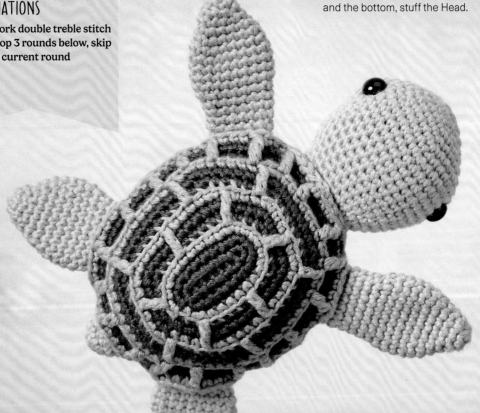

FRONT FLIPPERS (MAKE 2)

Using Yarn A, make a magic loop.
Round 1 (RS) Ch1, 6dc in loop. [6 sts]
Round 2 (RS) (1dc, 2dc in next st) 3 times. [9 sts]
Round 3 Dc in each st around.
Round 4 (2dc, 2dc in next st) 3 times. [12 sts]
Round 5 (3dc, 2dc in next st) 3 times. [15 sts]
Round 6 (4dc, 2dc in next st) 3 times. [18 sts]
Rounds 7-10 Dc in each st around.
Round 11 (7dc, invdec) twice. [16 sts]
Round 12 (6dc, invdec) twice. [14 sts]
Rounds 13-15 Dc in each st around.
Round 16 (5dc, invdec) twice. [12 sts]
Round 17 Dc in each st around.
Fasten off.

BACK FLIPPERS (MAKE 2)

Using Yarn A, work Rounds 1-13 of Front Flippers. [14 sts]
Fasten off.

TAIL

Using Yarn A, make a magic loop.
Rounds 1-3 (RS) As Rounds 1-3 of Flippers. [9 sts]
Round 4 8dc, 2dc in next st. [10 sts]
Fasten off.

TOP SHELL

Using Yarn C, ch8.
Round 1 Dc in second ch from hook, dc in next 5 sts, 3dc in next st, turn to work in opposite side of foundation ch, dc in next 5 sts, 2dc in next st. [16 sts]
Round 2 (2dc in next st, 5dc, 2dc in next 2 sts) twice. [22 sts]
Change to Yarn B.
Round 3 *1dc, 2dc in next st, 5dc, (1dc, 2dc in next st) twice; rep from * once more. [28 sts]
Change to Yarn C.
Round 4 (Working in bl only) *2dc, 2dc in next st, 5dc, (2dc, 2dc in next st) twice; rep from * once more. [34 sts]
Round 5 *3dc, 2dc in next st, 5dc, (3dc, 2dc in next st) twice; rep from * once more. [40 sts]
Change to Yarn B.

Round 6 *3dc, fldtr3d, 2dc in next st, 4dc, fldtr3d, 4dc, 2dc in next st, 1dc, fldtr3d, 2dc, 2dc in next st; rep from * once more. [46 sts]
Change to Yarn C.
Round 7 (Working in bl only) *5dc, 2dc in next st, 5dc, (5dc, 2dc in next st) twice; rep from * once more. [52 sts]
Round 8 *6dc, 2dc in next st, 5dc, (6dc, 2dc in next st) twice; rep from * once more. [58 sts]
Change to Yarn B.
Round 9 *Fldtr3d, 6dc, 2dc in next st, 1dc, fldtr3d, 8dc, fldtr3d, 1dc, 2dc in next st, 7dc, 2dc in next st; rep from * once more. [64 sts]
Change to Yarn C.
Round 10 (Working in bl only) *8dc, 2dc in next st, 5dc, (8dc, 2dc in next st) twice; rep from * once more. [70 sts]
Round 11 (Working in fl only) *9dc, 2dc in next st, 5dc, (9dc, 2dc in next st) twice; rep from * once more. [76 sts]
Change to Yarn B.
Round 12 (3dc, fldtr3d in next st) 19 times, ss to beg dc.
Fasten off.

BOTTOM SHELL

Using Yarn B throughout, work Rounds 1-11 of Top Shell. [76 sts]
Fasten off.

TO MAKE UP

Join Yarn B in first unused bl from Round 10 of Bottom Shell.
Round 1 Dc in each st around. [70 sts]
Flippers, Tail and Head are joined to the Bottom Shell over the next round. Flatten the final round of each piece and work across as indicated. Stuff pieces before joining them.
Round 2 Working through both layers of one Back Flipper and Round 1 of Shell, dc in next 7 sts, dc in next 10 sts of Round 1 only, working through both layers one Front Flipper and Round 1 of Shell, dc in next 6 sts, dc in next 2 sts of Round 1 only, working through both layers of Head and Round 1 of Shell, dc in next 9 sts, dc in next 2 sts of Round 1 only, working through both layers one Front Flipper and Round 1 of Shell, dc in next 6 sts, dc in next 10 sts of Round 1 only, working through both layers of one Back Flipper and Round 1 of Shell, dc in next 7 sts, dc in next 3 sts, working through Tail and Round 1, dc in next 5 sts, dc in final 3 sts from Round 1.
Fasten off, leaving a long tail.
Using the tail, sew sts of Round 2 to the unused bl from Round 11 of Top Shell, stuffing as you join.

Golden Frog

This gorgeous golden frog has a soft round belly and soulful eyes. What's not to love? Hook one up, and it'll soon be hopping its way into your heart.

YOU WILL NEED

• DK weight cotton yarn, approximately two 50g balls of each:
- Yarn A Yellow
• Approximately one 50g ball of each:
- Yarn B Light Yellow
- Yarn C Black

• A 2.5mm (US B/1 or C/2) hook

• 2 safety eyes, 12mm

• Toy stuffing

MEASUREMENTS

15x16cm (6x6¼in)

HEAD AND BODY

Using Yarn A, make a magic loop.
Round 1 (RS) Ch1 (does not count as st throughout), 6dc into loop. [6 sts]
Round 2 (RS) 2dc in each st around. [12 sts]
Round 3 (1dc, 2dc in next st) 6 times. [18 sts]
Round 4 (1dc, 2dc in next st, 1dc) 6 times. [24 sts]
Round 5 (3dc, 2dc in next st) 6 times. [30 sts]
Round 6 (2dc, 2dc in next st, 2dc) 6 times. [36 sts]
Round 7 (5dc, 2dc in next st) 6 times. [42 sts]
Round 8 (3dc, 2dc in next st, 3dc) 6 times. [48 sts]
Round 9 (23dc, 2dc in next st) twice. [50 sts]

Round 10 (12dc, 2dc in next st, 12dc) twice. [52 sts]
Round 11 (25dc, 2dc in next st) twice. [54 sts]
Round 12 (13dc, 2dc in next st, 13dc) twice. [56 sts]
Round 13 (27dc, 2dc in next st) twice. [58 sts]
Round 14 (14dc, 2dc in next st, 14dc) twice. [60 sts]
Round 15 (29dc, 2dc in next st) twice. [62 sts]
Round 16 (15dc, 2dc in next st, 15dc) twice. [64 sts]
Rounds 17-18 Dc in each st around.
Round 19 (3dc, dc2tog, 3dc) 8 times. [56 sts]
Round 20 (5dc, dc2tog) 8 times. [48 sts]
Round 21 (2dc, dc2tog, 2dc) 8 times. [40 sts]
Round 22 Dc in each st around.
Round 23 (2dc, 2dc in next st, 2dc) 8 times. [48 sts]
Rounds 24-31 As Rounds 9-16. [64 sts] Stuff as you work.
Round 32 (31dc, 2dc in next st) twice. [66 sts]
Round 33 (16dc, 2dc in next st, 16dc) twice. [68 sts]
Round 34 (33dc, 2dc in next st) twice. [70 sts]
Round 35 (17dc, 2dc in next st, 17dc) twice. [72 sts]
Round 36 (35dc, 2dc in next st) twice. [74 sts]
Round 37 (18dc, 2dc in next st, 18dc) twice. [76 sts]
Round 38 (37dc, 2dc in next st) twice. [78 sts]
Round 39 (19dc, 2dc in next st, 19dc) twice. [80 sts]
Rounds 40-42 Dc in each st around.

Round 43 (4dc, dc2tog, 4dc) 8 times. [72 sts]
Round 44 (7dc, dc2tog) 8 times. [64 sts]
Round 45 (3dc, dc2tog, 3dc) 8 times. [56 sts]
Round 46 (5dc, dc2tog) 8 times. [48 sts]
Round 47 (2dc, dc2tog, 2dc) 8 times. [40 sts]
Round 48 (3dc, dc2tog) 8 times. [32 sts]
Round 49 (1dc, dc2tog, 1dc) 8 times. [24 sts]
Round 50 (1dc, dc2tog) 8 times. [16 sts]
Round 51 (Dc2tog) 8 times. [8 sts]
Round 52 (Dc2tog) 4 times. [4 sts]
Fasten off.
Thread tail through the final 4 sts and pull tight to close.

EYES (MAKE 2)

Using Yarn B, make a magic loop.
Rounds 1-3 (RS) As Rounds 1-3 of Body. [18 sts]
Rounds 4-5 Dc in each st around.
Round 6 Ss in each st around.
Fasten off, leaving a long tail.
Insert safety eyes between Rounds 4-5.
Sew the Eyes to Rounds 8-13 of Head and Body stuffing as you join.

EYE LIDS (MAKE 2)

Using Yarn A, make a magic loop.
Round 1 (RS) Ch1, 4dc into loop, turn. [4 sts]
Round 2 (WS) Ch1, 2dc in each st across, turn. [8 sts]
Round 3 (RS) Ch1, (1dc, 2dc in next st) 4 times, turn. [12 sts]

Rounds 4-8 Ch1, dc in each st across.
Fasten off, leaving a long tail.
Using image as a gudie, sew Eye Lids to Eyes.

FEET (MAKE 4)
Using Yarn A, make a magic loop.
Round 1 (RS) Ch1, 6dc in loop. [6 sts]
Round 2 (RS) (1dc, 2dc in next st, 1dc) twice. [8 sts]
Round 3 7dc, 2dc in next st. [9 sts]
Round 4 4dc, 2dc in next st, 4dc. [10 sts]
Round 5 9dc, 2dc in next st. [11 sts]
Round 6 5dc, 2dc in next st, 5dc. [12 sts]
Round 7 11dc, 2dc in next st. [13 sts]
Round 8 6dc, 2dc in next st, 6dc. [14 sts]
Flatten the final round and work next row across both sides to join.
Round 9 7dc, turn. [7 sts]
Round 10 *Ch8, tr in third ch from hook, tr in next 2 ch, htr in next 2 ch, dc in next ch**, skip first 2 sts from Row 9, ss in next st, ch10, tr in third ch from hook, tr in next 2 ch, htr in next 3 ch, dc in next 2 ch, skip 1 st from Row 9, ss in next st; rep from * to ** once more, skip next st from Row 9, ss in final st.
Fasten off.

HIND LEGS (MAKE 2)
Using Yarn A, make a magic loop.
Rounds 1-3 (RS) As Rounds 1-3 of Head and Body. [18 sts]
Rounds 4-10 Dc in each st around.
Round 11 8dc, dc2tog, 8dc. [17 sts]
Round 12 Dc in each st around.
Round 13 15dc, dc2tog. [16 sts]
Stuff Leg as you go.
Round 14 Dc in each st around.
Round 15 7dc, dc2tog, 7dc. [15 sts]
Round 16 Dc in each st around.
Round 17 13dc, dc2tog. [14 sts]
Round 18 Dc in each st around.
Round 19 6dc, dc2tog, 6dc. [13 sts]
Round 20 Dc in each st around.
Round 21 11dc, dc2tog. [12 sts]
Round 22 Dc in each st around.
Round 23 5dc, dc2tog, 5dc. [11 sts]
Round 24 Dc in each st around.

Round 25 9dc, dc2tog. [10 sts]
Rounds 26-39 Dc in each st around.
Fasten off, leaving a long tail.
Sew the open side of one Hind Leg to one of the Feet, over Rounds 1-3. Bend the Hind Legs in a half and sew to lower side of the Body. Use the images a guide.

BELLY PATCH
Using Yarn B, make a magic loop.
Rounds 1-8 (RS) As Rounds 1-8 of Head and Body. [48 sts]
Round 9 (7dc, 2dc in next st) 6 times. [54 sts]
Fasten off, leaving a long tail.
Sew Belly Patch between the Hind Legs.

FRONT LEGS (MAKE 2)
Using Yarn A, make a magic loop.
Round 1 (RS) Ch1, 6dc in loop. [6 sts]
Round 2 (RS) 2dc in each st around. [12 sts]
Round 3 (3dc, 2dc in next st) 3 times. [15 sts]
Rounds 4-9 Dc in each st around.
Round 10 13dc, dc2tog. [14 sts]
Round 11 Dc in each st around.
Round 12 6dc, dc2tog, 6dc. [13 sts]
Round 13 Dc in each st around. [13 sts]
Stuff Leg as you go.
Round 14 11dc, dc2tog. [12 sts]
Round 15 Dc in each st around.
Round 16 5dc, dc2tog, 5dc. [11 sts]
Round 17 Dc in each st around.
Round 18 9dc, dc2tog. [10 sts]
Rounds 19-29 Dc in each st around.
Fasten off, leaving a long tail.
Sew the open side of one Front Leg

to one of the Feet, over Rounds 1-3. Sew Front Legs to sides of Body, below neck.

LARGE SPOTS (MAKE 3)
Using Yarn C, make a magic loop.
Rounds 1-3 (RS) As Rounds 1-3 of Head and Body. [18 sts]
Fasten off, leaving a long tail.

MEDIUM SPOTS (MAKE 5)
Using Yarn C, make a magic loop.
Rounds 1-2 (RS) As Rounds 1-2 of Head and Body. [12 sts]
Fasten off, leaving a long tail.

SMALL SPOTS (MAKE 5)
Using Yarn C, make a magic loop.
Round 1 (RS) Ch1, 6dc in loop. [6 sts]
Fasten off, leaving a long tail.

TO FINISH
Using the image as a guide, sew the Spots in place.
Using Yarn C, embroider the mouth.

Magnificent Mandrill

This striking primate is full of fun details, from his intricately shaped head to his cheeky colourful bottom. A delight to make and to look at!

YOU WILL NEED

- DK weight cotton yarn, approximately two 50g balls of:
- Yarn D Brown
- Approximately one 50g ball of each:
- Yarn A Red
- Yarn B Bright Blue
- Yarn C Yellow
- Yarn E Light Yellow

- A 2.75mm (C/2) hook

- 2 safety eyes, 7mm

- Stitch marker

- Toy stuffing

- Tapestry needle

- Cream felt, 6x4cm

- Fabric glue

MEASUREMENTS

17cm (6¾ in) tall

ABBREVIATIONS

2-tr pc 2tr in the same st, remove live loops from hook, insert hook in top of first tr, place loop back on hook and pull through st

HEAD

Using Yarn A, make a magic loop.
Round 1 Ch1 (does not count as st throughout), 6dc in the loop. [6 sts]
Round 2 2dc in each st around. [12 sts]

Round 3 (1dc, 2dc in next st) 6 times. [18 sts]
Round 4 (2dc, 2dc in next st) 3 times, dc in next st, 2-tr pc in next st, 2dc in next st, dc in next 2 sts, 2dc in next st, 2-tr pc in next st, dc in next st, 2dc in final st. [24 sts]
Round 5 (3dc, 2dc in next st) twice, dc in next 3 sts, (1dc, change to Yarn B, 1dc) in same st, dc in next 3 sts, 2dc in next st, change to Yarn A, dc in next 3 sts, change to Yarn B, 2dc in next st, dc in next 3 sts, 2dc in next st. [30 sts]
Change to Yarn A.
Round 6 Dc in next 4 sts, change to Yarn C, (2dc in next st, 4dc) twice, (1dc, change to Yarn B, 1dc) in same st, dc in next 4 sts, 2dc in next st, change to Yarn A, dc in next 3 sts, change to Yarn B, dc in next st, 2dc in next st, dc in next 4 sts, (1dc, change to Yarn C, 1dc) in next st. [36 sts]
Rounds 7-9 Dc in next 17 sts, change to Yarn B, dc in next 7 sts, change to Yarn A, dc in next 3 sts, change to Yarn B, dc in next 8 sts, change to Yarn C, dc in next st.
Round 10 Dc in next 17 sts, change to Yarn B, dc in next st, (1dc, 2dc in next st) 3 times, change to Yarn A, dc in next 3 sts, change to Yarn B, (2dc in next st, 1dc) 3 times, dc in next 2 sts, change to Yarn C, dc in next st. [42 sts]
Round 11 (Skip 1 st, 5tr in fl of next st, skip 1 st, dc in fl of next st) 4 times, change to Yarn D, dc in next 2 sts, (2dc, 2dc in next st) 3 times, htr in next 3 sts, (2dc in next st, 2dc) 3 times, dc in next 3 sts. [56 sts]
Round 12 Dc in 16 unworked bl from Round 10, dc in next 2 sts, (3dc, 2dc

in next st) 3 times, htr in next 3 sts, (2dc in next st, 3dc) 3 times, dc in next 3 sts. [54 sts]
Round 13 Dc in next 18 sts, (4dc, 2dc in next st) 3 times, htr in next 3 sts, (2dc in next st, 4dc) 3 times, dc in next 3 sts. [60 sts]
Round 14 Dc in next 33 sts, htr in next 9 sts, dc in next 18 sts.
Rounds 15-17 Dc in each st around.
Secure eyes between Rounds 11-12, approx 7 sts apart.
Round 18 Dc in next 16 sts, (skip 1 st, 5tr in fl of next st, skip 1 st, dc in fl of next st) 11 times. [82 sts]
Change to Yarn C.
Round 19 Dc in next 16 sts, dc in next 44 unworked loops from 2 rounds below. [60 sts]
Rounds 20-25 Repeat Rounds 18-19 another 3 times, changing to Yarn E at end of Round 20 and Yarn D at end of Round 22.
Round 26 (8dc, invdec) 6 times. [54 sts]
Stuff Head as you work.
Round 27 (7dc, invdec) 6 times. [48 sts]
Round 28 (6dc, invdec) 6 times. [42 sts]
Round 29 (5dc, invdec) 6 times. [36 sts]
Round 30 (4dc, invdec) 6 times. [30 sts]
Round 31 (3dc, invdec) 6 times. [24 sts]
Round 32 (2dc, invdec) 6 times. [18 sts]
Round 33 (1dc, invdec) 6 times. [12 sts]
Round 34 (Invdec) 6 times. [6 sts]
Fasten off.

Thread tail through final 6 sts, pull tight to close.

EYEBROWS
Using Yarn D, ch8.
Fasten off and sew above the eyes.

BODY
Using Yarn B, make a magic loop.
Rounds 1-3 (RS) As Rounds 1-3 of Head. [18 sts]
Round 4 (2dc, 2dc in next st) 6 times. [24 sts]
Change to Yarn A.
Round 5 (3dc, 2dc in next st) 6 times. [30 sts]
Round 6 (4dc, 2dc in next st) 6 times. [36 sts]
Change to Yarn D.
Round 7 (5dc, 2dc in next st) 6 times. [42 sts]
Round 8 (6dc, 2dc in next st) 6 times. [48 sts]
Round 9 (7dc, 2dc in next st) 6 times. [54 sts]
Rounds 10-17 Dc in each st around.
Round 18 (7dc, invdec) 6 times. [48 sts]
Rounds 19-23 Dc in each st around.
Round 24 (6dc, invdec) 6 times. [42 sts]
Rounds 25-27 Dc in each st around.
Round 28 (5dc, invdec) 6 times. [36 sts]
Round 29 (4dc, invdec) 6 times. [30 sts]
Fasten off, leaving a long tail.

LEGS (MAKE 2)
Using Yarn D, make a magic loop.
Round 1 (RS) Ch1, 6dc in the loop. [6 sts]
Round 2 (RS) 2dc in each st around. [12 sts]
Round 3 (1dc, 2dc in next st) twice, (ch4, dc in next st, ch4, 2dc in next st) twice, ch4, (dc in next st, 2dc in next st) twice. [18 sts, 5 ch-4 sps]
Round 4 Dc in each dc around, pushing the ch-4 to the RS for toes.
Round 5 Dc in next 5 sts, (invdec) 4 times, dc in next 5 sts. [14 sts]
Rounds 6-15 Dc in each st around. Stuff the Legs.

Row 16 Flatten Round 15, ch1, 7dc evenly across to close lower Leg. [7 sts]
Round 17 Ch1, dc in fl of next 6 sts, 2dc in fl next st, turn to work in bl, dc in next 6 sts, 2dc in next st. [16 sts]
Rounds 18-26 Dc in each st around.
Fasten off, leaving a long tail.

ARMS (MAKE 2)
Using Yarn D, ch6.
Round 1 (RS) Dc in second ch from hook and next 3 ch, 3dc in next st, turn to work in the opposite side of foundation ch, dc in next 3 sts, 2dc in next st. [12 sts]
Round 2 2-tr pc in next 5 sts, dc in next 7 sts.
Rounds 3-24 Dc in each st around.
Fasten off, leaving a long tail.

TO MAKE UP
Stuff the Body and sew to Head. Cut an oval shape from felt to fit the front of the Body. Using glue, secure in place.

Flatten the top of the Legs and sew to the Body between Rounds 9-10. Sew the tops of the thighs to the lower Body to allow the Mandrill to sit. Stuff and flatten the top of the Arms and sew between Body and Head.

Penguin Pal

This realistic design is based on the Humboldt penguin, native to Peru and Chile. This crochet pal stands at a height of about 30cm, making him a nice big project! Add some glossy safety eyes and embroider specs on the penguin's belly for a few extra-realistic touches.

YOU WILL NEED

• DK weight cotton yarn, approximately two 50g balls of:
- Yarn A Black
- Yarn C White
• Approximately one 50g ball of:
- Yarn B Pink

• A 2.75mm (US C/2) hook

• 2 looped glass safety eyes, 10mm (available from www.mohairbearmakingsupplies.co.uk)

• Toy stuffing

• 140cm craft wire, 2mm thick

• Long-nose pliers

• All-purpose adhesive

MEASUREMENTS

32cm (12½in) tall

BEAK

TOP BEAK
Using Yarn A, ch2.
Row 1 (WS) 3dc in second ch from hook, turn. [3 sts]
Row 2 (RS) Ch1 (does not count as st throughout), dc in each st to end, turn.
Row 3 Ch1, 1dc, 2dc in next st, 1dc, turn. [4 sts]

Row 4 Ch1, 1dc, 2dc in next 2 sts, 1dc, turn. [6 sts]
Row 5 Ch1, (1dc, 2dc in next st, 1dc) across to end. [8 sts]
Rows 6-13 As Row 2.
Row 14 Ch1, (1dc, 2dc in next st) twice, (2dc in next st, 1dc) twice, turn. [12 sts]
Row 15 As Row 2.
Row 16 (Working in fl only) As Row 5, do not turn. [16 sts]
Row 17 (RS) Rotate beak, work 15dc evenly along row ends, dc in tip of beak, 15dc evenly along row ends, change to Yarn B, dc in each st across working over the strand of Yarn A.
Fasten off, leaving a long tail of yarn.

LOWER BEAK
Using Yarn A, make magic loop.
Row 1 (RS) Ch1, 6dc into loop, turn. [6 sts]
Row 2 (WS) Ch1, 2dc in each st to end across, turn. [12 sts]
Rows 3-13 Ch1, dc in each st to end, turn.
Change to Yarn B and carry Yarn A, working over the strand.
Row 14 (1dc, 2dc in next st) 3 times, (2dc in next st, 1dc) 3 times, turn. [18 sts]
Row 15 Ch1, dc in each st to end, turn.
Row 16 Ch1, (1dc, 2dc in next st) 6 times, turn. [24 sts]
Change to Yarn A and fasten off Yarn B.

HEAD

JOIN BEAK PIECES
Row 1 (RS) Ch1, dc in next 4 sts, place Top and Lower Beak together with RS facing out, dc in next 16 sts on both pieces, dc in next 4 sts of Lower Beak, ss to beg dc to join edges, turn. [24 sts]
Row 2 (WS) (Working in fl only) Ch1, dc in next 2 sts, *(1dc, 2dc in next st, 1dc) 3 times, dc in next 2 sts; rep from * once more, ss to beg dc, turn. [30 sts]
Row 3 Ch1, dc in each st to end, ss to beg dc, turn.
Row 4 Ch1, (3dc, 2dc in next st) 3 times, 6dc, (2dc in next st, 3dc) 3 times, ss to beg dc, turn. [36 sts]
Row 5 As Row 3.
Row 6 Ch1, dc in next 3 sts, (2dc in next st, 4dc) 3 times, (4dc, 2dc in next st) 3 times, dc in next 3 sts, ss to beg dc, turn. [42 sts]
Row 7 As Row 3.
Rows 8-9 Ch1, dc in each dc to last 6 sts, turn. [30 sts at end of Row 9]
Rows 10-13 Ch1, dc in each st to end, turn.
Row 14 Ch1, dc in each st to end, ch12, ss to beg dc, turn. [30 sts, 1 ch-12 sp]
Do not fasten off.

BACK OF HEAD
Cont on in rounds.
Round 1 Dc in next 12 ch, dc in next 30 sts. [42 sts]
Round 2 Dc2tog, 8dc, dc2tog, (4dc, dc2tog) twice, 6dc, (dc2tog, 4dc) twice. [36 sts]

Round 3 Dc2tog, 6dc, dc2tog, (3dc, dc2tog) twice, 6dc, (dc2tog, 3dc) twice. [30 sts]
Round 4 Dc2tog, 4dc, dc2tog, (2dc, dc2tog) twice, 6dc, (dc2tog, 2dc) twice. [24 sts]
Round 5 Dc2tog, 2dc, dc2tog, (1dc, dc2tog) twice, 6dc, (dc2tog, 1dc) twice. [18 sts]
Round 6 (Dc2tog) 4 times, 6dc, (dc2tog) twice. [12 sts]
Round 7 (Dc2tog) 6 times. [6 sts]
Fasten off.
Thread tail through final 6 sts and pull tight to close.

SHAPE FACE
With RS of Head facing and Beak pointing downwards, join Yarn A in the fifth unworked front loop from Row 1 of Head.
Row 1 (RS) Dc in same st as ss, dc in next 15 unworked fl, turn. [16 sts]
Change to Yarn B and carry Yarn A.
Row 2 (WS) Ch1, 6dc, change to Yarn A, 4dc, change to Yarn B, 6dc, turn.
Row 3 Ch1, 3dc in next st, 5dc, change to Yarn A, 4dc, change to Yarn B, 5dc, 3dc in next st, change to Yarn A, dc in next 8 unworked loops of Row 1 of Head, ss to beg dc. [28 sts]
Fasten off, leaving a long tail.

NECK
With RS of back of Head facing, join Yarn A with a ss to the back of first ch of ch-12.
Round 1 (RS) Ch1, dc in same st as ss, dc in next 11 ch, change to Yarn C, 6dc evenly down edge of rows, dc in next 12 sts of Rows 7 and 8, 6dc evenly in row ends, ss to beg dc. [36 sts]
Round 2 (WS) Ch1, 24dc, change to Yarn A, 12dc, ss to beg dc, turn.
Round 3 Ch1, 12dc, change to Yarn C, 24dc, ss to beg dc, turn.
Round 4 As Round 2.
Round 5 Ch1, 12dc, change to Yarn C, 2dc, *(1dc, 2dc in next st, 1dc) 3 times, 2dc; rep from * once more, ss to beg dc, turn. [42 sts]
Round 6 Ch1, 30dc, change to Yarn A, 12dc, ss to beg dc, turn.

Round 7 Ch1, 2dc in next dc, 10dc, 2dc in next dc, change to Yarn C, 30dc, ss to beg dc, turn. [44 sts]
Round 8 Ch1, 30dc, change to Yarn A, 14dc, ss to beg dc, turn.
Continue with Yarn A and carry Yarn C.
Round 9 Ch1, 2dc in next dc, 12dc, 2dc in next dc, 30dc, ss to beg dc, turn. [46 sts]
Round 10 Ch1, dc in each st to end, ss to beg dc, turn.
Round 11 Ch1, 2dc in next dc, 14dc, 2dc in next dc, 30dc, ss to beg st, turn. [48 sts]
Rounds 12-14 As Round 10.
Do not fasten off.

BODY
Cont with Yarn A and carrying Yarn C.
Row 1 (RS) Ch1, 24dc, change to Yarn C, 13dc, ss in next st, turn leaving rem sts unworked. [38 sts]
Row 2 (WS) Dc in same dc as ss, 9dc, ss in next st, turn. [11 sts]
Row 3 Dc in same st as ss, 4dc, 2dc in next 2 sts, 4dc, dc in next unworked st from Neck, ss in next st, turn. [15 sts]
Row 4 Dc in same dc as ss, dc in each st across, dc in next unworked st from Neck, ss in next st, turn. [17 sts]
Row 5 Dc in same st as ss, 7dc, 2dc in next 2 sts, 7dc, dc in next st from Neck, ss in next st, turn. [21 sts]

The penguin has been designed to stand upright when the parts are assembled

Round 6 Dc in same dc as ss, 20dc, dc in next unworked st from Neck, change to Yarn A, 30dc, ss to beg dc, turn. [52 sts]

Round 7 Ch1, 30dc, change to Yarn C, 10dc, 2dc in next 2 sts, 10dc, ss to beg dc, turn. [54 sts]

Rounds 8 Ch1, 24dc, change to Yarn A, dc in each st to end, ss to beg dc, turn.

Round 9 Ch1, 30dc, change to Yarn C, dc in each st to end, ss to beg dc, turn.

Round 10 As Round 8.

Round 11 Ch1, 30dc, change to Yarn C, 11dc, 2dc in next 2 sts, 11dc, ss to beg dc, turn. [56 sts]

Round 12 Ch1, 26dc, change to Yarn A, 30dc, ss to beg dc, turn.

Round 13 As Round 9.

Round 14 As Round 12.

Round 15 Ch1, 30dc, change to Yarn C, 12dc, 2dc in next 2 sts, 12dc, ss to beg dc, turn. [58 sts]

Round 16 Ch1, 28dc, change to Yarn A, 30dc, ss to beg dc, turn.

Round 17 Ch1, 30dc, change to Yarn C, 28dc, ss to beg dc, turn.

Round 18 As Round 16.

Round 19 Ch1, 30dc, change to Yarn C, 13dc, 2dc in next 2 sts, 13dc, ss to beg dc, turn.
[60 sts]

Round 20 Ch1, 30dc, change to Yarn A, 30dc, ss to beg dc, turn.

Round 21 Ch1, 30dc, change to Yarn C, 30dc, ss to beg dc, turn.

Rounds 22-38 Rep Rounds 20-21 another 8 times, then rep Row 20.

Round 39 Ch1, 30dc, change to Yarn C, dc in next 2 sts, *(1dc, dc2tog, 1dc) 3 times, dc in next 2 sts; rep from * once more, ss to beg dc, turn. [54 sts]

Rounds 40-42 Rep Rounds 8-9, then rep Row 8.

Fasten off Yarn C only.

Rounds 43-44 Ch1, dc in each st to end, ss to beg dc, turn.

A space for the Legs is created over the next round.

Round 45 Ch1, 30dc, ch24, skip 24 sts, ss to beg dc, do not turn. [30 sts, 1 ch-24 sp]

Round 46 Ch1, 30dc, dc in next 24 ch, ss to beg dc. [54 sts]

Round 47 Ch1, (3dc, dc2tog, 20dc, dc2tog) twice, ss to beg dc. [50 sts]

Round 48 Ch1, (3dc, dc2tog, 18dc, dc2tog) twice, ss to beg dc. [46 sts]

Round 49 Ch1, (3dc, dc2tog, 16dc, dc2tog) twice, ss to beg dc. [42 sts]

Round 45 Ch1, (3dc, dc2tog, 14dc, dc2tog) twice, ss to beg dc. [38 sts]

Rounds 46-51 Continue decreasing 4 sts on each round as set. [14 sts at end of Round 51]

Round 52 Ch1, *3dc, (dc2tog) twice; rep from * once more, ss to beg dc. [10 sts]

Round 53 Ch1, (dc2tog) 5 times, ss to beg dc. [5 sts]

Fasten off.
Thread tail through final 5 sts, pulling tight to close.

LEFT THIGH

With RS of Body facing, join Yarn C in 18th unworked dc from Round 44 of Body.

Row 1 (RS) Dc in same st as join, dc in next 6 sts, dc in back of next 7 ch, turn. [14 sts]

Row 2 (WS) Ch1, dc in each st to end, turn.

Row 3 As Row 2.

Row 4 Ch1, (dc2tog, 1dc) 4 times, dc2tog. [9 sts]

Fasten off, leaving a long tail.

RIGHT THIGH

With RS of Body facing, join Yarn C in back of eighth ch from leg space on Body.

Skip the next 10 ch by the leg and join Yarn C with a ss to the reverse side of the next ch.

Row 1 Dc in same st as join, dc in back of next 6 ch, dc in next 7 sts, turn. [14 sts]

Rows 2-4 As Rows 2-4 of Left Thigh.

Fasten off, leaving a long tail.

FEET (MAKE 2)

Using Yarn A, make magic loop.
Round 1 (RS) Ch1, 6dc in loop, ss to beg dc. [6 sts]
Round 2 (RS) (2dc in next st, 1dc) 3 times. [9 sts]
Round 3 (2dc in next st, 2dc) 3 times. [12 sts]
Round 4 (2dc in next st, 3dc) 3 times. [15 sts]
Round 5 (2dc in next st, 4dc) 3 times. [18 sts]
Round 6 Dc in each st around.
Round 7 (2dc in next st, 5dc) 3 times. [21 sts]
Round 8 Dc in each st around.
Round 9 (2dc in next st, 6dc) 3 times. [24 sts]
Round 10 4dc, skip 16 sts, 4dc. [8 sts]
Round 11 Dc in each st around.
Fasten off.
Thread tail through final 8 sts, pulling tight to close.
Join Yarn A in first skipped st from Round 10.
Round 12 Dc in same st as ss, 3dc, skip 8 sts, 4dc. [8 sts]
Rounds 13-14 Dc in each st around.
Fasten off.
Thread tail through final 8 sts, pulling tight to close.
Join Yarn A in first skipped st from Round 12.
Round 15 Dc in same st as ss, dc in next 7 sts.
Round 16 Dc in each st around.
Fasten off.
Thread tail through final 8 sts, pulling tight to close.

FLIPPERS (MAKE 2)

UNDERSIDE
Using Yarn B ch26.
Row 1 Dc in second ch from hook, dc in next 2 ch, htr in next 3 ch, tr in next 9 ch, 2tr in next ch, tr in next 2 ch, (2htr in next ch, htr in next 2 ch) twice, 5htr in final ch, turn to work in opposite side of foundation ch, htr in next 6 ch, tr in next 6 ch, (2tr in next ch, tr in next 2 ch) twice, 2htr in next ch, htr in next 2 ch, dc in next 3 ch, turn. [59 sts]

Row 2 Ch1, 29dc, 3dc in next st, 29dc, turn. [61 sts]
Fasten off.

FLIPPER TOP
Using Yarn A, ch26.
Rows 1-2 As Rows 1-2 of Underside. [61 sts]
Position Top and Underside together with RS facing out. Work next round through both pieces to join.
Round 3 Ch1, dc in next 30 sts, 5dc in next st, dc in next 30 sts, 5dc evenly down row-end edge, ss to beg dc.

EYES (MAKE 2)

Using Yarn B, ch2.
Round 1 6dc in second ch from hook, ss to beg dc. [6 sts]
Row 2 Ch2, htr in first st.
Fasten off, leaving long tail.

TO MAKE UP

Stuff Body firmly, sew Flippers either side of Body, leaving a gap to insert legs.
Sew together seam of Beak and stuff. Sew edges of face shaping to Beak. Insert safety eyes through centre of Eye and sew to Head. Sew edge of Row 2 of Eye to face shaping.

LEGS AND MARKINGS

Using pliers, make a bend in the wire 17cm from end. Make first 2 toes by bending the wire back and forth at 5cm intervals. Make a 4cm third toe and 3.5cm fourth toe. Squeeze sharp ends around wire, so Legs are double thickness. Bend wire to fit inside Body. Bend tips of toes downwards to shape claws. Wind one layer of Yarn B around toes and 2 layers around Legs.
Apply adhesive to ends of the yarn at the base of the Foot and leave to dry. Position toes on foot and sew in place. Place Legs inside opening and sew the openingtogether.
Stuff Thighs and sew edges together. Thread yarn through stitches of last round of each thigh, pull up tight around leg and fasten off.

Adjust Legs so the penguin stands without tipping over.
Weave in all the yarn ends.
Using Yarn C, embroider lines over the Head and Body.
Using Yarn A, embroider small stitches over front of Body.
Weave in all ends.

Diddy Dinosaur

Say hello to this adorable diddy dinosaur. He may try his best to project
a fearsome image but, truth is, if you bumped into him at Jurassic Park, he'd
probably be relaxing by the lake eating cake rather than trying
to munch on any passing humans.

YOU WILL NEED

- 4ply weight cotton yarn, approximately two 50g balls of:
  - Yarn A Light Green
- A small amount of each:
  - Yarn B Coral
  - Yarn C Jade
- 2.75 mm (UK 11, US C/2) crochet hook
- Toy stuffing
- Two 8mm black safety eyes
- Stitch marker
- Tapestry or yarn needle

FINISHED SIZE

19cm (7½") high

FOUNDATION

Using Yarn A, ch8. Stitches will be worked around both sides of the foundation chain.

Round 1 Inc in 2nd ch from hook, 5dc, 4dc in next (last) st, continue on the other side of the foundation chain, 5dc, inc in last st. [18sts]

Don't forget to put the stitch marker at the first st in the beginning of each round.

Round 2 Inc, 7dc, 2inc, 7dc, inc. [22sts]

Round 3 2inc, 8dc, 3inc, 8dc, inc. [28sts]

Round 4 3inc, 10dc, 4inc, 10dc, inc. [36sts]

Round 5 (5dc, inc) 6 times. [42sts]

Rounds 6–10 1dc in each st around

Round 11 (5dc, dc2tog) 6 times. [36sts]

Round 12 7dc, (2dc, dc2tog) 6 times, 5dc. [30sts]

Round 13 (3dc, dc2tog) 6 times. [24sts]

Round 14 4dc, (1dc, dc2tog) 6 times, 2dc. [18sts]

Insert the safety eyes, using the image as a guide for placement. Fill the head firmly with stuffing and, from this point, continue stuffing as you go.

Round 15 8dc, 3dc2tog, 4dc [15sts]

Rounds 16–17 1dc in each st around

Round 18 2dc, inc, 12dc. [16sts]

Round 19 1dc in each st around

Round 20 3dc, inc, 12dc. [17sts]

Round 21 1dc in each st around

Round 22 3dc, inc, 13dc. [18sts]

Round 23 1dc in each st around

Round 24 4dc, inc, 13dc. [19sts]

Round 25 1dc in each st around

Round 26 5dc, inc, 13dc. [20sts]

Round 27 7dc, ch8 (to form the backbone of the dinosaur), you now work around this ch8 in the same way as the first round of the head (both sides of the new foundation chain, plus the neck). Place your stitch marker in the next st (as this is going to be the beginning of each round from this point), inc in 2nd ch from the hook, 33dc, inc in the last st. [37sts]

Round 28 2inc, 33dc, 2inc. [41sts]

Round 29 3inc, 36dc, 2inc. [46sts]

Round 30 (4dc, inc) 9 times, 1dc in last st. [55sts]

Round 31 1dc in each st around

Round 32 (5dc, inc) 9 times, 1dc in last st. [64sts]

At this point he'll look like Nessie emerging from the Loch!

Rounds 33–39 1dc in each st around

FIRST BACK LEG

Divide the work to crochet the four legs. In order to do this, you have to find the middle of the dinosaur body at the back. Continue crocheting 1dc around until that point (if you're not already in there).

Then work 2dc, place the stitch marker in the next st, 9dc, ch6. Join the last ch and the dc with the stitch marker with an ss.

The leg will be formed from the 9dc from the body and the new 6ch foundation chain.

Continue working the first back leg:

Round 1 15dc (9 from the body and 6 from the ch). [15sts]

Rounds 2–5 1dc in each st around

Round 6 (1dc, dc2tog) 5 times. [10sts]

Round 7 Dc2tog 5 times. [5sts]

Fasten off leaving a long tail. Using your yarn needle, weave the yarn tail through the front loop of each remaining stitch and pull it tight to close.

FIRST FRONT LEG

Count 9 sts along from where the first back leg is (this will become the belly) and attach the yarn to the next st (10th st along).

Work 9dc, ch6 and join the last ch and the first dc with a ss.

Repeat Rounds 1-7 as the first back leg.

SECOND FRONT LEG

Count 5sts along to the left from where the second front leg is (space between legs) and attach the yarn to the next st (6th st along). Work 9dc, ch6 and join the last ch and the first dc with a ss.

Repeat Rounds 1-7 as the first back leg.

SECOND BACK LEG

Count 9sts along to the left from where the first front leg is (this is the other side of the belly) and attach the yarn to the next st (10th st along). Work 9dc, ch6 and join the last ch and the first dc with a ss.

Repeat Rounds 1-7 as the first back leg.

BELLY

Between the legs you have 9st spaces along the sides and 5st spaces at front and back. The belly is made by creating flaps from these sts.
Start with the 9st space between the back and the front legs.
Attach the yarn to 1st st next to the first leg you made.
Row 1 9dc, turn
Rows 2-12 ch1 (does not count as st), 9dc, turn
Fasten off, leaving a long tail for sewing in later.
The back underbelly is made in the same way.
Attach the yarn to the 1st st after the last leg you made.
Row 1 5dc, turn
Rows 2-3 ch1 (does not count as st), 5dc, turn
Fasten off, leaving a long tail for sewing. Work the flap between the front legs in same way.
Using the tapestry needle, carefully sew the front flap to both front legs and the back flap to both back legs. Fill each leg with stuffing.
Sew the wide belly flap to the other side of the dinosaur.
Sew the belly flap to both the legs and the flaps between them, stuffing the body as you go.

TAIL

Round 1 Using Yarn A, start with a magic ring, 5dc in ring, pull ring tight. [5sts]
Round 2 1dc in each st around
Round 3 inc in each st around. [10sts]
Round 4 1dc in each st around
Round 5 (1dc, inc) 5 times. [15sts]
Round 6 1dc in each st around
Round 7 (2dc, inc) 5 times. [20sts]
Round 8 1dc in each st around
Round 9 (3dc, inc) 5 times. [25sts]
Round 10 1dc in each st around
Round 11 (4dc, inc) 5 times. [30sts]
Rounds 12–14 1dc in each st around
Fasten off leaving a long tail for sewing. Fill with stuffing.

LARGE SPIKES (MAKE 6)

Round 1 Using Yarn B, start with a magic ring, 5dc in ring, pull ring tight. [5sts]
Round 2 1dc in each st around
Round 3 inc in each st around. [10sts]
Round 4 1dc in each st around
Fasten off leaving long tail for sewing. Don't stuff.

MEDIUM SPIKES (MAKE 2)

Round 1 Using Yarn B, start with a magic ring, 5dc in ring, pull ring tight. [5sts]
Round 2 1dc in each st around
Round 3 inc in each st around. [10sts]
Fasten off leaving long tail for sewing. Don't stuff.

SMALL SPIKES (MAKE 2)

Round 1 Using Yarn B, start with a magic ring, 5dc in ring, pull ring tight. [5sts]

Round 2 1dc in each st around
Fasten off leaving long tail for sewing. Don't stuff.

SPOTS (MAKE 6)

Round 1 Using Yarn C, start with a magic ring, 6dc in ring, pull ring tight.
Fasten off leaving a long tail for sewing.

FINISHING

Stuff the tail and then sew it to the body. Sew the 10 spikes, descending from the largest to the smallest ones along the dinosaur spine towards the tail.
Finally, sew the spots to the body using the images as a guide for their placement.
There you go – your dino is ready for adventures!

Cosy Leopard

With that smile and those winter woollies, we've no doubt that this little leopard is a total softie. He's wrapped up warm to explore the woods nearby, but is sure to be home in time for tea.

YOU WILL NEED

- DK weight cotton yarn, approximately two balls of each:
-Yarn A Beige
- Approximately one 50g ball of each:
-Yarn B White
-Yarn C Light Blue
-Yarn D Peach
-Yarn E Pink
-Yarn F Brown
-Yarn G Black

- 2.75mm (US C/2) crochet hook

- Soft toy stuffing

- Four stitch markers

- Yarn needle

ABBREVIATIONS

BLO work st through back loop only

5-tr cluster 5 treble cluster – (yrh, insert hook in st indicated, yrh and pull up loop, yrh and draw through 2 loops) 5 times, inserting hook in same st each time, yrh and draw through all 6 loops on hook, ch1 to complete st

FPdc front post double crochet – insert hook from front to back, around back of indicated st and back through to the front, yrh and draw round back of post of indicated st, yrh and draw through 2 loops

BPdc back post double crochet – insert hook from back of work to front, around front of indicated st and back through to back, yrh and draw round front of post of indicated st, yrh and draw through 2 loops

FINISHED SIZE

15cm (6") tall

NOTES

- Stitch markers are important here as there are a few different elements to hook, but it's the incredible detail that makes this project so wonderful. The hat and scarf are removable, so you could make a few outfit changes.

SNOUT

The snout is made in two colours. When changing colour, do so on the last yarn over of the previous st

Round 1 Using Yarn A, make a magic loop, 3dc, change to Yarn B, 3dc. [6 sts]

Round 2 Change to Yarn A, inc 3 times, chage to Yarn B, inc 3 times. [12 sts]

Round 3 Change to Yarn A, (1dc, inc) 3 times, change to Yarn B, (1dc, inc) 3 times. [18 sts]

Rounds 4-5 Change to Yarn A, 9dc, change to Yarn B, 9dc. [18 sts]

Fasten off, leaving a long tail. Embroider the nose and mouth with Yarn G, using the images as a guide. Stuff the snout lightly

HEAD

Embroider the spots in Yarn F as you go, using the image as a guide

Round 1 Using Yarn A, make a magic ring, 6dc in ring, pull ring tight. [6 sts]

Round 2 Inc in each st around [12 sts]

Round 3 (1dc, inc) 6 times. [18 sts]

Round 4 (2dc, inc) 6 times. [24 sts]

Round 5 (3dc, inc) 6 times. [30 sts]

Round 6 (4dc, inc) 6 times. [36 sts]

Round 7 (5dc, inc) 6 times. [42 sts]

Round 8 (6dc, inc) 6 times. [48 sts]

Rounds 9-14 1dc in each st around

Rounds 15-18 Change to Yarn A, 10dc, change to Yarn B, 28dc, change to Yarn A, 10dc. [48 sts]

Round 19 (2dc, dc2tog) twice, 2dc, change to Yarn B, dc2tog, (2dc, dc2tog) 6 times, 2dc, change to Yarn A, dc2tog, (2dc, dc2tog) 2 times. [36 sts]

Round 20 4dc, dc2tog, 2dc, change to Yarn B, 2dc, dc2tog, (4dc, dc2tog) 3 times, change to Yarn A, 4dc, dc2tog. [30 sts]

Sew the snout between Rounds 11 and 17, positioning it so the colours match. Place it on the opposite side of the start of the round

Using Yarn G, embroider the eyes between Rounds 14 and 15, about 2 sts away from the snout then, using Yarn D, embroider cheeks

Round 21 Still in Yarn A, 3dc, dc2tog, 2dc, change to Yarn B, 1dc, dc2tog, (3dc, dc2tog) 3 times, change to Yarn A, 3dc, dc2tog [24 sts]

Round 22 2dc, dc2tog, 2dc, change to Yarn B, dc2tog, (2dc, dc2tog) 3 times, change to Yarn A, 2dc, dc2tog. [18 sts]

Round 23 5dc, change to Yarn B, 10dc, change to Yarn A, 3dc. [18 sts] Stuff the head firmly.

Round 24 5dc, change to Yarn B, 4dc, inc 3 times, 3dc, change to Yarn A, 3dc. [21 sts]

Round 25 Inc 5 times, change to Yarn B, 13dc, change to Yarn A, inc 3 times. [29 sts]

Round 26 10dc, change to Yarn B, 5dc, (inc, 1dc) 3 times, 2dc, change to Yarn A, 6dc. [32 sts]

Round 27 12dc, change to Yarn B, 14dc, change to Yarn A, 6dc. [32 sts]

Round 28 (1dc, inc) 4 times, 6dc, change to Yarn B, 10dc, change to Yarn A, 8dc. [36 sts]

Round 29 20dc, change to Yarn B, 6dc, change to Yarn A, 10dc. [36 sts]

Round 30 21dc, change to Yarn B, 4dc, change to Yarn A, 11dc. [36 sts] Continue in Yarn A

Round 31 (2dc, inc) 2 times, (inc, 2dc) 2 times, inc, 22dc, inc. [42 sts]

Round 32 1dc in each st around

Round 33 4dc, (inc, 3dc) twice, inc, 29dc. [45 sts]

Round 34 1dc in each st around Divide the work to crochet the back and two front legs of the leopard. First, using the 4 sts in white on the front as a reference, find the middle front st of the body and place a stitch marker there. Then, divide the work identifying 9 sts for each front leg – 27 sts remain for body

BODY

Round 35 22dc, ch8, miss 18 sts, 1dc, place the stitch marker in this last dc – it'll be the beginning of each round from this point. The body will be formed of 27dc of the body and the ch8, leaving the 18 missed sts for the front legs

Round 36 35dc (27 on the body and 8 on the ch). [35 sts]

Round 37 Inc 5 times, 17dc, inc 5 times, 8dc. [45 sts]

Rounds 38-41 1dc in each st around

Round 42 (7dc, dc2tog) 5 times [40 sts]

Round 43 1dc in each st around

Round 44 (6dc, dc2tog) 5 times [35 sts]

Round 45 (5dc, dc2tog) 5 times [30 sts]

Round 46 (3dc, dc2tog) 6 times [24 sts]

Round 47 (2dc, dc2tog) 6 times [18 sts]

Round 48 (1dc, dc2tog) 6 times [12 sts]

Round 49 (dc2tog) 6 times. [6 sts]

Fasten off leaving a long tail. Using the yarn needle, weave the yarn tail through the front loop of each remaining st and pull tight to close

FIRST FRONT LEG

Join Yarn A to the first st next to the body, which will be the first st of the first leg

Round 1 9dc, ch2 and join the last ch and the fourth ch from the body making a dc, 3dc. [15 sts]

Rounds 2-8 1dc in each st around

Round 9 2dc, (5-tr cluster, 1dc) 4 times, 5dc. [15 sts]

Round 10 In BLO, (1dc, dc2tog) 5 times. [10 sts]

Round 11 (Dc2tog) 5 times. [5 sts]

Fasten off leaving a long tail. Using the yarn needle, weave the yarn tail through the front loop of each remaining st and pull tight to close

SECOND FRONT LEG

Join Yarn A to the first chain st next to the first front leg, which will be the first st of the second leg

Round 1 15dc (2sts on ch between legs, 9 sts on front and 4 on ch made to make back of body)

Rounds 2-8 1dc in each st around

Round 9 3dc, (5-tr cluster, 1dc) 4 times, 4dc

Round 10 In BLO, (1dc, dc2tog) 5 times. [10 sts]

Round 11 (dc2tog) 5 times. [5 sts]

Fasten off leaving a long tail. Using a yarn needle, weave the yarn tail through the front loop of each remaining st and pull tight to close

BACK LEGS (MAKE TWO)

Round 1 Using Yarn A, make a magic ring, 5dc in ring, pull ring tight. [5 sts]

Round 2 Inc in each st around [10 sts]

Round 3 (1dc, inc) 5 times. [15 sts]

Round 4 In BLO, 3dc, (5-tr cluster, 1dc) 4 times, 4dc. [15 sts]

Rounds 5-9 1dc in each st around

Fasten off, leaving a long tail. Stuff firmly and sew the legs to the body

EARS (MAKE TWO)

Round 1 Using Yarn G, make a magic ring, 6dc in ring, pull ring tight. [6 sts]

Round 2 Inc in each st around [12 sts]

Change to Yarn A

Rounds 3-5 1dc in each st around

Fasten off, leaving a long tail for sewing. Embroider the white details using the images as a guide

TAIL

Round 1 Using Yarn G, start with a magic ring, 8dc in ring, pull ring tight. [8 sts]

Rounds 2-6 1dc in each st around

Change to Yarn A

Rounds 7-16 1dc in each st around

Fasten off, leaving a long tail for sewing. Stuff a little

SCARF

Foundation using Yarn C, ch59

Row 1 1dc in 4th ch from hook, *1dc, miss 1 ch, 1dc in the next ch; repeat from * to end, turn

Row 2 Ch2 (counts as 1dc, ch1), 1dc in the next 1ch-sp, *ch1, 1dc in next

1ch-sp; repeat from * to end, finishing with 1dc in the ch1 at the start of Row 1, turn

Rows 3-9 Ch2 (counts as 1dc, ch1), 1dc in next 1ch-sp, *ch1, 1dc in next 1ch-sp; repeat from * to end, 1dc in the ch1 at the start of the previous row, turn. Fasten off and weave in the ends. Make two pom poms in Yarn D and sew them to the scarf

HAT

Round 1 Using Yarn E, make a magic ring, 6dc in ring, pull ring tight. [6 sts]

Round 2 Inc in each st. [12 sts]

Round 3 (1dc, inc) 6 times. [18 sts]

Round 4 (2dc, inc) 6 times. [24 sts]

Round 5 (3dc, inc) 6 times. [30 sts]

Round 6 (4dc, inc) 6 times. [36 sts]

Round 7 (5dc, inc) 6 times. [42 sts]

Round 8 (6dc, inc) 6 times. [48 sts]

Rounds 9-11 1dc in each st around

Round 12 16dc, ch5, miss 5 sts, 6dc, ch5, miss 5 sts, 16dc. [48 sts]

Rounds 13-14 1dc in each st around

Rounds 15-16 (1FPdc, 1BPdc) 24 times. [48 sts]

Fasten off, weave in ends. Make a pom pom in Yarn E and sew it on

FINISHING

Place the hat on the head to find where the ears should go, using stitch markers to mark. Remove the hat, flatten the ears and sew onto the head. Sew the tail to the back, centred. Dress the leopard.

Designer Credits

Special thanks to all the wonderful designers
behind these patterns:

Beardie and Blondie
Socktopus p. 154

Kim Bengtsson Friis
Merry Macaw p. 62; Snuggly Red Panda p. 172

Kate Bruning
Circus Bear p. 142

Ilaria Caliri
Pretty Peacock p. 36; Sleepy Sloth p. 42; Rainbow
Unicorn p. 58; Superhero Dog p. 70; Little Lion p. 81;
Dashing Donkey p. 100; Otter Couple p. 113

MJ Carlos
Cute Quokka p. 135

Ellie's Craft Boutique
Sleepy Lambkin p. 126

Orsi Farkasvolgyi
Royal Swan p. 64

Becky Garratt
Woolly Whale p. 30; Deer Duo p. 78

Heather C Gibbs
Cuddly Schnauzer p. 55

Sara Huntington
Easy Bunny p. 18; Itty-Bitty Bat p. 29

Victoria Kairis
Clutching Koala p. 138; Busy Bees p. 157;
Dinosaur Family p. 160; Sea Turtle p. 176;
Magnificent Mandrill p. 180

Mary's Amiland
Beach Bear p. 26

Stephanie Lau
Baby Dragon p. 132

Erinna Lee
Adorable Axelotl p. 107; Tiny Deer p. 118;
Soft Seal p. 124; Gorgeous Guinea Pig p. 150

Eléna Leprêtre
Beautiful Butterfly p. 174

Mei Li Lee
Bear Brothers p. 45; Lovebirds p. 50;
Perfect Panda p. 52

Jhak Mercado
Playful Platypus p. 140

Vanessa Mooncie
Lovely Lamb p. 84; Sunshine Snail p. 89;
Sweet Rabbit p. 92; Puddle Duck p. 97;
Penguin Pal p. 182

Alanna O'Dea
Crafty Crocodile p. 168

Val Pierce
Sleepy Camel p. 73

Elisa Sartori
Baby Tapir p. 48, Interesting Iguana p. 60;
Golden Frog p. 178

Yan Schenkel
Dapper Fox p. 104; Diddy Dino p. 186;
Cosy Leopard p. 189

Irene Strange
Party Pug p. 110; Homey Hermit Crab p. 122;
Snug Penguin P. 145; Happy Hedgehog p. 152

The Crafty Mammy
Handsome Highland Cow p. 129

Rachel Wain
Sugar Mice, p. 19

Liz Ward
Puppy Pair p. 20; Owl Friends p. 23;
Chinese Cats p. 32; Frog Prince p. 38;
Jolly Giraffe p. 40; Cheeky Monkey p. 66;
Cat Pair p. 75; Dinosaur Duo p. 87;
Floppy-Eared Puppy p. 115